AF352460

QUEENS OF AFROBEAT

QUEENS *of* AFROBEAT

WOMEN, PLAY, AND FELA KUTI'S MUSIC REBELLION

DOTUN AYOBADE

INDIANA UNIVERSITY PRESS

This book is a publication of

Indiana University Press
Office of Scholarly Publishing
Herman B Wells Library 350
1320 East 10th Street
Bloomington, Indiana 47405 USA

iupress.org

Manufactured in the United States of America

First Printing 2024

Library of Congress Cataloging-in-Publication Data

Names: Ayobade, Dotun, author.
Title: Queens of Afrobeat : women, play, and Fela Kuti's music rebellion / Dotun Ayobade.
Description: Bloomington, Indiana : Indiana University Press, 2024. | Includes bibliographical references and index. |
Identifiers: LCCN 2023051677 (print) | LCCN 2023051678 (ebook) | ISBN 9780253068637 (hardback) | ISBN 9780253068644 (paperback) | ISBN 9780253068651 (pdf)
Subjects: LCSH: Fela, 1938-1997—Friends and associates. | Fela, 1938-1997. | Fela, 1938-1997—Relations with women. | Women singers—Nigeria. | Afrobeat—Nigeria—History and criticism. | Afrobeat—Social aspects—Nigeria. | Popular culture—Nigeria. | BISAC: BIOGRAPHY & AUTOBIOGRAPHY / Music | MUSIC / Genres & Styles / International
Classification: LCC ML410.F2955 A96 2024 (print) | LCC ML410.F2955 (ebook) | DDC 781.63092—dc23/eng/20231114
LC record available at https://lccn.loc.gov/2023051677
LC ebook record available at https://lccn.loc.gov/2023051678

For Yẹmí, Fèyí, and Ìfẹ́, my lodestars

CONTENTS

PREFACE

Erasure Takes Manifold Forms

Commissioned by the Lagos state government in 2011, the Kalakuta Museum bears distinct marks of erasure. This place once housed one of Nigeria's most iconic subcultures: Kalakuta Republic. I anticipate much of the museum experience from the smattering of chitchat with young men around the area, so I am little surprised when I witness the setup myself. The question on my mind as I navigate the museum is not whether its working class women artists would be erased but what form their erasure will take. Answers seep in as I ascend the stairs that lead though three floors of relatively sparse museum space. The stairs end at a penthouse bar, where Fela's Egypt 80 band rehearsed in the 1990s. Photographs of the storied Kuti family decorate the wall leading to the second floor—Fela, Remi, FRK, and Fela's children and siblings, one of whom was a minister of health in the 1980s. The black-and-white photographs tell a legend of one of Nigeria's most noted families. They feature the Kuti family but generally span Fela's childhood to his life as a young father. The museum's manager tells me that the women "added no value to themselves" and so had no place in the Kuti family. I do not know whether he seeks to clarify the curatorial choices of the museum or if in fact he believes these thoughts.

While curated to convey dignity and inspire nostalgia, the photographs achieve more: they craft a sanitized history of Afrobeat without excess—that is, no excess bodies or excess acts. I make a stop on the second floor. Fela's bedroom has been staged to convey pristineness, everything sitting ostensibly in the exact same position as when its world-renowned occupant lived here. A glass panel stands where a wall once existed, laying bare the room's contents (including a posthumous Grammy Award) while subtly encouraging the looker's voyeurism about what might have transpired in this space. The bed is laid in slightly rumpled multicolored fabric as through its owner, having only gone out for the day, will return here at night. This presence materializes for me at the confluence of sex and death. I peek through the panel into a laboratory of desire and contamination. This room is where the fluid states of passion and poison likely traveled between unequal bodies. This untold and untellable account of the space only wafts between the museum's rooms and walls. It is never made explicit.

The Afrobeat women who had been regularly derided in the press as the embodiment of excess needed to be tucked away. I ascend the stairs, increasingly anxious, in search of the Queens, Afrobeat's legendary and troublesome women, who find no space on the capacious "family" wall. Relief sets in as I finally locate them in a life-sized photograph of the women around Fela, who caresses a saxophone. Some women are smiling, and at least one is puffing at a joint. It is now an internet favorite, this photograph. It was destined for archival retrieval from the moment it was taken. Seeing the women in this way gives relief, which quickly gives way to frustration as I realize that none of the women bear names in the entire museum. No woman is named except one: "Fehintola Anikulapo-Kuti," etched on a large steel cauldron, an ìkòkò-irin. The pot intensifies the mystique about this remarkable woman, Fehintola Kuti. Why is she the only one named in the museum collection? What does it signify? Her son, Seun, conveys to me only fragments of Fehintola, who I learn died in 2007. Others I interview reveal as little of Fehintola as she appears to have of herself. The Fehintola mystique endures as I could only elicit few but important insights from speaking with others. The pot bears witness to its late owner. Perhaps it was the owner who inscribed herself into history. The pot illustrates one way the museum's curators sought to represent the past: show but tell little. Its owner sought another way to preserve the self—etch your name on a cauldron, whose sheer heft and usability as a symbol of gendered domesticity renders it, and its owner, difficult to discard.

—⁂—

The women about whom I write courted fame and controversy in the 1970s as an iconic collective of performers in the Africa 70 band led by Fela Anikulapo-Kuti (better known as Fela Kuti), Nigeria's most prominent musician and activist. These women were known as Afrobeat Queens (or simply Queens). While Fela is globally heralded as having invented Afrobeat music—a groovy blend of jazz, soul, highlife, and West African rhythms—the women were the true engines of the Afrobeat experience. In live performances at Fela's club, Afrika Shrine, they performed erotic dances and backing vocals to his most important musical compositions. They entertained the audience members, largely young men, who patronized Fela's work for its ideological and activist content as much as for its banal, sometimes vulgar, articulation of politics. The Queens were often regarded as "Fela's girls," a title used to derogate them as sex objects but that also quite patently named their youth, as many joined Fela's band in their teenage years. As such, the figure of the Queen—as much as the lives of the women who gave shape to said figure in the 1970s—is a density of unstable symbols and unresolved moral questions, marked as much by admiration and fascination as by discomfort and curiosity. Sexism and misogyny within Afrobeat and in larger Nigerian society have produced a distorted view of their creative labor and worth as artists, citizens, political subjects, and, crucially, as women who worked with one of Nigeria's most notorious antifeminist icons. With their youthful delinquency, quest for freedom, and disillusionment with the military state, these girls and young women fled parental control for a life in Afrobeat's associated subculture, filled with subversion, marijuana, experimental artmaking, travel, and polemic music. The Queens' courting of risk yielded understandably contradictory outcomes as they consequently became uniquely exposed to state violence and to the violence of patriarchy.

A crucial task I undertake in this book is to offer a critical framework for reimagining the presence, motivations, and struggles of the women that defined Afrobeat music. No book-length study currently exists on the Queens, but there are a few important works. Carlos Moore's 1982 biography, *Fela: This Bitch of a Life*, stands out on this front. Spanning fifty-six pages of text are interviews of the fourteen Queens. A full-page portrait prefaced by a concise biography accompanies each interview, which, as Moore describes it, was the "first time Fela's wives express[ed] themselves."[1] Moore offers a description of each woman's physique alongside a studied judgment of her temperament; details like facial features, demeanor, and relationships with the other women give nuance to the profile of each Queen.[2] Moore's interviews contain useful biographical information; important insights into domestic life in Kalakuta Republic, the urban commune and ideological hub for Fela's musical and political activities; and the often invisible operations of gender and class in Afrobeat. The interviews highlight when each woman met Fela and the length of her involvement. They also convey the visceral pain from the brutal state invasion in February 1977. Taken together, the interviews and portraits poignantly show the individuality of each Queen in what remains arguably the most valuable documentation of their lives in print. It is no surprise that Moore's text has influenced the production of two successful musicals—*Fela!* (choreographed by world-renowned African American choreographer Bill T. Jones) and *Fela and the Kalakuta Queens* (directed by award-winning Nigerian director Bolanle Austen-Peters). The productions cemented *This Bitch* as a decisive Afrobeat text. Yet Moore's work presents two key limitations I hope to address. The first is its unwitting transfiguration of the women absent during Moore's visit to the realm of the forgotten. This means that Queens who were absent for the interviews or who had parted ways with Fela—out of frustration, to reunite with their families, or to pursue a new life—have largely been especially susceptible to being forgotten. Second, Moore's interviews follow a formula that revolves around the Queens' intimate lives with Fela and their memories of Kalakuta's destruction. As deeply revealing and generative as Moore's questions are, the frames are also quite narrow—understandably so, as the women are featured as part of a larger story about Fela's life and the development of Afrobeat. Scholars have built on Moore's historic offering by ventilating the entry points into narratives of the Queens' lives.[3] Mine is a modest contribution to an already robust conversation.

ACKNOWLEDGMENTS

This book testifies to the staying power of a broad network of mentors, colleagues, institutions, friends, and family.

The project enjoyed its earliest and most focused support from faculty mentors in or affiliated with the Performance as Public Practice Program (PPP) at UT Austin. These include Charlotte Canning, Rebecca Rossen, Omise'eke Natasha Tinsley, and Omi Osun Joni L. Jones, about whom more will be said. My early articulation of this project also benefited immensely from Tejumola Olaniyan's sharp insights before his untimely passing. The careful reading and constructive feedback of these scholars helped sharpen my analysis and engagement with the material I collected. A host of PPP and UT Austin professors were instrumental to my growth as I honed the questions, methodologies, and texts pertinent to my work. The conscientious pedagogy of Meta DuEwa Jones, Paul Bonin-Rodriguez, Megan Alrutz, Andrew Ian Carlson, Toyin Falola, and Eric Tang was defining. Several Black Studies and African Studies scholars offered mentorship and support at different stages: Edmond T. Gordon, Christen Smith, Stephanie Lang, Hershini Bhana Young, James Yeku, Cajetan Iheka, Abosede George, Saheed Aderinto, Carli Coetzee, Shola Adenekan, Catherine Cole, Akin Ogundiran, and David Donkor.

Members of my PPP cohort were exemplars in collegiality and mutual support as we charted our respective paths: Abimbola Adelakun, Brianna Figueroa, Scott Blackshire, Amy Guenther, and Rachel Gilbert. Throughout my doctoral program, I enjoyed the privilege of collaborating with PPP colleagues, be it as classroom peers, in teaching teams, or in reading/writing groups. These peers were instrumental in supporting my growth in ways that are hard to put into words: Lydia Nelson, M'bewe Ninoska Escobar, Nicole Martin, Gustavo Melo Cerquiera, Cassidy Browning, Agatha Oliviera, Beliza Torres, Rudy Ramirez, James McMaster, Natashia Lindsey (to whom I am grateful for the invitation to present on the Queens at Central Washington University), and Katelyn Wood, who read a draft of the introduction and book proposal and offered invaluable feedback on how it could be improved.

The slow percolation demanded by this project benefited from the dispersed but defining input of peers and professors across many classes. My colleagues in the Subaltern Epistemologies cohort read early drafts of my ideas: Sheela Jane Menon, Mariana Sabino, Ogechukwu Ezekwem, Daniel Jean-Jacques, Cacee Hoyer, Shery Chanis, and Jenna Hanchey, who, in a peer review exercise, read a draft of the first paper I wrote on the topic. I am counting among my many blessings the support of two wonderful colleagues, Tsepo Masango Chéry and Bukola Aluko-Kpotie, both of whom showed up when it mattered and in ways that still have me in awe. Tsepo, a perceptive listener and wise Sotho *aussie*, gave grounded and candid advice for navigating crucial book-writing and career-transition challenges. Bukola, a big sister with a capacious heart and the most analytical of minds, read some of the thorniest sections of this book and gave insightful feedback—and, when I needed it most, honest critique. Bukola pushed me to write clearly and with my Yorùbá hat on; it is an invitation I am deeply grateful for. It was wonderful to count on the support of a cadre of UT Austin–affiliated Nigerian professors such as Omoniyi Afolabi, Moyo Okediji, and Augustine Agwuele as well as on colleagues and close friends such as Sam Okoronkwo, Otun Rasheed, and Olawale Egberongbe.

A network of centers at Brown University offered vital support at critical stages of reimagining my research as a book. Funds the Office of the Vice President for Research granted me from the Salomon Faculty Research Awards went into copyediting the manuscript; the Brown Arts Initiative (BAI) gave me a public presentation grant that covered the cost of travel to present at the Lagos Studies Association conference (LSA). Under the leadership of Tricia Rose, the Center for the Study of Race and Ethnicity in the Americas (CSREA) offered community and an intellectual home for my work. As part of the center's "What I Am Thinking About Now," I shared part of my book in progress and received invaluable feedback on areas of revision, particularly on Chapter 4. I worked with an exceptional cohort of colleagues at Africana Studies / Rite and Reason Theatre, all of whom pushed me to think and feel more deeply: Lisa Biggs, Keisha-Khan Perry, Francoise Hamlin, Brian Meeks, Tony Bogues, Paget Henry, and (the late) Anani Dzidzienyo. Elmo Terry Morgan, Karen Allen-Baxter, Kathy Moyer, and Alonzo Jones were relentless in their reassurance that the George Houston Bass Theatre was my creative laboratory, a space to put my research in creative motion. Elmo's keen directing eye and Karen's direct but generous prodding emboldened me to make artistic choices onstage that profoundly shaped the texture of the writing on the page. Indeed, Karen, with whom I made two trips to Nigeria, one of which included presenting a conference performance at the University of Lagos, made for the most joyous colleague. Matthew Guterl and Lundy Braun were exceptional mentors as I navigated the transition from graduate school to the tenure track at Brown. Colleagues beyond Africana Studies also supported my transition and work in important ways for which I remain grateful: Geri Augusto, Daniel Jordan Smith, and Jennifer Johnson. The administrative support of staff at Africana Studies—including Diagneris Garcia, Ellie Winter and Mariesa Fischer—was exceptional.

I am thankful for the gift of brilliant mentees as well as students I have had the privilege of teaching. Students who enrolled in *Performing Africa* and *Fela Kuti: Afrobeat to Afrobeats* routinely brought a keenness and energy to the study of contemporary Africa that expanded my approach to a range of Afrobeat-related topics.

On the invitation of Ramon Rivera-Servera and Mary Pattillo, respective incumbent chairs of Performance Studies and, at the time, African American Studies (now Black Studies) at Northwestern, I shared my ideas in progress with a highly engaged community. My two visits to Northwestern, in person and over Zoom, offered vital occasions for clarifying the nexus of research, creative work, and writing for myself and you, the reader. Graduate students and faculty in these departments and within Northwestern's African Studies community offered affirming feedback on excerpts of the manuscript. Many engaged me in a collegial and constructive fashion; others offered vital support as I made the transition between institutions while tidying up the book. They include E. Patrick Johnson (also Dean of the School of Communication [SOC]), Marcela Fuentes, Martha Biondi, Alexander Weheliye, Chris Abani, Jessica Winegar, Joshua Chambers-Letson, Mary Zimmerman, Shayna Silverstein, Bimbola Akinbola, Lori D. Barcliff-Baptista, Marquis Bey, Nicole Spigner, Nitasha Sharma, Sherwin Bryant, John Marquez, Barnor Hesse, Kennetta Hammond-Perry, Kent Brooks, Exal Ihareta, kihana miraya ross, Travy Vaughn-Manley, Cristal Truscott, and Connor Lifson. No sooner had I arrived at Northwestern than I counted as colleagues Nadine George-Graves, Melissa Blanco-Borelli, and Tommy DeFrantz, all of whom had supported my work in previous encounters. They have continued to be of exceptional support even as they navigate their own transitions to Northwestern. At the Dean's Office,

Associate Dean Bonnie Martin-Harris, LaShanta' Le'Sure, Theresa Bratanch, and Roderick Hawkins all worked to make my transition to Northwestern smooth and seamless. Deans E. Patrick Johnson and Adrian Randolph have made SOC and the Weinberg College of Arts and Sciences into nourishing intellectual homes. A cadre of Northwestern staff such as Dina Walters, Scottie Akines, Suzette Denose, Zoe McDaniel, Murielle Harris, and Gianna Carter in (or affiliated with) Black Studies and Performance Studies shared a standard of excellence in their administrative work that I greatly benefited from. Without their generous support, I would have been dazed more times than I can count.

Dee Mortensen saw the promise of the manuscript quite early and offered invaluable advice about its tone, even as she was retiring from an illustrious career at Indiana University Press (IUP). I benefited from Dee's extensive experience and incisive suggestions about giving the book its greatest chances at success. Ashante Thomas worked dedicatedly to keep the publication process on track, especially during those turbulent pandemic months when several institutions were navigating the sudden transition to remote work. Ashante made the peer review process appear seamless and maintained a clear line of communication during what, in the context of the COVID-19 pandemic, could have been an unsettling process. Anna C. Francis took over the manuscript and shepherded it to completion with extreme care and commitment. IUP director Gary Dunham helped oversee the process in a manner critical to moving the book toward publication. Their work in giving a sense of stability and assurance, especially in the wake of transitions at the press, is deeply appreciated. I am grateful to everyone at the press whose contributions, in modest and big ways, helped mold this book. I am equally grateful to the three blind reviewers who offered critical but generous feedback that guided my revisions. Shannon Wong Lerner's meticulousness and skill as a copyeditor and her critical eye for interdisciplinary scholarship helped give definition to the big picture and fine details of my writing. Shannon pushed me toward clear and engaged writing and was especially attentive to the nuance and sensitivity of the stories I wanted to translate on the page. Akiko Yamagata and Cathy Hannabach urged me to speak and write in my voice. They helped me establish a writing cadence that gave the book consistency, flow, and clarity. In the final stages of publication, the careful edits of Vinodhini Kumarasamy and Nancy Lila Lightfoot were instrumental in polishing the narrative and sharpening the intervention I sought to make. The hard work of editors at and outside Indiana University Press was support I did not realize I needed seriously. And to have tackled the final phases of the revision with writing partners like Fadeke Castor, Raquel Monroe, and Melissa Blanco Borelli was a gift.

Several librarians across different institutions played a pivotal role in facilitating access to archival materials and texts helpful to my research and writing. When I set out to map the initial outlines of this project, Beth Kerr at the UT Austin Fine Arts Library went to extra lengths to secure materials exactly when they were needed. The joy that Beth brought to searching for and suggesting resources made research an inspiring venture. Yetunde Zaid of the University of Lagos helped secure access to the troves of historical newspapers in the Gandhi Library. Justina Nduesoh patiently scoured uncatalogued cartons of newspapers (or pointed me in promising directions), an incredibly generous gesture during what was at that time an open-ended exploration of Nigerian dailies from the 1960s to the 1990s. Esmeralda Kale's support at the Herskovits Library for African Studies at Northwestern came at the critical end of the book-writing process. It has been a joy to be guided along the research process by these talented and thorough librarians and archivists. My longtime friend and collaborator Tunde Alabanla helped with logistical support for interviews and acted as interlocutor on day-to-day fieldwork planning. Aderemi Adegbite, Tokunbo Ogundipe, and Bukola George offered different levels of support, from transcribing interviews to locating copyright owners of images. It has taken an expansive community of friends and colleagues to arrive here.

The mentorsip of Omi Osun Joni L. Jones warrants more than a passing mention. She modeled Black feminist work as everyday praxis, showing me in the clearest terms what it might look like and accomplish in the world. I catch myself reflecting often on her hands-on mentorship, critical generosity, and on the friendship we now share, all of which exceed the conventional assignment of an adviser in the most inspiring and conscientious of ways. I have learned from her to strive for joy and meaning in academic work even when doing so might appear impossible. I am filled with the profoundest respect and the deepest gratitude for all you taught me and hope that this book reflects in its little way the excellent teacher and mentor that you are. Being under Omi's wings comes with the privilege of basking in the profound wisdom, perceptiveness, and big heart of her wife and collaborator, Sharon Bridgforth, as well as their wise and talented daughters, Leigh Gaymon-Jones and Sonja Perryman. It's been a blessing to walk with you all's light and to call you family.

I owe profound gratitude to my dear mother, Adebowale Ayobade (aka Mama Awon Boys), whose unconventional journey to and through the academy taught me all I needed to know about tenacity, creative thinking, and navigating intellectual work against debilitating odds. The many setbacks she confronted as a young woman and overcame as an adult student, a mother of three energetic boys, a scholar, and a university administrator are awe-inspiring.

She has remained the quintessential model for damning the odds and exemplifies all the ways in which brilliance can manifest. She harbored a clear vision of what she desired for herself and her sons; she pursued it relentlessly and often single handedly. Her support for this project extended to helping secure permissions for some of the images—a consummate expert at blurring the lines between mother and "senior" colleague. I cannot fully express how grateful I am for all you have given. My late father, Tope Ijiola Ayobade, showed me the joys of scholarship and the life of the mind. When he assumed storyteller mode, he regaled us with stories of student activism at the University of Ibadan, mimicked his former professors, performed mock intellectual debates, and did not stop writing even until his dying breath. My choice to become a college professor (as a teenager) owes in large part to how he modeled for me daily commitment to thinking and writing as well as the playful and ostentatious performance of intellectualism, the latter still being a work in progress. My wonderful mother-in-law, Olajumoke Lois Akinola, has been part of this project from the get-go. From extended visits and support during graduate school to helping locate "Fela's people" within her network, she has been a constant and deeply appreciated help in bringing this work to fruition.

Since the rainy day we met on the campus of University of Lagos, Olayemi has remained my best friend and most agile intellectual interlocutor. She was the one to let me know, in the clearest of terms, what worked and what could be improved about this project, including the writing style. The clarity she brought to the book extended to reminding me that it was time to let the manuscript go, which, in academic parlance, is nothing short of true love. I am deeply grateful for your keen intellect, for the wise friend and unflinching partner you are, and I hope you feel as loved and nourished to have me in your life as I feel having you in mine. The arc of writing this book has dovetailed with the lives of our two beautiful children, Feyisona and Ifedayo. These two are perfection. I have been moved by their encouragement and support, profound in their own ways, as I inched closer to finishing the project. They are the kids to give a few minutes of quiet (when sorely needed), and read a few sentences here and there (before inevitably discarding the page). Ultimately, they remind me of the gift and the privilege of fatherhood. I hope you two beauties, when you read this book, know how much you supported it. Also, thank you for that pesky question: "When will you finish your book?" I finished. This is it.

Several members of the Afrobeat community generously gave their time and offered access to a tightly knit, transnational group of artists, collaborators, family members, and Afrobeat afficionados. They invited me into this network and entrusted me with their life stories in Afrobeat, many of which lie at the core of this book's offering. They include the estate of Fela Kuti, Yeni Anikulapo-Kuti, Seun Anikulapo-Kuti, Theo Lawson, Duro Ikujenyo, Lemi Ghariokwu, Eludoyin Elutunde, Dede Mabiakwu, (the late) Yinusa Akinnibosun (Baba YS), Uwa Erhabor, Chinedu Onnebunne ("Sir Chay"), Cornel-Best Onyekaba, Adewale James Salako, Mallam Abdul Okwechime, Aya Yem, and Wunmi Olaiya, among many others. While the Afrobeat network I engage with exists primarily in Nigeria, its reach has extended to include collectives across the diaspora. I am indebted to Rujeko Dumbutshena and Nicole de Weever, both of whom were part of the Broadway ensemble in Bill T. Jones's critically acclaimed Broadway show based on Fela's life. Rujeko and Nicole were extremely gracious in not only granting my request for Zoom interviews in the middle of the pandemic but also sharing their rich recollection of the experience and artistic demands of performing as a Broadway Queen. Several artists, photographers, and archives permitted me to use their images, some free of charge. These artists include Kevwe Anikulapo-Kuti, Segun Osunla (and the estate of Femi Bankole Osunla), Weyinmi Atigbi ("Watigbi"), Sokari Douglas Camp, Lemi Ghariokwu, Adrian Boot, Bernard Matussière, and Getty Images.

Finally, I owe a profound debt to the Queens who, on the strength of trust and the promise to take care, gave me the permission to write this book and reweave their personal stories into the fabrics of Afrobeat history. The four Queens I interviewed—Olaide Babayale-Kuti, Kewve Anikulapo-Kuti, Najite Anikulapo-Kuti, and Omolara Shosanya—have led courageous artistic lives. I am filled with awe and gratitude that they entrusted me with some of their stories. I can never possibly repay this kindness. Other pioneering women artists such as Dele Salami and "second-generation" singer-dancers and artists like Pulchérie Ibilola Hoga, Mary Umude-Haverkamp and Ifeanyi Abuah also generously shared their life stories and invaluable insights into the longer arc of Afrobeat music and culture. I hope that you find this book worthy of the time and trust you invested in bringing it to life.

QUEENS OF AFROBEAT

Introduction

"The Enjoyment Was Too Much!": Gender and Serious Play in a 1970s Music Subculture

Approaching Najite: August 2014

All the Queens have an aura about them—a mixture of charisma, age, and the weight of life experience. This aura surrounds Najite as I saunter past her beer joint, situated about fifty meters from the Kalakuta Museum. Popular beer brands and stacked crates decorate the outside of the shop. Without breaking step, I do a mental scan of the joint. There are five customers, all men, sitting on two benches. If you stand at a distance, you can see right into the modest shop, which also hosts a small kitchen. My first sighting of Najite is of her shuffling between the customers in the meager space of the shop. She is light-skinned, full-figured and speaks in a high and assertive tone, the kind required to manage rowdy customers who may buy beer on a never-ending promise to pay. Here, she is known as "Mama Africa" or "Iya Motun." My quick glance fails to yield a mental match with the young women I have seen in Afrobeat photographs. Three people mentioned that one of "Fela's wives" runs a nearby joint. But failing to match her with the image in my head does little to change my intuitive sense that she is the woman I have come looking for, the kind of woman people in the area would know. I harbor no intentions of ruining what feels like one chance, so I stroll by as inconspicuously as possible.

I sight three middle-aged men in an area close to the museum. I approach them and introduce myself. One of them responds in smooth Yoruba, "Àwa n'ìyàwó Fela" / We are Fela's wives." He asks for identification. In the interval between his asking and my producing my student ID, he interjects, his tone one of mild annoyance, "Nǹkan tí change gan. O kọ̀ wá pé ò ń wá àwọn ìyàwó Fela. Kàní pé ìgbà tí Fela wá láíyé, a ma ti kọ̀kọ̀ lù ẹ́ ṣelése. / Things have changed much. You just approached us saying you are looking for Fela's wives. If Fela were alive, we would have beaten you up for the audacity." I am a little shaken as I produce my ID. They probably were here when Fela was alive, following his work with cultish dedication. At least one of them seems like he would have given his life for Fela if he had asked him to. Some probably would have without Fela's having to ask. "Give us money to smoke igbo [marijuana]," one of the two other men impatiently asks. As I hand them ₦500, the collector reassures me, "We are Fela's wives." I thank them for their time and make to leave when one of them catches up to me. He struggles to contain his excitement about my being an American student. When I presented my UT Austin student ID minutes ago, he sighted it, quickly handed it back and declared to his peers, "Àwọn ọmọ" Obafemi Awolowo University yẹn ni / He is one of those students from Obafemi Awolowo University." He's never touched an airplane, he explains. The closest he's come to an airplane is touching a television with the image of a plane on it. I appreciate the humor. This is when he shares his name: "Nwabueze." He's Igbo; his fluent Yoruba indexes a Lagos reality as much as it underlines the spirit of cosmopolitanism that was Kalakuta Republic. I reassure him that I am thoroughly Nigerian. The explanation does little to change how he conceives of me—as an outsider. "All the Queens don die finish," Nwabueze informs me casually, "but a few still dey alive." He counts them on his left hand. There is Najite, also Iya Motun, whose shop is close by. I need to approach her carefully because she's "illiterate" and, he adds, volatile. He proceeds to demonstrate how I might approach Iya Motun. Assuming the persona of a journalist or scholar, Nwabueze begins to speak in lively tones: "I dey see you for television. I don hear great things about you from my friends in America and Nigeria. Na why I come see you." I watch as he rounds out this monologue, assuring me that this is the only way to win her approval. If not, "she fit break bottle for your head" (she could crack my head with a bottle). This is not all to approaching Iya Motun. I also need to remember, he shares, that she loves Benson & Hedges cigarettes. Go with a pack and it will seal the deal. A voice cuts through Nwabueze's impassioned briefing. It's another young man around my age. His name is Tilewa. "Are you the one looking for Fela's wives?" he asks in crisp English. The two men in Nwabueze left behind have briefed him. When I respond in the affirmative, Tilewa offers to take me to Iya Motun. He leads without ceremony; he speaks little and walks officiously, his calmness making for an odd reassurance of his capacity to broker a meeting.

Iya Motun greets Tilewa warmly. He suspends both hands in greeting. I stand behind him and let him do the talking. Tilewa explains who I am and what I am here for. "This guy is a student who is doing his schoolwork on Fela and . . ." and before he finishes, Iya Motun begins a slow shake of her head, the kind that appears to be building up to a No. "I don stop to dey do interview with anybody," she responds before he finishes. She shares this thought matter-of-factly, without much visible emotion. "I no dey do interview again," this time a little more firmly. "Everybody don forget us." Tilewa, whom I met only minutes earlier, recognizes the opportunity. This is the point of his work, he explains. I agree, following up with an explanation of my work: it's not a project about Fela; it is about her, the other Queens, and their experience in Afrobeat. She contemplates my pitch for a couple of seconds. To my surprise, she asks me to return in a few days. I return home that night and decide to document the events of Day 1 of my journey searching for the Queens. The journal, excerpts of which are italicized throughout this book, are a compendium of some of my most impactful encounters in seeking out the iconic women.

The time was 1:10 p.m. on Monday, February 20, 1978. Unaccompanied by parents or legal guardians, twenty-seven young brides, some teenagers, filed into the lobby of Hotel Parisona, a little-known hotel in Anthony Village, a residential area in Lagos, Nigeria. Fela Anikulapo-Kuti, Afrobeat music superstar and husband-to-be, filed in with them; together, they settled on six mats before an *Ifá* priest, whose prayers yielded intermittent responses of "*Àṣẹ!*" Many of the girls and young women were artists in Fela's band, but they also maintained highly publicized romantic affairs with him. Some were striving toward stardom as dancers and singers, and Fela's fame and influence in the music industry likely played into their decision to marry him. The event was not without internal tensions. Besides the brides' parents, other crucial people were missing from the wedding, including Remilekun (Remi) Ransome-Kuti, the aspiring musician still legally married to Fela at the time, and Tunji Braithwaite, Fela's lawyer, whose best attempt at sabotaging the event for fear of his client's prosecution for bigamy yielded only a two-day delay of the original plans. The wedding took place on Fela's insistence. Fela placed a twenty-naira note on each bride's head, symbolic of the customary bride price, before handing it to the *Ifá* priest who replied with good news: the newly betrothed would live long together as "husband and wives."[1] Although the proceedings were far from a traditional Yoruba marriage ceremony, everything was in place as though they were. Sugar, sugarcanes, bitter kola, honey, palm wine, and an *Ifá* divination tray gave symbolic weight to the prayers (fig. intro.1). At the end of the formal proceedings, each woman received a marriage certificate designed by one of Fela's artistic collaborators and album art designers, Lemi Ghariokwu.[2] The certificates mimicked the official rituals of betrothal, giving the marriage mock legality. At the event, the brides were betrothed to a Nigerian superstar, someone whose music they had likely heard from a distance in teenage infatuation and whose mischief with the government they had learned about in the ubiquitous news coverage on Fela. With no evident guilt for marrying so many young girls and women, Fela gushed, "I am particularly happy that I have not betrayed my conscience and fatherland."[3] Certificates in hand, the newlyweds, for their part, danced out of Parisona and posed for photographs. When rumors broke of the wedding and the number of brides, a media frenzy began brewing. Unsurprisingly, the event consumed Nigeria's news cycle in the weeks that followed. Was this a proper ritual marriage? A business contract? A spectacle not unlike the rest of Fela's and his people's antics? And would any of these situations be considered legal, ethical, or acceptable? What of the girls? Did they consent to this? Could they, really? It seemed that the frenzy of the event overwhelmed these important questions. For the Lagos working-class public, Afrobeat music's core fan base for whom Fela was a folk hero, the communal wedding was an eye-gripping performance. It was a spectacle not unlike Fela's shows at the Afrika Shrine—or the women's titillatingly defiant enactment of the Black Power salute, topless, on the album cover of *Expensive Shit* (1975), or their nude genuflection on *Shakara* (1972), gestures that struck at the heart of a society invested in policing how the female body was publicly displayed, unclothing or clothing it according to the anxieties of the patriarchal order.[4] Many saw the wedding as a collaborative assault on social and political order by Fela as much as by the brides.

In the style of subculture that Fela's Afrobeat music and activism represented, the wedding became another social performance, willfully blending legal symbolism with the tropes of a Yoruba wedding. Instead of a wedding staged on the heels of rigorous protocols, the event was an incoherent garble of people and elements, equal parts scandal, farce, gossip material, and cultural atrocity. Its relentless fluidity lent the wedding multiple significations. For one, the mass wedding took place exactly one year after the public, violent, and spectacular destruction of Kalakuta Republic. Kalakuta was the creative and ideological hub for Fela's music; it was the urban commune where Fela, his bandmembers, young women, and sundry followers lived and from which they made music and Afrobeat-related art. During the horrible episode of Nigerian history now dubbed the "Kalakuta invasion," soldiers ruthlessly brutalized and raped Afrobeat girls and young women and followed this violation with an equally public and scandalous cover-up. In this vein, the mass wedding was the commune's comeuppance, a dissonant declaration of having survived the still-fresh wounds of the state's brutal assault. In the spirit of commemoration, the wedding helped to rejig the public conscience about the violation that had occurred in broad daylight a year earlier. The brides and groom hence took part in a highly visible social performance to contrast with the painful realities

Figure Intro.1. Fela (in lemon and brown clothing), two unnamed brides, and J. K. Braimah (in a bright red jacket) listen intently to an Ifá priest (bottom right) in a small wedding ceremony, February 1978. Photo credit: Femi Bankole Osunla. Permissions: Femi Osunla's estate.

of neocolonial abjection underscored by their personal experience, a bloody three-year civil war (fought over political secession) bordering on state genocide, and the rule of despotic regimes marked by quotidian brutality, coups, and, in the mid-1970s, high-level assassinations. The wedding also intervened symbolically in a long historical ideological battle produced by the colonial encounter. The ruthlessly polygynous spirit of the wedding scoffed at the ideals of Christian monogamous marriage, an institution that has been front and center in the profound tensions among Yoruba elites over what constitutes appropriate (heterosexual) marriage norms since at least the late nineteenth century.[5] At the Afrobeat wedding, sugarcane and bitter kola took the place of the white dress and ring, symbolizing the persistence of Yoruba rituals of betrothal despite colonial transformations of marriage.[6] Notwithstanding the marriage certificate as a nod to the state and written text as arbiter of legality, the wedding aspired toward a symbolic resistance of sorts. We could therefore interpret the event as yet another high-profile subversion of colonial notions of marriage, a willful, nonchalant appropriation and displacement of colonial signs, registers, moral codes, and logics in search of a soon-to-be-realized some-

Figure Intro.2. A photograph of the chorus line at an Afrobeat performance, taken January 1, 1983. Photo credit and permission: Ian Dickson via Getty Images.

thing new. The wedding appropriated the semiotics of betrothal to new possibilities of collectivity and being in a fledging neocolony.

By subscribing to Fela's Afrobeat music fusion of jazz, soul, and West African highlife music and embracing its corollary subculture, identified by marijuana, sex, and antiestablishment politics, the young brides, whom the public would come to know as Queens, publicized themselves as champions of a highly subversive notion of self, citizenship, and belonging. This book explores how the Queens, alongside an exhaustive list of little-known women (who did not all become Queens but either preceded them or followed in their footsteps), parleyed with Afrobeat by mobilizing various registers of serious play to negotiate individual and collective autonomy in shifting, contradictory, empowering, and self-sabotaging ways. The playful nature of their entanglement with Fela, of which the wedding was a prime example, was sometimes simultaneously subversive of and acquiescent to patriarchy and dominant conventions of femininity. For the most part, however, the Queens were noted for their brazen disruption of prescribed notions of decorum and subservience, not only troubling discourses of womanhood, female sexuality, and pervasive class apartheid but also actively mobilizing otherwise fragmented subcultural ideas and symbolism to query the very moral foundations of a neocolony. Although the young women's actions were liberating in many instances, their choice to live with and prop up Fela's image and work often amounted to substituting one form of patriarchy for another while standing apart from Nigerian conventions for middle-class or elite women. Because many were so young and made grave life decisions under circumstances in which their labors were exploitable, the public (and scholars of Afrobeat) have treated these women's contributions to the formation of a global musical genre as unremarkable or frivolous and have described the Queens as Fela's sidekicks (or worse, groupies). This book wades into the conversation with the goal of recuperating the women who have been buried at the bottom of the Afrobeat archives.

The Queens profoundly shaped Afrobeat art and activism, yet they remained in the shadows: not invited to cosign record deals, for example, or to articulate their own thoughts on Afrobeat ideas or their chosen lifestyle. Neither have they been highlighted in commemorative events around Afrobeat music. Therefore, when Kevwe Anikulapo-Kuti, a backup singer in Fela's band who was a young bride at the 1978 wedding, said to me during one of our interviews that she and her fellow backup singers had composed the hook for the song "Everything Scatter" (1975), I had to pause. "Do you think I am lying?" Kevwe challenged my initial shock at the notion. Four decades after its release, "Everything Scatter" opened *Fela!*, a musical choreographed by award-winning choreographer Bill T. Jones. The show, which opened off-Broadway and moved to Broadway before a global tour, is based on Fela's life; the Queens were not credited for their contributions to the music and live performance, as often is the case. Another Queen I interviewed, dancer Omolara Shosanya, recalled having casually uttered the phrase "uniform chance" in Fela's hearing, describing the pervasive intimidation of citizens by military and law enforcement officials in the 1970s. The uniform, in Omolara's thinking, preemptively tipped the balance of power in favor of state officials during routine encounters with civilians. It was the clothing itself, the thing, that symbolized the power of the state, that granted officials an unearned advantage in the event of a squabble, not infrequent in the 1970s. The phrase became the thematic anchor in the song "M. O. P. 1 (Movement of the People No. 1)." On the surface, Omolara's and Kevwe's belated claims to collaboration, if not unacknowledged co-ownership, appear suspect. The argument against giving them credit for their collaboration might sound something like this: Why did they wait all these years before claiming ownership of said songs? Where is the evidence that they contributed in these ways? Skeptics rarely pause to question how Fela could have *singlehand-edly* composed over fifty albums drawing neither input nor inspiration from the people closest to him. To be clear, discounting the aesthetic, intellectual, and political contributions of the women, Queens and non-Queens alike, who resided in the Kalakuta commune relies on the (mis)conception that they were passive actors somehow suspended from the internal logics of humor, subversion, and inventiveness that governed everyday life and manifested in Afrobeat songs composed, arranged, and published by Fela. This assumption could not be further from the truth. By taking residence in the commune, Kalakutans gave Fela access to the world of the underclass from which many of them sought escape. Their collective musings and interactions supplied Fela with unfiltered access to subaltern critiques of the Nigerian condition. In return, these girls and women found an outlet in Afrobeat music for creative expression unlike any Afropop music genre in the 1970s. It is true for Kalakuta women, as it is for Black girls in commercial Black popular music in the United States, that there would be "no royalties for the song-makers of double-dutch."[7] A sustained elaboration of the imbrication of gender, play, and musical creativity and the latter's susceptibility to appropriation has remained in the shadows. If Afrobeat history must be written with any eye toward clarity and fairness, we might begin by understanding these claims to mean the women's belated appreciation of their own roles as important coproducers, something that they, overcome by youth, exploitative labor relations, and the thrill of subversive artmaking, took for granted in real time.

Girls and young women affiliated themselves with Afrobeat music and its corollary subculture partly in response to the afterlives of colonial definitions of citizenship along the fields of maleness, whiteness, and wealth, a tripartite formulation that effectively excluded African women from full status as citizens.[8] When girls and young women participate in subcultures, they may do so in the pursuit of a sense of community and belonging or, in the context of massive upheaval, as rebellion against a dominant order. The young women who subscribe to subcultures might embody said rebellion through any combination of sexualized self-expression (considering that male-defined subcultures often limit the scope of female expressiveness of their sexuality), through spectacular styles of dress and bodily adornment, or by becoming outspoken activists who challenge the norms around family, work, and leisure. Early scholarship on girls in subcultures underscored that girls' invisibility in subculture studies derived less from their objective marginality within those subcultures than from their structurally different situation than young men. Girls in postwar British subcultures, for example, were active in fan clubs that were pivotal and complementary but subordinated to male-coded arenas of subcultural activity, such as school, work, and leisure. The marginal attention to girls in early postwar subcultures mirrors a general subordination of women in mainstream society while reflecting scholars' tendency to focus on youth violence, an area of subcultural activity in which girls are least likely to participate.[9] The historical convergences that spurred the Afrobeat subculture were distinct, as were the specific ideas that defined propriety and deviance in 1970s Nigeria. Yet the observation that young women occupy structurally distinct and underappreciated locations in subcultures is relevant to Afrobeat. Fela controlled pivotal areas of Afrobeat activity and coded them as masculine through his art and lifestyle: technical knowledge and orchestration of music, public oration and sensational confrontation, showy intellectualism, individual creativity, and populist heroism. Scholars, for their part, have tended to take these domains as the fullest and most valid range of aesthetic and political possibility within Afrobeat. The distortion that ensues is not simply of active absence (though it sometimes is), but, more specifically, of losing sight of "a whole alternative network of responses and activities through which girls negotiate their relation to the subcultures."[10] Even though girls and young women excelled in alternative pursuits of artistic excellence such as collectivized backup singing, collective dancing, and the application of facial makeup, they did so from a position of structural disadvantage imposed by age, gender, and social class disparities relative to Fela. It was from this structural position that they also performed domestic labor in running Kalakuta Republic, the communal home, even if the homeliness and privacy conventionally attached to ideas of home appear incompatible with an urban commune. Additionally, the collaborative, sacrificial labor that unfolded in Kalakuta and beyond the public eye was, quite unsurprisingly, overwhelmingly performed by women. It was offstage that they struggled, thrived, and expressed the most complex version of themselves to bold if paradoxical effect. Their actions in these aesthetic, social, and political domains stretched the moral and ideological range to which Afrobeat laid claim and, in a most tangible sense, the power of Fela's performances and the soundscape of his music. The invisibility of the Afrobeat women's labor equally laid the foundation for separating the women from the fruits of their work. It is along the open-ended and interanimating fields of play, survival, pleasure, resistance, possibility, and oppression that we must read the scope of these women's entanglements with Fela and the production apparatus of Afrobeat music. Such exploration of broad fields of engagement requires a reenchantment with the everyday, the space in which they gave impetus to the meaning of community, creativity, and gendered citizenship. When considered alongside public stage performances, fluid and contested spaces of everyday life contained for Afrobeat women opportunities to self-express and flourish despite the internal and external constraints they confronted. Excavating Afrobeat's "secondary" domains also offers a way out of what appears to be a theoretical conundrum that imposes a victim/agent binary on women's work in Afrobeat, despite the varying temporal scales of their involvement, from a few weeks to as long as three decades. A sustained excavation of the everyday reveals many of the women's actions as constantly negotiated and historically contingent acts. This is a processual approach to social and aesthetic performance that foregrounds capacity and agency in the construction of social realities, including gendered experience.[11] Attending to the everyday as a domain of female creativity, negotiation, political action, leisure, solidarity, contestation, and contingent freedom offers an entry point into alternative, women-centered visions of Afrobeat. Tejumola Olaniyan urges us to consider the women beyond "two opposite extremes," outside the absolute categories of victimhood or agency.[12] This book builds on the contributions of Olaniyan and several Afrobeat scholars who have sought out ways to consider the presence of women in Afrobeat, a salient musical form and subculture with enduring relevance in the lives of Nigerians and West Africans.

In addition to conducting interviews with Afrobeat band members, Fela's closest collaborators, two of his children, and numerous Kalakutans, I conducted multiple oral interviews with four Queens (Omolara Shosanya, Najite Mukoro, Kevwe Oghomienor, and Olaide Babayale). During these interviews, the Queens consistently privileged the positive experiences of Kalakuta Republic and its everyday world as a space of play and of activism. They spoke unanimously of the "drama" in Kalakuta Republic, even though they did not always narrate specific events to corroborate this characterization and though their memories of specific events were sketchy at best. It quickly became clear that the everyday offered abundant room for verbal and embodied self-expression in ways the Afrobeat stage did not. This book therefore gives equal salience to the spectacular and the everyday in the historiography of gender and performance in Afrobeat. Privileging everyday life as performance productively complicates an approach to Afrobeat that routinely privileges the stage, the music, and the spectacular. Thinking of the everyday as a holding space for feminist and nonfeminist possibilities, I engaged the Queens about the range of meanings attached to their stage performances and lives in Afrobeat. I became interested, following their lead, in how they lived within Kalakuta, mainly in the 1970s and 1980s, and in the trajectory of their post-Afrobeat lives. It became clear from our conversations that the mundane lives of Afrobeat women, lives marked by boredom, cooperation, or conflict, seeped into Afrobeat music through codified acts such as *yabis* (playful abuse). Of relevance here is Kyra Gaunt's exploration of how Black girls play; their everyday acts of amusement such as hand clapping, jive talk, chants, dance, colloquial gestures, and body thumping mapped out the initial textures of commercial Black musical forms like hip-hop. Gaunt urges: "Listen in on girls' daily broadcasts from the playground and you'll hear more than 'nonsense.' . . . watch their daily routines. . . . you'll be hooked on their fascinating rhythms."[13] In the uneven playground that was Kalakuta Republic, Fela likewise paid attention to girls' and women's embodiment in self-serving ways. Fela described the process of composing a song's bass line from the vibration of a woman's backside: "I was just watching a girl pass by. . . . Suppose I write a bass line whose rhythm matches the movement of her backside. When I get that bass line, then I can work out the other parts and a new tune is born."[14] Clearly, Fela centered his gaze and creative agency in this telling; the Queens on the contrary often described a communal state in which everything—from sleep states to the semiconsciousness of being marijuana high, debates, and active jostling for Fela's attention (which they described as "hustling")—generated a state of reverie, underscoring the multiple ways that women's mundane lives spurred the sonic, moral, and theoretical propositions of Afrobeat music and problematized the status of solo male genius often ascribed to Fela.

The questions I pose throughout the book tackle why archivists, scholars, and the public have overlooked the Queens' and Kalakuta women's accomplishments even though these largely working-class women artists had a real impact on Afrobeat art and culture and, I would add, on the textures of activism in 1970s and 1980s Nigeria. Also, why have the moral questions associated with their unequal and exploitative entanglement with Fela often gone unremarked? Were the women ignored because of the largely unspoken thought that Fela had used his superstar power and influence to take undue advantage of the twenty-seven young brides as well as other Afrobeat women, a position that might not sit well with posthumous constructions of Fela in philanthropic and messianic terms? Did the women's identities seem too fused with a hypermasculine figure, leaving them too blemished for rigorous feminist and liberatory projects? Furthermore, when Fela married these young women and girls, did it somehow inaugurate a platform for them to express themselves, in a political sense? The commonplace characterization of the women as "Fela's Queens" goes to the heart of these problematics. On the one hand, this characterization expresses Fela's objectifying claims over the women's bodies, labors, and activist actions, and it does so in ways that erase the women as autonomous social agents. On the other hand, "Fela's Queens" underscores the women's differential and shifting relationships to the idea of "Fela," especially as the brand accumulated nostalgic value that continues to circulate in popular music. The resurgence of interest in Fela on the global stage—on Broadway, in his nomination to the Rock and Roll Hall of Fame, and in the rise of global Afrobeat stars like Burna Boy, who strategically fashioned himself after Fela at the outset of his career—has likely contributed to a pragmatic reclaiming of Fela and Afrobeat music by the Queens themselves, even if this connection risks reproducing the Queens' flattened subjectivities. Fela, therefore, materializes in the expression "Fela's Queens" not simply as macho superstar but also as a floating signifier in a contested marketplace where proximity to Afrobeat could potentially translate into other forms of capital. It is in this context that we might understand the women who continue to narrate themselves as "Fela's Queens."

It is guaranteed that every major event involving the Afrobeat subculture generates competing explanations. As such, no consensus can be reached about the rationale behind the 1978 wedding or its many implications, but a few explanations have nonetheless flourished. I list four here to illustrate how an Afrobeat event can easily lend itself to multiple, conflicted perspectives (often undergirded by complicated interests). Conflicting rationales given for the wedding also illustrate how I have written this book as an attempt to foreground the voices of the women, even when those voices compete over meaning or fail to cohere neatly to historical evidence.

A first narrative around the wedding emphasizes its commemorative ethos. The explanation goes that the occasion reinserted the bodies of Kalakutans into the public space, becoming for Fela and Kalakutans a way to publicly recall the destruction of the beloved Kalakuta Republic and acknowledge the women's suffering at the hands of soldiers. A second commonly held view argues that Fela used matrimony to broker the dignity of the Queens. According to this view, the erotic dancing and marijuana smoking that defined Fela's work had ostensibly sullied the reputation of the girls and women. Their image needed revamping, which Fela provided by marrying them. Indeed, part of the ideological work of the designation "Queens" was to discursively revamp the women's mischaracterization as sex workers.[15] The critiques of this line of thinking around moral redemption were swift; a few vocal critics point to the unequal and troubling basis of Fela's sexual and moral relationship to the girls and women, an uneven relationship brought into sharp relief at the wedding. Caro Nwankwo, a Nigerian feminist, spoke of the girls as hapless victims of Fela's manipulation, whose public relationships with Fela had the potential of setting dangerous precedents capable of setting back the fight for women's rights in Nigeria.[16] Tai Solarin, a prominent human rights activist, addressed an impassioned open letter to Fela when rumors emerged of the wedding, challenging the upper-class, British-educated musician about his interest in barely educated, largely working-class Lagos girls and women. Part of the letter reads: "There must be some of the girls who hoped to learn to sing and dance in your team and then look forward to becoming film stars and live independent lives of their own. . . . Would you as a torchbearer say any [of] tomorrow's 27 wives is worth more than a twenty-seventh of you?"[17] Citing Fela's class privilege, his age relative to the brides' youth, and his fame, Solarin argued that the wedding violated the principles of equity and justice that Fela presented himself as championing. The issue was a moral one all right, but it was hardly one of redeeming the women's reputation; the issue was of exploitation by a man with gender and class privilege of girls and women without those privileges. These important critiques often neglected to engage with the young women's perspectives and examine the conditions that made close affiliation with Afrobeat music and, specifically, the Fela-led Kalakuta Republic attractive propositions. The diversity of the young women in Afrobeat's ages, social classes, and backgrounds accounted for the variety of their motivations, some of which overlapped. Many of the women rationalized their affiliation in terms of what they gained in terms of access to the arts, subversive politics, an escape from homelessness, an opportunity to experience the world while on tour, and a place in which they could assert something of a political voice. The fixation on the number of brides, twenty-seven, and that they required saving from society or the state took precedence over a more nuanced narrative that held Fela to account for the few, the vulnerable young, whose presence in Kalakuta was indefensible even when held under the light of the women's shifting and varied investments in his music.

A third position centers the agency of the brides, speculating that they leveraged marriage to Fela to cement their status as public figures and stars in their own right. Their visibility and social status held the capacity, however narrow it might seem, to inspire a view of working-class women and girls not as victims but as empowered in a manner unprecedented in Nigerian pop music culture. There is ample visual evidence to suggest that the young women's self-fashioning, their individual and collective aesthetic choices, fashioned them into pop icons particularly within the Black diaspora and, more recently, in Nigerian pop. They staged striking visual ripostes to critiques levied against them in a manner reminiscent of third-wave feminist self-fashioning. They appeared boisterous and often wore outlandish makeup. The girls hijacked social spaces like nightclubs, hotels, and airport lobbies with brutal unrestraint. In this way, and because of their own power and influence in the public venues they frequented, they accumulated enemies, small and powerful—something only people with some power could achieve. By marrying Fela, relatively unknown girls and women passed through a threshold from ordinary Nigerians to the status of pseudo royalty. They could lay claim to celebrity status through their affiliation with Fela, a status heightened by the quasi-cultural rituals of marriage to an acclaimed pop star and political activist. This view is at best double edged. For one, it considers the public image of the Queens without accounting for how this image germinated from and often fed a patriarchy that hardly nourished them over the long arc of their lives. Also, although the Queens achieved fame as a collective, they confronted lives altered specifically by being entangled at such a young age with a much older, controversial figure. Such a view of the transformative effect of the wedding fails to consider the afterlives of the glossy acts of defiance.

Yet a fourth perspective contends that the mass wedding was little more than a logistical ploy or a publicity stunt—that neither the brides nor the groom harbored serious conjugal intentions.[18] The media frenzy that trailed the event contrasted with the solemnity that such an occasion should command. Because Fela had staged the wedding in secret from his brides' families and from the media, the publicity amplified excitement. Skirting important protocols and excluding family members gave weight to Omolara Shosanya's insistence, decades later, that Fela "did not marry me. He married his work."[19] This was a running theme across two interviews with Omolara. In a marked departure from the other women, Omolara insisted on being addressed by her family name, Shosanya, and sporadically rejected the label of "Queen." (On one occasion, she retorted *"Queen òṣì wo"* / *What worthless Queen.*) Omolara went a step further to draw an explicit connection between Fela Kuti and Hubert Ogunde, a pioneer of modern Nigerian theater who, in 1946, married more wives to subsidize his commitment to full-time theater making.[20] Marriage for these men in popular theater and music appeared to solve the problem of retaining women's scarce artistic labor. Ogunde opted for marriage after failing to recruit women artists through formal advertisement. Fela resorted to marriage at a time when he was losing female talent after the destruction of his assets. The logic is consistent between both figures. By October 1969, twelve women, all wives, were married to Ogunde[21]; roughly a decade later, Fela claimed twenty-seven. As a bride and worker, Omolara offered the less frequently considered fact that the wedding was a way for Fela to reenlist women's labor and affective investment in his work, especially in the wake of massive financial and material loss. Marriage, in this sense, became a culturally recognizable way of rekindling enthusiasm within the commune and, more crucially, the women's belief in the Afrobeat project. For the young brides, the personal and material losses they suffered during the invasion weakened the prospects of returning to their familial homes soon after. "Nobody left [Kalakuta] with a pin," Olaide Babayale-Kuti mused, recounting the scale of personal loss when soldiers set the commune ablaze in the attack's culmination.[22] Although a few Kalakuta women were able to reunite with their families or seek a new life beyond the commune,[23] many felt that they could not return empty-handed without being the object of ridicule. Others stayed a little longer; some never left.[24] Marriage to Fela earned them cultural capital in the sense that becoming a wife papered over some of the post-invasion wounds. For his part, Fela milked the publicity generated by the infamous wedding as well as the sense of renewed investment that the women, as wives, might have felt in its wake. The wedding occasioned a new dynamic in the commune: being a wife implied ownership and submission to patriarchy, which in turn occasioned the performance of new gendered subjectivities as Queens *and* wives.

I engage to different degrees the thinking that undergirds each of the rationales attached to the wedding, but I have found it most analytically useful and consistently applicable to this work to consider the women's affective investments and agency as aesthetically expressed acts; the domestic and artistic labor that underpin their public performances; and the social and structural fields from which those labors and investments are extracted.

The four perspectives I've outlined illustrate that the sensationalism around the wedding obscures a deeper appreciation for the young women's pragmatic decisions and motivations. That the Queens silently enacted roles that reinforced the stereotype of themselves as victims also obscures the possibility for more nuanced perspectives. While women like Olaide Babayale-Kuti and Najite Anikulapo-Kuti celebrated the social and cultural capital they gained from the wedding, others like Omolara Shosanya offered the important perspective that the young brides might, in fact, not have been mature enough to appreciate the full ramifications of their choices on their lives. What also appears critical in this discussion is that competing narratives help transcend the binary of victimhood or agency; each represents a totalizing position that circumscribes a nuanced accounting of the past and its many afterlives. The women's stories illustrate that a complete history of Afrobeat cannot simply be a history of Fela in which women appear as afterthoughts. I therefore am exploring largely uncharted territory by opening a conceptual, theoretical, and narrative space in which the Queens' many stories can be told and heard, hopefully with candor. While I reflect throughout about how I exist in relation to the women and men I interviewed, this work is not a story about my positionality as a relatively young, heterosexual Nigerian man who resides in the United States and studies dance, performance, and African popular culture. Neither is this book a repetition of stories told by other scholars who stake claims on the bodies, identities, experiences, and perceptions of the Queens. I have made a conscientious attempt to convey the Queens' stories in all their complexity, with an awareness of the failures that attend my effort. I collected these stories through interviews, fieldwork, and archival research and have woven together a critical but coherent mapping of gender in Afrobeat through a close reading of a variety of musical and visual texts, from album covers and photographs to songs and song lyrics, live concert performances, and material culture. The archival and ethnographic approaches that inform this book are given narrative coherence and critical meaning through the concept of serious play, which I mobilize to excavate subcultural and feminist themes in Afrobeat in a decidedly Nigerian historical context.

To show the complexity of the Queens' lives within and beyond Afrobeat, "serious play" reframes their stories from a wide berth of Afrobeat-related experiences, ranging from everyday self-fashioning practices and quotidian enjoyment to trauma occasioned by state violence and domestic abuse. A handful of scholars have attended to play in formulations of social life in the afterlives of colonialism. Political theorist Achille Mbembe has argued for an understanding of the African as postcolonial subject endowed with a capacity for play and indulgent enjoyment. For Mbembe, play functions as a method by which Africans negotiate the inversion of order marked by the state's overreach in everyday life, an overreach so mundane and engulfing as to be banal.[25] To play in this condition is therefore to shapeshift with and within the matrices of power, acquiescing, surviving, or destabilizing its everyday operations. To play is to immerse the self in the moment, to enjoy. It is to experiment with new narratives, icons, symbols, and imaginings of the self and of collectivities and to experiment with novel rituals, geographies, and practices of intimacy. It is at once to simulate deference to state rituals and to "say the unsayable and to recognize the otherwise unrecognizable" under the guise of frivolity.[26] Immersed in states of play, the subject laughs, sings, dances, gossips, and loves, activating registers of being beyond categories of dystopia and in spite of biting realities of material abjection. That African studies scholarship has reckoned meagerly with the potency of play or the ludic conceived more broadly hardly undermines the salience of these practices to the construction of African lifeworlds or the subjective experience of Africans. After all, African youths constantly seek opportunities for "the free play of the imagination."[27] To play as such is to enact slippages, troubling the banality of power and doing so with relish.[28] When, like the Afrobeat Queens, working-class women play, they shapeshift and enact slippages within the geometries of patriarchy, state power, economic abuse, and a broad system of gendered dispossession. Aimee Meredith Cox's articulation of Black women's shapeshifting within and beyond the grammars of resiliency and casualty is instructive. Cox writes of performers whose narratives are informed by "what it feels like to live in bodies that are given multiple unstable identifications," including Blackness, femaleness, youth, class, and nationality.[29] *Queens of Afrobeat* underlines how Afrobeat's women performers, over drawn-out periods, instrumentalized play in aestheticized and everyday social performances as they negotiated competing subcultural and neocolonial imperatives.

The Wedding as Serious Play

With the mass wedding, the brides ceased to be "Fela's girls"; they became *Queens*. In a highly cited explanation for the wedding, Fela described it as appreciation for the women's having endured many troubled times: "These girls have suffered plenty-plenty for me-o! For years. Some for eight years! Fearless women, these my girls. Good women, man. And I said to myself: 'Fela, these na good women o! Shiiiiit!'"[30] As discussed earlier, this explanation flattens the complex and competing motivations behind the women's participation in the wedding to token appreciation. Beyond Fela's reasoning, Kalakutans, including young men who worked for Fela or found a mentor in him, sought to stage the wedding as intentionally absurd. It was in this spirit that the wedding came to showcase neither the pageantry of a middle-class Lagos wedding nor the rigorous protocols of its Yoruba equivalent. To be sure, a combination of belated access to formal education for girls and the traditional role of women as caretakers implied that early marriage of girls and women was not an uncommon practice in 1970s Nigeria.[31] However, such marriages were attended by elaborate and unbending protocols, enlisting the support of key stakeholders in the lives of the individuals. In place of parents or family, Fela's childhood friend J. K. Braimah was "father" to the twenty-seven brides and doubled as groomsman. No parents or family members of the brides were present or invited, as would have been customary Yoruba practice, neither were they presented with the opportunity to decline their wards' involvement in the marriage. The wedding's proceedings repurposed as fluid and contingent a stable and policed cultural practice. The wedding drew on tropes of Yoruba matrimony augmented with *Ifá* divinatory practice, incoherently and illogically appropriating enough of the rituals of customary and colonial-derived marriage practices to be considered a troubling sociocultural precedent. It was the nonchalant subversion of the institution, the toying with marriage, the number and age of the brides, and the cultural assault implied by the absurd ritual that many observers found concerning. The implications of the wedding were serious for those involved and for observers in society. By the same token, it postured as playful, a happening not to be taken too seriously. The ambiguity inherent in this serious play has critical application across a host of Afrobeat-related events and performances.

Play is understood to carry cultural potency,[32] but what does serious play achieve or imply? It has been observed that young women tend to join subcultures in a search for "pleasure and excitement" as much as to mark themselves apart from a dominant culture.[33] Consistent with the pleasure-inducing experience at the heart of subcultural affiliation, I conceive of serious play in the Afrobeat context as an array of structured, subversive, and improvised pursuits that amused and absorbed Kalakutans and dialectically shaped Afrobeat music and subculture. The Afrobeat subculture imbued the absurd, the trivial, and the jocular with potency and derived pleasure from teasing the military state and Nigerian cultural elites. I also use the term "serious play" to underscore three interrelated propositions: playing as political, as generative, and as subversive enough to elicit an outsized cultural response. Because what is being toyed with are the ideas and institutions that society holds sacrosanct, serious play tends to elicit backlash; it is particularly potent in flipping the underbelly of cultural and political power and in deconstructing culture. Creative activism scholars have used "serious play" to describe the "ludic and playful actions that agitate in support of a social movement,"[34] and organizational behavior researchers have taken up the concept to describe "the intentional use of playful behavior to achieve work-related goals."[35] Afrobeat women's activism was characterized by intentional experimentation with aesthetics and with a blurring of the boundaries between work, leisure, and activism. The women illustrate how groups might juxtapose frivolity and work as experiments in ambiguity and adaptation.[36] Improvisation, self-indulgence, and enjoyment thus take on political and generative forms. Engaging Afrobeat through the work/play/activism triad disrupts singular narratives of genius often attributed to Fela.

I build on existing conceptions of serious play as political and generative action by underlining how in the context of class, age, and gender inequities and the state of precarity of inhabiting all these subject positions, the ludic posture might assume repercussive dimensions. The "serious" in serious play, as such, implies its potential to produce a stark response. This sense of danger, stoked by Nigeria's fraught political climate in the 1970s, underscored the women's public and private acts in Afrobeat. Olaide Babayale-Kuti seemed overcome by a deluge of memories of fun and adventure when she shared, *"Aiyé ti pò jù! / The enjoyment was too much!"* I had asked her "How would you describe Kalakuta to a stranger?" to help me visualize the everyday world of subcultural living. *"Aiyé ti pò jù!"* was her emphatic response. Olaide used *aiyé* to suggest a state of being overcome by pleasure, the irreducibility of communal life in the mid-1970s to a single story. What story, after all, can contain or convey the experience of being completely enraptured? It is hardly a negation of Olaide's explanation that Tony Allen, Fela Kuti's lead drummer and one of his most important collaborators, remembered the Kalakuta Republic area as "a war zone" during this same period.[37] This differential accounting suggests that Olaide, like her peers, refused to reduce risk and pleasure to mutually exclusive categories. It is fitting that Olaide's refusal to sum up her Kalakuta experience would frame my thinking about the potency of ostensibly frivolous pursuits in forging a meaningful understanding of the women's lives in Afrobeat. Women in Afrobeat freely appropriated and riffed on an endless array of indigenous and colonial-derived symbols, discourses, rituals, and codes to make claims on their subjectivity and presence, to insert their bodies and voices in a context in which they were made invisible and unheard. As an immersive mode of everyday life performance, the Queens (and non-Queens alike) mobilized serious play in willful acts of refusal, pleasure, troublemaking, creativity, and freedom. They performed acts that had an ideological weight and that provoked ostracism, moral panic, and physical violence. The women's playfulness manifested an array of stage and everyday life performances and responded to the pressures of intersecting patriarchies—of the Fela-led commune in which they lived and of the patriarchy embodied in normative formulations of family and state. The public did not simply read their acts of serious play as symbolic disruptions of culture but as acts that demanded a forceful response, even punishment. The wedding, the state violence it memorialized, and the frantic coverage it provoked illustrate the convergence of three elements crucial to understanding the women's presence in the Afrobeat subculture: the generative and subversive nature of playing; the ever-present risk of violence and retribution that attended the activity of playing; and the capacity of said activity to reinforce a subculture's processes of self-knowing.

The Queens

Only a few genres of music are nearly synonymous with specific individuals. A funky medley of soul and jazz improvisations, West African highlife, scat singing, and call-and-response vocals, Fela's pioneering brand of Afrobeat music combined derisive humor and inflammatory social critique. Throughout his life, Fela embodied a public persona that shaped reception of Afrobeat: playboy, musical genius, social crusader, and prophet of the downtrodden.[38] He projected charisma within each of these roles (separately or combined) and onto the political aims of his music, which explored themes such as institutionalized corruption, the psychology of the so-called African subject, the lingering structural effects of colonization, and the entrenchment of autocracy in its wake. Fela dispelled the myth that music should have only entertainment value and not a deeper message: "As far as Africa is concerned," Fela famously offered, "music cannot be for enjoyment; music has to be for revolution."[39] Fela's weapons in this revolution were satire, parody, and creative subversion, all of which rode on the back of groovy musical arrangements. Nigeria's sprawling underclass embraced Afrobeat music for the clarity with which it portrayed and critiqued the realities of contemporary social life.

The most decisive transformation in Afrobeat ideas can be dated to 1971, when Fela opened his mother's two-story home in the working-class Mushin neighborhood to members of his band. What began as a logistical move to conveniently house dancers and bandmembers, who would otherwise endure long travels in the notorious Lagos traffic, ended up taking ideological valence as the house evolved into an artist commune, a critical move in Fela's broader experimentation with harmonizing talent management, musical form, and the ideological character of his blended form of pop music. By the time the home became widely known as Kalakuta Republic in 1974, it had also become Nigeria's most iconic urban commune and a subculture in its own right.[40] The commune assumed a bohemian character, transforming into a subcultural space beloved and reviled for its loose experimentation with sexual freedom, artistic self-expression, marijuana smoking, irreverence, ideological polemics, and groovy pop music. It was not long before Kalakuta assumed near-mythical character and loomed large in the Nigerian and, soon enough, African imagination. Nigeria's cultural elites viewed Kalakuta and its charismatic leader as morally bankrupt. Their posture was one of distance from Kalakuta because being seen as close to Kalakuta (let alone in it) or as affiliated with Fela was a taint. Kalakutans were too bohemian for middle-class and elite Nigerians, whose cultural disposition leaned toward mimicry of Eurocentric values and mores. The broader publics of Afrobeat music tended to be fascinated by Kalakutans for their daring, the disruptive nature of their artmaking, and the individual freedom, Black liberation, and youth agency that undergirded much of their creative output. These progressive positions—radical at the time—blinded many to a critical assessment of inequity within Afrobeat, especially as it pertained to young girls. What is more, that the Nigerian military state, itself resistant to free expression, viewed the nonconformist attitudes of Kalakutans as decidedly problematic only heightened empathy for Kalakutans by the end of the decade. Kalakuta's very existence as a "republic" implicitly questioned the legitimacy of a military state.

If Kalakuta registered to visitors as a generative rebellion against the state and elites, its affiliated nightclub across the street, Afrika Shrine, staged performances that gave aesthetic and architectural form to sometimes inchoate ideas. Like the commune, the now-iconized Afrika Shrine began modestly, in a courtyard at the Empire Hotel, in the Idi-Oro/Moshalashi area of Lagos. The area's physical geography mattered for the notoriety that accrued to the nightclub and commune. Surrounding Kalakuta Republic and the Shrine were a host of hotels, brothels, and nightclubs stretching from the Moshalashi area to the middle-class Surulere area of Lagos. Kalakutans immersed themselves in the Moshalashi area as a vibrant hub for youth culture and late-night entertainment, amplifying the area's vibrancy.[41] Popular clubs like Phoenicia and Surulere Nightclub, both of which had housed Fela's band, Africa 70, prior to the Afrika Shrine, dotted the scene between Kalakuta and the working-class neighborhoods that included Mushin, Akoka, Surulere, and Ojuelegba. Afrika Shrine was unique in this area marked by abandon, sexual freeness, booze, music, and enjoyment precisely because of what it did differently. The Shrine, as it was often called, projected Afrobeat music's ideological character. A blue neon sign that read "Blackism: A Force of the Mind" acted as the backdrop of the stage. Fela's keyboard or saxophone stand sat center stage, while a raised platform carried percussionists and Africa 70's horn section, as well as women backup singers. Four netted, cylindrical cages were central to the Afrobeat spectacle. Two stood at the foot of the stage; two others were positioned deeper in the audience. Each contraption, about three meters high, could only contain one dancer at a time. During extended grooves, four women danced in the cages, rotating between solo dancing onstage and resting in the wings. The orchestra pit conveyed the Shrine's spiritual character. It housed a worship area bearing the portraits of Pan-African icons: Kwame Nkrumah, Patrice Lumumba, Malcolm X, Martin Luther King, and, after 1977, Funmilayo Ransome-Kuti (FRK), Fela's mother. During comprehensive shows, Fela took worship breaks to propitiate this pantheon of political ancestors, sometimes offering animal sacrifice in full view of the audience.[42] The Shrine hosted a vibrant weeklong program that attracted university students, the urban working class, day laborers, and soldiers alike.[43] Soldiers at a nearby military outpost, Abalti Barracks, patronized the Shrine along with businesses in the bustling area. The proximity between Abalti and the Shrine came to color their quotidian and symbolic interactions, including the 1977 violence between Kalakuta Republic and the state (elaborated in chap. 4). The density of imageries, acts, sonic vibrations, and symbolism contained within and facilitated by the Shrine and Kalakuta Republic underscored the creative rebellion of Afrobeat music as a genre that relied on the restless, the erotic, and what was commonly understood as the radical in the 1970s.

Fela and Africa 70 performers gave shape to Afrobeat ideas through their bodies. Young women in Afrobeat were at first dismissed as "Fela's girls," but by the end of the 1970s, they had become cultural icons of their own. They forced this reckoning through virtuosic dancing and backup singing at the Shrine as well as creative application of Afrocentric facial makeup. In some cases, the women's dancing allowed them to cultivate a dedicated following among Shrine goers. These domains of women's creativity became cornerstones of Fela's music, giving credence to the view that Afrobeat was not simply a musical genre but also "a whole lifestyle."[44] Compared to the singers, the dancers loomed large in the public imagination. Their dance routines involved controlled vibration of the hips and buttocks in the dancing cages at the Shrine. The erotic nature of their performances earned them a denigrating label: prostitutes. If Afrobeat music was the vehicle through which Fela conveyed his ideas around African liberation, women's dancing located those ideologies in the realm of the banal. Their sensual dancing propelled Pan-African ideology through the libidinal, channeling the intellectual through the affective power of the erotic via what Vivian Goldman pointedly describes as "the primeval pussy power."[45] Their contributions transcended their stage performances when, in 1975, they formalized the use of bold facial makeup to great effect, using *efun* and *osùn* (white and red organic body paints).[46] Embracing their faces as canvases for creativity and self-expression, the women expanded their makeup routines to include cowries and miniature plastic discs, token expressions of cultural authenticity. Because these bodily adornments became part of everyday life, the bodies of Afrobeat-affiliated women became itinerant statements of the genre's subversion.

The women of Afrobeat emerged on the music scene straddling the spaces of girlhood innocence and adult transgression during a time when the meaning and boundaries of girlhood were still very much contested. Because many of the Queens joined the subculture as teenagers, they became figures of moral controversy. Resistance to their presence in Fela's work was expressed through sporadic criticism in newspaper writings and in court cases filed against Fela. The teenagers / young women associated with Fela were in the eye of the storm as their parents either sued Fela for child abduction or sponsored police officers to retrieve daughters consumed by the Afrobeat lifestyle. Folake Oladeinde, the twelve-year-old daughter of a former police commissioner, was at the center of one of the earliest state incursions into the commune. On November 4, 1974, Folake's widowed mother, Juliet Oladeinde, led eight policemen in a third attempt to retrieve her from "somewhere called Kalakuta Republic."[47] Members of the commune, including other girls and young women similarly estranged from their families, resisted by pelting the officers with bottles, tree branches, and stones. Oladeinde successfully retrieved Folake from the commune. Relieved, she enrolled her daughter in school at the recommendation of the chief magistrate who presided over Folake's child abduction hearing. Folake's subsequent actions were at odds with the wishes of the court and of her mother, who lamented how Folake "did not say a word before running back to Fela's house."[48] Folake's story illustrates that it was not for lack of trying that parents gave up on their impressionable daughters. Lacking effective measures from the state and faced with weak child protection laws, parents tried futilely to mobilize meaningful support for retrieving their daughters from Fela's clutches. Kalakuta lured both daughters and sons deeper into a world of marijuana, sex, travel, music, and an elusive pursuit of freedom. Folake did not enjoy a monopoly on this kind of teenage rebellion; others were even more ambitious. Serwaa Akosua, a young Ghanaian woman with a talent for dancing, journeyed from Accra across three national borders to join Kalakuta Republic. How girls and young women forsook their homes baffled observers, fueling speculation that they had no agency over their circumstances and did not understand the full ramifications of their actions on their lives. It was certainly true that the precarious thrill of Kalakuta life, especially as it entailed psychedelic drugs, blunted their perception of living under the fangs of exploitation. Plus, some girls were actual *girls*, too young and still developing their bodies, brains, and identities; for them, Kalakuta and Fela represented toxic models. So it should come as no surprise that when parents sued, a few girls testified in court in Fela's favor, not only embarrassing their parents but also effectively invalidating the child abduction charge, the only applicable law on the books. The absence of coherent federal legislation on child marriage or child rights made prosecution practically impossible.[49] These highly mediatized legal spectacles, for which Fela received praise, came to a tragic head quickly. When tensions came to a boiling point in February 1977 and soldiers invaded Kalakuta Republic, they took to sexual violence, leaving many girls and women with enduring scars. For some, the invasion reinforced their resolve to resist dominant society, lengthening their affiliation with Fela and Afrobeat. The invasion was one of

Figure Intro.3. A portrait of Kevwe Oghomienor taken in Paris, circa 1985. Photo credit and permission: Bernard Matussière.

several vicious attempts at silencing Fela and the cohort of women performers, whom the state deemed not victims but dangerous accomplices to the musician's mischief. By the 1978 wedding, Nigerian society viewed Kalakutans in a polarized fashion: either as iconoclasts worthy of adulation or as morally bankrupt undesirables whose actions needed to be punished before they upturned society altogether. The Queens would bear the brunt of the tensions between subculture, mainstream society, and a volatile state.

Kevwe Oghomienor (see fig. intro.3) was a flashpoint in these tensions. Hers is a well told and easily distorted Afrobeat story. Kevwe's parents failed in their attempts to lure her away from Kalakuta. They purchased a piano to satisfy her passion for music.[50] Kevwe evolved into a vocal powerhouse for Fela's work, featuring in virtually every major album released between 1972 and 1997. Her singing role was interrupted only by sporadic exits and returns after the Kalakuta invasion on February 18, 1977.[51] Today, Kevwe, whose piercingly sonorous voice earned the admiration of her peers, lives with a complicated memory of the past. On many levels, her voice demonstrates the backup singers' centrality and erasure—and more so, the haunting dialectic of being listened to but not heard. Kevwe's story illustrates untold aspects of Afrobeat history, the familiar and the terrible, the fascinating and the traumatic, aspects that laid themselves bare during my initial meeting with her in July 2014 and our subsequent interactions.

I encountered suspicion, painful retrospection, ostracism, and mourning from the Queens at the start of the project. However, as I came to know them, to listen to them (even if only through brief messages or short exchanges between long periods of silence), and to align myself with their stories and struggles as a fellow Nigerian who also cares deeply for collective flourishing, they slowly let me into their fold and allowed me to tell their stories, with a commitment to respect and their integrity. By encountering the Queens one by one and seeing their initial resistance to talk about Kalakuta, I came to realize that I could recreate their experiences while keeping an eye to complexity. At the start of the project, one of my main aims was for readers of this book to take the Queens *seriously*. To do this, I knew I would need to show them as conscious cultural agents and everyday performers. I had to describe their pursuit of pleasure and their love of the Afrobeat project (and their intimate relationships with Fela Kuti as host, friend, husband, employer, and, in some cases, oppressor) accurately and respectfully as sites of critical exploration. My deepest hope is that this book takes steps toward restoring the women to their proper place in Afrobeat history while guiding future research toward a more ethical, thoughtful, and rigorous treatment of their lives and presence in such an important political movement and music subculture.

Methodology

I conducted multiple interviews with four Queens—Olaide Babayale, Kevwe Oghomienor, Omolara Shosanya, and Najite Kuti. I also interviewed a host of individuals close to Fela, including two of his children, Yeni and Seun Anikulapo-Kuti; Egypt 80 musicians including Dede Mabiakwu and Yinusa Akinnibosun (who passed away in 2018); and two cofounders of Young African Pioneers (YAP), Lemi Ghariokwu and Duro Ikujenyo. My interviewees included men (such as Eludoyin Elutunde) and younger "non-Queen" women who either worked closely with Fela or resided in Kalakuta Republic between the 1980s and 1990s. These women performers came to Afrobeat at a later juncture, were younger than the Queens, and offered perspectives on Afrobeat that Queens did not have due to departures or positionality. Three women in this group include Mary Umude-Haverkamp and Pulchérie Ibilola Hoga, singers who joined in the 1980s, and Ifeanyi Abuah, an entrepreneur who frequented the commune from the late 1980s to the mid-1990s. The interviews with Hoga, Umude-Haverkamp, and Abuah revealed crucial information about the different and sometimes overlapping relationships that a successive generation of women maintained with the Afrobeat project. Interviewing younger women also revealed patterns and deviations over the long term, which proved particularly illuminating in understanding not only shifts in gendered power dynamics but also rehearsed organizations of labor, talent, and expectations around gender. Taken together, interviews with Afrobeat-affiliated women revealed designs and differences in their trajectories, including exoduses, hiatuses, returns, and, in some instances, deaths. Alongside Kevwe Oghomienor, Najite Mukoro, nicknamed "Fire Dancer," was one of the women with the greatest longevity in Afrobeat. Having joined Kalakuta Republic in 1972, she worked as an Afrobeat dancer for decades, her run interrupted by motherhood and aging out. Najite's dear friend Fehintola Kayode was a highly talented backup singer from Ipoti-Ekiti, a small town in southwest Nigeria, who also boasted a long career in Afrobeat (over thirty years). Fehintola's extensive work entailed ensuring the band's survival after Fela's death (chap. 7). Alake Adedipe was known as the intellectual among the women: she read books and engaged in debates often considered the preserve of men. Kalakutans compared Funmilayo Onilere with Fela's mother, FRK, reading meaning into their shared name and prominent cheekbones. The younger Funmilayo performed impromptu impersonations of the revered activist to the commune's delight, especially following FRK's death in April 1978. These nuances of these women's characters, desires, and motivations have largely eluded scholarship and public discourse. To gain a sense of the Queens' entry and presence in the Broadway show, *Fela!*, I interviewed two performers, Rujeko Dumbutshena and Nicole de Weever, both of whom played Queens in the Broadway production centered around Fela's life. Those interviews revealed crucial insights into Black women's aesthetic and political reinterpretation of the Queens' lives and activism.

I have distributed autoethnographic reflections throughout the book. The purpose of these narratives is to take stock of my positionality and share with the reader affecting moments in my journey searching for the long-forgotten Afrobeat Queens. The stories narrate triumph, dread, disappointment, chance connections, difficult discoveries, and musings on how the Afrobeat past inflects the women's present realities. The stories are intimate and vulnerable, and they sidestep an approach to knowledge production that prizes empirical observation and critical analysis from a distance.[52] Rather than assuming an "objective" tone, I have favored a ground-level telling of encounters that are personal and processual and aspire to work in service of the women's goals of reconstructing narratives of the past. Those stories variously contain ambivalence and certitude, chance meetings and design, discomfort and laughter; they convey, as transparently as I can afford in this form, the messiness of ethnographic work. The punctuating pattern in which the stories interrupt, amplify, or cut through the narrative is deeply inspired by the powerful jazz-form writing of Omi Osun Joni L. Jones in *Theatrical Jazz: Performance, Ase and the Power of the Present Moment.* My hope is that these autoethnographic stories facilitate a reenchantment with Afrobeat temporalities. They invite the reader to a stocktaking of a postrevolutionary moment, a return to the Queens since the last time society checked in on them, a meeting after iconicity and beyond the spotlight. I use ethnography to make legible subjugated aspects of the Queens' lives I experienced firsthand beginning in summer 2014, when all I had were untested interview questions for my doctoral dissertation. Music journalism has historically probed the private lives of women artists to critique or construct them as sexually loose and, if straying too far from maternity, deviant. This kind of framing of the lives of women in popular music undercuts women's talent, ambition, and achievements while reproducing male dominance.[53] When the Queens shared intimate details about their lives and deeply personal struggles, they did so to lay bare the anatomy of their oppression as working-class women navigating an industry on their own and without usable precedent. They spoke about their lives to underline an ongoing struggle for more just and inclusive Afrobeat narratives that facilitate an improvement in their material conditions. The reproduction of the details of their personal lives in the ensuing pages serves the similar end of flipping the underbelly of gendered oppression in Afrobeat and the powerful gatekeeping that permeates the community.[54]

Archival research complemented and informed my core ethnographic approach. Exploring the newspaper archive of the Gandhi Library, known officially as Research and Bibliographic Department of the University of Lagos Library, revealed how 1970s and 1980s print media indexed deep cultural anxieties around women's autonomy. Newspapers and magazines promoted their publications partly by fanning controversy around the facts and fabrications of young women's sexual lives; evidence of interest in the young women's well-being is in short supply. Archival discoveries sometimes served a corroboratory role in the research; in some cases, newspaper articles confirmed the stories that Queens had shared during interviews. Olaide Babayale-Kuti, for instance, was thrilled to receive an old newspaper photograph that I shared with her. The clipping showed Olaide in the company of FRK, reinforcing Olaide's claims in our first interview about being the closest Queen to Fela's late mother. "I was not lying to you," Olaide added in a reaction that was half delight, half vindication. Archival discoveries helped to frame or deepen interview questions, to fill in critical gaps in reconstructing key events in the past, and to understand the contemporaneous motivations of a variety of actors. Occasional gaps emerged between past events and the women's recollections. These gaps were sometimes confusing but often rich and generative. In some instances, they exposed deliberate elision of specific historical details, contemporary revisions to past events, new interpretations, or renewed sensitivity to the retrospective significance of a person, event, or subject matter after many intervening years. Interviews offered space for sensitively fleshing out gaps between past and present. In short, silences were often more generative than not, especially when read alongside archival evidence or absence. The question of absence and erasure was particularly striking when I visited the Kalakuta Museum, a repository of Afrobeat print and material culture converted from the actual building that last housed the Kalakutans. The range of distortion in that official curation helped reinforce the value of the counterdiscourse the women often offered in their stories. These stories represent a multitude of lives that the archive tends to distort or silence. In addition to exploring institutional archives and conducting interviews, I closely studied a wide-ranging array of materials including lyrics, album art, artworks, photographs, concert performances, and lesser-known hagiographies like Mabinuori Kayode Idowu's *Fela: Why Black Man Carry Shit* and Majemite Jaboro's self-published *The Ikoyi Prison Narratives: The Spiritualism and Political Philosophy of Fela Kuti*. These two books proved helpful for reading through the silences around the women because the authors, both of whom lived in Kalakuta Republic, exhibit far less narrative restraint than traditional scholarly analyses. The combination of archival, ethnographic, and close-reading methods aided my painting of a richer portrait of Afrobeat women's lives than is currently found in the literature.

Chapters

Fela inaugurated the commune that became Kalakuta Republic shortly after the 1971 release of the song "Jeun Ko Ku." That the commune was free and open to the public attracted a trove of disaffected youths; it became the permanent home of girls and young women, many of whom became performing artists in the Africa 70 band. Chapter 1, "Birth of a Restless Collective: How the 'Girls' Converged," attends to crosscurrents that drew girls and young women to the commune at its inception. The chapter examines local circumstances—for instance, disillusion marking the years following the Nigerian civil war (1967–

1970), celebrity, and marginal opportunities for women artists—as well as global events such as the rise of postwar youth subcultures and the Pan-African ethos that suffused the political and intellectual culture of 1970s Nigeria. In this chapter, I read the youths attracted to Kalakuta Republic as impressionable but alert to the prevailing circumstances.

Only a handful of women activists rival the grassroots activists organized by Funmilayo Ransome-Kuti (FRK, Fela's mother), who in the 1940s rallied against the colonial administration in Abeokuta and helped oust a colluding local king, the Alake. While elite women such as FRK take center stage in Nigeria's feminist roster, the parameters for appreciating their activism require adaptation when engaging the lives of women in the Afrobeat subculture. The prominence of privileged women raises a question: Is the lens for interpreting the lives of elite African women capacious enough to accommodate the aspirations, desires, struggles, and actions of working-class African women? The dynamics that set FRK apart from the Queens are not often considered. Not only did FRK live in Kalakuta Republic in the mid-1970s alongside many of Fela's "girls," she also offered tacit approval of the girls' and young women's entanglements with her son, a dynamic reminiscent of how influential women can become part and parcel of, or conscripted into, projects of male dominance.[55] In chapter 2, "From FRK to 'Lady': A Revised Genealogy of the Music's Other Women," I weigh in on discussions of women's contributions to Afrobeat by including in this pantheon working-class women artists such as Fela's first dancer, Dele Salami, who is often written out of Afrobeat histories. The chapter proposes a rethinking of the scope of working-class women's involvement with the emergence of the genre of Afrobeat music. Thus, this chapter takes as its imperative the separation of different subject positions to ensure that a plenitude of women's voices are given more ventilation.

Africa 70 implemented modest initiatives to professionalize women artists, such as hiring a choreographer and a voice trainer. These initiatives demonstrated Fela's desire to run a functional and internationally recognized band. And yet this vision was readily complicated by Kalakuta's embrace of subversion and rule breaking. Women Afrobeat artists therefore lived neither exclusively as professional artists nor as wives in any traditional sense. Rather, they inhabited a complex and shifting combination of these identities, embodying Kalakuta's work-play ethic. Chapter 3, "To Improvise a Precarious Freedom: Before FESTAC 77," examines how the gray area between formal labor relations and the cultivation of rebellion manifested a form of quasi-professionalism. This structured improvisation characterized everyday life in Kalakuta and laid the groundwork for a living and artmaking strategy that embraced individual creativity and collective rebellion. In this chapter, I elaborate on three serious play tactics—yabis (derisive, sometimes playful verbal abuse), solo dancing, and iconic facial makeup—to reread the women's subtle but strategic attempts to assert individuality and creative agency on stage and in Kalakuta. I demonstrate how the women's individual and collective acts gave the Afrobeat music and subculture political significance, refashioning the women into important political actors, especially in the events leading up to Nigeria's hosting of the Second World Black and African Festival of Arts and Culture (FESTAC 77), a Pan-African cultural celebration that also became the landmark initiative of the Obasanjo regime.

One week after the festival closed, on February 18, 1977, the state struck with violence. Hundreds of soldiers descended on Kalakuta Republic. They severely brutalized the commune's residents before setting it ablaze. A common way of narrating the invasion reads it as an act of state rebuttal against Fela's critiques, especially his lampooning of the military complex in songs like "Zombie" (1976). This is true only to a certain extent. Narrating the invasion from the viewpoint of musical provocation is grossly inadequate in explaining the state-sanctioned rapes and gendered violence targeted at the Kalakuta girls and women. I proceed with an obvious but overlooked geographic fact, namely that the Afrika Shrine and Kalakuta Republic sat a mere four hundred meters from a major military installation, Abalti Barracks. Chapter 4, "Unknown Soldier: The 1977 Kalakuta Invasion and the Geopolitics of Intimacy," argues that the historical significance of this proximity figured in the blatant instrumentalization of sexual violence at the invasion. The violence of 1977 became a brutal culmination of confrontations between Kalakuta and the military establishment.

After the invasion, the commune moved to a makeshift block of apartments. Afrobeat music and everyday Kalakuta culture reflected still-fresh trauma up through the early 1980s. The commune's recovery floundered in the wake of a new set of economic and political upheavals, namely emerging neoliberalism and two military coups. It is therefore fitting that Afrobeat music underwent profound artistic and spiritual transformations under the weight of these experiences. Chapter 5, "'Spirit Catch Am': Possessions, Paranoia, and the Tumultuous Egypt 80," focuses on women's role in fomenting those changes amid a wave of spiritualism that swept through the commune. Queens were routinely "possessed" by spirits, notably of FRK or of Fela's Ghanaian friend and spiritual guide Kwaku Addai (known as Professor Hindu). The "spirit years"—the interval between September 1980 and September 1984—culminated in an exodus of women and Fela's imprisonment. This chapter examines how the possessions reshuffled power along gender lines and led to profound transformations in

women's involvement with Afrobeat, changes that reverberated across the decade. A few Queens, especially the mothers, rode out the Afrobeat exodus and
continued to defy hegemonic norms through affiliation with Afrobeat. Following years of strategic shapeshifting between acquiescence and resistance, these
women faced a moment of reckoning when Fela died suddenly in August 1997.
Chapter 6, "Facing the Music: AIDS and Alienation after Fela," examines the
implications of Fela's AIDS-related death for the women alongside the ensuing
feud between Queens, non-Queens, and the Kuti family over legitimacy, ownership, and belonging. Class differences between the women and the Kutis that
had lain largely dormant erupted in the wake of Fela's death, shaping determi-
nations about his legacy. Because the Queens were not legally or conventionally
deemed widows or documented collaborators with authorship and copyright
over their contributions, the public treated them as inconsequential. They were
further stigmatized as pariahs when they were rumored to be AIDS carriers by
virtue of association with Fela. This chapter argues that a combination of AIDS
stigma, family intrigue, and wealth consolidation around "legitimate" heirs
laid the groundwork for the Queens being sidelined from (and perhaps stated
more boldly, robbed of) Afrobeat's commonwealth. Even as they confronted
their mortality, the Queens suffered deep ostracism, but this only unleashed an
indomitable will to survive against the odds. The book's final chapter, "'Where
We Fall Is Where We Pick Ourselves Up From': A Legacy in Fragments," considers the first public concert in Fela's memory to explore emerging patterns
in framing the legacy of the Queens as figures of cultural, moral, and political
consequence in Nigerian and Black cultural production. Motherhood became
the basis for a provisional truce—a final reproduction of the structural integrity of Afrobeat patriarchy—between a few women, such as Fehintola, and the
Kuti family, and how children became both targets for critique and surrogate
actors in constructing the legacies of specific women in the ongoing struggle
for fairness. The chapter considers the broader cultural impact of Bill T. Jones's
reimagination of the Queens in the musical *Fela!*

1

—ɯ—

Birth of a Restless Collective

How the "Girls" Converged

Since the 1950s, youth subcultures have emerged from London and Los Angeles to Lagos and Kinshasa to express disaffection with mainstream culture. Nigeria's most lively contribution to the transnational eruption of post–World War II youth subcultures came in the form of Kalakuta Republic, a group of bohemian artists who converged in an otherwise bland, tan-colored duplex nestled along a rail track running to the Lagos Island Port. For a collective that embraced intellectualism, creative self-expression, individual capacity, and freedom, it is poetic that the commune counted among its neighbors Abalti Barracks, a major military cantonment a few hundred yards away, from which it drew patrons. The commune was also only a few miles from three institutions of higher education, including the University of Lagos; it constituted part of a network of Lagos nightclubs that housed bands experimenting with fusions of local and foreign musical styles (the output described by the capacious category "Afropop") and was engaged in key debates of the time such as African autonomy in the wake of formal colonialism, the nature of citizenship, freedom under authoritarianism, and the role of culture workers in forging (or contesting) national identity. Kalakuta's spare appearance contrasted wildly with its reputation. The commune and its affiliated nightclub, Afrika Shrine, literally across the street, offered a synergy of best-selling Afropop music with lucid and original critiques of the organization of Nigerian society. Within a few odd years, Kalakuta had asserted itself as a crucial West African node in the loose network of global youth subcultures, especially as one animated by a strong Pan-African sensibility. Kalakuta symbolized the potential of Africa's young people as much as their capacity for creative disruption at a time of political ferment. Theirs was an urgent desire to impose a reengineered social order on Nigeria, or at least on a tiny patch of Lagos, at a time when such an elusive political vision appeared tantalizingly realizable. This possibility, galvanized by music and popular performance, partly explains why an expanding cast of young people chose to make an unlikely home out of a relatively obscure artist commune.

West African collectives such as Kalakuta Republic emerged as articulations of youth dissatisfaction with the state and elite culture. Mamadou Diouf writes about how certain African youth collectives capture social margins to assert autonomy beyond the state's ambit. These spaces await, Diouf concludes, "ready to be filled, conquered, and named" and to express, through artistic and spiritual means, a desire for recognition.[1] When otherwise marginal subjects hold spaces open using art, play, and symbolism, they construct alternative worlds that transcend their concrete realities. In these special worlds, communities can "make the rules, rearrange time, assign value to things, and work for pleasure."[2] The artists who populated Kalakuta cut a generally consistent profile. With few notable exceptions, they hailed from working-class homes, expressed frustration with the colonial curriculum of schools they had abandoned, had an appetite for artmaking that dwarfed their artistic training, and publicly expressed cynicism about Nigeria's dominant social and moral order. Kalakuta morphed seemingly overnight from an artist commune into a vibrant subculture where young Nigerians, mostly teenagers, converged and devised an alternate world that gave breath to Fela Kuti's music and imbued a wide range of creative acts—from everyday self-fashioning practices to live-music performance—with political meaning.

Drawn to the allure of subversion and to Fela's charisma and musical output, girls and women played a decisive yet misunderstood role in the rise of Kalakuta Republic and its public character. As in other urban subcultures, women influenced the sway subcultures held in the public imaginary at an elemental level. Early scholarship on girls and young women in subculture misconstrued their presence and motivation for partaking in these groups.[3] In the Afrobeat example, a more complete appreciation for the particularities of the historical moment, or what V. Y. Mudimbe describes as the "conditions of possibility," the sociohistorical and epistemic context of discourse,[4] requires an empathetic encounter with the enchantment of such marginal spaces—what they promised, what they defined themselves against, as much as the imageries by which they were made intelligible. Bodily epistemes underpin the broad and specific significations attached to gestures, movements, states of dress or undress, vocality, and bodily states and arrangements, all of which assume meaning within the particularities of time and place. In the context of the 1970s, the female body and women's bodily deportment acquired gendered, ethnic, classed, sexual, and racialized meanings, many of which were subject to intense public debate. Painting a picture of the 1970s makes legible the bodily epistemes in which Afrobeat dancers and singers performed, foregrounding why the expression "dancing girls" encoded a moral problematic and why the female dancing body in Afrobeat entered an ambivalent public discourse as an object of simultaneous fascination, discomfort, adulation, and revulsion.

Without an elaboration of the conditions that characterized the early 1970s as context, the contemporary reader might be confounded by why young women gave up significant opportunities—afforded by tertiary education and, for some, elite social standing—for an antisocial life of polemical music, subversive art, psychedelic drugs, and the free and public expression of sexuality. Why did young women rebel against a powerful social script, choosing a more precarious subcultural belonging to Kalakuta? Such a reader might also wonder how the lackluster duplex populated by scarcely educated youth gripped the military state's attention so intently, provoking it to unthinkable violence later in the decade. The seeming incommensurability between the social script presented to young women and the subcultural belonging to which Kalakutan women subscribed becomes less jarring when read in the context of a palpable longing for an alternative, if precarious, order. It is relevant that Kalakuta Republic and Fela's Afrobeat music emerged during the years immediately following Nigeria's genocidal civil war, at a moment of uncertainty around the moral legitimacy of a Nigerian state still structurally organized by colonial interests, mores, and orderings.

Afrobeat music's rise in the early 1970s coincided with the coming of age of a generation of Nigerians living through the bitter early years of African independence, an episode marked by authoritarian rule, stark inequities, misuse of public funds, and the consolidation of a powerful and extravagant elite class.[5] Afrobeat music drew its sting from the clarity with which Fela put Nigeria's woes to music even as he reveled in the swamp himself.[6] The interplay between man, music, and moment is well documented in extant scholarship. The question, however, of why a critical mass of youth, especially young women, found a home in Afrobeat music and its associated subculture remains less well understood. I argue that a complex of forces beyond celebrity life galvanized young women's subscription to a life in Kalakuta. This chapter contextualizes the steady gravitation of young women to Fela's work and home in the early 1970s and why, despite protracted efforts by families and state agents, Kalakuta continued to welcome them and young men alike. In well-circulated interviews with scholar and Fela biographer Carlos Moore, many women offered rare reflections about their motivations for fraternizing with Fela. Reasons ranged from personal ambition and passion for music and the arts to Fela's activism and generosity. Artistic collaborators like singer Alake Adedipe cautiously implied a desire for freedom from stifling mores around womanhood.[7]

Neither the idealization of communal life nor the growing number of women at Fela's home was well received by every segment of the public. In addition to cultivating admirers, the Fela-led commune attracted the attention of a tiny but vociferous set of critics who levied dissenting views against the inchoate and, with what little was known at the time, potentially exploitative relationship he maintained with girls and young women. Mostly Western educated and middle class, these critics saw the singers and dancers in Fela's band as abductees oblivious to Fela's politics and their own exploitation. Caro Nwankwo, a Nigerian feminist, argued in a magazine article that the continued association of the "girls" with Fela was consistent with the behavior of victims of domestic abuse; it was some sort of Stockholm syndrome. Mental manipulation had not only inflicted damage on their grasp of objective reality, she continued, but also robbed them of the capacity for self-liberation. What woman would choose a life in Kalakuta Republic, after all?[8] Nwankwo was hardly a lone voice. In an open letter published a day before a wedding in which Fela married twenty-seven of the young women who also worked with him, renowned Nigerian activist and educator Tai Solarin penned an impassioned open letter to Fela. He wondered about the puzzle of the "dancing girls" and their impending marriage to Fela. "Many people had been wondering what the relationship between you and . . . the dancing girls, were [sic]. Opinions differed. But tomorrow after you will have gotten married to them, opinions would coalesce. Friends would pull one another by the sleeves of their dresses—'I am proved right, am I not': 'when I told you it couldn't be otherwise you said Fela was too sophisticated for my ugly suggestions.'"[9] Solarin described the "dancing girls" in such a way to conflate the act of public dancing with stolen innocence.[10] These public commentaries named a real but legally unenforceable concern about pedophilia and sexual exploitation of impressionable girls and young women. And the failure to extract them from Kalakuta and from Fela's grip was not for lack of trying. Some parents sued Fela on grounds of abduction or of their daughters having fallen victim to his manipulation. When those daughters testified in court that their residence in Kalakuta was an exercise of free will, their testimonies drowned out parents' lawsuits and strengthened Fela's case. The musician eagerly parroted the young women's testimonies, only furthering, for some, the suspicion of manipulation. Indeed, the weight accorded to the testimony of girls and young women, including teenagers, revealed the law's ambivalence toward them as potential child victims or capable adults, an ambivalence colored by the unresolved space between colonial and indigenous ideas of the boundaries of modern girlhood.[11] The law notwithstanding, the public antics of the young women had the trappings of silent abuse. In the minds of many critics, those acts joined a litany of failures of public institutions to protect the vulnerable. The language alleging Fela's manipulation named a genuine concern harbored by critics for the young women; chapter 6 contains an extensive reflection on how degrees of maturity, inflected by youth, figured in a long, paternalistic, and exploitative relationship. Perhaps Fela's greatest defense lay in the theatricality of Kalakuta life itself. Kalakuta appeared too fantastic and entertaining to pose a real threat to anyone, too carefree to be taken seriously.

Biting criticisms against Fela had fizzled out by the end of the decade due to public admiration of his antics and activism, incessant raids on the commune by the state (painting Fela himself as deserving sympathy), and the theatrics of the mass wedding, which gave the sheen of legitimacy to a patently unequal artistic-social arrangement. One reason well-intentioned criticisms failed to land any serious blows was the perception that these attacks oozed the puritanism of elite society and painted all young women in Afrobeat with the broad brush of incapacity and girlhood innocence. Such a move elided the age diversity in the ranks of Afrobeat women as well as the creativity and political alertness of the young women to the circumstances of their time. The conflation of age with innocence and incapacity also undercut cultural references marshaled by the commune to justify the creative and political work of young and impressionable women. The assumption of innocence appears at odds with the Yoruba sense of the porousness between childhood and adulthood, a fluidity shaped more by maturity, experience, and responsibility than by numerical age. Proceeding from these premises allows for the interpretation of the historical moment from the expressed and implied worldviews of young women who understood themselves as equipped with a flexible range of cultural resources as they grappled with structural constraints. Just as my first interview with Olaide Babayale was kicking off, she gestured to photographs of her parents on the wall and explained her fraught relationship with them because of Fela: "That's my father; that's my mother. They hated me because of Fela. But I made them to understand that my life is about enjoyment. Life with Fela is about enjoyment, but the uniform people [soldiers and police officers] turned it into something else."[12] In addition to enchantment and enjoyment, it is impossible to grasp the women's affinity with Fela without the contrasting context of military autocracy. As infantilization became the dominant critical lens for reading young women's convergence in the 1970s, narratives effaced the self-articulated intentions of this community of performers, occluding how they understood their creative work as supporting an impactful music band and movement that many perceived as potent enough to threaten Nigeria's social order. I approach the story from two perspectives: that of the women I interviewed and that of the scholarly literature on the broader local/global circumstances that defined constraints and opportunities for them. I hope that this telling encourages an empathetic appreciation of the active deconstruction of ideas and symbols by Fela and members of the Kalakuta community.

Even as skepticism prevailed, the young women continued to articulate their choices using the language of activism underpinned by gestures of playful defiance. This chapter offers a historicizing perspective gleaned from contemporaneous news reporting about them, critical literature on the gender context of the early 1970s, and the women's stories, told in real time and to me, about their arrival at Fela's house and their decision to join his Africa 70 band. It also teases out the crosscurrent of local and global conditions that characterized the birth of Kalakuta Republic as an urban commune that nurtured and thrived on the creative rebellion of otherwise voiceless young women. This is a telling of the commune's formation that proceeds from the young women's interpretations together with the promise that Afrobeat music and its ancillary commune held at a time of national ferment.

Shifting Grounds

Afrobeat's assertion of dissent and difference dovetailed with the global spread of African-derived musical genres such as blues, jazz, reggae, and soul—musical conduits for the lived experience and political thought of people of African descent. Crucially, Black consciousness encoded in music offered African musicians a template for rethinking the political potency of music and the popular arts. African American artists engaged with Africa for musical and political inspiration as they mirrored the elasticity of Black sounds back to African artists and audiences. Fela's political transformation and the Afrobeat women's Africanist self-fashioning embodied a deeply Pan-African ethos that flourished throughout the Black world in the 1960s and 1970s. Insurgent declarations of racial pride in art accompanied by community-level organizing that clamored for structural reform were running themes of US public life in the 1960s. It was in this context that Sandra Izsadore, a Black Panther Party member, guided Fela to reimagine the form and purpose of his music. The relationship between Sandra and Fela represented a microcosm of the reenergized cultural, political, and intellectual ties between newly independent African nations and the African diaspora. Following Ghana's independence from Britain in 1957, Kwame Nkrumah became instrumental in bridging the Pan-African and anti-neocolonial struggle by supporting a fruitful exchange of ideas between artists, thinkers, and political figures from West Africa to the Caribbean to the United States. A series of state-sponsored Pan-African festivals also shaped the zeitgeist of this period. These large-scale, public-funded festivals helped African nations construct shared pasts and imagine futures beyond the colonial with the Black diaspora. Festivals occurred in Dakar in 1966, Algiers in 1969, Kinshasa (in Zaire, now Democratic Republic of the Congo) in 1974, and Lagos in 1977.[13] Consistent with the spirit of the times, Africanist histories took a keen intellectual interest in African royalty. The Afrobeat appellation "Queen" mirrored a tendency among historians at the time to write about glorious African pasts, including a search for histories of African women, especially royalty, in indigenous political structures.[14] Afrobeat music came to reflect the global racial politics of the period. What has gone underappreciated is how the Fela-led Kalakuta reflected, rather incongruously, a different development in global youth culture: subcultures.

Post–World War II social and economic transformations in the global North spurred iconic youth subcultures, collectives of youths who embraced distinct fashions and mannerisms to signal difference from mainstream culture. Subcultures expressed disillusion with the destruction of war and with social transformation in metropoles such as London. Race was a factor not only in the membership of these collectives but also in the root of their angst—for example, Caribbean migration to London—from the 1950s onward. A plethora of white male British subcultures in the midcentury formed in part as a response to the surging Black immigrant population in Britain.[15] Fela was a student at Trinity College of Music in 1958 and remained in the United Kingdom until 1963. This period saw a succession of youth subcultures in London, teenagers dealing with the shocks of postwar industrial change that reshaped established notions of family, work, leisure, and neighborhood. As members of a white-dominant subculture in the United Kingdom, Teddy Boys (also known as the Teds) notoriously spearheaded racist attacks against Caribbean immigrants, whom they viewed as portents and easy targets for anxieties about the destabilizing effects of economic forces on their working-class identity. This destabilization was expressed, for instance, in the breakup of traditional housing patterns, changing modes of capitalist production that displaced working-class jobs, and the proliferation of affordable but poorly resourced urban housing.[16] For their part, Caribbean immigrants who found themselves hemmed in by racial discrimination, unemployment, and poverty turned to reggae music and Rastafarianism, among a broad range of cultural resources, to register disaffection and articulate belonging to the West Indies and Ethiopia. The expressive choices of these migrant youths ranged from the use of patois, weed, and biblical symbolism to wearing prominent locks and, among younger West Indian immigrants, a pep in their walking. These expressions animated individual and collective personhood counterposed to racial scripts in Britain. These assertions of cultural identity were also instrumental in transforming the soundscape and style of Britain's urban working-class communities. Reggae music, perhaps more than any other medium, allowed youths to activate imaginative worlds that affirmed their personhood.[17] For the Nigerian subculture still years in the making, the 1960s was therefore incubatory.

Kalakuta Republic refracted the resistive aspects of Black youth style with the media-gripping creative strategies of working-class British youth collectives. A similar imperative absorbed Afrobeat music. Its experimental sounds contained the Kalakuta ethos of post–World War II British youth subcultures and the media attention they commanded by virtue of style, on the one hand, and the fierce urgency of Black creative self-expression against structures of domination, on the other. Fela's London was one shaped quite profoundly by migrants' creative responses to racism as Caribbean style and music flourished among West Indian immigrants. Groups such as the Mods, Skinheads, and Teddy Boys exemplified white youth subcultures dealing with postwar social change. Fela's time as a student and aspiring musician coincided fortuitously with the rise of these youth groups.

White British subcultures and Black youths' creative cultural responses to racism were driven by diametrically opposed impulses. Yet they all distilled the power of cultural performance in shaping identity and believed in youth as capable agents. These lessons were reinforced during Fela's tour to the United States between 1969 and 1970 with his Koola Lobitos band. The tour was a disaster by all professional standards; it nonetheless proved definitive in Afrobeat's formation. Koola Lobitos struggled to secure regular gigs because the band did not belong to a union; a bandmember filed for asylum in the United States, depleting the meagre pool of talents—some of whom, threatened by homelessness and starvation, overstayed visas and faced the possibility of deportation. Koola Lobitos members took low-paying jobs to survive.

Crucially, the fabled tour was auspicious as it overlapped with two critical turns in US youth culture: the civil rights movement and the rise of hippie subculture. Hippies cut a public image as peace activists who rejected mainstream American culture. Not unlike their London peers, hippies created a recognizable brand of rebellion that included "long hair and beards, colorful style, psychedelic drug use, love of rock music and eco-conscious lifestyle."[18] Nudity and sexual libertarianism constituted an important if controversial aspect of their activism. In 1967, one hundred thousand hippies marched to Washington, DC, in vocal but peaceful opposition to the bloodshed of the Vietnam War. Antiwar efforts began at the dawn of the decade as dispersed protests across college campuses; by the end of the decade, thousands of youths had joined the ranks. For some, hippies embodied the culmination of a decade of young, mostly white Americans embracing a distinct style for self-expression, protest, and spirituality. When hippies protested America's involvement in Vietnam, they wore flower-patterned attire and handed out flowers to symbolize their philosophy of peace and free love. They kept a grip on American media from the mid-1960s to the early 1970s, overlapping neatly with Fela's botched tour.[19] The consensus among Afrobeat scholars is that Fela's racial awakening also occurred during this tour, coinciding with the civil rights struggle. The 1969–1970 tour took place during a period of public protests and community-level programming around education, public safety, and public health in Black communities. A more specific form of Black agitation was underway, namely the rise of the Black Panther Party, a networked community of Black youth who, frustrated by the peaceful resistance of the civil rights struggle, embraced self-defense and organized resistance against racist policing and anti-Black racism in education, housing, and employment. Black student activism intensified pressure against predominantly white colleges and universities to revise curriculum and diversify the faculty.[20] The Black Power movement imagined a radically different approach to the welfare and education of Black people to such a degree that it attracted intense espionage, infiltration, and unlawful imprisonment and persecution of activists by states and the federal government itself. At the urging of Black Panther activist Sandra Izsadore, Fela's music came to reflect the radical spirit of the Black Power movement. His work assumed a political bent as it incorporated race, class, and empire as lenses for reading the history and political economy of contemporary African societies. The critical intimacy between Africa and Black diasporas, fostered by 1960s activists in the United States, transformed Fela's thinking in the most profound of ways. Grappling with Fela's rearticulation of radical politics into a significant subculture requires an appreciation for the subcultures and youth groups that were staples of his travels as a student and, later, as a struggling musician.

Reckoning with Fela's political awakening demands an acknowledgment of his racial ignorance in the years preceding the US tour. A quick illustration will suffice. Remi Taylor was an aspiring musician when she met Fela at a London party in 1959. Their meeting kick-started a romance that led to marriage and, in quick succession, three children. Remi's initial assessment of Fela at the London party reveals something important about his outlook as a young man. Remi was mildly irritated at Fela's Teddy Boy outfit at the London party, likely because she interpreted it as awkward assimilation into British culture. His style at the London party would appear incongruous with his later political image as a champion of African consciousness. That Teddy Boys viewed Caribbean (and likely African) immigrants with disdain and targeted them with mob violence resonated little with young Fela. A Trinidadian migrant recalled, for instance, how "Teddy boys hung out on street corners, and at night they took to 'hunting' black men who they perceived to be 'taking' their women."[21] Racially motivated attacks of this kind culminated in the August 1958 Notting Hill riot, arguably the worst riot in British history.[22] This racist and violent history notwithstanding, the impressionable Fela felt compelled by the Teddy Boy style as a student. Fela's naive style choice reflected the remove with which he navigated London's charged racial climate and his refusal to internalize first-hand racist encounters. Two decades later, Fela reflected laughingly about his student days in London, confessing to having seen the racist rental advertisements of landlords who wanted "No blacks. No dogs."[23] The power of youths as agents of social transformation and the salience of style in public persuasion took hold in place of a reasoned response to racism. Style as politics became the denominator that crossed time and place—from Caribbean youth to Teds and Mods, Hippies to the Black Panther Party.

Black political organizing and postwar subcultures crystallized the agency of the youth into what would become an Afrobeat collective. Yet Afrobeat did not merely imitate better-known collectives. Nigeria was ripe for its own home-grown youth rebellion. The imagined future of prosperity and autonomy that had propelled African independence struggles had all but collapsed. Nigeria's civil war became a continent-wide symptom of this failure. Led by Major General Johnson Aguiyi-Ironsi, Igbo soldiers launched a 1966 coup and offensive, which became perceived as an attack against Nigeria's northern elites, who claimed an outsized share of political and military power. When the Hausa retaliated in a massacre that claimed thousands of Igbo lives, the federal government failed to abate the killings. Perceptions of state complicity in the violence led to clamors for Igbo secession from the Nigerian state. Under the leadership of Lieutenant Colonel Chukwuemeka Ojukwu, the Igbos declared the Republic of Biafra in 1967, taking up arms against federal forces (jointly constituted by the Hausa-Fulani block to the north and Yoruba political elites to the west). When war finally broke out, it lasted for three years and claimed over one million lives.[24] Whatever lingered of the euphoria of Nigerian independence, gained in 1960, was supplanted by utter disillusion by the end of the decade.

The civil war's aftershocks were varied. The federal army had claimed triumph in the war, but its public image was battered. General Yakubu Gowon, who had led the war, became the leader of a state willing to slaughter and starve its citizens on the scale witnessed in the war. His adoption of a policy of reconciliation ("no victor, no vanquished") fed the perception that the government was refusing to reckon meaningfully with war crimes in a war it could have averted. The ethnic mistrust that had fueled the war lingered long after the Biafrans surrendered dreams of autonomy and self-rule by taking up arms. Beyond Lagos, travel across ethnic-spatial lines came with the risk of violent attack.[25] In this climate, the moral legitimacy of the state itself was under question from many quarters.

Popular music reflected the shifting grounds of citizenship, from the uncertainties of war to the shaky consolidation of state power.[26] That Nigeria came out of the war with Africa's largest army had real implications for contact between citizens and state in virtually all strata of society. Fela lamented how victorious federal soldiers strutted around "with fuckin' guns and sticks; pushing people around and acting so big-o!"[27] Contact between state and citizen ritualized itself through violent bodily contact, a form of political subject making routinized through quotidian violence. Police, soldiers, and traffic officers beat offenders or provoked offense to call forth, to hail, citizens into everyday theaters of state power. Suspension of electoral politics consolidated the exercise of political power through violence, or the threat of it, transforming political life into a playground of martial masculinity and by implication, eroding decades of women's political organizing. That the state increasingly imagined and sought to produce pliant citizens who reflected its ostensible penetration into the collective psyche only generated slippages to be exploited by artists; and the economic woes of the 1970s expanded the terrain of legitimate critique. Gowon's dismal reconciliation efforts might have appeared tempered by Nigeria's seemingly overnight oil fortunes. In 1973, Arab states placed a temporary embargo on the sale of crude oil to the United States in retaliation against American support of Israel in the Yom Kippur War. Oil-exporting African nations like Nigeria and Angola were poised to meet the supply shortfall. Demand for Nigeria's low-viscosity crude oil increased fourfold during this period, a shift that repositioned the country as a geopolitical force in Africa. A combination of state incompetence and lack of coherent economic policy for absorbing revenue surpluses made monies from the oil boom a corrupter of Nigerian public life. In a now-iconic statement, the governor of the Central Bank of Nigeria declared that the most pressing national problem was not generating revenue but seeking projects on which to splurge public funds. The statement was indicative of the economic policy, or lack thereof, that undergirded the ensuing public waste, corruption, and unlawful enrichment. Sensational accusations of embezzlement against key public figures became a staple of the Gowon administration.[28] The mismanagement of wealth worsened public confidence, underscoring the 1970s as a hodgepodge of postwar trauma, wasted promise, and discontent.

Key to Afrobeat's traction among Nigerian youth was the notion that a subculture's latent function is to somehow magically resolve contradictions hidden or unresolved in the parent culture.[29] The civil war, shifting grounds of citizenship, and collapse of trust in the state and elite culture fertilized the ground from which an Afrobeat subculture germinated. Otherwise important criticism of Fela's ambiguous relationship with the "dancing girls" in his band drew blanks in the face of the mass-scale atrocities that had occurred during the war and the ensuing quotidian brutalization of citizens in the streets. Concerns about Afrobeat paled in comparison to the more pressing moral atrocities of the Gowon government. Against this backdrop, Fela assumed hero status, and his relationships with multiple young women seemed inconsequential. The zero-sum logic behind such thinking went something like this: In what universe could topless young women on album art outweigh a pogrom? Could loose sexual mores compare morally with the tactics of mass starvation used against the Igbo in the war? Incommensurability gave steam to critiques levied by Fela's music. The naming of Fela's Afrika Shrine in 1971 and Kalakuta Republic in 1974 was symbolic but registered as ripostes to the moral deficiency of the state and Nigerian elite culture.

"Shortage of Female Artists"

Although reeling from the war, Nigeria found itself awash with petrodollars, a significant amount of which funded the cultural vitality of Afropop music. Relatively untouched by the civil war, Lagos emerged as the public theater for a cultural renaissance fueled by fatigue with the musical landscape and by postwar petrodollars. Local and international record labels mushroomed around mainland Lagos. Bands expanded in size just as nightclubs harvested disposable income among Lagosian youth. Public corruption fueled by the oil boom had an ironic side. When the wealthy threw lavish parties, they enlisted the services of praise-singing musicians, many of whom immortalized the objects of their praise in vinyl through hagiographic song titles and lyrics. In this way, oil money through patronage helped fund the rise of musical megastars. And while Fela abhorred the practice of praise singing, he benefited from a booming, oil-dependent economy that sustained live music. Advances in music consumption technology at the turn of the decade were also fortuitous for the consolidation of Fela's brand of music.[30]

A dismal number of bands were women controlled. Because women seldom led bands or recording businesses, this oil-dependent culture boom brought only meager dividends to Nigerian women performers. The rank and file of bands and their public faces were overwhelming male. The incentives for women to join a precarious, male-dominated industry were few, worsened by stigma attached to "showgirls" as moral deviants. The few women who ventured into the industry tended to "occupy the lowest rung in the popular band's hierarchy" even when their performances are vital to attracting and retaining a paying audience.[31] Their creative labor was not only tokenized but also conscribed to low-wage dance acts, a role attracted only working class, out-of-state migrant women in desperate need of a wage. Even here, they confronted sexism and abuse. Only a dismal number of bands had women meaningfully integrated into their hierarchy. And locally owned record labels frustrated women's craft in ways that paralleled the malpractices of foreign labels such as EMI and Decca, whose executives were accused of treating women artists as prime candidates for exploitative record deals. The Lijadu Sisters, an Afro-funk and Afro-soul music duo led by Taiwo and Kehinde Lijadu, was one of a handful of women-led bands based in Lagos.[32] The Lijadu Sisters were backing vocalists with Ginger Baker and later sang on Tunji Oyelana's album *Tunji Oyelana, A Nigerian Retrospective, 1966–1969*.[33]

Not only were the Lijadus two of the few Nigerian women bandleaders signed by a major international record label, but they also succeeded in carving out a recognizable sonic space for their craft. The Sisters deftly blended soulful vocals from Yoruba folk music with funk-style beats to command widespread appeal for both Yoruba and non-Yoruba listeners.[34] The cosmopolitan, Pan-ethnic character of the Sisters' music also lied at the heart of their formula for commercial success. Kehinde put it succinctly: "If we make a million Naira today, I won't be surprised because we had planned and worked hard for it and we don't give up. One thing I'll want to see us achieving is giving a concert with at least ten different Ethnic groups around and reaching them. Taiwo and I have different diversifications [*sic*]—We are like Nigeria."[35] Despite their distinct sound and pioneering efforts, the duo struggled to find major international success. Their relationship with Decca Records symptomized their struggle for an elusive popular music breakthrough that appeared on the horizon with the release of their second album *Mother Africa*. "We've waded through a lot of turbulent waters…. Now that things are a bit alright, people tend to forget what we had been through," Taiwo reflected in 1977.[36] One of the sisters explicitly laid the blame for their struggles on the industry's sexism and misogyny.

> In the past, our men believed that the wife stick to the kitchen and bring kids into the world. That's all. … But now women are telling their men that they no longer want to stick at home and live a dull life, empty one. … It is only this industry that has the problem of *shortage of female artists* [my emphasis]. … You should be the baby to these [recording] companies because you are actually making the money for them. But the other side of the coin is that they don't care, they don't give one fick [*sic*] about the artist. They can sap and sap [you].[37]

Underreported album sales and unpaid royalties lay at the heart of Fela's scuffles with Decca Records, another illustration of the exploitative tendencies of foreign record labels or, at least, of artists' perceptions of the labels' practices as shady. In a desperate attempt to be paid his fair share of royalties, Fela, accompanied by Kalakutans, famously protested by flooding Decca's head office with buckets of feces. This confrontation is monumentalized in "You Gimme Shit I Give You Shit." The incredulity of Fela's desperate act to confront Decca's lack of transparency about his record sales received favorable press. Brazenness of this kind was a privilege only men like Fela could exercise. For pioneering women artists like the Lijadu Sisters, whose participation in music was deemed aberrant, the constraints on such spectacular forms of protests were potent and layered. They confronted the limiting images of the modern woman as restrained and could not count on male allies to support such a fight.

If popular musicians and record labels distrusted one another, the tensions appeared to worsen between 1973 and 1974 with the proliferation of cassette tapes and, with them, the market for pirated music.[38] Negatively affected by the shifting distribution landscape of the mid-1970s, artists increasingly relied on live performance as a revenue stream over which they could assert near-absolute control. Because of the widespread reliance on live concerts for music revenue, women artists, skimmed of recording profits, faced challenges heading their own bands, including cultivating the dedicated clientele of audiences required for stability and recruiting instrumentalists, often men, willing to join a women-led band and appreciate women's artistic and organizational leadership. As such, the consolidation of live music as a response to piracy only further marginalized women in the booming music industry. Indeed, popular performance and women's music had the valence of a paradox. Women across the Islamic Sahel region found themselves conscripted to roles of domesticity, which produced a sense of interiority that materialized sonically.[39] Across Nigeria, women-dominated musical genres circulated largely in rural enclaves, deriving legitimacy from long-standing ritual and ceremonial practices. In cities like Lagos, women-dominated genres of music were in terrible scarcity, and when they were present, they existed within niche ethnic or religious circuits. Waka music was one such women-dominated genre. Mostly during Islamic celebrations, musicians performed waka drawn from Qur'anic chants, melismatic texts, and nasalized singing.[40] Waka's circulation was limited, however, to social events held by Yoruba groups on Lagos Island as well as by patrons in neighboring Yoruba towns. Waka did not aspire to appeal to Lagos's heterogeneous public; it was sung largely in Yoruba, heavily inflected with Islamic verses, and did not have the cosmopolitan character suited to Lagos audiences versed in global pop tunes of the time. Waka's sonic, aesthetic, and affective character placed it beyond the social ambits of the elite Yoruba and non-Yoruba women of Lagos, thinning the pool of potentially dedicated followers.

African feminist scholarship has documented the persistent neglect of women's writing.[41] Musical form, language, sonic properties, audiences and reception, embodiment, and ownership carry gendered significations that render women's craft and struggles in popular music a poignant site for feminist theorizing. Women musicians found themselves contending not only with the shifting technologies of production and circulation of 1970s Afropop music but also with entrenched cynicism around women and their contribution to culture and society. Just as spoiling was the widespread conflation of visible forms of women's artistic labor with prostitution, the locus of moral contestations throughout the early twentieth century. With only a handful of widely known African women musicians—including Miriam Makeba, South African vocalist and antiapartheid activist, and Oum Kalthoum, Egyptian singer and songwriter—boasting global renown the picture looked bleak across the continent. Consequently, Makeba and Kalthoum loomed on a continental scale as notable exceptions. Kalthoum dominated North Africa from the 1930s onward, her legend spreading as far as major cities in the Middle East. By the time of Kalthoum's death in 1975, she had become widely known by the honorific title "Star of the Orient." Miriam Makeba's lucid and soulful rendering of Black social life under apartheid rule in English, Zulu, and Xhosa language resonated in different contexts than did Kalthoum's work. Makeba was widely beloved by fans in newly independent African nations that harbored fresh memories of colonial rule. Makeba's itineraries included live performances at 1960s and

1970s Pan-African festivals, not least at Nigeria's FESTAC 77, performances that bore witness to her stellar profile and the esteem in which progressive African governments held her music. Makeba's international profile only grew when, exiled from apartheid South Africa, she relocated to the United States in 1959. While in exile, Makeba used live performances and concerts, Shana L. Redmond argues, to act as a "mobile and recognizable proxy for Black South Africans and the ANC in countries like Angola, Ethiopia and Liberia."[42] In New York, she befriended United Nations delegates of newly independent African states and, in 1962, performed in a benefit show in Kenya for orphans of the Mau Mau uprising. She testified in 1963 before the United Nations Committee on Apartheid on the evils of the racist South African regime. Makeba recorded international hits such as "Pata Pata," a catchy dance song performed in English and Xhosa. As Makeba became more involved with the civil rights struggle, she found uncomfortable parallels between apartheid and US racial segregation. Her overt political stance on US racism, punctuated by her affair with Black Panther activist Stokely Carmichael (later Kwame Touré), led to Makeba's blacklisting by US record labels.[43] These circuits not only boosted Makeba's already stellar profile as an African performer but also consolidated her status as an important Pan-African activist and African ally of the civil rights struggle. Makeba's soulful voice, maternal aura, and commanding presence onstage as a musician and orator cemented her place in an elite class of twentieth-century Black artist-activists.[44] Kalthoum and Makeba were exceptions in African popular music, which remained hostile to female stardom. Nigeria was no much different. Lead vocals were the preserve of men, leaving a band like the Lijadu Sisters the striking outlier. The industry, as one of the sisters noted, had a gender problem. The glass ceiling for most women in Nigerian pop was as show dancers in nightclubs, backup singers in bands, or in a combination of these supporting roles. Performers hailed almost inevitably from working-class homes, and their art was tied to urban survival. Show dancing, for some, became a last-ditch effort at earning a living in Lagos. When they performed in a band, they did so as sidepieces hardly integrated into the group's identity in a coherent fashion.

The conditions were ripe for the convergence of a cohort of young women seeking a shot at music and the performing arts, unsatisfied with the limiting circumstances imposed on their lives as young women in larger society. Fela's Afrobeat offered a potent outlet for these desires. In Afrobeat, they could pursue a range of artistic endeavors, from the familiar show dancing and backup singing to disc jockeying. Afrobeat afforded a rare opportunity for women to embrace public artistic pursuits in advancing a largely activist cause. It also implied that their craft elicited more curiosity and admiration than outright rebuke.

So when young women erupted onto the Nigerian pop scene via Afrobeat, they did so as a function of multiple interanimating, albeit volatile, events, from postwar policy failures to the specific constriction of women's craft in popular music. If the dearth of artistic, and specifically musical, opportunities urged young women's affinity with Afrobeat, Fela's emergent role as a social critic and musical megastar amplified Kalakuta's appeal for impressionable young women seeking an outlet. In the next section, I explain how Fela came to be seen as an important social critic with the release of his popular song "Jeun Ko Ku" and how this song springboarded him into star status.

Before and Beyond "Jeun Ko Ku"

Fela harbored a long-standing desire to play sophisticated dance music without sacrificing widespread appeal. What appeared to be an elusive musical vision coalesced in *Afrodisiac* (1972), an album that sold over two hundred thousand copies in the space of six weeks. *Afrodisiac* owed its success in large part to its signature song "Jeun Ko Ku" (Chop and Quench), a parody of the glutton, a figure that was itself a riff on the familiar Yoruba literary fascination with the habitually drunk.[45] Fela masterfully layers upbeat horn phrases and solos on a rolling percussion of conga and snare drums. The sway of the groove has a hypnotic feel. At its core, "Jeun Ko Ku" declared Fela's breakaway from the mellow highlife music that had dominated the West African social scene for at least three decades. Riding on the album's success, Fela organized a national tour of campuses and city halls, quickly carrying the infectious song far. Riots reportedly broke out at the venues in Kano and Zaria after fans who had purchased tickets found no space in the overpacked halls.[46] The success of the *Afrodisiac* album was amply supported by Fela's irreverent public persona. Throughout the early 1970s, he increasingly played the role of jester, critic, and truth teller to construct a complex persona revered by Nigeria's intellectual class, inner-city youth, and university students but reviled by traditional and urban Yoruba elites.[47]

Students, intellectuals, and the urban working class became the most important constituents for Afrobeat. This group bought wholesale the innovation that was signaled in "Jeun Ko Ku." Its satirical and edgy but danceable sound wove together sonic strands of soul, jazz, funk, and highlife music but laid claim to a new idiom. The avid listeners of this hybrid sound in Lagos, Ibadan, and Accra materialized one author's description of "the Afrobeat generation":

urban youth with some formal education who showed resistance to orthodoxy. The Afrobeat generation, the anonymous author argued, found satisfaction in soul music, harbored subtle resentment toward highlife music, and deemed local Yoruba genres like *àpàlà* and *jùjú* beneath their cosmopolitan tastes.[48] The writer expressed a generation's impatience with established genres while defining the prevailing sense of disenchantment with the national project, feelings not unlike those harbored by the "second-generation of African writers," who aimed their frustrations at the "postcolonial state" and its agents.[49]

The tone for "Jeun Ko Ku" had been set by the earlier "Na Poi" (1971), a song whose title contains a not-so-subtle description of coitus. Teenage students emerged as an unlikely fan base for this irreverent song. Nkiru Nzegwu recalls how, as a high school student, her girlfriends sang along and engaged in playful banter about the inexpert sex captured rather vividly in "Na Poi." The song has the kind of lyrics, Nzegwu muses, that are censored by mothers, even as it became for schoolgirls a choice weapon in a growing "repertoire of mischief songs."[50] The song's lewdness is tempered by the hilarity with which Fela describes fumbling lovers exploring the mysteries of sex. At its height, "Na Poi" found a home on university campuses, themselves important sites of gender performance; male students reportedly bellowed it at every opportunity, while some female students relished the pleasure of private listening.[51] Although "Na Poi" and "Jeun Ko Ku" failed to generate critical, international acclaim, they set the tone for Fela's musical career.

The songs helped catalyze changes in Fela's Africa 70 band, the most profound of which were set in motion by young women seeking work with his band. Young men and women, many of whom had danced to "Na Poi" and "Jeun Ko Ku" and witnessed Fela's ascension to stardom, responded when it became public knowledge that Fela was recruiting dancers. In a later defense of the Kalakuta commune, Fela's brother Beko Ransome-Kuti, a renowned medical doctor and activist in his own right, reflected on the circumstances that led to the population and character of the band and an emerging commune. It "started when some of his dancers had been unable to find housing in Lagos. Now the Kalakuta Republic was a haven for many who would otherwise be on the street. . . . Fela not only paid salaries to these persons, but also gave each daily pocket money."[52] Clearly, the growing ranks around Fela's band made little sense logistically because an inflated staff placed additional pressures on the organization's limited resources, notably on feeding and safety. Only a handful of individuals other than Afrobeat ace drummer Tony Allen could bear better witness to the evolving (if uncomfortable) dynamics that created the gradual swell in the number of women: "Up until 'Jeun K'oku,' we had the same formation, which was a ten-piece band plus one dancer [Dele Salami]. Then the band started to grow. Fela started to recruit more dancers and singers. We soon had about forty people around us on payroll. Then Fela decided that, since he was recruiting so many people, he wanted to bring the whole thing under his control inside his house. That's when he changed his way of living."[53] It was in the spirit of incorporating the labor of everyone in Afrobeat's ranks that Fela adopted a collective approach, each person contributing time, talent, or sweat to the survival of the commune. Women who took creative work with the band tended to do so as dancers; others invested their energies into the daily running of the commune. Young men who did not work as instrumentalists tended to work in technical capacities or as Fela's assistants. It was not until 1972 that women's artistic roles became defined more squarely as singers / dancers / disc jockeys and men's expanded to include foot soldiers for Afrobeat's ideological work. Many young women began their journey in Kalakuta tentatively, but they came to dominate an industry that was iffy about female participation. What the band lost in overstaffing, it gained in free press time. Afrobeat stories routinely made frontpage headlines of major newspapers. Fela's innovative music and utterances, communal life in Kalakuta, and curiosity about the nature of Fela's relationship with the women who danced for him were all fodders for public interest. When it became clear that the "girls" were also romantically involved with Fela, the realization hurt at least one person deeply—Fela's first wife, Remi Taylor. Their relationship had always been rocky, but sharing a roof with her husband's "girlfriends" proved too much. In a weak attempt at a tribute to Remi two years into their marriage, Fela stated, "I seem to have many girl-friends. But I know I have only one—my wife." In the same breath, he added, "Girls admire me when I am playing on the stage. Naturally I am happy about it and as an artist, it is only natural that I should return admiration for admiration."[54] Remi moved out of the matrimonial home, a move that by some accounts a key historical accident in the birth of an Afrobeat commune. In a timeline consistent with Tony Allen's recollection, Fela's daughter Yeni Kuti reminisced that Remi's exit triggered the transformation. Her exit also signaled a transition in the institutional family model that underpinned Afrobeat music. A defining feature of early subcultures was the active search for forms of living and social arrangements outside the nuclear family model.[55] Remi's exit marked a rupture of the nuclear family as the basic support structure underpinning Afrobeat music. What followed was a transition to a communal lifestyle and a reshaping of Afrobeat music aesthetics. No sooner had young women begun living with Fela than they showed up in his music in the form of vocal support, firming up his observations on Nigerian society. *Shakara* (1972)

Figure 1.1. Album cover art for *Shakara* (1972). Photo credit and permissions: Fela Kuti's estate.

offered the first real experiment in women as backup singers. The album was an instant hit. The album cover art (fig. 1.1), in which the young women appear topless, combined well with the crisp vocals, which offered a soaring counterpoint to the huff of male vocal singing that had marked Afrobeat music until that point. Consistent with 1960s communes that embraced a return to the land and wilderness, the Kalakuta commune contained contradictory impulses embodied by the women. When they appeared nude on album covers and in everyday communal life, they symbolized and rehearsed an idealized return to rural, even precolonial life while gesturing toward a future in which women could reclaim ownership of their bodies from arbitrary colonial and neocolonial inscriptions attached to the female body in public.[56] Afrobeat women embraced nudity and, soon, erotic dancing in ways that attached new and revitalized moral and political meaning to their bodies. The growing collective of women was intentionally unruly in everyday conduct, even to exaggerated levels, in ways that resonated with the restiveness of many young Nigerians. For this reason, the women were admired by some and reviled by others. Their irreverent deportment challenged middle-class Yoruba values of decorum and propriety that had endured in the face of rapid urbanization. The women's titillation and musical sophistication of Afrobeat underpinned the steady stream of Africa 70 songs that contained reflections on gender, sex, and Lagos social life—songs such as "Open and Close" (1971) "Roforofo Fight" (1972) and "Yellow Fever" (1976). The Kalakuta commune and Afrobeat music consolidated their charm on Nigeria's young.

An Uneasy Convergence

Young men and women united by risk, adventure, and promise arrived individually, and later in droves, from near and far. The influx of young, passionate women was singular in transforming the Ransome-Kuti home into one of West Africa's most iconic subcultures. It was in the duplex—situated on 14A Agege Motor Road—that a subculture that embraced nudity, marijuana, sexual liberalism, and agitational music flourished. Fela had spent the previous decade seeking out the limelight for his music; with help from the young women who flocked around him, he consolidated the formula he had initiated in early 1970s songs like "Jeun Ko Ku" (1973). As the decade progressed, Afrobeat lyrics grew lewder and more irreverent while nude women appeared on album covers (like *Shakara*, the first of at least two Africa 70 albums with topless women in the cover art). Afrobeat posed a moral concern precisely because it threatened to institute a regime of the erotic.[57] Imageries of female irreverence saturated the visual fields of Afrobeat, from onstage dancing and photography to live performance. The women's fierce vocal support in *Shakara* combined with the provocative album art to signal a long decade of defiant self-fashioning. Quite predictably, the women's publicness and discourtesy provoked unease when they reached beyond the orbit of the stage and album art and became a staple feature of leading newspapers. A series of photographs published in a 1978 newspaper feature in the *Punch* illustrates how the young women induced discomfort, especially because of their age. The five photographs capture young women in poses or in off-guard moments of domestic work in what appears to be a shaky construction of them as conforming to a dominant idea of female domesticity. And yet it is the last photograph on the bottom right of the page that brings unease into sharp focus. The photographic subject is identified simply as "Miss Ngozi." Her round face and prominent eyes imply that she is in her early teens, her look troubling the newspaper's prefixing her with the prenuptial "Miss" rather than "Ngozi." But it is her gesture that makes the photograph a curious encounter between the subjectivity of young women, their public construction by the male-dominated press, and the moral ambivalence about their presence in Afrobeat. Miss Ngozi tugs at the rim of her tank top with her left hand, while with her right she points her index finger to a breast. She returns the camera's gaze as though oblivious to the tug, her look something between innocence and calm defiance—a teenager negotiating puberty while confronting her over-sexualization, in concert with her peers, by the press. One encounters in this uneasy photograph a moment of self-assertion. The photographic subject stares focused but expressionless into the journalist's camera as though knowing that its interest is not in herself, her feelings, or her interior life but in her barely formed body. She looks at the viewer while directing the viewer's gaze away from her probing eyes. In *Listening to Images*, Tina Campt reads photographs as "deeply affective objects" that impress themselves on us through multiple forms of contact, including visual (seeing), physical (touching), psychic (feeling), and sonic (listening).[58] These registers of photographic contact alert us to an array of affective frequencies through which to sense a photograph and, conversely, invite readings of the photographic subject beyond the register of control and capture.[59] The photograph of Miss Ngozi is intended to construct her as deviant, enchanting, and dangerous but certainly not innocent. And yet the affective power of the photograph lies in her corresponding gaze at the camera, forcing the viewer to see back at her, not innocent but capable of innocence. The quiet frequencies of the photograph facilitate an archival encounter that challenges "the facticity of the archive and interrupt, at least temporarily, [the archive's] power to constitute subjects through the visual tropes and archetypes it so frequently naturalizes."[60] The press might have sought to frame the photo-graph as a titillating capture of lost girlhood, one from which it profited, but it also captured its own complicity in the exploitation of a girl. One of the haptic frequencies, to stay with Campt a little more, in which to read the photograph is the interval between the photographic capture and its life and circulation in print, mediated by the physical touch of the rank and file of the press as they editorialized, passed around copies of, and judged the photograph's suitability for public consumption. The subtle pose and returning gaze force the viewer to look at her, indicting in that look a network of complicit adult actors including Fela, the photographer who held up the camera and took the shot, the editorship of the press, and the Nigerian public as having let down this and many girls like her.[61] It was one thing for this kind of photograph to appear on Fela's album cover and yet another altogether for a major national newspaper to pass it on for public consumption. Indeed, editors in print media constituted a key part in stoking controversy around Afrobeat women. Papers actively courted Afrobeat women to pose as "Page Three" girls. Controversy and titillation sold papers, but they also implicated newspaper elites as active participants in widening the publics that consumed the girls' and women's bodies.[62]

Beyond nudity and facile erotic appeal, a key reason for public interest in the lives of Afrobeat women stemmed from their being unlikely cultural catalysts. The twentieth century saw an extensive and underappreciated list of women in Nigerian popular theater.[63] Their work in theater, however, is unified in being almost inevitably couched in polygamous marriage arrangements. Their husbands tended to be the directors, producers, and actors of family-run theater groups of which the women became part. Offstage, women who married into theater practice had the dignified deportment of wives in a polygamous arrangement. Marriage shielded them from the moral judgment that attended being a woman in popular theater. Kalakuta women appeared to conform to this mold, but only to an extent. They performed artistic roles consistent with the longer practice of wife-performers, but their general social deportment strutted into the dangerous terrain of urban *sirens*, unrecognizably wayward women who seize the public's attention with sonorous singing and barely clothed bodies. For most of the decade, they maintained an ill-defined relationship with Fela that incorporated the work ethic of traditional bands with cohabitative sex, almost "an orgy playground."[64] Most Afrobeat women harbored unrequited passion for music and the performing arts, had some form of postprimary education (only a handful completed secondary school), and hailed from a mix of working class polygamous homes.[65] People from working-class homes intermingled with the few peers who had abandoned the comforts of a sheltered upbringing. In Kalakuta, they shared sticks of marijuana with young people whose parents were judges, police commissioners, and top-level civil servants. Fear of collapse in the class divide played its part in amplifying the moral panic. If only symbolically, Kalakuta threatened class boundaries that underwrote Lagos social life, a mirroring the divide etched into the city's colonial-spatial mapping that separated the posh Lagos Island from a mainland teeming with the poor.

Public discourse embraced zero-sum thinking in which the young women could only be one thing or another: candidates for social intervention or, on the flip side, sentient artists. The former view—embodied, for instance, by Tai Solarin's open letter—underplayed the women's creative rebellion, its impact on the evolving shape of Afrobeat music, and how their presence and embodied acts transformed Kalakuta into a hub of creativity and controversy. This thinking also neglected how women expanded the creative currency of Afrobeat music, which became a legitimate voice for millions of young Africans. These young women found kinship in Kalakuta that evinced a collective reckoning with the zeitgeist of a moment Tejumola Olaniyan poignantly characterized as "the postcolonial incredible." But the dominant expression through which the Afrobeat women engaged this infraction manifested in the form of a visceral sensuality, reclaiming the African female body from its colonial coding as grotesque and excessive.[66] Popular songs such as Christie Essien Igbokwe's "Seun Rere" (Do Good) and Mike Okri's "Time Na Money" were beloved by middle-class and elite Lagosians; the songs projected the middle class's self-conscious ethics of hard work, discipline, professionalism, and focus, ethics through which this privileged class also wielded disciplinary power. These songs, along with the efforts at populist didacticism of the time, captured a dominant anxiety that underpinned the socialization of the young: the dangers of keeping "bad" company. When young women erupted on the popular music scene in the early 1970s—performing erotically charged dances in go-go cages, singing sonorously in denunciatory, often sexual songs, posing nude on Fela's album covers—they achieved more than simply carving out a space for themselves in a male-dominated music industry. They challenged the terms on which women's bodies would be permitted in the public space. They were also subverting the oblique policing of women's bodies through moralizing nationalist projects that only conceived of women in the roles of domestic nurturers or moral harbingers. Kalakutans and all the commune stood for seemed to embody the very antithesis of these values. The commune constituted what Yoruba Lagosians might have described as an egbẹ́kẹ́gbẹ́, roughly "dangerous collectives." Ironically, Kalakutans could only elicit strong reactions from Nigerian society by intensifying the gender stereotype that, if not contained, girls and women would go wild and corrupt the soul of a society striving to construe itself as modern in the wake of colonialism.

The other side of the coin, which takes them as absolute agents exercising free will, is equally dangerous. It underplays the impact of maturity (or lack thereof) in the young women's decision-making and the manipulation that attended working in Fela's band and idealizes patriarchy and the reproduction of oppressive gendered practices in everyday communal life. Neither of these categories are as helpful as a careful unpacking of specific moments, contexts, motivations, and effects pertaining to the imbrication of gendered identity in the making of a musical genre and subculture as dynamic and complex as

Afrobeat. Biographical sketches productively complicate a binary understanding of girls' and women's Afrobeat arrivals.

Itineraries of the Restless

Najite Mukoro was fourteen when she took a one-way trip from Warri, an oil-rich southern Nigerian town, to an address she had acquired by word of mouth: 14A Agege Motor Road. It was Fela's home. Najite arrived at Kalakuta shortly after the release of "Lady," a song whose lyrics idealize a "fire-dancing" African woman in cheeky contrast with the Western-educated "lady." Najite earned the title "Fire Dancer" because she moved with skill and youthful gusto when she mounted the stage. Her dance solo at the 1978 Berlin Jazz Festival, Africa 70's first European tour, bears out the reputation Najite garnered for herself. Her arrival marked the start of a nearly thirty-year career as a dancer in Fela's Africa 70 band. The journey of Ihase Obotu, a young woman and soon-to-be singer, was fueled by a different impulse: escape. In a journey quite like Najite's, Ihase traveled from Benin, a city with a rich dynastic and cultural history. In Benin, Ihase attended a Fela concert that convinced her to join the Africa 70 band. The promise of escape into the arts was matched only by the assurance of housing in Lagos, a city that takes little pity on the unhoused. Rumors that the musician recruited women artists and housed them only amplified Ihase's enthusiasm. She pilfered just enough of her father's money to fund the journey into a life as a singer.[67] Hers, too, was a one-way ticket to Lagos.

Najite Mukoro and Ihase Obotu intermingled with young men and women their age, individuals who left heartbreak in the homes they fled. Some *jùjú* musicians felt that Fela was taking undue "advantage of young migrant women from the village,"[68] a charge that was only true to the extent that it ignored the overwhelming contingent of Lagosians who gravitated to Afrobeat music. Najite Mukoro and Ihase Obotu traveled from beyond Lagos, but the young women who converged on Fela's home in the early 1970s overwhelmingly resided in Lagos. The travelers and their Lagosian peers discovered a shared disdain for the doldrums of everyday life. Alake Adedipe deemed her family "too colonial," a thinking that inspired her affinity with the working class–dominated commune.[69] She was the rebellious and intellectually curious daughter of a federal judge, one of the few Kalakutans from elite homes. Alake's father, a lawyer who rose to become a high court judge, tried futilely and with help from his powerful network to pry his daughter from Kalakuta life.[70] Kevwe Oghomienor, an Itsekiri girl born in Sapele, a town in the southern part of

Nigeria, also belonged in the group of Lagos-based, Kalakuta-bound non-conformists. Like many of her peers, she was raised in a polygamous home—Kevwe's father had two wives who bore seven children between them. Both teachers, Kevwe's parents, relocated to Lagos when she was four. And like most middle-class Lagosians her age, Kevwe had been raised by the tenets of Christianity and exposed to music at home and in church. When her parents discovered Kevwe's more-than-passing interest in music, they hoped she would opt for a more socially acceptable outlet to express her talents, like church. Their calculation was misplaced. Kevwe quit her education in favor of a life singing in Africa 70. At sixteen, she began a career as a backup singer in Africa 70—which would soon become one of Africa's most well-known bands. Sonorous and piercing, Kevwe's voice first appeared in the *Shakara* album. After joining Fela's band in 1972, she sang in most hit Afrobeat songs. If Fela was Afrobeat's driver, Kevwe was one of its engines. By the 1978 wedding, she was twenty-two years old and a six-year member of Afrobeat's inner community.

Afrobeat women's itineraries had a transnational dimension, as Kalakuta welcomed young men and women from Nigeria's westward neighbors: Ghana, Togo, and Republic of Benin. Two Ghanaian women, Naa Lamiley Lamptey (Lamiley henceforth) and Serwaa Akosua, embodied a larger pattern of migration between Ghana and Nigeria from at least the 1960s. Lamiley was assertive but well liked, while Serwaa Akosua, a dancer with an electric stage presence, became widely disliked because some Kalakutans perceived her as shifty. Serwaa was a buxom, fast-talking woman who invested in few albeit committed friendships. She was generally quiet, only unfurling her power through dancing when provoked by Afrobeat's instrumental ensemble. Onstage, Serwaa oozed confidence and sensuality, self-assured in the carnal athleticism of her movement. Much of Serwaa's actions were governed by grit and the need to survive a hostile environment that included Nigeria's migration climate. Her Ghanaian counterpart had a different temperament and biography. Even in the thick of anti-immigrant sentiment in the early 1980s, Lamiley's formal education and professional exposure tempered some of the usual anxieties associated with constraining circumstances faced by Ghanaian immigrants. Whereas Kalakutans perceived Serwaa as calculated in her dealings, they saw Lamiley as more restrained and seasoned. Lamiley and Fela met in Accra in 1971 while she was studying to become a museum technician. The two reunited in 1973 when she won a UNESCO fellowship to study museum techniques in Jos, a city in central Nigeria.[71] Throughout her fellowship, Lamiley made brief leisure trips to Lagos sponsored by Fela. Lamiley finally moved to Lagos at his invitation, but she did so from a position of privilege. When Afrobeat women earned their high school diploma, they accomplished a great milestone because many discontinued their education for a life in Afrobeat. Afrobeat women did not necessarily conduct themselves professionally because of their contingent status as Fela's workers and girlfriends. Lamiley was set apart from others in this sense. Fela reportedly feared Lamiley's forthrightness.[72] To her, Fela was her contemporary. "When I met him," Lamiley insisted, "I met him as any other man," underscoring the importance of age and emotional maturity in how women comported themselves in relation to Fela and his business.[73] Perhaps Lamiley also represented the challenge matured women might present for Fela's brand of male authority. While younger women often tiptoed around their host, Lamiley clearly expressed herself in conversations with Fela. Lamiley enjoyed the benefits of limited artistic demands in the organization. She never performed onstage, choosing to act beyond the ambit of Fela's exacting artistic control. When Afrobeat women mounted the stage at the Shrine, they could assert some artistic freedom but were always under the gaze and judgment of Fela. Uninterested for the spotlight, Lamiley took the low-stakes role of Kalakuta disc jockey. To underscore how she managed to live as part of the Kalakuta community but just beyond Fela's reach, Lamiley lived by herself in a hotel close to Kalakuta.[74] That Lamiley and Serwaa seldom socialized in Kalakuta had little to do with Serwaa being an Ashante woman and Lamiley being Ga. The women were separated by temperament and class mobility.

Boys and young men were also enchanted by Fela's charisma and unconventional lifestyle. Ndubuisi Okwechime, for instance, was a student of mass communication at the University of Lagos and a newly employed journalist with the *Punch* newspaper when assigned to conduct an interview with Fela. After the interview, Ndubuisi promptly abandoned formal education to embrace ideologies of Pan-Africanism, self-discovery, and critical thinking in Kalakuta and, in turn, showed a general bent toward Afrocentric thought.[75] Okwechime became one of many boys—such as Lemi Ghariokwu, Duro Ikujenyo, Mabinuori Kayode and Eludoyin Elutunde, to name a few—who, spellbound by Kalakutan ideas, visited and never left. Ndubuisi realized in a short period that he needed to eschew ideologically weak education at the University of Lagos. His journey into Kalakuta Republic was not an isolated one for college students on similar journeys of questioning the status quo. Many of the women Okwechime met in Kalakuta had taken varied, daunting journeys to start a new life in the arts and on the social margins. He continued a tradition of Lagos-based middle-class boys who rescinded college education for subcultural living. Other young men without the social capital bestowed by a path to higher education took menial jobs like electricians, or security guards in Fela's organization. Others in this class performed feminized labors such as cleaning and waiting on Fela. While women were discouraged from deep intellectual pursuit, this group of men took little interest in the intellectualism that delighted young men like Ndubuisi. Observers may have been baffled by these restive youths some of whom left elite colleges or stable social positions to come to Kalakuta from near and far; however, it was the collective energy, shared social values for activism, and heterogeneity as West Africans of Kalakutans as a pan-ethnic and class-diverse collective that helped cultivate the unencumbered creative synergy at the core of Afrobeat music—a collective effort of Nigerian and African youths that competing bands failed to decode as the substance of Afrobeat music. This synergy, too, was a reason to feel a sense of belonging to a community of strangers.

Working-class migrants have historically shaped Lagos's cosmopolitan identity. But in Kalakuta, migrants interacted with their urban counterparts on equal footing, a relationship that contrasted sharply with middle-class and elite Lagos circles where mannerisms perceived as rural exposed new migrants to mockery.[76] Migrating women embodied for Afrobeat a psychic connection to Nigeria's hinterlands and to "timeless" rituals and cultural practices that fired up Fela's cultural nationalist message.[77] Afrobeat women who had migrated from the hinterlands and were relatively unexperienced about city life bolstered Kalakuta's ideological claims because they appeared to embody pristine notions of an African womanhood untouched by the *corrupt* external contact, even though live performances readily complicated this reading. For instance, Najite Mukoro explained her use of facial makeup as being "from [her] village."[78] Often Westernized in their educational backgrounds and urban lifeways, Lagos-bred Kalakutans learned from migrants indigenous beautification practices, including invented ones, that urban living denied them. Migrants, in turn, learned the ropes of urban life in the relatively safe space of Kalakuta Republic. In these ways, Afrobeat music did not simply assimilate the aesthetics of rural and suburban life. The music transformed and beatified the aesthetics.

Even a cursory look at the historical context of the 1970s complicates the idea that Kalakuta Republic was populated by abductees. Misinformation about the numerous young men and women converging on Kalakuta implied that they could only have been manipulated into doing so. It is crucial, as LaRay Denzer notes, that Kalakuta gave women the latitude to develop their talents in ways largely unavailable in competing bands, formal institutions (such as school, church, home, and marriage), or existing youth collectives. Afrobeat women often cited freedom as an impetus for their association with the subculture.[79]

When asked to describe or define Afrobeat freedom, the women nonetheless struggled for words. They almost invariably described experiences such as nightclub surfing, self-indulging beyond parental control (in substances, sex, and music), meeting new people, and exploring the world within and beyond Nigeria. These ostensibly banal articulations of freedom, I think, mask a deeper desire to transcend an intersection of constraints germane to Nigerian reality— military dictatorship, quotidian state violence, gendered domesticity, moral contradictions of elite culture, and economic uncertainty in the wake of a civil war. The women's seemingly banal apprehension of freedom might be understood as politically productive if scholars attend to the equilibrium between one's wishes and one's capacity to act, or between the impulse to rein in one's imagination or expand one's capacity for action.[80] That this brand of freedom did not extend to a critique of patriarchy however entailed the loss of certain capacities for action.[81] And still it was a politically loaded action, radical even, to be seen in Afrobeat company. By taking residence in *this* commune, the women did not simply seek to expand their capacity to act—they also refused to rein in the imagination in some aspects of their lives, becoming like surrealists experimenting with "new social relationships, new ways of living and interacting, new attitudes toward work and leisure and community."[82] On a certain level, Kalakuta Republic might be understood as a collective formed not only in response to acute postindependence disillusion but also in an elusive pursuit of true autonomy. It was within these crevices that the women made art.

"My Life Story Never Finish": August 2014
My stride is steady on the return to Ikeja. The prospect of a chat with Najite (now in her sixties and known Iya Motun) has left me restless with anticipation. It's late morning and there are no customers in her shop. I am greeted by a gentleman who asks my mission. "I dey find Mama Najite," I explain, unsure what to make of his authority. She does not return until two thirty p.m., he replies with the confidence of someone tasked with conveying this precise information or fixing uncomplicated orders, like a cold drink. There are two hours to fill before then, so I attempt to reconnect with Nwabueze and his "co-wives." It's been about a week, and the men left me with lingering questions. I proceed to the Kalakuta Museum when I fail to locate them. The penthouse bar feels like a place to dally.

I pause for several minutes in front of Fela's bedroom, trying to take the space in anew. I am struggling for focus when I meet and become fast, if uneasy, friends with the museum manager, who's excited to learn about my work. Around here, he's called by his role: Manager. He is slightly talkative, which is beneficial in this instance. It permits me to listen more and speak less; around him, I feel no need to ask questions. Maybe, I do not know what questions to ask. He escorts me to his office, where he engages in lengthy musings about "the mystery of the man" called Fela. He was like "a kind of Jesus Christ," Manager repeats three times over the course of our hour-long exchange. I steer the conversation toward the Queens. He offers tips for cautiously approaching Kevwe, who resides at the Shrine. It is a familiar refrain about how I need to exaggerate my excitement about hearing about her exploits in America. He assures me that Iya Motun, whom I inform him I would love to interview, has little to add to my work. I needn't waste time speaking to her. In his opinion, the Queens no longer have a place in the contemporary outlook of the Kuti family. He qualifies this scathing assessment with a striking observation: the women added no value to themselves and could not keep up with the Kuti family's progressive pace. As the Kuti family has invested a lot of energy and strategy into managing the Fela brand, I cannot hear Manager's assessment outside of the neoliberal rhetoric of personal responsibility that places blame on the individual for structural impediments to their flourishing. But what strikes me immediately is that he expresses these views about the women without grasping the irony that he has a job precisely because of the value with which women endowed Afrobeat. Still, I appreciate that he put words to a sensation that permeates the museum, from curatorial choices of the collection to casual praise of the Kuti family. Like Manager, the disposition of many around the museum, including the young cleaner, is that the women have little worth in today's Afrobeat. By contrast, Manager showers eulogies on Fela's children with sycophantic fervor. One should speak no ill of one's employers, but Manager goes the extra mile with his Jesus Christ reference as with his Queen-bashing. He's been the only one to put words to this unspoken notion of value that I could only sense up until our meeting.

Manager leads me to Fela's former recording studio on the second floor. It holds historical mementos such as the complete and, up to now, elusive political manifesto of the Movement of the People (MOP), the Fela-led party. The manifesto is digitally reproduced in typewritten form and laid out sequentially, by page, to convey a sense of originality. The typewriter on which Fela ostensibly typed the document (circa 1978) interrupts the sequence of pages, but a visitor could begin the first page at the left end of the room and read the entire the manifesto by panning right in an arc across a room with a high density of Afrobeat history per square inch. On the walls above the manifesto are newspaper clippings, mainly from the 1970s, about Fela's melodramatic life. The clippings feature news about the revered Funmilayo

Ransome-Kuti (FRK); the 1978 mass wedding; and contemporaneous coverage of the registration of MOP, an inclusion that deepens the significance of the party's manifesto on display. I think this aspect of the museum is particularly well curated. Manager leads me to a "photograph room" down the hall. The curators have represented the women in this room but, unsurprisingly, in unlabeled, anonymous portraits and concert photographs on four walls. An adjoining room contains Fela-related paintings and hagiographic artworks by young artists. We come to a huge three-legged pot on which is engraved "Fehintola Anikulapo-Kuti," the name of a notable Queen. Manager explains that they used the pot to cook for Fela. I question his explanation not only because pots of that size and style feature in ceremonial more than everyday cooking but also, more pressingly, because minutes ago he failed to positively identify Sandra Izsadore in the picture room. I fear what else he might misrepresent after failing to identify Sandra, an iconic figure in Afrobeat history. His explanation appears to rely on a notion of domesticity at odds with Kalakuta life. Notwithstanding Kalakuta's mirroring of many aspects of Nigerian patriarchy, the notion of a wife bound to daily cooking on that scale does not chime with Kalakuta as I understand it. I am still thinking about the pot when I express my gratitude to Manager.

From a distance, I sight Iya Motun, her face locked in a grimace. She mutters inaudibly as I cautiously squeeze past three customers. I explain that I visited last week; she might not recall my face. "I no dey do any interview again. I dey vex! I no do any interview. I no dey talk to any journalist again," her frustration catches the attention of customers. Hoping to salvage the situation, I offer, "I fit come back later in the week." "No come back," she fires back. "I say I no dey do interview again," she assures me, this time turning to attend to her business, a signal that I have overstayed. It would be regrettable to leave and return after this verdict. It's a heartbreaking dead end. I must act quickly, and I do. It happens sometimes: words spilling from one's mouth before they are fully processed. This is one of such fieldwork occasions. I blurt, "You get Guinness stout?" without much time to think. "E dey," her voice softens ever so slightly as she rises to retrieve a bottle. I'm still rattled by the exchange but say, "Make I take one stout before I go." A customer who's been listening to our exchange bursts into laugher at my swift transition. I do not care for him or what he considers funny. Being in the shop affords me a little more time. It will take time to convince her or anyone that my work is not journalism, let alone the kind that has sensationalized Afrobeat women and governed their exposure to print publics since the 1970s. When Iya Motun enters a tight negotiation with a goat-meat seller, I offer to break the deadlock on price by covering some of the cost. She expresses gratitude and makes prayers. If she reads my gesture as bribery or an attempt at winning her trust, she gives nothing away. She insists that my Guinness is a gift from her; I insist on paying and promise to return the next day for goat-meat pepper soup. We laugh. I leave her shop penniless but pleased.

A day later. When a customer issues a complaint about the volume of goat meat on my plate, Iya Motun checks him quickly: "If you know wetin this man do me yesterday, you go know why I serve am like that." The gentleman wraps himself a joint and puffs away as we share the meal on my invitation. The conversation between Iya Motun and her customers touches on Ebola, a theme around Lagos these days. It's been devastating for merchants of bush meat, a male customer complains. Iya Motun, now in a relaxed state, shares a little of her struggles with the men. "I don fight many battles for this life," she expresses, but "I still dey stand strong." She makes her point by flexing both arms, fists clenched, and stamping both feet from her sitting position. She is seated at the entrance of her shop, flanked by men on benches on either side. This modest shop is a space over which she holds sway. She narrates a dream she had to make the point that her battles were also metaphysical. It was of a fierce fight with a creature the form of a long-haired, light-skinned girl with a tail about fifteen meters long. The tail doubled as a lash with which the creature-girl whipped Iya Motun, who only gained the upper hand after a prolonged rumble. She seized the creature-girl by the neck and challenged her, "Wetin I do you? Wetin I do you?" By now, Iya Motun has her right hand outstretched, holding tight to the creature-girl suspended in the air by the defendant's grip. The muscle around her forearm tightens as she shakes the creature-girl, hoping for an explanation for why she-it launched the attack. The creature-girl says nothing as the two stare at each other. We, Iya Motun's customers, are fully immersed in the recounted dream as she picks up the creature-girl and rolls and slams her-it to the ground, her hands recreating the encounter with vivid precision. A third character, an angel, enters the scene, de ex machina style, to wrestle the creature-girl. The men's faces, our faces, show rapt enchantment. There are too many bad people in this world, she concludes, but she sleeps soundly now knowing that victory is certain. We agree. Other stories mix with beer parlor talk, but none comes close to the melodrama of Iya Motun and the creature-girl.

Nwabueze gives Iya Motun a tuale, a gesture of respect and surrender in which the greeter stands still and suspends both hands in the air from a distance. When he asks about my progress, Iya Motun seizes the opportunity to repeat gently but emphatically that she will not be granting any interviews. "My life story never finish. E still dey unfold. If e finish, I go fit talk about am." She adds: "Come back in a

*year or two years," maybe the story will be ripe enough to be shared. I am grateful
for her invitation.*

*We reconnect three years later, in 2017, in the cozy sitting area of her daughter's
home. Photographs of Iya Motun share wall space with those of her daughter, Motun. It is quiet here, our conversation interrupted only occasionally by her animated
granddaughter, also prominently featured on the wall. Iya Motun opens our chat by
recalling our first meeting in 2014. She shares that I visited her shop at a distressing
time. She'd been struggling to keep the business afloat and had to shut it down for
a full year. The story of her fight with the creature-girl three years prior might have
signaled a deeper struggle after all. She permits me to record our hour-long interview
then eases into a casual pose. I take a photograph of her at home.*

2

From FRK to "Lady"

A Revised Genealogy of the Music's Other Women

Misogynistic lyrics in "Lady" (1972) and "Mattress" (1975) cast a shadow over an expansive rendering of the lived dimensions of gender in Afrobeat. While salient entry points, the discourses those lyrics generate constrict a field of view that would otherwise include the multiple and shifting structural positions women inhabit in relation to the production of Afrobeat music. This chapter presents fuller biographical profiles of a few Afrobeat-related women, including Funmilayo Ransome-Kuti (FRK), a pioneering anticolonial feminist and Fela's mother; Dele Salami, the first professional dancer in Fela's 1960s band; Koola Lobitos, whose virtuosity as a performer created the template for women's dance in Afrobeat; two Africa 70 dancers, Olaide Babayale and Funmilayo Onilere, both of whom came on the heels of Salami; Sandra Izsadore, the Black Panther activist credited with radicalizing Fela; and Remi Taylor, an aspiring musician who became the first woman to marry Fela. These women inhabited different social positions but were united by a will to transcend the gender, race, and class regimes that confronted them. The lives of some of these women are well documented; others are not.[1] The historical archive and parameters of public memory are the products of power and precinct of the privileged, even when subaltern groups constitute the agents of momentous social action.[2] FRK, for instance, left personal papers that have informed biographies about her storied life. A coauthored autobiography entitled *Fela and Me* chronicles Sandra Izsadore's memories of her life work and, as the title suggests, her momentous encounter with the Afrobeat musician. By contrast, little is known of Remi Taylor and Dele Salami, let alone of the women who followed in Salami's footsteps as dancers. In this chapter, I attempt to ventilate the entry points into Afrobeat gender discourse about the women whose lives were entangled with a musical genre that defined a generation. My first effort is to sketch a genealogy of Afrobeat-affiliated women, performers and nonperformers alike, whose talents, visions, and activism defined the genre up to the early 1970s. In so doing, I chart a genealogy that sidesteps narratives of pure origins in favor of history "in what we tend to feel is without history—in sentiments, love, conscience, instincts."[3] This is a history of Afrobeat women that scripts "unlikely" protagonists like Dele Salami and dancers whose last names escape recall, whose photographs failed to make the cut for the museum wall. The ensuing pages embrace often-told stories of Afrobeat women as well as serendipitous encounters, retellings that assume no internal logic, narratives that cautiously stitch a slice in time in one woman's life to another to create a mosaic of women's contributions to the evolution of the music up to the early 1970s.

The second entry point is to problematize the impulse toward Afrobeat exceptionalism. Thinking about misogyny in Afrobeat music as exceptional obscures the commonplace ways in which misogyny permeated 1970s Nigerian public culture. It obscures critical lessons to be gleaned from how gender regimes produced Fela and, crucially, how society underwrote the male privilege that Fela sometimes crudely embodied for popular entertainment. In place of exceptionalism, I historicize Fela's thoughts on gender, communicated through music, as expressing male anxieties around the increasing autonomy of women, anxieties stemming from the late colonial era to at least the 1970s. Far from exonerating Fela, I argue that one can discern in the 1970s a set of gender discourses and parameters around gender circulating in an uneven public domain. Such a long view clarifies the conversations into which "Lady" entered as well as the intentionally polarizing positions that Fela assumed through his music and public utterances. Emerging from such a view is a picture in which the seeds sown by chirpy horns and crisp vocals in "Lady," for instance, shaped the public's mistreatment of some of the women with whom Fela satirized gender equity. Instead of circumscribing the gender question to, say, the interval between "Lady" and "Mattress"—1972 to 1975—there is more to be gleaned from understanding the calibrations of gender of specific historical moments. We should be alert, as Oyèrónké Oyěwùmí urges, "to the continuous ways in which gender is made and remade in everyday interactions and by institutions."[4] Afrobeat's gender project was not resolved in a time capsule defined by album releases. More controversial songs that explicitly intervened in gender debates of the day were geared toward stoking controversy and publicity, shedding only partial light on the everyday landscape of Afrobeat in mid-1970s. The songs were released during what, relative to later trajectories of Afrobeat women's lives, could be argued was a high point in their collective experience as workers, artistic and political interlocutors, partners, and agents in the life of the commune. The subculture's most significant gender projects—by which I mean the most defining and coherent mobilization of bodies, ideas around gender roles, resources, talents and expectations, and rewards and punishments based on gender identity and everyday gender performance—were consolidated later in the decade and well into the 1980s.

Funmilayo Ransome-Kuti (FRK): Arts of the Yoruba Feminist Anticolonial Struggle

When Fela's mother, FRK, urged him to compose music in the language and idiom of ordinary Nigerians, she did more than rescue his struggling career. In that pivotal exchange, FRK codified for Fela the tactics for grassroots mobilization she had applied to great effect as a young community organizer. As a student at Abeokuta Grammar School in the 1910s, FRK came of age amid consolidation of and resistance to British colonial power in southwest Nigeria. In 1914, a proposed tax by Abeokuta's central administration sparked an uprising in the Ijemo area, even though the proposed tax was a last-ditch response to a British threat to stop collecting import duties on Abeokuta's behalf at the British-controlled Lagos port. The protest was the first in a series of mass political actions in the town. In June and July 1918, another uprising engulfed the Adubi area in response to "illegal and oppressive sanitary fines."[5] In what has been dubbed the Adubi war, protesters wrecked massive havoc on railway and telegraph lines, prompting British retaliation including the opportunistic destruction of local shrines. The British-backed Alake of Egba, Oladapo Ademola II, was an influential figure in the evolving colonial administrative structure. Ademola II earned an annual salary of £3,000, which included remuneration for overseeing the Egba Native Authority that enforced the collection of colonial taxes.[6] Targeted colonial policy drastically tipped the balance of power in men's favor, speeding up what appeared to be women's exclusion from public and political life. Spaces and symbols of female autonomy and authority shrank because of gender-specific colonial reforms. Colonial maneuvering diminished the status of Iyalode and Erelu, important chieftain and advisory roles held exclusively by women. A watchful and impressionable FRK observed as a series of mass actions unfolded against taxes and the systematic diminishing of indigenous institutions such as the Ogboni society.

It became clear to FRK, as to most Egba women, that the success of colonial rule hinged on willing local chiefs and patriarchs—essentially a collusion of men. This lesson informed Funmilayo's lifelong commitment to political activism, public education, and community organizing. She became instrumental in the resistance against women's taxation in Egba and went on to fight for universal adult suffrage, and, on the international scene, revisions to the 1946 Richards Constitution, a crucial precursor to negotiations for Nigerian independence.[7] As a child, FRK was assertive and self-assured, qualities developed partly by her protracted stay and study, by herself, in England. But her journey to becoming a feminist icon was gradual and began locally. In 1932, alongside twelve other women, FRK helped found the Abeokuta Ladies Club (ALC), a civic outreach group that hosted social and athletic events (like picnics, games, and lectures) for teenagers. The club was much evolved from an earlier organization that, consistent with colonial domestication policies, had taught girls social etiquette and handicrafts. The activities of the ALC betrayed its members' status as Christian, middle-class, Western-educated women.

Early 1944 was defining for FRK as for the club. The story goes that FRK made the acquaintance of an elderly market woman who stockpiled old newspapers in the hopes of being able to someday read them. FRK's interaction with this woman inspired her to lead literacy programs for poor, uneducated women (uneducated in the sense of not having attended Western-style schools). She recruited two of her children, Olikoye and Dolu, as tutors alongside her nephew, Wole Soyinka, and his mother, Eniola Soyinka, a schoolteacher. FRK's solidarity with market women did more than lead her to expand the curriculum of the ALC; she came to a greater appreciation for the challenges faced by women without class privilege. The ALC became Abeokuta Women's Union, signaling a renewed commitment to "an activist orientation," an attention to women's labor, and an expansion of its ranks to include working women.[8] At her residence at the Abeokuta Grammar School, FRK hosted strategy sessions with women from every stratum of society. Market women aired their grievances before the gathering, the most pressing of which, in 1945, were price controls and the confiscation of foodstuffs by the colonial administration for Nigerian soldiers (to buffer the shortages caused by World War II). FRK, with other ALC representatives, conveyed these grievances to the colonial authority and its Abeokuta cronies. FRK's commitment to the market women only deepened with the imposition of tax on women, which was foreign, exploitative, invasive, and humiliating in its enforcement (particularly the voyeurism involved with stripping young women naked to determine their age). The sexual undertones of the practice only stoked Egba women's fury.[9] The women combined a variety of tactics including a press campaign, public protests, and a sit-in at the Alake's palace, pressuring the Ogboni society to expel him. The women celebrated their hard-fought victories through the streets of Abeokuta; they danced and sang protest songs they had composed. They brokered representation in an interim government through which they abolished taxes on women and pursued fiscal reforms toward transparency and equity.[10] FRK became known as the "Lioness of Lisabi," named after a nineteenth-century warrior who rescued Abeokuta from invasion by the neighboring Ijebu.

How FRK's feminist credentials sat with Fela's misogyny has confounded many. Scholars have ventured hypotheses to find a harmony between FRK and Fela's ostensibly paradoxical positions on society's treatment of women. One explanation is that Fela's gender politics was a direct consequence of an excessively strict upbringing in which his mother was a looming presence. If we ignore how this position absolves Fela of responsibility and places blame on FRK's strictness, it still paints only part of a complex picture, at best. A few other explanations have been ventured for what appears to be mother and son's irreconcilable gender ideologies. Michael Veal offers the explanation that FRK "accepted his contradictions in light of his overall contribution to Nigerian culture and his upholding of her legacy of radical activism."[11] While all of FRK's children committed themselves to activism and public service, Fela came the closest to embodying her politics of insurgent activism, which may have explained in part her tolerance for his excesses. That Funmilayo moved into Kalakuta in the mid-1970s and, in 1975, changed her surname from Ransome-Kuti to Anikulapo-Kuti (becoming FAK) provides ample evidence of her solidarity with Fela, who had previously changed his name to Anikulapo-Kuti, in alignment with his anticolonial self-fashioning. (I refer to FAK for the rest of the chapter except when referencing events before her name change.) But FAK's name change should be read as a continuation of her own long-standing cultural self-reclaiming (as a Yoruba woman) like her allegiance with the Egba market women.[12]

FAK's feminist and Fela's gender legacies are further complicated by another fact: FAK lived in Kalakuta at the height of its fame and notoriety in the 1970s and enjoyed the lavish devotion of a few of her son's girlfriends, many of whom competed for her attention and approval. Olaide Babayale and Funmilayo Onilere stand out in this regard.

Both chance and a desire for adventure contributed to Kalakuta's draw for Olaide. A student at Our Ladies of Apostles (OLA) in Ijebu-Ode, Olaide Babayale was outgoing and had a penchant for rule breaking. She stayed on top of her classwork but played hooky with equally audacious friends. Her jaunts saw her attending parties and nightclubs far from her boarding school in Ijebu. It was during one of these illicit adventures that a senior (who at that point was a

Kalakuta regular and featured routinely as a "Page Three" girl in glamour magazines) planted the idea of Kalakuta in Olaide's adolescent head. Tales of freedom and adventure enraptured the impressionable Olaide. Chance and Fela's
eye for impressionable but restive girls also contributed to luring the teenager
into subcultural living. Olaide's family lived in the Shitta area in Surulere,
opposite Surulere Nightclub, where Fela's band played. From her apartment
and the surrounding areas, you could hear Fela's band playing; only adults or
the boldest young dared visit the club. Olaide had been fending off boredom,
getting "fresh air," as she put it, while Fela performed the Sunday Jump show.
She was at a vendor stall being managed on the day by her teenage friend when
a pair of customers came calling. The girls soon discovered their new customers to be "Fela's boys," young men who assisted Fela directly or were Africa
70 hangers-on. The exchange between seller and customer turned sour when
one of the men bullishly insisted on being given more than they had paid for.
The seller refused; Olaide sided with her. The ensuing dispute drew the attention of Fela who, fresh from the stage, was approaching the scene. Each side
narrated its case and Fela promptly disciplined his boys. Fela insisted that the
men apologize for their unruly behavior. "Fela never wanted any woman to be
cheated in his life," Olaide capped her recall of the encounter, "so when he heard
the story, he called the man [who spearheaded the confrontation] and Fela
disciplined him in the presence of everybody. That was what I liked about in
Fela. I liked the disciplinary action."[13] While Fela's celebrity profile might have
factored into Olaide's decision to meet him a day later, and while their mutual
public predisposition toward fairness certainly informed their getting together,
a less savory aspect of Olaide's joining Kalakuta lay in Fela's opportunism. "The
following day," Olaide added, "he sent a car to" pick me up.[14] Fela's invitation
highlights the diversity of tactics he used to recruit young women, a relevant
complication to the glamorization of the women's free will and initiative. The
choice made by many young women to fraternize with Afrobeat was influenced
by invitations such as this and by Fela's exploitation of his star profile. The
seeds for a life at the edges of society were planted by Olaide's girlfriend and
pollinated by the excesses of Fela's boys. Thus began Olaide's decade-long life
of professional dancing, living at the edge of social norms, and ongoing trouble
with the military state.

Olaide was a three-year Kalakuta resident when FAK moved into the commune. The pair grew close. The stately distance FAK maintained from the
Kalakuta women partly reflected her mission for relocating there: to contain
Fela's excesses.[15] But FAK was seldom fruitful in her efforts at fending off girls
she deemed too young for Kalakuta life. FAK persuaded the young women who

stayed to complete their high school education. FAK ensured, for example, that Olaide completed her schooling, a decision that assumed importance in Olaide's later career transition into the civil service. Olaide resisted FAK's suggestion that tertiary education was the next step—not that the schedule of an Afrobeat dancer was particularly suited to the rhythms of higher education. Olaide and FAK developed the kind of obligatory closeness and deference common between a Yoruba bride-to-be and her potential mother-in-law. Olaide ran errands for FAK and accompanied her on a few of her travels. "I was with Fela's mother for years . . . years!" The Kutis showed their gratitude for Olaide's devotion to their mother. When FAK died in 1978, the family was instrumental in setting Olaide up for a career at the Ministry of Health, where she spent twenty-seven years, eight as a contractor and nineteen as a staff member. Olaide danced on and off at the Shrine in her early years working in the health sector.

Few could resist the pull of the commune's shenanigans, and FAK was no exception. The commune's residents lived by rules that encouraged play and revelry (see chap. 3). Before long, the septuagenarian succumbed to the little marvels that made up a typical day in the commune. Her storied life as a young activist became the raw material for one such spectacle; an unlikely figure, Funmilayo Onilere, was the protagonist. The younger Funmilayo would enact spontaneous impressions of Fela's mother. Her demeanor would become prim, her speech flowery, accenting the syllables of the older Funmilayo's pretentiously delicate English. A pair of spectacles accented her act. The dramatic enactment could be of FAK reading a newspaper or offering a dignified rebuke to an erring soul. As the older activist seldom engaged with many in the commune, Funmilayo likely drew her material from personal observation or from the stories that Fela enthusiastically told about FAK's political adventures in Abeokuta. That the younger Funmilayo was endowed with prominent cheekbones much like her muse lent credibility to her act. These moments of spontaneous performance enlivened the everyday and softened the edges of social difference in the commune. Eludoyin Elutunde, a Kalakuta resident, reminisced about how much delight Funmilayo's mimicry elicited in the commune's members. "She [became] just like the mother," he mused. Although FAK deemed Funmilayo's imitations amusing, she seldom remarked on them.[16] Joseph Roach in *Cities of the Dead* describes these acts as surrogation, a concept that explains how embodiment fulfills the need for cultural regeneration. The process of reembodiment, or surrogation, Roach explains, is continuous and reiterative in that it unfolds "as actual and perceived vacancies occur in the network of social relations that constitute the social. Into the cavities created by loss through death of other forms of departure," survivors rehearse and attempt sometimes ill-fitting alternatives.[17] Funmilayo's acts assumed heightened significance as the commune mourned FAK's death in 1978. In a gesture that underscored the commune's impulse toward surrogation, Fela bequeathed FAK's eyeglasses to Funmilayo after his mother's death. Redoubling on the commune's surrogating gesture, Funmilayo named her first child Olikoye, the name of FAK's eldest son. But the biographies of the two Funmilayos could not be more different. Funmilayo Onilere was fifteen when she stopped her formal education in 1971, at Form 3, joining Fela's band shortly afterward. Her father worked in the shipping business, while her mother traded clothes. Enchantment with the arts and a refusal to abide by her mother's desired line of work for her, in trading, were key drivers in Funmilayo's joining Fela's band.[18] Like Olaide, with whom she became a codancer, the idea of Kalakuta was planted by a girlfriend. "I went to a friend's house and from there we went to Fela's house. That was in 1972," Funmilayo shared in an interview with Carlos Moore. "I know [*sic*] about Fela before, but I did not know that I can stay in his house . . . that my friend, she was living there, before me. She was living with Fela."[19] Following a brief informal interview with Fela, Funmilayo began her Africa 70 career as a disc jockey, with the primary role of curating and playing nonstop music in Kalakuta. Although music and disaffection pulled the young women together, they continually constructed their alterity in everyday contexts through music. "It was a nonstop groove," reminisced Olaide Babayale. Disc jockeys helped cultivate the sonic textures of Kalakuta everyday life; they helped make Kalakuta feel like a party that seemed to never end. Music played continuously in the ground-floor living room, into which fifty to seventy people regularly crammed themselves. The speakers boomed, filling the building with pop songs from Africa and its diasporas. Funmilayo Onilere made a belated foray into dancing, a role she performed for roughly ten years.

The celebrated activist, FAK, however seldom consorted with the younger women. But when she did, it seemed to be a measure of the younger women's efforts to make a connection.

Sandra Izsadore: A Black Panther Activist

As an African American woman and former Black Panther Party member who came of age during the civil rights movement and was involved in California race riots, Sandra Izsadore's activism put her in the crosshairs of the police, resulting in two arrests. Sandra's fortuitous meeting with Fela happened while she was on a personal quest to forge a cultural and ideological connection with Africa. Fela ill-fittingly embodied the potential for such connection. Their romance joins an exclusive list of high-profile relationships between African artists and African American activists like Miriam Makeba and Kwame Touré. Over the course of six months of romance and nightly dialogue, Sandra shared with Fela books, poems, songs, and speeches by African American artists and activists, from Angela Davis and Martin Luther King to Nina Simone and Nikki Giovanni. *The Autobiography of Malcolm X* astounded Fela, who, Sandra recalled, simply listened to her musings and "never said anything."[20] Quite unlike Makeba and Touré, who projected dignity and grace and whose union powerfully conveyed and idealized harmonious, heteronormative relations between Africa and the Black diaspora and in the narrow frame of the nuclear family, Fela and Sandra's relationship was combustible, characterized by equal parts vibrant intellectual exchange and fights, including one occasion when Sandra slapped a philandering Fela in full view of a Los Angeles audience.[21] In remarks strikingly reminiscent of those of Naa Lamiley (chap. 1), Sandra shared, "I was already walking on high ground when I met Fela."[22] Sandra matched Fela in drive and conviction. Fela owed a lot to Sandra; her benevolence housing Fela helped salvage an otherwise disastrous tour with his Koola Lobitos band. Sandra's helping the band is not only celebrated in "My Lady Frustration," a song Fela composed in her honor, but she has also received lavish and deserved credit for her pivotal influence in Fela's political transformation.

Sandra Izsadore towers in Afrobeat history, and for good reason. Even for women with well-rehearsed biographies like Sandra, there is a less studied aspect, namely the interaction she maintained with other women in Afrobeat. Sandra visited Nigeria for the first time in 1972, but her visit was marred by visa troubles and brushes with Nigerian immigration. FAK sheltered Sandra away from the authorities in her Abeokuta home. FAK did not interact with Sandra often, but their limited interactions were impactful. FAK shared a plethora of books with Sandra, everything from Lenin and communism to Erich von Däniken's *Chariots of the Gods*, about ancient human-alien encounters. FAK's trip to communist China and her oft-recounted meeting with Mao Zedong were fodder for discussion. It was during one of their limited communions that FAK expressed quiet disappointment in Fela's choice to become a musician instead of pursuing medicine like his brothers.[23] FAK became instrumental in securing Sandra a two-week visa extension. Sandra's cordial relationship with FAK stood in stark contrast with Sandra's relationship with the women who worked with Fela, many of whom perceived her as a threat. The differentiated structural positions and levels of precarity that women inhabited in relation to society and to Afrobeat mythologies defined the possibilities and limits of solidarity between them. "There was a lot of hatred too among the women living at Fela's because they didn't want me there. Call it obeah, juju, or voodoo. They were using everything against me."[24] Tensions were amplified by the perception that Sandra was privileged and by her being ill equipped for the intrigue and negotiations that attended polyamory in the commune. (The same can be said of polygamy in Yoruba culture; a light take is found in Lola Shoneyin's *The Secret Lives of Baba Segi's Wives*.) The tensions were somewhat tempered during Sandra's second six-month visit (fig. 2.1). When the American returned to Nigeria five years after her first visit, she came with better cultural sensibility and succeeded in forging more cordial relationships with the women in the commune. It had become clear to many in the commune that Sandra was more an occasional visitor than a potentially powerful competitor. During her 1976 visit, Sandra took vocal lead in "Upside Down" (fig. 2.2), a pointed musical critique of the sordid state of Nigeria's public infrastructure, backed by Africa 70 singers. The song became a fleeting vision of what Afrobeat could be with women musicianship outside of the gendered delineation of voices Fela generally favored.

When dancer Aduni Idowu said she "don't have brain for book," she captured a common sentiment among Afrobeat women artists toward intellectualism or, at least, toward the posturing of it.[25] Unlike with Sandra, the exchange of intellectual ideas and books between FAK and other young Afrobeat women was nearly nonexistent. There is little in evidence to suggest that the older activist saw Olaide Babayale, who tended to her, and Funmilayo Onilere, who imitated her, as protégés. There was a notable gulf in the exchange of ideas between FAK and the women who lived in the commune. The interactive gap established by differences in education, exposure, and maturity was only deepened, perhaps, by FAK's tenuous distance from communal life in general. Still, FAK's presence in Kalakuta provided silent endorsement of Afrobeat's edgy brand of rebellion—and the role of young women in it. Perhaps the elderly activist admired the young women. We might venture that FAK, as an activist, saw in the young women the same insurgent creativity that had propelled her to renown. The way Kalakuta women seized everyday life and endowed the body, through art, with meaning was politically impactful. The everyday world they wrought in the commune contained random bursts of singing, self-curated body drawings, debate, and animated vocalizations, teasing, and playing that vibrated beneath the live and recorded music they performed. These sonic textures of Kalakuta everyday life and their translation into agitational music were likely also familiar to FAK. Abeokuta Women's Union under her leadership composed over two hundred songs of protest, songs deployed to boost morale or to ridicule or articulate grievance against the marginalization of women under colonial rule.[26] In this sense, one finds echoed in Alake Adedipe's disdain

Figure 2.1. Left to right: Queen Olaide, Sandra Izsadore, Queen Najite (performing the Black Power salute), and Yeni Kuti, circa 1976. Photo credit and permission: Adrian Boot / Urban Image.

of class oppression—"I don't like how they (the bourgeoisie) treat the workers, the common people. . . . Like in my family, the driver, the servants, they treat them badly"[27]—traces of FAK's class-based activism. She, did after all, elect a public life of activism and advocacy over domesticity, even at great personal expense.[28] The young women in Afrobeat charted a similar course of publicness and activism that had potent resonances with FAK's earlier life. She may have admired them and the vitality they certainly brought to her son's work.

If FAK's early activism was driven by resistance to the agents and mechanics of colonial expansion in Abeokuta, the women in Afrobeat dealt with an African state that, as Achille Mbembe poetically describes it, lured its citizens into a frenzied dance and preyed on their flesh.[29] The neocolonial entity that was the state assimilated the colonial logic of authoritarian repression, rendering the citizen more a disposable nuisance than a subject endowed with rights. Afrobeat women deployed body and voice in ways that some misconstrued as reflecting their lack of social refinement. On the contrary, their crude antics vividly mirrored the political reality in which they found themselves, a reality

Figure 2.2. Sandra Izsadore (bottom right) on the album cover of *Upside Down* (1976). Photo credit and permission: Lemi Ghariokwu.

quite different from, but no less urgent than, that of the Abeokuta market women—a postwar dystopia overseen by a rabid military establishment and entangled with a misfiring state. The neocolonial state weened itself of the moral pretensions of the colonial state, which, no less exploitative, engaged in moral arguments about colonial obligation to those it determined *needed* civilization.[30] That the neocolonial reconfiguration of African societies happened alongside the Cold War, during which African states were ping-ponged between competing imperial alliances, created further fissures in the social contract between Nigeria and its citizens. Indeed, the looking outward that entailed the political economy of neocolonialism and navigating Cold War imperatives rendered the exercise of violence a staple of statecraft. As working-class citizens who received the short end of the stick in state-citizen encounters, Afrobeat's women came to know the state intimately; they could read its reflexes in ways that had not fully materialized as targets for political resistance for earlier generations of feminist activists. Afrobeat women had something to teach FAK about their crude tactics for engaging a state eager to spill blood. Yet while the women's tools of resistance were more visceral than cerebral, more volatile than organized, they shared with FAK and the Abeokuta market women a rejection of the coalescing conditions of coloniality that governed their respective historical moments.

The entanglement between FAK and the expanding ranks of young women in Afrobeat makes the case for viewing her involvement through a frame more expansive than uneasy tolerance. FAK played an active role in protecting her son and the commune, not least from questions about his relationship with girls and young women. On more than one occasion, FAK used her influence to bail Fela out from face-offs with authorities. And when the gender question was posed more pointedly, she vigorously defended him publicly. Following a 1974 police raid of the commune to rescue one of its female residents, for instance, FAK, who seldom spoke publicly about Fela's lifestyle, argued in his defense in an interview: "I challenge the police to disclose the name of the girl and to find out why it was that after I had personally driven the girl out of the house she had to come back again. . . . If people cannot properly train their children to stay in their houses, who is to blame when they take to the streets." Casting doubt on the police's rescue mission account, FAK argued that her son was the victim and pinned the accusations against him on "jealousy and hatred."[31] FAK's defense of Fela was hardly an isolated instance. When pressed elsewhere on the same subject, FAK urged that Fela be praised for his social rehabilitation efforts in Kalakuta, for picking up the slack when Nigerian society failed its delinquent youth. Afrobeat surfeit found vigorous support in FAK, who once challenged a journalist: "Fela will never make a million at all. What he is doing now is providing for many destitute children who are not cared for by their parents. They accuse him of abducting teenagers. There will be more and more coming to his house because he feeds them. The government should emulate European governments and register every child so that when anything goes wrong they can trace them. Fela should be thanked by the government for helping them do their job." Later in the same interview, FAK complicates the narrative of welfare and philanthropy when she explicitly states, "If you are doing anything and don't get women involved you will never get on. . . . Would you go to Fela's show if only boys danced for him?"[32]

On one level, FAK's support for Kalakuta culture might be read less as an endorsement of Fela's problematic ideas about women and more as her affirmation of "his right to express his views."[33] If this was the case, then her affirmation of Fela's right to free expression assumed that this right was equally available to everyone, including the women who worked with him, making Fela's pronouncements understandable as participating in a culture of open debate. This was not the case. In fact, such a position helped to obscure the unequal relations Fela maintained with girls and young women who worked with him, the uneven access to shaping public discourse around gender, and the disproportionate power Fela held over his collaborators. Importantly, pinning the blame on parental neglect in no way supports the sketchy moral premise on which Fela recruited, housed, and maintained affairs with the young women in his band. In other words, had there been solid moral premises on which to defend her son, FAK would have consistently ventured such a position. The moral deficiencies of other actors—state or parents—were her repeated defense for Fela's relationship with the women in his music. With her son, FAK showed an unlikely tolerance for patriarchy by avoidance and deflection, an image that stands at odds with the firebrand feminist image that formed a decisive part of her legacy. Perhaps a more accurate description of FAK's entanglement with Fela on the sticky question of gender is that she succumbed to affection, the critical blindness that only love can inflict, not less so on a mother for a treasured son. Love roped FAK into the web of contradictions that Fela spun around himself. That the terrain of Afrobeat activism appeared to be broader than the damning gender aspects of Fela's work, or that the controversy generated by Afrobeat's gender question amplified publicity for and curiosity about the other aspects of Fela's activism, seemed to temper some of the unease she might have felt. Either way, we cannot sustain belief in a passive relationship between FAK and her son's gender politics, nor should biographies overlook the complex human entanglements between mother and son. FAK's only daughter, Dolu, put it clearly: FAK would "rather die than see Fela suffer."[34] FAK and Fela shared an abiding love that fed her patience with excesses she may have elsewhere rejected. Fela returned his mother's affection despite her high-handed discipline: "I dug her. I liked to hear her talk, discuss. Something always made me sit with her, to listen."[35] While FAK helped protect younger women who wandered into Kalakuta, her ultimate interest was in protecting Fela. Consequently, her vociferous defense of Fela's brushes with the state worked against the interests of the women around him. Maternal endorsement of the kind FAK brought to Afrobeat has long afterlives; her untimely death in 1978 meant she could no longer act as a counterweight to Fela's combustible relationship with the young women in his charge, young women who were still finding their way in the world.

Remi Taylor: A Quiet Force

Remi Taylor shrouded herself in mystery.[36] Hers was mystery born of equal parts cultured deportment and melancholia. Like Sandra, Remi related to Fela in a way that stood at odds with the musician's public persona of ostensible authority over women. Asked about the dynamics of her relationship with Fela vis-à-vis other women, Remi responded: "Most of the [other women] are younger. I would say he doesn't treat me any differently. He treats each person how he sees them. I feel he treats us the same. Like Lamiley, she's a senior wife too. I think we are all treated individually. I don't think we are classed, like this is Remi, she is up there and they are down or anything like that. I'm more or less his age and I've lived with him longer, so I know him more."[37] Remi's comments about age foreshadow her wavering diplomacy on the question. Moments later, she remarked quite pointedly, "I sometimes feel Fela's a bit afraid of me. I really do. [*Laughter*] He may never show it or admit it, but I feel it."[38] Clearly, being Fela's peer set Remi apart. She was on par with Fela not simply because of for her age but also because of the social capital she wielded through education, family, nationality, legal marriage, and, in the Yoruba context, motherhood. Born and raised in Britain, Remi had social and cultural capital that ostensibly immunized her from Fela's ridiculous pronouncements on women. Remi was the daughter of a mother of Native American and African American heritage and a Nigerian father, both of whom lived in Britain. Remi was eighteen when she met Fela at a party in 1959. While she initially found his Teddy Boy style off-putting, they eventually kicked off a romantic affair that culminated in marriage on January 7, 1961, two years after their meeting. "At first she did not think much of me," Fela confessed, "but when we met again, my music did it, although I was then more mature and experienced."[39] A mournful Fela is said to have wept throughout the wedding ceremony, promising anything but fidelity in what appeared to him a loveless marriage. He interpreted the marriage much later as forced cultural assimilation into whiteness: "By the time I got married in London, I was thinking like a whiteman [*sic*]."[40] As the first legal wife and mother of Fela's first three children—Yeni, Femi, and Sola—Remi towered over the other women working with her husband. Remi's stately demeanor helped her maintain an "Olympian detachment" from the younger women.[41]

For all they differed on, Remi and Fela both expressed an unlikely cynicism about women's liberation over the course of their lives. Remi's view of gender difference was more nuanced than Fela's, however. She believed in equity but did not want to perform "masculine" tasks like driving a bus; she shared Fela's embrace of biological determinism as the basis for gender hierarchies. Remi's lived experience might have evolved to complicate her cynicism about women's liberation as she became the target of the inevitable petty indignities that attended marriage to Fela. Marrying arguably the most sexually irreverent public figure in Nigeria might have had its perks, but privacy and decorum were not among them. If Remi was predisposed to a life of quiet, she doubled down on this tendency in the face of media scrutiny. Zealous journalists sniffed for any hint of marital distress. Her marriage to Fela became an open sore, but Remi dissembled, denying anyone or the public the pleasure of bearing witness to her struggle. Remi projected a sense of being unbothered, a demeanor that starkly contrasted with the rollercoaster of controversies that surrounded Fela and his publicity antics, not least the mass wedding. When asked her feelings on the mass wedding in an article whose title, "Fela's Wife Okays Mass Wedding," bore witness to the journalistic baiting to which Remi was exposed, Remi retorted in usual fashion, "I don't think Fela's actions will have any adverse effect on me and my family."[42] She defended the wedding as well as Fela's right to legal compensation after a brutal state crackdown. It was only as a grown woman that her first daughter, Yeni, came to grips with what her mother might have endured. "For me, as a kid, it was fun having so many stepmothers, though now, at 49, I wonder how my mother Remi, who was born and raised in England, really felt."[43] Clearly, Remi's dissembling showed cracks. Awakened to the reality behind the excitement of her dramatic childhood, Yeni eventually recognized her mother's emotional distress. Whatever hurt Fela's lifestyle did not inflict, scrutiny around her improbable calm and the burden of posturing as the eternally forgiving wife did.

Remi's anguish had roots in betrayal of another kind. She made personal and career sacrifices on the promise of respect and reciprocity. Remi had been an aspiring musician, though she spoke little over her lifetime about her career aspirations or passion for music. Precious little is known about Remi, which is ironic given the plethora of music biographies in which she makes an adjacent appearance to Fela. Relocating to Nigeria after marrying Fela appeared incompatible with her dreams of becoming a musician herself. She supported Fela nonetheless through his early days as a struggling musician. Watching Fela play to a packed crowd at Afro-Spot (the nightclub that housed Fela's band prior to his relocation to the Afrika Shrine), one regular recalled Afrobeat's humble beginnings and Remi's visible place in it. "Sitting back and watching the scene, I could not but recall the several evenings five short years back when the audience strength was constantly FOUR: Fela's brothers, his wife and I."[44] It is likely that Remi invested in Fela's career as a struggling musician on the promise that his big break would mark their shared success. It could not have panned out more differently. Fame and success transformed not only Fela but also their relationship as partners. In 1972, Remi moved out of their home and into a separate residence with her children, separating herself from Fela's philandering and from a budding commune that only blossomed in notoriety with her departure. Saddled with the sole responsibility of parenting, Remi dedicated most her life to raising her children. "Love, discipline . . . I got all of that from my mother and it played a defining role in childhood," Femi Kuti reminisced.[45] When Remi returned to the Kuti home in 1980, she found a subculture that had seen some of its best days. Her marriage to Fela showed signs of stability only to the extent that Remi maintained her distance from Fela and his entourage. Their troubles peaked in August 1981, when dancer Funmilayo Onilere bore Olikoye, Fela's first child mothered by a Queen, signifying yet another rupture to the nuclear family model Remi embodied. Fela requested Remi's blessing of the newborn, which she rightfully interpreted as a mark of disrespect. Slaps were exchanged at the naming ceremony before Remi separated from Fela. It is the sole documented instance of an outburst attributable to Remi. Before her death in 2002, Remi requested a quiet burial, commanding in death the same reserve she cultivated in life. Remi found solace in silence and restraint. Both came at a price she was willing to pay, or so it seemed.

Dele Salami: A Fire of Her Own

The working-class women who constituted the majority at Kalakuta Republic, and were arguably Afrobeat's most impactful collective sit in the shadows of women like FAK and Sandra, whose biographies dominate Afrobeat histories.[46] It is remarkable that the women are credited with tolerance and sacrifice to Fela (Sandra's credit circulates around her ideological impact, but not without mention of her support of Fela and his Koola Lobitos band in Los Angeles). Yet it is possible to chart a genealogy that pertains to the artistic impact of women on Afrobeat music performance itself. This genealogy not only enriches Afrobeat women's history but also historicizes women's artistic innovation in terms beyond uneasy sacrifice. Such genealogical approach brings into sharp focus Dele Salami, the first and, for a long time, only dancer in Fela's band, especially in the late 1960s, critical years of experimentation and identity formation. Dele played a crucial but seldom-referenced role in the development of the Afrobeat aesthetic.

Dele was the sole dancer in Koola Lobitos beginning in 1969, accompanying the band on its tumultuous 1969–1970 US tour. The solitary female artist in a male-dominated group, Dele was primarily responsible for her own choreography, tailoring her solo dance routines to the band's repertoire of songs; she enjoyed great latitude in this role. At the height of Dele's short but impactful career in Afrobeat, Fela was preoccupied with developing a musical form that would successfully blend local idioms and musical styles with the sophistication and freedom of jazz and the funk of soul music. Focusing on music meant that interfering with Dele's choreographic process was a privilege unavailable to Fela. The persona he later cut for himself as Afrobeat's singular creative muse was in scarce evidence in the Koola Lobitos band, where relationships were mostly horizontal and the compositional process more open and collaborative. This said, Dele's autonomy derived ultimately from the power of her craft to "make the audience go wild."[47] Her autonomy would appear alien in Afrobeat's subsequently fraught relationship with female artistry. True to the improvisatory spirit that marked these early times, Dele wore no special costumes. Instead, she switched between everyday clothing and, for major shows, tailored pieces. And as with her dances, she made most costume decisions alone, with minimal input from the bandleader. Dele was largely self-taught, driven by passion and grit, yet she managed to eke out a living through dancing. For women like Dele, lack of formal training and society's cynicism about professional dancers did little to help them on their path. It might have worked to Dele's benefit that Koola Lobitos did not have a fraught reputation with female sexuality the way subsequent iterations of Fela's bands did. In Koola Lobitos, she found ample room for artistic experimentation.

Congolese popular *danseuses* earned fame and notoriety through their artful blend of grace, stamina, eroticism, and sensual control of their bodies during solo and group dance routines. The women regarded as skillful *danseuses* attuned their bodies to the fine, real-time ebbs, flows, and textures of live instrumentation. Instead of performing from memory or pursuing a faithful repetition of past and familiar routines, they oriented their performances toward the drummer's cues, who "must be perceptive to a dancer's hints" about pace, tension, and rhythmic breaks. Together, and when well executed, ensembles enacted a push and pull between percussion and dancing body that drew as much from practice as from in-the-moment improvisation; they riffed on a familiar structure to continually generate exciting dance solos that inspired the band and entertained the audience.[48] Dele Salami, as Koola Lobitos's inaugural dancer, mirrored the potency of *danseuses* as critical creative agents in the lives of popular dance-music bands. Dele became heralded by Koola

Lobitos drummers as highly attuned to their rhythmic pulse and as an inspiration that urged instrumentalists to the creative limits. Tony Allen, Fela's most celebrated drummer, was enthused about Dele's dancing: she could "dance to anything," Allen confessed. "She could dance to solos; she could even preview where you were going in the music. You can imagine such a dancer in front of you—she inspires you all the time."[49] Allen's words remain a rare tribute—only documented five decades later, long after Dele's time, they powerfully underscore the scant consideration given to women in popular culture and, more pointedly, the undercounting of women's craft as dancers in Afrobeat music. As such, Dele's absence from Afrobeat narratives is as gendered as the belated critical attention given to most nonelite women in the field of African history,[50] to androgenic hagiographies of popular Afrobeat scholarship, and to the idea that dance is "the last of the arts to be recognized within both academia and the art world as a valid subject of study or legitimate art form."[51] Misogyny and the construction of Fela as a singular genius consolidate the silencing of the creative agency of women as dancers. Such an ambivalent view of dance—one that marvels at dance's power to enrapture the viewer but holds the dancer in contempt—is particularly ironic in Afrobeat, a genre that rode to the mainstream on the back of "grooving," a musical and performative code that both invokes and is expressed in the dancing body.

Dele honed her craft through practice, improvisation, and close consultation with band members. Observation was also a key aspect of Dele's arsenal of learning techniques. The story goes that during the 1969–1970 Koola Lobitos tour, Dele had been taken by an impromptu dance routine performed by an African American woman. Inspired by the music and likely by Dele's interpretation, the freestyling Black woman leapt onstage and delivered a quick dance improvisation to the same song Dele had performed. Tony Allen recalled that by the next stop of the tour, Dele had incorporated elements of the woman's style into her own. The result was a movement vocabulary at once new and distinctly Dele's, expanding through her body the dance spectacle that Fela's live performances relied on so heavily.[52] Dele sharpened her craft while helping the band adapt to the tastes of the American audiences it encountered during the turbulent tour. Dele was, in short, indispensable to the band's survival on that tour and to Afrobeat's trajectory well into the 1970s. It was with Dele that Fela gained his first real appreciation for the power of women's artistry as dance collaborators. When Dele separated from the band in the early 1970s, she left a void. Decades later, Fela described Dele as "my first dancer, the [original] Afrobeat Queen," but he gave scant credit for the value she brought to his music.[53] Dele was a pioneering artist in mapping out the contours of the female dancing body and the emerging Afrobeat aesthetic. Her skills came to define not just the power of dancing women in generating visual spectacle but also, and just as critically, the generative power of women's dancing in the production of Afrobeat sound itself. It was after all the case that instrumentalists, per Allen, drummed to follow the dancer's bodily prompts as much as she responded to theirs. Dele's artistry and pioneering efforts distinguish her in a genre filled with uncelebrated women talents. During her tenure, the notion of "dancing girls" had not yet coalesced in the public's consciousness as the signature of Fela's work. In fact, one of Dele's successors was a man, Daniel Koranteng (aka JB), a Ghanaian soul dancer who briefly worked alongside Dele. Fela employed Daniel Koranteng permanently, placing him on a weekly salary of five pounds.[54] Having Koranteng on the payroll following Dele formalized dancers as part of Fela's band structure.

But Dele's entanglement with Fela transcended dancing. They had also been romantically involved. With Dele, the Africa 70 band (newly evolved from Koola Lobitos) caught its first glimpse at a unique approach to managing women's talent. Dele suggested to Fela that they separate business from romance, especially considering Fela's philandering. "Business first before friendship,"[55] Dele recalled in a tone that illustrated how these women, although often young, advocated for themselves in an industry dominated by men who set their own rules. When asked how she felt about Sandra Izsadore's involvement with Fela, she insisted on this separation between romance and work: "I don't feel anything, because me and Fela are in business. . . . Fela was no longer my boyfriend." Fela signaled his comfort with Dele's proposed separation when she asked, but he was reportedly not pleased when she got pregnant by another musician.[56] It is unclear what upset Fela exactly: the pregnancy with another musician (potentially a rival bandleader) or that the pregnancy might get in the way of her dancing and, by extension, his work. Perhaps both possibilities were true. When Dele left Koola Lobitos, she took a dancing job with a highlife band, Harmony Kings, where Tony Benson, the father of her child, played. These entanglements with male band leaders reveal the delicate balance, if at all conceivable in these terms, that women had to strike when pursuing a life in the popular arts. The social pressure to settle down and become wives and mothers often rubbed against the unspoken requirements of their employment as dancers/singers. An unwritten clause implied that they gave up a certain degree of bodily autonomy, part of which entailed romantic involvement with male bandleaders and, if desirable, the choice and timing of pregnancy (and the choice of with whom to get pregnant). Dele's exit exemplified this tension. Her experience nonetheless appears to have consolidated the idea that women who were sexually and emotionally involved with Fela might make for more yielding laborers than women who worked in a strictly professional relationship. This notion of talent management was refined as more women joined the ranks of Africa 70. That Dele and Fela were erstwhile lovers and artistic collaborators implied that romance, flirtation, and sex coexisted with, and perhaps propelled, artistic collaboration resting on a skewed power dynamic. To be clear, romantic affairs between bandleaders and female talents were rampant at the time, yet Fela's Africa 70 was public and singular in the unabashed deployment of sexual intimacy in its modus operandi. Dele, who worked from paycheck to paycheck, crystallized for Fela the dividends of blurring the boundaries between work, play, labor, sex, and pleasure. This lesson stuck even if the experiment failed with Dele, who, as an expecting mother, ultimately parted ways with Fela because of his tendency to delay or withhold pay.

Experiments in the Erotic

The spectacle Dele brought to the band confirmed an emerging trend in Nigerian pop: the centrality of "showgirls" to a band's success. Fela advertised for women dancers in a bid to attract valuable new talent. Two dancers, Paulina (likely also known as Pauline) and Evelyn, joined the band not long before Dele left. Fela played at the time at Kakadu Nightclub alongside this powerful trio of women dancers; one reporter effusively called them "useful catalysts when Fela is in his Afro-laboratory doing his musical experiment."[57] In their short time together, Dele mentored the two women, ensuring that they could excel in what was likely their first gig in the industry. "I taught them how to dance" to Fela's music, Dele mused. They observed Dele's movement, practiced it, and ultimately brought their own improvisations to bear.[58] Two more women, Kemi and Adia, joined in quick succession. Together, the four new dancers became what we might call second-generation Afrobeat dancers (Dele being the first). This group enjoyed only a brief stint, barely appearing in musical or archival records after 1972, but seems to have championed experiments with the erotic.[59] Their stage names were suggestive. Adia, for instance, was fondly called *Nyash Controller*, Buttocks Controller. Kemi was *Shakibo*, a rough translation of which would be "just put it inside." Perhaps the names were casually attached to each dancer after a specific dance routine and never intended to encompass techniques or temperaments as dancers. But the names signaled at the least an endorsement of unabashed eroticism. The shifts in sonic and visual textures of early 1970s Afrobeat music, reflected in "Na Poi," for example, signaled an embrace of sexual play in Afrobeat performance. Also in a first for Fela's band, new women dancers appeared in uniformed costumes: short skirts, about four inches above the knees, with deep slits. Dancing women adorned skimpy costumes during special appearances.[60] Nicknames and costumes not only mirrored Afrobeat's increasingly erotic tenor in lyrics, album art, and live performance but also reflected Fela's domestication, also happening in other bands, of women's glamor and objectifying sexual presence as trends in global pop. When Dele Salami was the band's sole dancer, eroticism or sexual appeal were largely downplayed in favor of her skill, innovation, and rhythmic control. By the end of her tenure as an Afrobeat dancer, an erotic transformation was well underway. Dele considered returning after having her child, but the landscape had changed, with "too many girls" around Fela, as she remembered her final Afrobeat stint.[61]

Few documented instances of live improvisation capture the erotic brazenness of second-generation Afrobeat dancers. One such document is *Ginger Baker in Africa*.[62] Producing the documentary took Ginger Baker to Calabar during Fela's national tour in 1971. The documentary provides rare filmic archive of a crucial transition in Afrobeat women's aesthetics between Dele and the succeeding cohort of dancing women. Baker's documentary features other Nigerian and Lagos-based musicians, but its most extensive and unbroken sequence is Fela's live show on a rainy night at an unnamed Calabar nightclub. The audience is composed of young men, many of whom appear to be in their twenties, with only a sprinkling of women. The audience sits under canopies on all three sides of the outdoor performance area. The band is located upstage, leaving ample room for Fela and the backing dancers. A sweaty Fela commands the center stage area with his funk-inspired "Je'Nwi Temi" (Don't Gag Me). Four women and two men are gyrating close to Fela. Together, they shuffle smilingly downstage in a half-hop as saxophonist Igo Chico leads the ensemble by firing stuttering notes to prod their choreography. The women gyrate in place upstage as the singing begins; their routines feature flexed torsos and sudden shifts of their upper body, their legs planted. Fela leads the vocal section of the song, transitioning to improvised and playful dancing with the two men, each playing the ṣẹ̀kẹ̀rẹ̀ (a gourd-shaped instrument wrapped with stringed beads that produces a hissing effect) and the wooden clef as they accompany Fela downstage. The three men build up the excitement, but it is the women casually dancing behind them who crown the night's spectacle. Fela guides each woman to the center to perform a roughly two-minute solo dance, after which he leads her back to her position on the stage. This sequence continues until all four dancers have had their moment. Solos are demarcated moments for each woman to break free from the collective to showcase her individuality, virtuosity, and declare herself a visible artistic agent within the overall structure of the dance-music ensemble. These slices of performance time-space also present dancers with unique, if fleeting, opportunities for subversion.[63] At the Calabar show, each woman's freestyle solo features different degrees of hip control as well as flexing and releasing of the torso to the trumpet's staccato notes. The last solo dancer is the highlight of the night. After her solo, Fela moves to usher her back to the dancers' rectangular formation. She refuses to concede the spotlight too easily. She suspends her hands behind Fela's neck and thrusts her groin into his aggressively (fig. 2.3). The audience is thrilled, but she is not done yet. She flicks her buttocks at Fela with rhythmic precision at the urging of the trumpet. A mildly surprised Fela feigns surrender. This display delights even her fellow dancers who, in the moment, become as much onlookers as coperformers to a moment of subversion in which a woman performs masculine-coded act of dominating the space and doing the mock thrusting. It is moments such as these that illustrate popular performance's elasticity and capaciousness to fleetingly accommodate queer visions and women's power in otherwise masculine-coded spaces. Two men appear from the audience; they paste naira notes to her forehead and disappear as quickly as they emerged. This unscripted moment marks Afrobeat's shifting grounds into lurid sexual politics, a shift reflecting its growing embrace of populism (entertainment targeted toward "the people") and the string of moral controversies that trailed the women who were key agents of this kind of erotic entertainment. The historical record is scant on these dancers and pinpointing the precise circumstances of their departure is difficult. But it is quite plausible that their visibility and artistic power helped advertise Fela's band as the place for interested women dancers to showcase their talents. Singer Kevwe Oghomienor described a certain "Pauline" (likely the "Paulina" who danced with Dele) as having introduced her to Fela's work. It became a refrain that other young women were attracted to Fela's work because of the presence and creative prowess of the women in his band.

The introduction of dance solos into Fela's live shows equally demonstrates a logistical leap in the dramaturgy of live Afrobeat performance. Solos not only generated spectacle, but they also became a modular device for managing performance time. Women's solos could be lengthened or shortened, performed once or recursively, based on the band's specific needs for any outing. Because dance solos were often accompanied by instrumental solos, they were ripe for exciting dialogue between specific saxophonists and trumpeters (like Igo Chico, Yinusa Akinnibosun, and Lekan Animashaun) and talented dancers (like Lara Shosanya, Najite Mukoro, and Serwaa Akosua), pairings that, by themselves, generated audience anticipation and applause. The showoffs between instrumentalists provided much-needed variety and unpredictability

Figure 2.3. Still image of a dancer suspending her hands behind Fela as she thrusts her groin into his in a Calabar performance. *Ginger Baker in Africa*, circa 1971.

to the band's routines and, crucially, reduced Fela's playing time, which made his appearances more impactful. Solo dances later evolved into long interludes for the musician and backup singers to take backstage rest before returning onstage. Baker's documentary captures both Afrobeat's budding erotic revolution and critical leaps in the dramaturgy of Afrobeat performance. Baker also renders in real time the development of a performance idiom that became refined over the decade: dance solos amid group choreographies.

While the 1970s cultural renaissance fueled by the oil boom failed to proliferate women-led bands, this period witnessed heightened recruitment by bands and nightclubs of women artists on their payroll. Competing bands recruited women as dancers and singers, on a per-show basis, alongside all manner of spectacular acts to augment live music, including magicians, contortionists, and ventriloquists. Women performing visible artistic roles of some sort became the baseline for competing at the highest level in the industry. Segun Bucknor, who helped popularize soul music in Nigeria in the late 1960s and struggled to shake off comparisons to Fela's success,[64] signed on Funlayo Shyngle, a graceful and promising singer whose voice, one writer gushed, projected emotion "as if she invented it."[65] Bucknor's Revolution band enlisted a contingent of women dancers whose choreography was sometimes frenetic and showed hints of primitivist aesthetics.[66] In 1974, a reporter described a dancer named Rita Ajilo, who danced on Saturday nights in Sir Victor Uwaifo's

Melody Aces highlife band, as "the best show dancer around Lagos now." Rita was mesmerizing, this reporter enthused in prose that conceals little of the author's prejudice: "Mouths go agape, sighs and hisses fill the air, male eyes go dim, and female faces grow green with envy [when she dances]."[67] The Ozzidi band by Sonny Okosun, a close rival to Fela in terms of political ideology, featured a duo named the Christie Sisters, whose "highly explosive and sexually aggressive" dancing enlivened Okosun's stage performances.[68] The Christie Sisters were hardly the first dancers in the Ozzidi band. A show dancer named Adia, whom the press eulogized as having a strong personality and plenty of charm, preceded them. "Those who have had the opportunity of watching Adia on stage . . . will agree that this star had a star-studded future," a reporter wrote.[69] A full-page magazine feature on Adia titled "Star in Her Eyes" nonetheless underscored the press's role in exploiting women's sexuality and broadcasting their bodies as much as their art to publics exceeding the nightclub space and the weekend night out. The full-page feature shows a photograph of Adia topless; she flashes a bright smile and bare bosom to the camera (in a fashion reminiscent of "Miss Ngozi," chap. 1), raising the question of the fraught relationship between showgirls who performed at nightclubs and newspaper editors with the potential to prop up or exploit their insecure careers. Writers and editors of entertainment news became vital witnesses to popular culture's serious reliance on creative women—even if newspapers sensationalized the women whose craft they also celebrated. Magnified by the pornographic gaze of journalists' cameras, imageries of nude young women suffused multiple music genres.[70] Afrobeat women belonged to a set of working-class women artists whose voices and dances lit up Lagos nightlife and Nigerian public culture. But despite the dispersal of key women across other bands, no competing musician succeeded at harnessing the erotic for commercial advantage like Fela. Afrobeat dancers infused Fela's outings with an erotic charge that other A-list bands tried without much success to reproduce.

Antifeminism and Male Anxiety in "Lady"

Fela's *Shakara* had the trappings of a hit album. On the B-side song "Lady," Tony Allen delivers intermittent half beats and deft strokes of the high hat that meld with the hiss of the ṣẹ̀kẹ̀rẹ̀, producing a sleek groove. The keyboard alternates with the horns in a tightly arranged call-and-response sequence; each musical phrase is separated from the next by a stripped-down pause filled in by a smooth, airy beat. Just as this pattern feels like the new stasis, the horns scramble into the arrangement. Stoked by calculated breaks, the chirpy beat's purpose appears to be to goad the listener to move.[71] "If you call am woman, African woman no go gree, she go saaaay, she go say I be lady o." Fela delivers the song's first vocal salvo. He repeats the phrase with rhythmic scats, ending on a third go at "saaaay." This break ushers in a major invention in Afrobeat music: a chorus of women vocalizing crisp musical notes. This sonic shift in Afrobeat music is difficult to miss but easy to underestimate. The brand-new chorus responds in unison, "She go say I be lady o." Fela leads the chorus in a lighthearted call-and-response, echoing the dialogue between the instruments themselves. The "shrill, businesslike, and penetrating" backup vocals by women, Tejumola Olaniyan notes, "set up a meaningful dramatic counterpoint to Fela's gruff bellows, playful yaks, and witty scat singing," enriching the listening experience.[72] The singing women in "Lady" represented more than a breath of fresh air in a pop music landscape defined by the bellow of Afrobeat instrumentalists who had previously doubled as vocal backup. It signaled an exercise in re-sounding contemporary Nigerian social life.[73] *Shakara* became arguably the most astute, multisensory engagement with the feminine—as an aural, visual, and tactile force—in postwar Nigerian popular culture. Through live performances and crisp vocals, the women offered a fierce counterpoint to one of the most sampled antifeminist songs in postindependence Nigeria. A string of publicity-generating controversies around the lives and lifestyles of the young women who produced this art transformed Afrobeat permanently into an artform dependent on feminine energy.

Shakara evokes the visual aesthetics of Jimi Hendrix's *Electric Ladyland* (1968),[74] underscoring Fela's attentiveness to global pop icons and announcing Lagos as an emerging destination for pop erotica. But it was what the album signified locally that lent it moral importance. The nineteen topless women in *Shakara*'s cover art extended the conversation into the domain of the visual. Their bodies are arranged to create a pictograph of "Africa 70" (fig. 1.2). The pictograph captures the women kneeling in supplication (in the pictograph's second image, each woman cups her breasts, ostensibly offering them to the viewer) or sitting in a fashion that opens their bodies with legs crossed. A grinning Fela basks at the center of the "o" of their "Africa 70," a posture that conjures the imagery of penetration as much as engulfment by the yonic "o." Read as an insertive sign, Fela's situation paints a less than subtle hint at phallic penetration of the yoni, a reading Fela would have embraced. An equally generative read, however, is that his body (of work) is encircled by an unbroken chain of unnamed women, a reading that shifts the focus to the women whose bodies grace the album, bodies endowed with the capacity to nurture, protect, and smother what they hold in their grip. The album art becomes a potent visualization of the Yoruba awe and enchantment with àjé, the generative power of womanhood and female sexuality.[75] Both readings of the album art's bodily signification are compelling, but the first, aided by the lyrics of "Lady," was destined to dominate Afrobeat debates.

Controversy and invention guaranteed commercial success for "Lady." The lyrics were redeployed in some of the most vibrant debates of the 1970s about the emerging class of Western-educated, professional women, often perceived as a threat to patriarchy. Partly in jest, Fela satirizes the Western-educated African woman who refuses traditional gender roles of nurturer and subordinate partner. In a simplistic characterization, he lists her egregious offenses as ranging from refusing to cook, embracing gender equality, and, for full effect, wanting to be waited on by a man. She is the antithesis of the African woman who, by contrast, serves her master and does his bidding without question or complaint. The irony of women singing the lyrics (in Afrobeat's new sonic innovation) and giving beautiful melody to these ideas adds to the song's sting. Reinforced visually by a masculinist reading of the album art, the women singers performatively embody the African woman who fire-dances for male visual pleasure, avails her body (for penetration), and is made intelligible only in deference to male authority. The song's pitching of the Western-educated woman against an imagined African woman in such melodramatic fashion set the tone for its deployment in debates about gender. "Lady" has been invoked as the lyrical antipode to the fictional Wakanda in Marvel's critically acclaimed *Black Panther.* The song also emerged in efforts at situating Fela in the company of Bill Cosby, the fallen American comedic icon found guilty of drugging and sexually preying on multiple women.[76] Although the comparison to Cosby might be misinformed, it underscores the divergent critical projects to which "Lady" lends itself. This said, feminists have offered the most nuanced critiques of the song and its implications for gender. Nkiru Nzegwu astutely interprets "Lady" as a work that appears "intuitively true about African women yet is fundamentally Western," pointing to Fela's ironic ignorance of the role of colonialism in producing the strand of male hegemony he extols. Fela misses the irony that the submission and dependence he ascribes to African women were Victorian notions that became the hallmark of nineteenth-century elite Lagos women pursuing assimilation into British womanhood—a willful oversight that comes into sharp relief when read against the deep and expansive histories of Yoruba women in kingship, local and international markets, spirituality, and social life writ large.[77] Nkiru lauds the song's sophisticated instrumentation without missing the oppressive ideas it propagates. "Lady" has remained the stuff of polarizing debates on the limits of Fela's radical politics.[78] If humor by exaggeration produces a sense of ambiguity in "Lady," the less-melodious "Mattress" (1975), whose lyrics include "Woman na mattress" (women are mattresses), reinforces a sense that Fela was a misogynist or, at the least, that Afrobeat music lacked a liberatory agenda that included women. Teresa Washington has argued that even in Fela's songs that advertise shameless sexism, Fela "weaves threads of irony and sews swatches of truth."[79] One might thus include "Lady" in the company of songs like "Ikoyi Blindness" and "Johnny Just Drop," songs that highlight Fela's potent class critique. And yet it would be misleading to clear Fela of accusations of misogyny on the grounds that "Lady" contains some truth or because he eulogizes Sandra Izsadore in "My Lady Frustration."[80] Such a maneuver elides the structural advantage that Sandra enjoyed as a function of class and nationality.

While Fela gave oxygen to antifeminism, it would be a mistake to conflate excess with exception. "Lady" illuminated the anxieties produced by the threat that women's liberation posed to male privilege in Nigerian society. These anxieties percolated through 1970s public culture. Postindependence military regimes not only extended the gender logics of colonialism but also entrenched them in a way that concentrated power and opportunity in the hands of men. Women with national profiles as community organizers and politicians from the 1950s and 1960s retreated from life in politics as violence, and the threat to exercise it, became the dominant means of seizing and retaining political power. Margaret Ekpo's life (as well as that of her political mentor, Funmilayo Ransome-Kuti) vividly illustrates women's retreat from national politics.[81] The concentration of political power in the hands of men derived from the systematic marginalization of women through colonial policy, but specific policies of the late colonial era around public welfare and schooling for girls reverberated through Nigerian social life for decades. When confronted with clamors for self-determination, the British colonial government introduced significant reforms, including new child labor laws (such as banning street trading by girls) and increased access to Western education for girls, even though these initiatives often conflicted with local sensibilities.[82] The impact of said reforms materialized in vivid fashion in the 1970s in the form of increased women's participation in the civil service, formal economy, and public culture. Lively public discourse around women and gender relations was informed as much by local transformations as by the United Nations' declaration of the Decade of the Woman (1975 to 1985).

When Western-educated African women asserted their autonomy, they triggered male anxieties that manifested in the form of vitriol, if not violence.[83] The rise and constitution of African print culture became implicated in producing gender discourse. With a few exceptions, elite men dominated print culture across Africa and dictated deliberations over gender roles.[84] For their part, Nigerian newspapers and magazines featured lively columns and op-ed pieces debating gender and sexual relations in the 1970s. The modern Nigerian woman, as much a historical subject as an imagined one, cut a figure of disruption. With formal education, access to the formal economy, and cosmopolitan tastes, this figure had social and, by implication, sexual mobility, stoking fears about an ongoing gender revolution, particularly in urban areas. How she dressed, if/when she got married and to whom, how she expended her earned income, and with whom she slept and at what frequency became fodder for frenzied public discourse throughout the decade. The modern woman embodied all that was undesirable about unchecked modernity. Print media lit up with the "Pandora's box," as one writer put it, of so-called women's liberation.[85] The shifting landscape of even marginal autonomy for Western-educated Nigerian women nonetheless produced an obsession with regulating their bodies.[86] In this context, "Lady" can be read as a historical document of sorts, a sonic repertoire of an evolving social world. One finds the anxiety of newspaper columnists echoed in the song's lament of the Western-educated woman who has repudiated domestication at a material level ("she would dance the lady dance") and a discursive level ("she would say, 'I am a lady o'"). The narrator in Fela's "Lady" inhabited the same cultural universe as patriarchs, from emirs and husbands to Idoma male migrants in northern Nigeria, in the late colonial era.[87] Their methods varied, but they shared a similar goal: containing independent modern women.

Flexible Misogyny

Misogyny in Fela's music did not translate seamlessly into misogyny as an unwavering part of his relationship to women. Lyrics offered transparent access to some of Fela's deeply held beliefs, but this was not always the case with gender or the relationship between gender discourse (in lyrics, rhetoric, and album art) and the lived experience of gender relations in Kalakuta. On the one hand, Fela has been described as "humanizing," caring for, and showing empathy toward vulnerable women, a posture strikingly at odds with any lyric or rhetoric about gender. Beside the *humanizing* Fela sits the Fela who, at other times, struck women (or had them punished) for misdemeanors.[88] The commune he led encouraged freedom of a kind that shamed even progressive movements of the time, but he also argued that fecundity and homemaking were a woman's ultimate purpose. He revered certain women and lorded it over other women, a gesture modulated by a woman's structural advantage, her capacity to resist, and a host of contextual circumstances that define who wields power regardless of gender. We could fairly accurately describe this shifting gender posture as *flexible misogyny*. In interviews of those who knew him, Fela appeared variously as an object of effusive praise or as a source of distress from the women who closely worked with him. The ostensibly bifurcated image of defender and abuser could not have been more striking than in my interview with Olaide Babayale-Kuti. She was fervent in sharing that "Fela never wanted any woman to suffer in his life." She mentioned, in the same interview, that Kalakuta had its system of discipline supervised by Fela, a system that saw women punished (sometimes through floggings and isolation in a mock prison). Even though Olaide was a teenager for most of her time in Kalakuta, she blamed her many beatings on her own truancy. Flexible misogyny in Afrobeat describes Fela's adaptive approach to gender. The goal was to manage the differentiated resources and expectations of Afrobeat women as well as those of the listening public, and the central purpose was to stoke a sense of notoriety and sell songs. In a shifting array of contexts, Fela adulated his mother, serenaded his wife Remi, and exercised near-absolute power, with notable exceptions, over the plenitude of working-class women around him. The adaptiveness of this gender approach contorted and reproduced patriarchy without disrupting it in any sense. Keen to even the faintest pulse of popular trends, Fela attuned himself to a cost-benefit deployment of misogyny in music and daily life, a model of gender management that buried him in contradictions and produced what appears at the surface to be a bifurcated posture on gender.

Afrobeat music revealed little about the differentiated social positions that women inhabited in relation to its production. A revised genealogy takes Afrobeat history as unsettled and contingent. Social class, nationality, age, and seniority were salient variables in how women navigated their relationship to Fela and to the music machinery he oversaw. The women who had arguably the most defining impact on the Afrobeat style and aesthetics were the working-class women. Volatile, relentless, edgy, and brazenly sensual, the "girls" followed the lead of Dele Salami and early Afrobeat women artists like Evelyn, Pauline, and Adia to unleash verve on Afrobeat and Nigeria's popular music scene. These young women remained unfettered by Funmilayo's age and measured wisdom, and they were devoid of Remi's cultivated detachment and Sandra's intellectual forthrightness. Their energy and controversial presence, coming on the heels of Sandra's intervention, proved decisive for the trajectory of Afrobeat music. If Remi promised decorum and Sandra unraveled the transformative power of intellectualism, the Queens, as many of them would later be known, reveled in a form of resistance that was at once quotidian and spectacular. Through a collective embrace of sensuality and personal style, they championed a shameless rebuke of convention. Dress, nudity, song, and an ever-expanding vocabulary of urban slang became choice weapons against the tedium of conventional femininity. FAK passively nurtured these different iterations of female rebellion, especially as they advanced her son's musical and political agenda. It should be clear that Fela was not responsible for awakening a latent capacity for rebellion in these women, who were separated by age, class, and nation. The case of Sandra quite easily refutes this conclusion, but the same was true for others. The young women, just like Sandra, discovered in Fela a fertile conduit for the expression of their individual impatience with quotidian oppression. Through him, the women discovered and made uneasy connections to one another, expanding in the process the creative possibilities entailed by what true rebellion lay on the horizon. Of all Afrobeat women, these working-class creative workers of Afrobeat performed a mix of docility and irreverence, submission, and unpredictability, bolstering Fela's public persona as a neotraditional chief and triggering moral crusaders and cultural purists. Their defiance was expressed in small acts unbecoming of "decent" women—a stick of marijuana held casually, wayward flesh sensually displayed in daylight. Their irreverence animated Afrobeat music, tipping it beyond the boundaries of propriety.

The tenuous convergence of FAK, Sandra, and the ranks of working women in Kalakuta Republic reveals its transnational potential as an incubator of Black and anticolonial feminist struggle. That this convergence was enabled in part by affective ties to Fela equally underlines what could have been true political solidarity between women who spanned age, nation, class, and culture.

A historicity of everyday life, the marketplace where gender is trafficked, transacted, contested, and where it accumulates meaning, can help ventilate gender discourse in Afrobeat.

3

To Improvise a Precarious Freedom

Before FESTAC 77

> The life in Kalakuta is an irresistible life.
> Once you get into Kalakuta you cannot leave
> anymore because it was a free land.
>
> **—Olaide Babayale-Kuti, former
> Africa 70 dancer, in an interview**

"One day I decided to join any musician that has name and get the sense of music," Fehintola Kayode (fig. 3.1) mused regarding when, at seventeen years old, she acted on her love for music.[1] High-profile bands that played what she deemed "sensible" music were based in Lagos, requiring five hours of travel from her village in Ipoti-Ekiti. The Fela-led Africa 70 band fit her criteria on several fronts. By 1975, Fela's popularity had reached epic proportions, his critique of military politics had grown more acerbic, and his stature was on the upsurge. Fehintola was convinced to take her talents to his Africa 70 band. Quite unlike many of her peers, however, Fehintola did not abscond home. She instead sought the consent of her supportive parents before journeying "straight to Fela's house in '76."[2] Another factor might have informed Fehintola's decision: irrefutable evidence of women as creative agents in Afrobeat. A few months before Fehintola's arrival, Kalakuta women had begun sporting bold facial makeup that became a punctum in Afrobeat's medley of beauty and resistance. An unnamed Kalakuta woman recalled being enchanted by the sensuality and fame of Afrobeat's women performers and how, as she put it, they would "sing and gyrate their buttocks to the admiration and applause of viewers."[3] The sensuality of women enchanted other women into what, from the outside, appeared like a world of magic and freedom.

96

At Kalakuta Republic, Fehintola began a tumultuous career as an amateur backup singer, a career that spanned roughly three decades. Fehintola could not have known that she was joining the Fela-led commune at a time of intense political ferment with ramifications for Fela's work. Neither could she have known that Fela and his cohorts had truly begun to upset the Nigerian military establishment. Not to posit that a safe time existed to join Kalakuta—put simply, certain moments were more precarious and volatile than others. The mid-1970s was one such precarious moment for Nigerians and Kalakutans. In the span of two years, 1974 to 1976, Nigeria witnessed a military coup that ousted the General Yakubu Gowon regime and another fatal coup attempt that, while unsuccessful, saw the cold-blooded assassination of Brigadier General Murtala Muhammed, Nigeria's head of state until his death in February 1976. These events made an already fraught climate even more delicate at the highest levels of power. The military had to be wary of restive soldiers within its ranks and of a citizenry that, disgruntled by failed governance, began clamoring for a return to electoral politics. In the political atmosphere of the mid-1970s, civilians and soldiers alike were threatened by violence. High-profile assassinations were commonplace, as were state-sanctioned killings of soldiers suspected to have participated in coups. Besides using his music as running commentary on the political situation, Fela also inserted himself into the fray when, following a newly amended constitution, General Olusegun Obasanjo lifted the ban on political parties, signaling Nigeria's transition to democracy after thirteen years of military rule. Fela floated a political party, Movement of the People (MOP), to support his candidacy for president and used his music and rhetoric to advance his candidacy.[4]

The actions of Kalakutans as a collective helped to stoke friction with the nervous autocratic state. Kalakutans were a raucous bunch who not only performed in a plethora of artistic and logistical capacities to help Fela consolidate his public profile as *enfant terrible* but also were emboldened by the band's popularity, commercial success, and public approval to clash with state actors in one-on-one encounters. Save for a handful of rescue raids on the commune, Kalakuta Republic was at most a mild irritant for the police and, to a lesser extent, the military for the first half of the decade. That profile changed dramatically, and Kalakutans appeared and stayed on the state's radar in the second half of the decade. Interest in the commune's political activities spiked in January 1977 (especially between January 15 and February 12, 1977), when Obasanjo's administration hosted its signature Pan-African culture project, the Second World Black Festival of Art and Culture (FESTAC 77). State actors reviled Fela, Kalakutans, and his political mentees in Young African Pioneers (YAP) for their alleged attempt at sabotaging FESTAC. So, the Supreme Military Council held a meeting on February 17, 1977, five days after FESTAC, with Fela Kuti, Kalakuta Republic, and the YAP on their agenda. At this meeting, Chief of Army Staff T. Y. Danjuma is reported to have issued the directive that Fela be captured, "dead or alive."[5] This escalation to extreme violence can be understood as a culmination of the commune's mild irritancies and the state's belief that, left to their own devises, Fela and the kangaroo republic he led could blossom into untamable creatures capable of undermining an already fragile polity.

Within a few odd years, Kalakuta had transformed from a commune of "reckless bohemians" to an agenda at the Supreme Military Council; Fela's music and razor-sharp pronouncements on political anomie combined with the everyday acts of especially the young women who gave shape to his art and elevated Afrobeat to "a whole new phenomenon."[6] By the end of the decade, powerful state actors considered the girls and women in Afrobeat persons of interest—they could no longer be dismissed as puppets of Fela's ideas. This chapter explores the density of interanimating acts that accounted for the shift in perception of the young women as candidates for public welfare and rescue to their being perceived as dangerous accomplices against the state. Aesthetic deployments of body and voice laid at the heart of said transformation. Afrobeat women embraced a plethora of self and collective and improvisations occasioned by blurred boundaries between play and resistance, pleasure and labor. Their improvisations were not just aesthetically innovative but also politically subversive, fashioning them into social threats. Fela had sought to professionalize the women in the band, for instance, by enlisting a choreographer and voice trainer. However, the women showed little interest in becoming professionals in any strict sense. Instrumentalists were invariably men who maintained a well-defined, waged relationship with Africa 70; they tended to reside outside Kalakuta Republic, some with their families. For these men, playing an instrument in Fela's band was a job above anything else. On the contrary, the women who performed in the band maintained a dynamic, slippery, and ever-shifting number of domestic and artistic roles. This ill-defined status became fodder for frenzied speculation about the exact nature of their relationship to Fela and, in the absence of clarity on the question, whether they were of value to the Afrobeat enterprise. As noncontract workers, they lived on daily wages susceptible to cash-flow issues from their near-daily performances at the Shrine. Each day was lived on its own terms. The flexibility that attended the women's lives informed their art and was informed by it, leaving many with a highly refined capacity for improvisation and code-switching. These were important reflex responses for confronting the buffoonery of cynical elites, the military

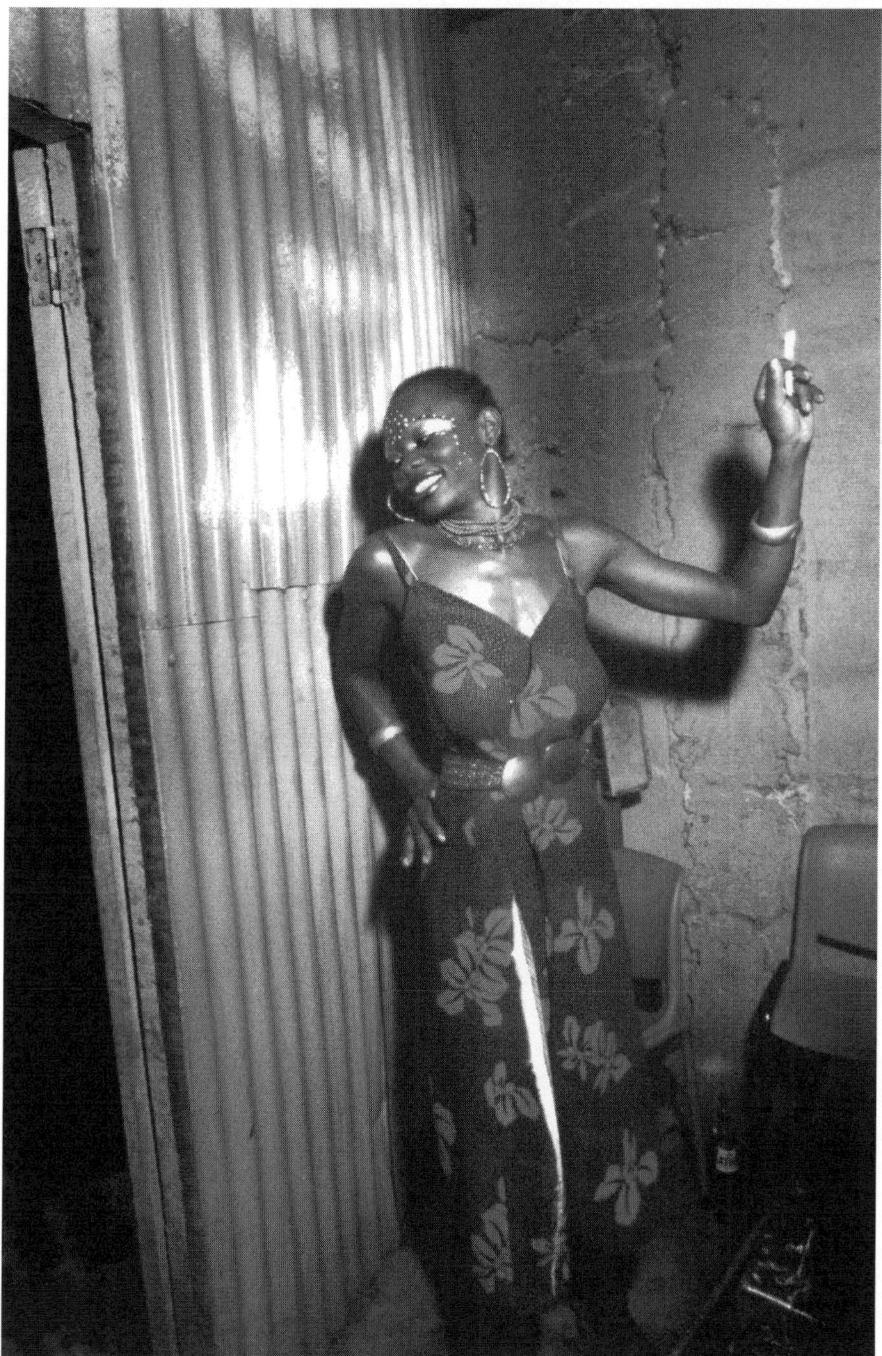

Figure 3.1. Fehintola Kayode poses for a photograph with a joint in her hand, circa 1976. Photo credit and permission: Adrian Boot / Urban Image.

complex, and the so-called colonial mentality that pervaded mainstream Nigerian society. Writing about the Oyin Adejobi Theatre Company, Karin Barber concludes that actors in Yoruba popular theater worked with a desire to realize their full artistic potential in ways that inspired novelty in every dimension of performance.[7] Barber's insight on collective improvisation, on how each actor's creative muscle strengthens the collective, is instructive in the Afrobeat context. Appreciating the creative muscle that women flexed in forging Afrobeat music into a powerhouse of youth culture and activism under the nose of autocracy requires pulling back the veil on the idea that women were props of little worth to Fela's work. The women were, to borrow from performance studies scholar Omi Osun Joni L. Jones, crucial catalysts of the *àṣẹ*, the life force,[8] of Afrobeat music and its affiliated subculture.

To tell a narrative about self-crafting and improvisation and to illustrate the generative power and limits of these strategies, this chapter draws a link between the aesthetic choices of Afrobeat women, as individual artists and as members of an artist collective, and their transformation of a genre. I attempt to capture as well as possible the theatrical ambience witnessed by a Kalakuta visitor who described life in the commune as "just like the movies."[9] Conveying the subtle and overt ways in which everyday acts shaped Afrobeat's mid-1970s mode of alterity demands an examination of three performative practices where women's creativity, improvisation, and negotiation flourished: (1) *yabis*, Kalakuta's entrenched practice of jocular abuse, a form in which the women were champs; (2) Afrocentric facial makeup; and (3) solo dancing, which I contend provides clear insight into the principle of structured improvisation and negotiated freedom within set boundaries that pervaded much of the women's life in Afrobeat. This push and pull between structure and spontaneity, rules and subversion, in multiple domains of Afrobeat performance provided a crucible for the fierce innovations evidenced in Africa 70's creative output and in its notoriety as a political force.

"Yabis Is No Case"

Ethnomusicologist John Collins was intrigued, during his visit to Kalakuta in January 1977, by the spirited drama that characterized everyday life in Nigeria's shadow republic, headed by his friend Fela. "Everyone [was] supremely self-confident," Collins noted, "but lots of friction and skin-pain between them. Much stupidity and hurt, but much of it [was] dramatic overstatement. Everybody's a born actor."[10] It was not Collins's first visit to the commune. In November 1974, Collins and members of the Accra-based band Basa-Basa and Bunzu

Sounds had been guests at the Empire Hotel (in whose courtyard Fela housed the Shrine) when sixty riot police officers had invaded and "teargassed" hotel guests and, subsequently, residents of the Kalakuta commune across the street. The purpose of the operation had been to "rescue" a runaway Kalakuta girl.[11] It was the second major raid that year. The operation was not the only striking aspect of Collins's first Lagos visit. Heightened encounters between state and commune punctuated an already theatrical everyday life shaped by ethnically diverse and class-diverse young women and men who smoked marijuana in daylight, worked for play, and could be mistaken as perpetually idle save for their highly public work as performers in Fela's band. At the hands of a woman disc jockey, visitors and residents in the commune listened to music produced by artists in a host of genres, from jazz and soul to highlife and soukous, songs that captured the social and revolutionary zeitgeist of the Black world in the 1960s and 1970s. The self-fashioning practices of Kalakuta women—notably their Afrocentric makeup and penchant for nudity—contributed to an image of the commune that might have puzzled visitors. But these were not the only notable aspects of the women's public persona. They were also a notoriously loud crew. In his extensive study of Fela and Afrobeat music, Frank Thurmond Fairfax III lamented the women's lack of discipline and "wifely" comportment. "There is considerable bickering, and constant 'yabbis' or verbal abuse among them. The hospitality and dignity of the ideal African household, whether monogamous or polygynous," Fairfax III protested, "is little in evidence."[12] Kalakuta visitors like the writer saw a clear link between the women's noise and yabis as a recognized form of playful abuse. And yet they often underplayed or altogether missed how "loud talk" masked a formulaic and codified mode of address, a practice that sharpened verbal reflexes in inevitable negotiations with the state and everyday antagonisms. Yabis belongs in the same verbal, aesthetic, and social register as *the dozens* in African American culture that E. Patrick Johnson offers operate "as a source of ritual insult and survivalist strategy or both depending on the context."[13] In Afrobeat, yabis resembled and called forth unprofessional behavior—like bickering and rivalry—but it also was a unique verbal and performative practice that fed Fela's music.

Yabis (pronounced "yah-bees") is a pidgin English derivative of the verb "yab," which itself is a corruption of the English "yap," meaning shrill or noisy talk.[14] While Fela did not invent yabis, he is credited with popularizing the practice in Nigerian vernacular discourse through songs like "Roforofo Fight (1972) and "International Thief Thief" (1980). The former prefaces a musical critique of neoliberal, state-sanctioned corruption with "Make I yab them?" to which the studio audience enthusiastically responds with a cacophonous "yab them!" In "Roforofo Fight," yabis unfolds near a mud puddle as two Lagosians' tempers flare. The argument escalates into a brawl, leaving the two muddied yabbers undifferentiable from one another. Onstage, Fela used yabis as an occasion for sardonic musings on ongoing local and global events as well as scathing reflections on public institutions and officials.[15] The dialogic spirit of yabis carried over to its manifestation in live performance, as errant audience members became targets of Fela's spontaneous barbs. But his exceptional talents in yabis did little to discourage members of the Shrine's audience from returning his yabis in kind, even at the risk of public humiliation.[16] An audience member once roasted Fela when his brother accepted an appointment as minister of health under the notorious Babangida regime. Fela responded by rebuking the timidity of Nigerians about directly addressing such concerns to powerful officials, including his brother. Extending the landscape of yabis, Fela purchased "Chief Priest Say" columns in major newspapers to advance critiques.

The Afrobeat public did not widely possess knowledge about yabis' figuration in Kalakuta everyday life or about the role played by Kalakuta women in how it unfolded. If yabis manifested in live performance as a form of public, dialogic commentary, it operated in Kalakuta as a regulated play code with its own rule: "Yabis is no case, first touch na case." The rule implied virtually no limits to the subject of verbal abuse; everything, with the exception of Fela's mother and children, was fair game. Physical assault ("first touch") from being provoked was punishable under the yabis rule. The Kalakuta saying "Yabis is no case" came to underscore the practice as both civic engagement and policer of otherwise volatile everyday interactions. A newcomer who lacked city smarts could elicit yabis ridicule, as could an individual perceived as too prim for Kalakuta life. Unscrupulous behavior, questionable choices in any set of daily encounters, encroachment on others' spaces, or shifting alliances among friends were yabis triggers. For the most part, yabis stung someone at the same time as it entertained others. But it did not require bite or a specific target to entertain. If the commune was too quiet, Omolara Shosanya shared, someone might scream, out of the blue. The commune would come alive if this individual succeeded in provoking a reaction, be it laughter, surprise, or disgust. Yabis might be obvious or veiled in innuendo, leaving space for retreat or evasion. When yabis came disguised, expressed in song or proverb, "the opponent ran the risk of appearing foolish or offensive should [they] respond in an overt way."[17] In these ways, yabis allowed Kalakutans to collectively articulate the ideal communal subject. This imagined subject was expressive, self-assured, nimble, and intolerant of slights against their person. Understanding one's skill level at yabis required engaging others in the art, fostering interaction and self-regulation within the commune, while also shaping on an ongoing basis Kalakutans' sense of acceptable conduct.

As was true about many Kalakuta practices, yabis was double edged. Although Kalakutans were often lighthearted when performing yabis, viciousness was commonplace: mudslinging, body shaming, and gaslighting were common unsavory strategies. For example, when dancer Olaide Babayale was struck in the belly by soldiers and feared damage to her internal organs, especially her womb, she made for an easy target of a fellow dancer's yabis. These verbal barbs after an attack struck a nerve. The hurt lingered for decades, well after her aggressor's death. In another instance, Fela's suspected infertility several months after the mass wedding caused disgruntled women to target him with yabis. An eyewitness described a scene in which "about ten women were talking virtually at once and Fela was in the middle of them all, soaking abuses which were centered in the main on his sexual prowess, like sponge."[18] Yeni, the musician's eldest daughter, who formed the habit of eavesdropping, sometimes overheard and was quietly enraged by the women's scathing evaluation of Fela's offstage performance.[19]

Attempting to gain a handle on the people with whom he lived and produced art, Fela paid close attention during yabis to learn about plots or clandestine behavior. Active participation spelled courtship with betrayal; precious personal secrets easily became public entertainment. By the same token, critical information about happenings in the commune entered the communal space. In the heat of yabis, Kalakutans levied serious accusations of infidelity, betrayal, or collusion with enemies of the commune, all of which, true or fabricated, revealed or confirmed something important about the parties involved. This volatile transparency was one reason for Fela's reluctance to stop yabis altogether, despite the rancor it sometimes produced. The personal nature of yabis prefigured more significant confrontations with larger society.

Dexterity for play in the verbal arts of ritual insult, such as in *the dozens*, is known to slide easily into "a critical technology of self-assertion and resistance."[20] Yabis was regularly personal and petty, but it assumed wider Afrobeat connotations, such as "to expose one's wrongdoing in public, to discomfit, humiliate, deconstruct."[21] Yabis was often deployed by Afrobeat women to articulate their views on unfolding political events. Yabis conveyed themes such as daily human rights violations and the material consequences of urban poverty, some of which caught Fela's ear and formed the conceptual seeds for new musical compositions. The dancer Omolara contributed to such influential yabis: as mentioned in the introduction, Omolara used the phrase "uniform chance" to describe how uniforms functioned as a badge of authority that implicitly granted officers undue power over unarmed citizens. Soldiers and police officers harassed citizens in ways that would have been impossible without uniforms, simultaneously symbol and material cultural artifact of state power. Such were the vernacular deconstructions of power that the women put forward during yabis and from which Fela drew for his music. Yabis figured in a spectrum of musical noise: from idle banter, argumentation, gossip, and hum to choral singing and scat. The practice of yabis might seem to favor women's autonomy and free expression. However, the women were working within a gender hierarchy shaped by sexism—although they came to this realization late. Fela monopolized yabis, giving the practice a formal and public outlet on the stage, and his monopoly of this node in a larger Afrobeat world of sounds encouraged a misreading of yabis as a men's form of discourse.

In the public imaginary, Kalakuta Republic was a space of alterity—reanimating, to borrow from Homi Bhabha, an ambivalence reminiscent of colonial mimicry, the desire to produce a recognizable Other "almost the same, but not quite."[22] Kalakuta Republic boasted its own mock court system, adding to its symbolic mimicry of the neocolonial state. Fela acted as chief justice, overseeing cases that yabis failed to resolve or matters that required nuanced adjudication. An appointed leader of the girls or chief of staff also helped resolve common disagreements. Serious accusations such as theft, debt, dereliction of duty, and "first touch" were escalated to the chief justice, who listened to grievances, admitted witnesses, and pronounced judgment. Penalties varied by infraction, including wage forfeiture, public apology, flogging, and increased chores. The chief justice might sentence serious offenders to imprisonment in Kalakuta's makeshift prison, "Kalakondo" (called "Kalakusu" at a different time), for a period lasting between a few hours and overnight, depending on the gravity of the crime. Cases without clear-cut guilt or with equally compelling eyewitnesses could simply be dismissed. Through its justice system, the Fela-led Republic—whose existence parodied the illocutionary power of colonial state formation—did not simply refute registers of difference that were relics of colonial othering. Instead, the commune mobilized a more potent strategy of mirroring the slippages and absurdity of mimicry performed by Africans in the wake of colonialism.

The staging of justice through mimicry of court procedures became a familiar image in Kalakuta everyday life, as in live performances. Fela's 1985 "Cross Examination" is set in a fictive court in which Fela performatively prosecutes a former colonial soldier. Not unlike his role in Kalakuta's mock court, Fela casts himself as judge and prosecutor delivering a verdict on behalf of Africans: "I will now pronounce the judgment / And the people will now comment /

You are guilty." The repetition of legal performance was likely the outcome of Kalakutans' serial brushes with the law or their fascination with its theatricality, the power that court pronouncements (a relatively recent historical practice) have on the fate of people. As Dwight Conquergood argues in "Lethal Theatre," rituals act out abstract concepts such as justice; the embodied performances that materialize around criminal punishment—such as arrest, trial, conviction, detention, sentencing—derive their power from actuating the unseeable concept of justice, helping citizens *see* "justice done."[23] The dramatization of justice illustrated Kalakutans' enchantment with the ease through which rituals pronounce justice or, as was a common condition of military rule, the miscarriage of the concept of justice. Enactments of justice in fictionalized courts or in the commune's mock courts equally reveal an intimate appreciation of the fissures, paradoxes, and pressure points glossed over by colonially inherited, state-sponsored rituals of justice. Indeed, both the object of their critique and their own performed critiques of justice were revelatory as much as concealing of the commune's contradictions, the incoherence of and challenges to its own articulation of justice and fairness. The commune's mimicry of justice thinly concealed Fela's above-the-law posture; as chief justice, he pronounced judgment and could not be tried in the Kalakuta system. This does not imply, however, that there were no challenges to his pronouncements or posturing as chief justice. When audiences or outsiders observed Fela's exercise of judicial authority in the commune and his dominant stage presence over the band and the women, they recognized him as reinforcing elements of the authoritarianism he relentlessly critiqued. Audiences and outsiders seldom saw explicit or gendered challenges to his authority, which were often enacted in the absence of visitors. Here is a story of a young woman whose case was adjudged in Kalakuta court and who was given the penalty of general beating (GB): "One day, after they give one girl GB (general beating) the girl (name given) jumped on Fela and tear his pant. Fela was naked, and they brought another pant for him. He ordered another general beating for the girl. And after they beat the girl, she jumped on Fela again and tear his pant. The girl is very stubborn, she fight Fela that day."[24] The story of the young woman's resistance to Fela's bogus justice system parallels a scene from the muddy brawl in "Roforofo Fight," described earlier. Fela sings about how "she tear trouser, e tear pant / she pull the thing commot, e tear the thing." This semblance between a real event involving a Kalakuta woman and the lyrics of "Roforofo Fight" raises the possibility that Afrobeat women drew inspiration from Africa 70 songs or, conversely, that a woman's challenge to Fela was the subtext for the actions described in the song. Such assaults against Fela's "justice" were not commonplace, but they were important instances of self-advocacy as well as ruptures of the commune's ordering.

Kalakuta women asserted ownership of Afrobeat songs through reappropriation. When women played with and exchanged musical idioms in their everyday lives, they channeled into Afrobeat the same ludic energy generated through Black girls' games of Double Dutch, hand clapping, and cheering. These everyday forms of play have shaped the sonic textures of Black popular music in forms such as hip-hop, R&B, and neosoul, male-dominated genres that Kyra Gaunt points out "exclude or simply incorporate the communal or everyday forms of popular music that cannot be assigned individual authorship or ownership," especially not to the Black girls from whose games they derive musical inspiration.[25] Despite Fela's claims to sole authorship, the women recycled Africa 70 songs in public circulation back into communal life. In the 1982 documentary *Fela Kuti: Music is the Weapon* (by Jean-Jacques Flori and Stéphane Tchalgadjieff), Fehintola Kayode was notably filmed singing a sonorous rendition of Africa 70's "No Buredi" (1976): "Look-u you / You stand-i for ground your leg dey shake" (Look at you / You stand but your legs wobble).[26] Individual women weaponized Africa 70 lyrics, imageries, and metaphors for new, if petty, effects. They also addressed concerns of greater political significance. Fehintola casually sings the lyrics to "No Buredi," which include "You no get the power to fight." These lyrics are multi-edged, a barb targeted at fellow Kalakutans or a reflection on a festering dysphoria. Recycling of songs required an astute read of scenarios and the strategic selection or recombination of particular lyrics, musical hooks, melodies, or Kalakuta sayings to the new context. This kind of reappropriation also took place even in the throes of the state. So was the case of Pulchérie Ibilola Hoga, an Egypt 80 dancer, who when arraigned before a judge sang a section of "Army Arrangement" to the judge's hearing. "Army Arrangement" was one of Fela's most scathing diatribes about high-level collusion and staggering public corruption. In the song, Fela also mused about "police particulars" to talk about bribery and quotidian sexual exploitation by law enforcement. Hoga had sung "Army Arrangement" (1984) to her inmates while awaiting her court hearing. "When I went to that court, I saw them with wig. Blonde wig, the judge, and the man was blowing English that people could not understand. . . . Nonsense, so Fela sent his lawyer, and we were free. When I was in jail, I sang for them 'Army Arrangement' there. Even in the court I sang 'Army Arrangement' for them there too. When they see me, when I talk, they know this one is not one of us."[27] The same section of the song, performed in court and in the cell, would signify differently, shaping not only the song's reception but also the singer's exposure to admiration, indifference, or retaliation. Hoga was likely refencing her French-inflected accent as a marker of difference, but also, before she spoke, the visual aesthetic of the makeup was a signifier not only of difference but also as a demarcative signal that it was performance time. Behind the makeup—which in Hoga's case would have worn off a bit after a night in jail—Afrobeat women occasionally enjoyed the benefit of being perceived as being suspended from the scripts of the everyday, as performing, even if they were staging patent critiques. This arbitrary state of suspension made the process of musical recycling in everyday yabis both possible and potent.

Clearly, Kalakuta women found uses for yabis in their negotiation of life outside the commune. "There is nowhere we don't yab," Olaide Babayale reminisced,[28] elaborating further on how everyday modes of play aggregated into larger negotiations for citizenship and justice. As a codified form of verbal abuse, yabis became a rehearsal for inevitable confrontations with state actors. Yabis figured in a flexible toolkit of embodied resistance, considering how exposed the women were to abuse from law enforcement and moral judgment from everyday citizens. At police stations and airports, public spaces fraught with impingement on citizens' rights, the women used yabis to assert themselves and address injustice. Olaide reflected:

> If we are outside, we behave
> But if the person wan pass im boundary; we give it to him or her . . .
> "Wetin dey happen?
> What's wrong with you?
> Wetin you think say you be?
> You think say you be human being?
> Abi wetin you carry for hand?
> The thing wey dey you carry for body, na im I carry for body!
> You dey crase!
> You no get eye?"[29]
>
> If we are outside, we behave ourselves
> But the person wants to cross boundaries [or oversteps]; we give abuses to
> him or her . . .
> "What is going on?
> What is wrong with you?
> What do think you are?
> Do you think you are a human being?
> Or, what do you have in your hand [referencing a gun]?
> What you have on your body is what I have on mine

Are you crazy?
Are you blind?"

Kalakuta women performing yabis to address a soldier or police officer showed remarkable bravery, as they did so at the risk of personal injury. They figuratively exposed their bodies in dance and yabis and, by extension, to batons and battery. Most of them did not share Fela's command of English, but they effectively weaponized insults in pidgin English or their respective native tongues. Police officers are reported to have retreated from the women's verbal barbs when they lacked proper reinforcement. The Kalakuta women in turn used yabis, although benign compared to the hegemonic state, as a crucial form of Kalakuta defense. The public continued to praise Fela for his physical and rhetorical confrontations with the state. But Afrobeat accounts of heroism routinely elided women's deployment of these modes of discourse in engaging the state during instances of heightened exposure to violence. The women instrumentalized yabis to escape potential harm, to stage counterharassments, and to defend the commune's integrity.

"Fuck You": Tension in the Room, June 2018

Omolara Shosanya and I are scheduled to meet for the first time at Olaide Babayale-Kuti's place. We've neither met nor spoken before, so she is honoring my invitation to a filmed interview only on the weight of Olaide's word, saying something perhaps about her sense of trust. The modest living room brims with anticipation. It holds the video crew; my friend and assistant, Tunde Alabanla; a caterer; and two of Olaide's acquaintances who will soon excuse themselves. I enter the space with a level of anonymity. I sight Omolara sitting by herself in a corner. One would be forgiven for thinking Omolara Shosanya walked right off a 1970s concert stage. Whatever little has changed about her physique is perfunctory, and she looks utterly absorbed by her thoughts. Now a devout Christian and a caterer, Omolara sports a bright yellow lace ìró and bùbá (a loose-fitting traditional blouse and a wrapper worn by Yoruba women) complete with a head wrap that conceals all her hair. Her hair is tightly bound, one of the first signs of her faith, as Olaide has informed me. Omolara wears matching yellow earrings and her top is puffy at the shoulders, which appears to accentuate her slender face. Her slim frame remains virtually unchanged from what it was forty years ago, at least from what I've seen of how she moves in archival footage. "I can still dance," she gestures to her torso as though she's read my thoughts.

Omolara speaks in a low, emphatic tone. When she suspects that you may have missed a crucial thought, she shoots a focused look to convey the gravity of the story.

She sometimes speaks in a whispery voice, which I soon learn is her way of getting across her version of the past, especially when in the company of another Queen who might insist on a different account. There is a feeling of incompleteness after our hour-long chat, so we meet again a year later, this time at the home of her elder sister who's just lost her husband. Omolara's head wrap is still bound into a knot. The air of mourning is conveyed by the heavy silence that courses through the space when neither of us speaks. The smacking sounds of carpenters doing woodwork filters in every once a while, the only disturbance to an eerily quiet Sunday afternoon. Aunty Lara, as I sometimes call her, fetches bottled water and juice to welcome me. Here, too, she speaks in the now-familiar whisper when she finally sits for the interview. But she whispers for a different reason. Her mourning sister despises hearing "Fela" and wants none of it in her home. The rest of her family harbors similarly strong feelings about the Afrobeat musician. They are convinced that he ruined Omolara's life. Aunty Lara communicates some of these feelings of betrayal, of having been sacrificed to pave Fela's and his family's fame and wealth. Some of Aunty Lara's stories are gloomy; others are amusing accounts of life in the Kalakuta commune. Yet others are still incredible to her, at sixty years old. Some of it feels, she muses, like having lived an adventure, a dream with plenty of nightmarish days. But most of her stories call for pauses and deep reflection as she tells them. We wait at intervals when the weight of the story demands it or when footsteps announce someone is approaching. It's quite the task to complete the interview in hushed tones; we spend the exchange cautioning one another about the loudness of our voices, careful to not mention Fela's name too loudly—if at all.

Omolara speaks with intention. Early in our first interview a year earlier at Olaide's home, she takes care more than once to ensure that I document the correct surname: Shosanya, not Anikulapo-Kuti. Her right elbow digs into her thigh as she leans in. With her eyes pressed on me, she says, "Fela did not marry me. He married his work. Fela knew what he was doing; he knew that he could not do it alone." Our initial encounter at Olaide's place is significant because it is my first and only experience sitting in a room with two Queens. It does not fail to amuse. The first time Omolara shares these thoughts on her marriage is during our preinterview briefing in Olaide's bedroom. Olaide will have none of it. Without skipping a beat, she retorts, "But o ró ìró now. Ìyàwó Fela ni ẹ / But you wore a ceremonial wrapper. You were Fela's wife." Omolara delivers her own riposte with lightning speed, "Fuck you!" flicking her left wrist in Olaide's direction without so much as turning to the offender. The room tenses. I fear that things have gotten out of hand and worry about if and how to intervene in a fight between women my mother's age, one of whom I met minutes ago. Then, in precise synchrony, the women burst into laughter. "It is all yabis. I love it," Omolara deflates the tension, smiling. I am confused but relieved. They are not done. She launches her own offensive when Olaide shares about her limping. Olaide pins her mobility problems on soldiers' brutality; Omolara pins some of it on fatness, reminiscent of the edginess of yabis. They maintain a loving but combustible friendship: their interaction teeters on the brink of conflict, but it never quite tips over. Such moments of eruption and stasis intersperse the interview. Theirs is sisterhood tested by fire and wrought by shared memory.

—⧖—

Omi Osun Joni L. Jones's study of Black queer theatrical jazz artists reveals how everyday practices of leisure and pleasure constitute playgrounds in which artists rehearse and sharpen techniques of resistance. Everyday improvisations strengthen the creative muscle that artists require for performance.[30] Yabis operated on a similar logic. The practice thickened the skin, stretched the wit, and strengthened the muscle of dialogic speaking. Counterposed against a larger political reality marked by restricted expression and mobility, Kalakuta women's everyday practice of yabis translated into civic engagement beyond the commune. The women were notably sharp mouthed not simply due to natural predisposition but because yabis was a practiced form of Kalakuta discourse, reflexively shaping their responses to actual or potential threats. Kalakuta women acted on the cumulative experience of serial verbal wordplay occasioned by yabis. Outside, they deployed yabis as on-the-spot improvisations during verbal duels with state officials and aggression from the public. Words and phrases from Afrobeat songs were adopted in their arsenal of survival tactics to fend off different shades of violence. They repurposed punch lines from yabis heard in Kalakuta, aided by the proficiency of reading a scene and quickly profiling an aggressor for potential weakness. When individual women used Kalakuta yabis, they boosted their psychological fortitude against insults to the collective, the most common being their perceived sexual looseness. Indeed, when placed alongside one another, Kalakuta yabis and the women's embrace of yabis to assert their somebodiness show a clear, functional link in a context where, African art scholar dele jegede informs us, "Journalists were harassed, whole newspaper editions were seized and destroyed, media executives were invited for 'a chat' by security operatives, and, on the flimsiest excuse, media houses were peremptorily sealed up at the pleasure of whichever 'head of state' Nigeria was saddled with."[31] In little ways, Kalakuta women embodied creativity and freedom as a rejoinder to relentless censorship. As jegede reveals, state and political elites invested their creativity into containing restive citizens and civil society. But the target of the commune's yabis was multipronged, including privileged elites who, though victims of the state, weaponized taste and notions of propriety to maintain status and power. Members of this class of Africans, the historical product of a colonial situation, oriented their disciplinary impulses into culturing *less civilized* Africans. Their resistance to colonialism was largely assimilatory, deriving from a desire to be at par with Europeans. They embraced the liberalism that undergirded colonialism in Africa, distinguishing the human from the "not-yet-sufficiently human," the cultured from the native.[32] Colonial discrimination exceeded mere classification, delineating certain people and cultures as rational and civilized and others as outside the purview of humanity.[33] In embracing otherness, Kalakutans behaved in ways that magnified their refusal of elite expectations of personhood and Eurocentric acculturation; Kalakuta women enacted defiant personas that exaggerated their rejection of so-called proper femininity. In the eyes of the public and high-ranking military officials, their conduct and refusal of gendered expectations fueled undesirable stereotypes of them as lousy, unprofessional, and impulsive. For the women, however, inhabiting the subjective positioning of the uncouth native was an act of self-integration beyond the conditioning of the state and elite culture. This refusal is clarified in Olaide's brazen declaration: "There is nowhere we don't yab." In these ways, Kalakutans flirted with imperfect attempts at the decolonial. Little acts aggregated into larger moral meaning on relating ethically with others in the wake of colonial interpellation.[34]

Yabis fostered intimacy across social class in ways that fed Fela's musical creativity. Fela's upper-class status had the potential to disconnect him from the lived experience his music trenchantly captured. Likewise, his celebrity status could have alienated him from an on-the-ground view of everyday oppression. Potentially furthering Fela's distance from the social world of the urban working poor was his reduced number of public appearances for most of the 1980s and his reclusiveness in the 1990s. However, even as Fela seemed to recede from public view, his music continued to reflect an intimate appreciation of the grievances of Nigeria's oppressed class. While criticisms of the military's absurd rule in the 1970s were commonplace in public discourse, Fela musicalized the precarious existence of the urban poor with striking clarity, and the public appreciated Fela's music as capturing their socioeconomic realities. Kalakuta yabis played a key role in the musician's unique grasp of the pulse of the evolving neocolonial and neoliberal moments that defined his time. At a basic level, yabis refreshed Kalakuta everyday life with energy and Lagos street lingo. Fela's open-door policy encouraged emergent slang, images, and gestures to rapidly enter and emerge from and through the commune. This traffic through Kalakuta, each person embodying their unique mannerisms, personal histories, and articulations of cityness,[35] supplied endless material for music. Fela sang to the public the stories of Lagosians, some of whom traveled in, out, and through Kalakuta Republic, acting as itinerant ethnographers of Afrobeat music.[36] Established Kalakutans and new arrivals trafficked Lagosian vogues as well as news of the city's greatest nuisances, such as potholes, traffic congestion, sanitation, crime, and the like. Lagosians continue to evoke the enduring imagery of "forty-nine sitting, ninety-nine standing" passengers in the notoriously rickety, overpacked *molue* buses. This image, the visual and sonic cornerstone of the song "Shuffering and Shmiling" (a vernacularization of "suffering and smiling"), came from the YAP Boys who rode the *molue* and, back at the commune, vented about their horrific experiences.[37] The Lagosian public listened to Fela's song and recirculated his expression "suffering and smiling" into an expanding descriptive and critical lexicon of Nigerian urbanism. Earlier, Kalakutans had described urban subsistence using the metaphor of bread, which Fela repeated in his lyrics. The musician described how this listening method shaped other compositions: "Like 'Yellow Fever,' it was the people at Mushin who first called traffic wardens Yellow Fever. So I decided to call the [skin] bleaching people 'Yellow Fever.' It was not my original idea. Even 'Shakara,' it was from the Mushin people. I don't work in isolation from the society.... When I want to write lyrics, I think about my environment, I think about catchy words, words that can be easily be identified with society.... this is why they are very successful."[38] Deep listening reflected through musical creativity progressed in other ways. Dede Mabiakwu, one of Fela's protégés, recounted to me a story about an unnamed Kalakuta woman's response to a press conference held by Fela. Dede recalled how said woman casually informed Fela how much she had enjoyed his flowery use of the English language. She described his big words and his interjective use of the Americanized slang "men!" as entertaining.[39] Whether she intended the comment as a compliment or as a veiled yab seems less important than what she clearly revealed: the limits of standard English as a vehicle for popular struggle, and the ever-present possibility of miscommunication between Fela and the urban underclass whose perspectives he claimed to voice. Fela had a lot of empathy for working-class Nigerians' social struggles and was willing to suspend his class standing to be counted in their ranks. However, Fela's self-demotion, which has been described by scholars and the public as "class suicide," might have been more strategic than these observers assume.[40] Fela's social immersion could have been a function of radical empathy; it was also true, however, that Kalakutans helped him bridge the gulf of class and celebrity that threatened to separate them from the musician, sustaining his career.

Makeup as Micropolitics

> Fela just tell us one day say im want us to dey paint Af-
> rican face. You know say all those things, dem dey do
> am for my village. Na im everybody start im own de-
> sign. . . . You go do your own design as you want.
>
> (Fela just told us one day that he wanted us to begin paint-
> ing "African faces." You know, we did these things in my
> village. That was how everyone began their own designs.
> . . . You create the makeup design of your choice.)
>
> —dancer Najite

By 1975, Najite's so-called African face had become idiomatic of Afrobeat style. The women's now-famous body and face painting was an important dimension of Afrobeat's visual creativity, a space in which women wielded tremendous creative autonomy. The documentary *Fela Kuti: Music Is the Weapon* provides perhaps the best surviving illustration of their makeup *in process*. The documentary captures the breadth of styles employed by Afrobeat women in their distinctly personal makeup. The sequence of shots opens with Kevwe, who casually gazes into space having brushed white powder around her eyes (fig. 3.2a). Aduni, who appears in the next shot, is shown meticulously applying black lines onto her left wrist using an eye pencil (fig. 3.2b). Fehintola transforms her left eye with metallic blue paint (fig. 3.2c), while Ihase continues pasting multicolored plastic disks above each eyebrow (fig. 3.2d).[41] Each woman holds up a mirror to her face as she transforms it into a canvas, which could extend to the rest of her exposed skin. "Hours of the afternoon would pass," Vivian Goldman explains of the sometimes-meticulous process, "with them lounging across the bed or sprawling in the armchair, intently anointing themselves with tiny, perfectly positioned spots of white, yellow or red."[42] Alake, who appears in the final shot of the documentary's makeup sequence, culminates the filmic fragments of the women's transformation. The final shot in the sequence captures Alake in a distracted pose, lounging in an armchair with a marijuana joint between her thumb and ring finger. It is an elegant pose for Alake, who appears to be half aware of the camera's gaze (fig. 3.2e). Her left wrist bears about four inches of beads, an adornment matching the thick rings of beads around her neck. The shot of Alake's face is the highlight of the sequence: it is an art piece. She has drawn red bean-like motifs on each cheek, surrounded by two dotted

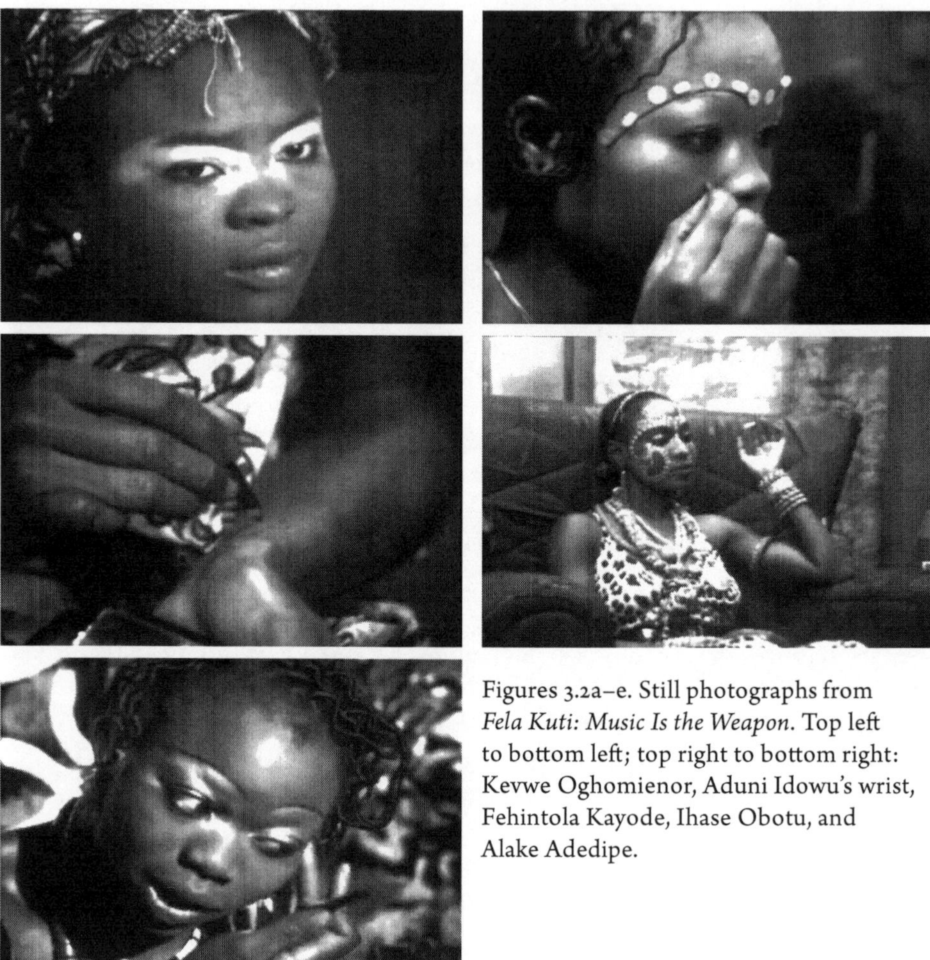

Figures 3.2a–e. Still photographs from
Fela Kuti: Music Is the Weapon. Top left
to bottom left; top right to bottom right:
Kevwe Oghomienor, Aduni Idowu's wrist,
Fehintola Kayode, Ihase Obotu, and
Alake Adedipe.

lines. The same dots travel in an upward curve around her eyes and temple to right above her brows. They intersect with another that runs down her nose from a red petal on her forehead. Her lips mirror the bright red of her forehead and cheeks, perfecting the balance of white dots and solid red ornamentation. Alake showcases an intricately rendered design, a delicate balance of beauty and strangeness that declares the self. The body art was an invitation and a dare to "look at me" to the state, the public, and Kalakuta visitors. Alake wears this bodily art, joint in hand, with panache.

Each woman would decide on the degree of complexity to adopt in each makeup style. Mood, time, and the day's itinerary would modulate this choice and the aesthetic each woman would pursue. "Different styles na im I dey do," Najite explained to me, "Sometimes I fit do 'V.' Sometimes I fit do round round, ball ball. Sometimes I fit do flower for this side and this side. . . . E just be like drawing. When you want to draw, it will come to your mind" (I could do different styles. Sometimes I could draw a "V." Sometimes I could draw a round-round, or ball-ball pattern. Sometimes I could do flowers on either cheek. It was just like drawing. When you want to draw, the inspiration comes to your mind). Najite compared the makeup to drawing because it was in fact *art*, a creative practice requiring the principles of composition, proportion, and, no less than any other art form, imagination (Fig. 3.3). On the body, this art assumes a kinesthetic quality that enhances the symbolism of other embodied art forms, such as dancing, singing, or yabbing. The body of a Kalakuta women would thus become a canvas whereon she could express, Goldman argues, her "highest self" within the scope of possibilities at her disposal.[43] In an attempt to adopt a similar aesthetic for himself, Fela began his painting own face by 1980; his style paled by comparison. Fela favored a simple white circle around either eye, accompanied by motifs that can only be described as rudimentary. He explained his painted eye in spiritual terms, as evidence of extraterrestrial vision. Perhaps this explanation also revealed his skill level compared to complex designs of the women who advanced Afrobeat makeup as a complete art form.

The makeup was not the transplant of a timeless idiom, nor was it altogether the women's invention. The connoisseurs of Afrobeat makeup borrowed from and riffed on beautification practices from disparate African cultures, far and near, to create distinct makeup designs. They drew inspiration from sources such as books about ancient Egyptian makeup and the body painting of ethnic groups in Kenya. Some found inspiration in a "great-great-great grandmother"; others turned to Hausa *lali* body art or to actual or imagined "village" art practices.[44] Afrobeat makeup, in other words, derived from and reflected an array of body art practices reinterpreted to make salient statements about beauty, womanhood, citizenship, and politics in 1970s Lagos. In this sense, Afrobeat women fit the wave of postindependence cultural nationalism in which artists articulated the narrow and broad strokes of postcolonial modernism "from individual, national and Pan-African perspectives by seeking recourse to longstanding artistic traditions, and reclaiming or repurposing assumed cultural roots."[45] In the Kalakutan view, painting the African face meant ornamenting the performer's face beatifying the bearer using Afrobeat makeup to construct the "African face" was also about troubling African elite sensibilities. European

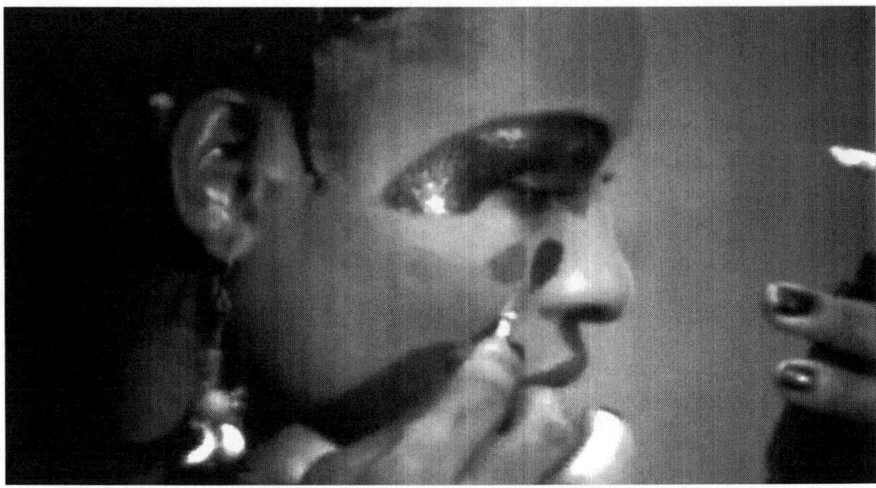

Figure 3.3. Still photograph of Najite painting her face in red and black. Photo credit: *Music Is the Weapon.*

assimilation and mimicry characterized the dominant cultural orientation of urban elites, and Afrobeat makeup performed both resistance to and an incorporation into the frames of this orientation. "The versatility and irrepressible exuberance of popular African cultures and creative arts, their irreverent and exhilarating yearnings for all-inclusive liberation," Paul Tiyambe Zeleza argues, "mocks and subverts the singular elite narratives of African nationalism, their aspirations for social uniformity and conformity as they go about ransacking and ravaging the wealth of their nations."[46] Visually, makeup registered the plurality of Afrobeat's counterstrikes, variously and incongruously embodying African beauty and the primitive—sure to produce feelings of discomfort, even dread, among elites—in service not of nationalism but to declare youth agency, urban self-styling, and general restlessness with an elite orientation. Afrobeat makeup became potent, if reactionary, political art, especially when read alongside the broader activist statements in which it participated: lyrics, rhetoric, live performance, and everyday encounters with the state. Reading Afrobeat makeup as inherently African often misses how the practice mirrored ongoing constructions of African culture by state actors in the 1970s. Andrew Apter has argued that artistic directors and cultural officers at FESTAC 77 invented traditions with precolonial pedigrees. "In a fundamental sense," Apter writes, "the customary culture which FESTAC resurrected was always already mediated by the colonial encounter, and in some degree was produced by it."[47]

As much as the Afrobeat makeup drew inspiration from established cultural practices, it also signaled a rearticulation of those practices in a context where a broad spectrum of dispositions labeled "precolonial" were put in service of decidedly modern ambitions.

Like yabis, facial ornamentation prefigured how Kalakuta women navigated the world beyond the stage.[48] Afrobeat makeup became coextensive with their presence, simultaneously advertising Africa 70 and marking Afrobeat's incursion into public spaces. In the context of the everyday, the women modulated how to use the Afrobeat makeup vis-à-vis expressing sensuality and negotiating sexual interests. When romantic adventures took them beyond the commune, for instance (not uncommon prior to the mass wedding), the bold facial makeup helped to signify them as artists who earned a living through music and dance and *not* through sex work. This kind of signaling was unnecessary with familiar romantic partners. For Fela, Afrobeat makeup represented a publicity strategy as much as it staged ideological positions. For Kalakuta women, however, public display of Afrobeat makeup worked to plural, dynamic ends. The makeup granted the women a greater sense of physical mobility, not unlike a mask that disguises the habitual self and frees one's true personality.[49] They embraced the masked self to access an unencumbered artistic self. Even the shyest Kalakuta woman might behave differently, with a little more spunk, behind the makeup. Onlookers gazed at the women with fascination or unease, reactions elicited by the makeup; the anticipation of being gazed on heightened the women's sense of performing beyond the concert stage. For this reason, the performer behind the makeup, as I have suggested elsewhere, assumed a heightened sense of aesthetic consciousness, requiring an expansive understanding of the stage and everyday life as interanimating spaces that extended the platforms available to Afrobeat women to make bodily statements.[50] This self-aware state of being suspended in performance was sustained by literal spectators who hung around Kalakuta, sometimes for hours on end, to watch rehearsals or witness the commune go about its business. In a vivid complication of a break between the stage and the everyday, one journalist described how "between 50 and 200 people could be seen standing around [Kalakuta's fence] stretching their necks to peep into the compound"; they waited day and night for glimpses of Fela or "the bevy of beautiful girls in the compound."[51]

City life anonymized young women who sought to assert social agency outside accepted mores. Even when women in Afrobeat acquiesced to heteropatriarchy and played roles that resembled those of their peers, their close association with politically subversive music, marijuana, nudity, and sexual freedom put them squarely at odds with the prevailing scripts of proper womanhood.

Concerns about city women were captured in popular arts produced by men who, consumed by ambivalence and anxiety, imbued their women characters with a tragic impulse that discouraged ambition and autonomy in cities.[52] For the young women who worked with Fela, Lagos's teeming population and cultural heterogeneity alone would seem to provide the ideal conditions for anonymity. Indeed, city life allowed migrating young women to rearticulate their own understanding of modern womanhood. It was against the backdrop of urbanity that their onstage and everyday life performances facilitated flexible degrees of being. The makeup made the women legibly different from the largely Westernized fashion style of 1970s Lagos youth. Their *African* makeup was worn in live performance as for performing everyday chores. The makeup venerated "bush-ness" in the city. As such, it became a powerful tool for modulating individual women's bold self-expression or self-effacement, as the occasion demanded. If Lagos granted anonymity to most of its inhabitants, Afrobeat makeup became a second-order act for negotiating the poles between being anonymous and making a spectacle of oneself. As the makeup obscured each woman, it enabled the freedom that comes with being unidentifiable, prompting a series of subversive acts that became attached to the women as a collective. Design elements such as complexity, brightness, balance, density, and contrast were therefore also techniques of differentiation—choices that authorized modulation between states of visibility and obscurement, which the women shrewdly deployed as a matter of personal enjoyment and social and political survival.

By 1978, the makeup had become regarded as "Queen" makeup. Even if Afrobeat makeup was politically useful, the sometimes-dense layer of facial makeup became double edged. By wearing exotic facial designs, each woman unwittingly participated in concealing distinct aspects of her personality conveyable via facial recognition. The face painting shrouded individuality because of its capacity to depersonalize. Individual identities bled into each other, and by 1978, the personhood of Afrobeat women coalesced around the collectivized figure of the Queen (not a plurality of different Queens). Concealed behind Afrobeat makeup, the task of exploring the nuances of each woman's public persona became rather tricky. Erasure of individuality was heightened by the women's quiet public profile, as they seldom spoke about their art or political views in formal platforms. For some, modest levels of formal education meant they did not always articulate themselves in "good" English.[53] But the makeup played its part in the process of obscuring who they were. Yet while concealment produced erasure, it might have simultaneously helped to evade surveillance. Obscuring facial features complicated the military regime's efforts, for example, to build coherent individual profiles on Kalakuta's women and deliver targeted punishment. This protective quality partly explains the persistent qualification of the women, collectively, as "Fela's girls" rather than by their individual names or specific artistic and political actions. Despite this potential advantage, Afrobeat makeup did obscure the women's autonomous political actions, a fact that underscores the urgency of naming and personalizing them in Afrobeat historical projects. Collective acts were vital, as were individual ones.

As powerfully as Afrobeat makeup registered Black/African female strength and beauty, it also operated against a backdrop of aesthetic control. In the Afrobeat scene of the mid to late 1970s emerged a silent ideological transformation within Kalakuta, a war waged on cultural and political desires with the women's faces acting as a key site in the ideological ferment. For Fela, the early 1970s marked a transition from "apolitical hustler" to cultural nationalist.[54] The political and intellectual works of Marcus Garvey, W. E. B. DuBois, and Edward Blyden popularized Pan-Africanism as a political philosophy rooted in Black racial solidarity. The writings and policies of Kwame Nkrumah, Ghana's first president and a fierce advocate for African unity (resulting in his establishing the Organization for African Unity), gave rise to Fela's interest in Pan-Africanism. By the mid-1970s, Fela leaned more toward Afrocentrism, an ideology committed to raising consciousness around the histories of great African empires and kingdoms, slave revolts, Black cultural resistance, African challenges to colonial domination, and Black Power movements in the United States.[55] By the late 1970s, Fela condensed these ideological threads into one formulation: Africanism.[56] His decade-long reenchantment with Africa manifested itself in the musician's concept of African female beauty as embodied by dark-skinned Black women, an idea he famously satirized in his 1976 album *Yellow Fever*. In the eponymous song, Fela ridicules skin bleaching, a practice he viewed as violating an essential notion of African beauty. The song title playfully conflates the yellow-skin symptoms of jaundice, a physiological condition resulting from a viral infection, with the mental disease of inferiority at the nexus of gender and race. These two conditions are metaphorized; in a highly effective dislocation, they are placed back onto the bright orange uniform worn by 1970s Nigerian traffic police, who were popularly dubbed Yellow Fever. This gendered critique of women's self-fashioning was not uncommon in revolutionary discourse of the day. African cultural nationalists mobilized women and their bodies to uphold idealized notions of womanhood even as men consolidated control of key social and political institutions.[57] Afrobeat makeup operated against the backdrop of similar ideological tendencies.

Fela's push for Africanist aesthetics by the mid-1970s did not sit well with all the women in Kalakuta. The so-called Africanist aesthetics curtailed, among other things, the predisposition of some women toward cosmopolitan ideas of beauty. In a move seemingly incongruous with Fela's view of Africanness, dresses grew sexier and shorter, to what some women felt were uncomfortable lengths.[58] Some women dissented as hairdos and makeup became increasingly regulated. Fela instrumentalized books to build an ideological defense of his shifting positions. When, for instance, he encountered a book containing images of Kenyans wearing heavy makeup, he retorted, "This MUST have existed in Africa! What is everybody [complaining] about the makeup for? Now I insist—MAKE UP."[59] While some women embraced the shift, others grumbled, to little effect. Fela led the band, controlled its purse, and housed everyone. So the rule stood: make up or leave Kalakuta. Such hard-lined threats were effective only in the context of ostensibly abundant women's labor. The makeup might not have been a difficult compromise, especially for women who had already made incalculable personal sacrifices by severing ties with their families to work in Fela's band. The so-called African face or Queen makeup was destined to become a staple of Afrobeat music aesthetics. Elaborate makeup had become an everyday requirement by 1980, regardless of performance itinerary. The coercive nature of the requirement usurped the relative democracy of taste that had existed in Kalakuta Republic in the early 1970s. City-born women with little experience with rural life and aesthetics might have been inhibited by Fela's narrow and shifting vision of African beauty, but they somehow empowered themselves within its strictures. The women who remained in the band or continued to reside in the commune adapted by improvising new patterns and possibilities, helping to popularize the style within and beyond Nigeria. That Fela required every woman on his payroll to wear the makeup often obscures the plethora of ways that the women reimagined it as a full-blown artform to navigate the world around them. The makeup became its own form of Afrobeat agitation, an embrace of a particular articulation of Africanness. By extension, it also became a declaration against the relegation of rural and suburban women's aesthetics to the margins of cosmopolitan culture. In many ways, the makeup underlined the fundamental dynamic that undergirded Afrobeat's creative process: the dynamic between structure (Fela's imposition of his idea of African beauty) and improvisation (the women's ownership and, ultimately, expansion of this narrow idea of beauty into plural political statements through experimentation and revision). Understanding how the makeup became a site for women's expressivity and agency demands an appreciation of the strictures within which it operated.

"My Solo, No Be Teacher Teach Me"

Dance solos were the women's most celebrated modes of bodily expression at the nightclub, Afrika Shrine. Dance solos, because they had an erotic edge, tended to be a key source of the women's notoriety and unease about their craft. Solos offered breakaway moments for dancers to assert individuality, claim aesthetic freedom, and cultivate fandom from the Shrine's audience. Onstage, Najite Mukoro moved with skill and gusto. The 1978 Berlin Jazz Festival was Africa 70's first major tour abroad, and from it comes some of the band's most well-preserved archival footage of an international concert. In this footage of the festival, Najite's dance solo matches her reputation as the Fire Dancer. Accompanied by two musicians playing the gourd-shaped ṣẹ̀kẹ̀rẹ̀. Najite seizes her moment in the spotlight in one of the band's most important outings in terms of musical exposure and financial earnings. With both arms suspended in front of her, Najite flexes her torso center stage and punctuates these movements with quick footwork. The attack of her movements rouses the band from its lethargy—the band begins to pick up the tempo. To match Najite's energy, Tony Allen delivers a rolling rhythm on the jazz drum, dramatized by spaced-out strokes. The saxophonist sputters high-pitched notes before rejoining the orchestra. Her lean frame contorts to her will as she delivers a solo at once athletic and taxing. The entire band comes alive, but it is a difficult pace to maintain. Najite runs out of steam and transitions into a slower dance that resembles jogging. Although her entrance is fierce, her transition from high-energy dancing to slower movements lacks a smooth transition. Her efforts earn her applause. Afrobeat instrumentalists anticipated Najite's lively dance solos at festivals such as the Berlin Jazz Festival. Her instincts for dancing and keen ear for musical breaks had been cultivated long before Najite made the fateful journey to Lagos in 1974. As a girl, she looked forward to Christmas and local festivals, when, in the company of other girls, she would dance at the village hall and in the streets. ("That was my native Urhobo dance that I danced," Najite explained as she delightedly reflected with me on her famous Berlin Jazz solo.) When Najite joined Fela's band, she earned the nickname Fire Dancer, not because she fit the image of the stereotypically servile African woman Fela sang about in "Lady"—far from it—but because of the fierceness of her dancing, a quality captured in footage of her Berlin Jazz solo. Najite's story illustrates how Fela's political project relied on the creative agency of young women, whose individual creativity enriched the overall performance experience and lifted the band's profile.

Without exception, Africa 70 instrumentalists were men, and their typical route to Afrobeat was as crossover artists from competing bands like Bongos Ikwue and the Groovies or King Sunny Ade and his African Beats. Live performance of Afrobeat music could therefore have become a showcase solely of men's instrumental virtuosity. But live performance also became a crucial domain of women's creativity. Africa 70's infectious bass lines and complicated jazz solos were accompanied by the expectation that each woman dancer would maximize her moment in the spotlight and match the skill level of seasoned instrumentalists. This calculation had a transformative effect on the band's live shows. The dancing women, therefore, need to be approached as more than "locomotive artists," one writer's half-mocking description.[60] Rather, we might understand their dancing as charging the energy fields of live-music performance; in movement, their bodies amplified the affective resonance of Afrobeat sound and lyrics. Afrobeat dancers translated music into controlled bodily vibrations that affected even the most passive onlooker. "I love the fact that the women control. They controlled it," explained Wunmi Olaiya, a jazz-funk-Afrobeat singer, songwriter, and costumer. Olaiya did not leave her observation at the women's domination of the live performance experience. "You can talk about Fela all day long, but when you went to the show, you went to check the women out."[61] Afrobeat women confronted the audience with masterful hip control within a choreographic structure that entailed leading, riffing off, and following the instrumentalists. Sensual bodily articulations fleshed out the groove, visually and affectively. The women gave credence to the notion that feeling and understanding a groove in a host of African-derived musical forms occurs neither in thought nor in listening alone "but through the body."[62] Backup singers were also often in motion, swaying while and after rendering song lyrics. Some singers gyrated to great effect: Alake did so in the band's rendition of "Teacher Don't Teach Me Nonsense" at the 1984 Glastonbury Festival. With these dance moves, women singers revealed the maneuvering possible within Afrobeat's tight musical structure, where the aesthetic form of live performance produced constrained movements for backing vocalists. Fela's scrutiny of every aspect of Afrobeat performance factored into how Afrobeat women artists considered their choices, including the artistic dynamics of choreographic space and time, body orientation, and audience temperament.

Africa 70 imposed strictures on the women's onstage creativity, limitations organized around the instrumentalists' performance of Afrobeat's tight-knit arrangements. However, the band's restrictive dynamics were different for

women singers and dancers. While the dancers worked with a choreographer—
Ajayi Ogunde, son of acclaimed Nigerian theater director Hubert Ogunde—
the backup singers worked directly under Fela's strict oversight. Fela recruited
Ogunde as a choreographer to train the women in dance technique, while the
musician exacted control over the band's overall aesthetic. The singer Alake
Adedipe mused, "Fela designed everything. . . . It all came from him. He taught
us himself and engaged choreographers. I had three teachers for my voice."[63]
Alake's comment paints a partial picture of the authority Fela exerted over
performance design. The level of autonomy of Fela's earliest dance collaborators, such as the pioneering Dele Salami, might have been unavailable to most
Africa 70 dancers; more regulation had been introduced into the creative process, limiting the spaces for generative risk. Yet Alake appears to underplay
the subtle ways in which the women's improvisations shaped the look and feel
of Africa 70 live performances, including how women imposed themselves on
multiple layers of Afrobeat structure through dance solos. Najite made this
case more clearly: "Ogunde pickin, na im be our teacher. Im come dey teach us
how to dance. The teaching helped me. And me too, I put my own knowledge.
My solo, no be teacher teach me, but the [group choreography] na teacher teach
me. But the dancing when I go enter stage display, no be im teach me. Dat one
na from my own mind, from my own experience. When I listen to the song,
the spirit will come to me about how I go dance" (my emphasis).[64] Within the
allotted time for dancers to shine, some women seized instrumental solos to
contribute bodily statements of their own; others used solos to cultivate a following among Shrinegoers. Afrobeat scholar Sola Olorunyomi recounts how,
after being goaded by the audience, Dodo (also Dodomaya but her real name
is Ndudi), an Egypt 80 dancer, took aesthetic control of the band to deliver an
entertaining display within the narrow timeframe of her solo. Olorunyomi's
poignant description, arguably the most detailed and attentive documentation
of Afrobeat dance available in print, attests to the power of solo dancing in
shaping the experience of live performance at the Shrine. Olorunyomi's words
are worth quoting in their rich detail.

The audience is anxiously awaiting the last dancer, Dodo. Shouts of "Dodo"
momentarily drown the speakers as she is "called" forth to mount the stage
for her solo performance. There is deep anxiety both on the part of fan and
band, over the anticipated contest. She takes her time, acting oblivious of the
revelry around her as she knots the Nigerian Midwestern, neo-traditional
popular dance histrionic of white kerchief around her waist. The suspense is
in good effect as the audience is closing in around the stage. . . . Everybody

knows: it is Dodo's day. She descends the rungs in brisk rhythmic movement, then stops to enact a brief fore-dance and, again, shouts of accolade rend the air. Aware that they cannot hurry her up, the ritual "summoners" begin to clang more vigorously in circles around her. Done, she proceeds to the central stage and takes fast rhythmic strides across its breadth, as if defining the space as hers, and challenging the instrumental soloist and the entire ensemble to a contest. . . . Fela triggers the contest by first releasing short, sharp and angular chirping notes, which Dodo duplicates with an ease of corresponding dance steps. . . . Within the short time allotted to her, Dodo executes diverse varieties of Fire Dance: at once doing the swivel dance, and at other times, pelvis gyration—a motion based on the contraction and release of the groin, or alternation with a hop-step and shoulder blade movement. Even when her arms complement the dance, they are also constantly in aid to keeping the balance of a highly stylized athleticism.[65]

Dodo's intricate response to instrumentation reminded the audience of how dancer and drummer maintain a competitive interrelatedness. Dodo masterfully demonstrated not only how drummers might intensify or ease the complexity of music based on the dancer's skill level but also how the "dancer can also move beyond the limits of the drummer's skill, to underscore their superior knowledge."[66] In Yoruba performance, musicians and dancers compete, sometimes playfully, for the spotlight, endowing each improvised performance with a quality of freshness within a recognizable form and style.[67] In her performance, Dodo demonstrated performance competence through her grasp of the aesthetic significance of the "last dancer"[68] and, more complexly, of the Shrine's audience as crucial interlocutors in negotiations of power and space. Her dance makes a crucial point—that the dancing women had the freedom to improvise while negotiating the boundaries of appropriateness in the heat of improvisation.[69] Dodo created the desired effect not despite but because of the time-space limitations imposed on her, illustrated by the growing impatience of the "summoners" and anticipation of the audience. Dodo's solo also exemplified the symbiosis between sound production and dance, an African-derived cultural phenomenon that has enjoyed widespread critical attention.[70] The role of the dancing women in activating the creative power of improvisation propelled instrumentalists into yet-to-be-explored crevices of musical possibility and, by implication, stretched out the soundscape of Afrobeat itself. In the context of African musical production, dialogic improvisation that aspires toward collective excellence occurs on a horizontal plane, gesturing for the need to dismantle the discursive hierarchies between dance and music, between movement and musical instrumentation. Here, the drummer, whose primary role is to produce sound, must engage in active dialogue with "the people who listen, dance, chant, and get possessed" during performance.[71] The dancer enters the dialogue by activating the felt, gestural, and sensorial registers of embodiment, translating music into practiced and improvised movement that impacts the lived experience of witnesses to the live event. The dancer acts as a crucial if also chronically underestimated mediator of the Afrobeat musical experience.

Dancers displayed their individuality onstage but could not operate outside of Fela's authority. Olorunyomi notes that Dodo's performance occurred under Fela's gaze. Quite notable is that Fela played the first note for Dodo's solo, confirming her level of skill, as instrumentalists preferred playing solos to the most talented dancers. This selection and judgment of aesthetic quality illustrate how dance solos became imbricated in the broader politics of band management. As bandleader, Fela judged the quality of the solos, even if in informal ways. He was known to suggest movement changes to specific dancers, especially newcomers adapting to the Afrobeat dance aesthetic. When Dodo was new to the organization, Fela advised her to tame her impulse to hop while dancing.[72] Dodo's early freestyle, Fela mused, was better suited to reggae music and, by implication, was ill suited to Afrobeat's choreographic demands. Clearly, Dodo had evolved her style, illustrating the dynamism of the women as dance artists across time.

Fela needed the women's improvisations because of his loose composition style. As such, dance solos were shaped by practical calculations, which meant Fela's ceding a level of aesthetic control to dancers over their movements. When recorded, Fela's songs were lengthy, many hovering around thirty minutes. But recorded songs were extremely condensed versions of iterations in live performances, where they easily spanned hours in length. These loose, extended compositions made the task of tightly rehearsed group choreographies impractical. Not only was it impossible to create group choreographies to correspond to the length of any one song, but it would also be tasking on the stamina of the dancers, who performed about four nights a week. The dancers performed more hours per week, and sometimes to more new compositions, than one choreographer could handle. The compromise married short, well-rehearsed, and aesthetically pleasing group choreographies with individualized dance solo routines, giving dynamism and unpredictability to the band's appearances. This compromise economized everyone's energy: dancers took breaks when they were out of rotation, Fela could take breaks during instrumental-dancer solos, and the choreographer had no need to choreograph an hour-long routine, giving his contribution a sense of freshness. In other words, a composition style that produced long and complex songs meant that Fela simply could neither disregard dance solos nor involve himself in fine-tuning the details of dance routines. Najite once again underscored this point by recalling her solo dance appearance at the 1978 Berlin Jazz Festival: "When Tony Allen played the drum, you see the way I come out and display. . . . Nobody dey tell each other anything. You will go and show your own experience there. Your own talent. Fela no know what we will do . . . but the group [choreography], he will see that one. Then when you finish the solo, if you do it well, Fela will hail you. Say 'Very nice.'"[73] Solo improvisations were therefore not simply a desirable performance option for Fela's band—they were a practical necessity given the length of songs in live performance. Despite the women's ingenious exploitation of spaces in musical structure, however, Afrobeat performance rested essentially on gendered hierarchy, order, and form. The balancing act between structure and improvisation became the cornerstone of women's artistry. As generative and impactful as was the women's creative work onstage, ending the analysis there heightens the risk of losing sight of the complex lives they pursued beyond the spotlight and in everyday spaces over which they held sway. Kalakuta Republic shared some of the principles of hierarchy and orchestrated order, but the commune also embraced disruption, rule breaking, and a veneration of individual capacity. If Fela had insisted on running Kalakuta Republic in the same manner as his structured stage performances, he might have produced spectacular failures that would have fed the commune's endless appetite for ridicule, buffoonery, gossip, and self-amazement. The Shrine's more policed balance between freedom and form might have worked in Kalakuta Republic. But if Fela had strictly enforced the logics of the stage in Kalakuta Republic, he would have violated the unwritten codes of subversion that Kalakutans held dear. Such a position would have sabotaged the creative energy on which the commune thrived. Kalakuta visitors were delighted to witness the dialectic between rules and rule breaking. What emerged from this negotiation was strange to non-Kalakutans and sometimes spectacular. Fela found this to be a desirable effect for his brand. Visitors should be forgiven for their enchantment with Kalakuta life—that said, their admiration of Kalakuta life did not always equate with a desire to see its logics and ethos spill over into larger Nigerian society. The state was especially motivated to keep the commune's "excesses" contained.

Alagbon Close: Police, Army, and Kalakuta

The military regime staged a bloody invasion of Kalakuta Republic in February 1977. It was the first incursion by the military, but it was not the first raid on Kalakuta Republic. Three years prior, on April 30, 1974, fifty police officers had stormed the commune on a tip-off about rampant marijuana use. It was a successful operation by their count: they discovered marijuana everywhere, "under the carpets, in toilets, in kitchen . . . every fucking place."[74] At the time, marijuana possession carried a ten-year jail term. The raid led to Fela's arrest, but he read it as the government's abortive effort at sabotaging his first international tour to Cameroon. The encounter inspired *Alagbon Close* (1975), Fela's first album directly criticizing Nigerian law enforcement. (He called these "direct attack" albums.[75]) Another raid followed days after his release on bail. It was an early morning follow-up raid; at about 4:00 a.m., five detectives conducted this second search and, this time, planted a joint after making no incriminating discovery. A quick-thinking Fela grabbed and ingested the joint, leading to his second arrest. The police awaited a sample of his feces as evidence in his prosecution. The court discharged Fela for lack of evidence when his stool returned no traces of marijuana's active ingredients.[76] This 1974 raid—and the "rescue" raid of November of the same year—led Fela to fortify Kalakuta Republic with barbed wire and an electric fence, both of which featured prominently in Kalakuta's weak defense in the 1977 military operation.

The police patronized the women they encountered in Kalakuta, treating them not as the potent women artists they were but as misguided girls lacking morals and good parenting. In fact, the police placed some of the girls and women in the custody of welfare services, a vivid illustration of how they were seen as politically insignificant. This perception eroded quickly as the young women refused state custody. After two months in welfare, all but five of them made a clean escape by scaling the facility's fence. "Those, my girls. That's why I had to marry them, man. They were a bunch of wild motherfuckers, man," Fela bragged after their audacious escape.[77] One year later, some of those women appeared on the cover of *Expensive Shit* (1975), fists raised in the Black Power salute, topless and smiling (fig. 3.4). The women continued such defiant gestures in ways that countered the government and media's dismissal of them as passive objects of Fela's whims. The women acted for themselves and did so in bold strokes. However, even with this proof of strength and empowered performance, the government set its eyes on prosecuting Fela Kuti.

Sunday Adewusi, chief of the Criminal Investigations Department, was desperate to prosecute Fela. After trying futilely to pursue child abduction charges against Fela, Adewusi doubled down on his efforts by hiring two people to falsely testify in court as the parents of a young woman named Ibekwedi.[78] Adewusi's serial failure to successfully prosecute Fela only inspired further attempts at containing Fela and the women around him. It was in response to these failures that on November 27, 1974, Adewusi ordered a police invasion of

Figure 3.4. Album cover for *Expensive Shit* (1975). Photo credit and permission: Fela Kuti's estate.

Kalakuta Republic. It was up to that point the most brutal encounter between commune and state. The police pinned the raid on a mission to rescue Folake Oladeinde, the daughter of a police commissioner. Her refusal to cooperate with the police aggravated tensions between Kalakuta and law enforcement. An unrelenting Adewusi continued to use his elevated position to act on the desire to see Fela put away. The police chief masterminded yet another ambush of Kalakutans in February 1975, on their way to a concert in Ilorin. Ironically, Adewusi's serial and desperate attempts at silencing Fela only amplified his popularity in the mid-1970s.[79] After his acquittal in the Folake Oladeinde incident, thousands of supporters are reported to have escorted him from the court to Kalakuta Republic, where he climbed on top of a car, played antigovernment songs, and delivered incendiary speeches through a loudspeaker. Fela continued lambasting the government at the Shrine later that evening.[80]

After the foiled Folake Oladeinde rescue raid, Kalakuta's contact with the state went beyond run-ins with law enforcement. High-ranking military officials became increasingly involved—specifically General Olusegun Obasanjo, the head of state and a well-known adversary of Fela. Not only did both men hail from the same hometown, Abeokuta, but they also attended secondary schools near each another, and their families knew of each other. Although Fela denied having any childhood memories of Obasanjo, the musician did not discount the possibility of their having met prior to becoming public figures.[81] The tension between the two men devolved into full-fledged hostility after FESTAC 77, putting Afrobeat's audacious women squarely on the state's radar alongside their host. Obasanjo rose to the highest political office after Lieutenant Colonel Buka Suka Dimka, a high-ranking officer, led an unsuccessful coup against the incumbent head of state, Murtala Muhammed, in February 1976. (Dimka had been implicated in another coup exactly a decade earlier.) Dimka's forces ambushed a Mercedes Benz containing Brigadier General Muhammed while Muhammed's car was stuck in Lagos traffic. Although unsuccessful, the attempt saw the widely beloved Muhammed assassinated, his body filled with a hailstorm of AK-47 bullets. Muhammed had a penchant for simplicity; he eschewed the usual trappings of power, such as an ostentatious lifestyle and a heavy security escort. This simplicity facilitated his killers' access to his unescorted car. Muhammed's death cast a shadow among progressive forces on the continent. Mariam Makeba composed a tribute song, "Murtala," in his honor, underlining his support for Black majority rule in South Africa, Zimbabwe, and Namibia. Murtala's Pan-Africanist vision endeared him to Fela and led him to occasionally visit the Shrine. He replaced the jail term for marijuana possession with a nominal ten-naira fine, a move whose aim, some believed, was to ease Fela's marijuana-related troubles with the authorities.

Muhammed's death set the stage for the rise of his second-in-command, Olusegun Obasanjo, one of three assassination targets in the failed coup. Obasanjo not only evaded assassination but also foiled the plot with the support of loyalists within the military. A counterstrike took place in the interval between the plotters' declaration of their takeover of the government at Radio Nigeria House in Ikoyi and the planned hit on Obasanjo. Once discovered, the conspirators were killed by a public firing squad, but not before they confessed. The coup attempt was then traced to General Yakubu Gowon, who had been ousted by Murtala Muhammed and exiled in London. The coups and countercoups of the 1960s and 1970s fueled deep suspicion within the military. Mid- and high-level soldiers eyed political power and its promise of personal enrichment. Political ambition fueled paranoia and clientelism within the military ranks.[82] It was during this time, the early to mid-1970s, that Kalakutans became more than mere irritants to the political establishment; they began pointing out rot and contradiction within law enforcement and the military in critiques that would later crystallize in Afrobeat classics like "Army Arrangement" (1985) and "Overtake Don Overtake Overtake (ODOO) (1990)."

Africa 70's evolving public image and the messages in its music paralleled Kalakuta Republic's more socialist ideological leanings. Its influence on public opinion through music, controversy, and Fela's rhetoric fomented interest not only from Nigerian governmental figures but also from political actors in parts of anglophone West Africa.[83] Expanding political appeal to these new discursive communities often took the form of Fela couching his rhetoric in the prevailing Cold War discourse, promising in his political party's "Manifesto of the Movement of the People" that he would pursue an agenda dissuading African women from giving "their children over to colonial, British, American, and Chinese or Russian mannerisms."[84] While Fela often commented on the Cold War and African politics, his interviews, writing, and song lyrics suggest that he understood himself and his community as significant if subaltern interlopers in everyday politics, especially in light of his continued antagonism of Obasanjo, a staunch US ally. Obasanjo continually expressed disapproval of Fela and his cohorts.[85] Kalakutans enjoyed a brief peace between July 1975 and February 1976, the interval between Murtala Muhammed's takeover and his assassination. The Obasanjo era marked an end to the momentary truce. The shift also meant a renewed interest in Kalakutans, women included, as treasonous combatants.

The creative lives of Afrobeat women convey individual and collaborative creativity that shaped overall performance aesthetics. The broad domain of women's creative practice should put to bed the obsolete image of the lone creator slaving away in a studio.[86] The array of improvised, partly structured everyday aesthetic practices, from yabis and makeup to dance solos, constituted them into an important political force in their own right and in cahoots with Fela. These collective acts need to be understood as accumulating political meaning in tandem with Fela's songs, rhetoric, and actions, all of which drove Afrobeat's ascendance as a musical and political force, especially in the lead-up to FESTAC 77. When the state struck, it did so with the understanding that the women were crucial agents in Fela's success. "How the infamous attack was decidedly gendered is unpacked in the next chapter."

4

Unknown Soldier

The 1977 Kalakuta Invasion and the Geopolitics of Intimacy

> We were happy those days, before they came
> and burned the house.
>
> **—Kevwe Anikulapo-Kuti, former Africa 70 singer, in an interview**

My goal here is not to rehash the spectacle of state repression or the trauma of sexual violence it often leaves in its wake but to reconsider settled narratives about one of Nigeria's most well-known instances of military infraction on civilian life outside of the context of war.

On February 18, 1977, the Nigerian state, led by General Olusegun Obasanjo, brazenly invaded and destroyed Kalakuta Republic. This chapter analyzes the invasion of the Afrobeat commune in relation to three interrelated phenomena: (1) everyday Kalakuta-state interactions and the national events that gave intensity to those interactions; (2) the spatial context and barracks culture that produced opportunistic sexual assault and rape as part of the state's administration of suffering to Kalakuta women; and (3) the gendered silences produced by the state and by Fela, both of whom rendered invisible, in different ways, the trauma of Afrobeat women. Throughout the 1970s, Fela's Africa 70 band continued to prodigiously produce high-quality, politically relevant, radical music. During this same period, the mid-1970s, Afrobeat women consolidated their profile as important cultural agents while featuring in a series of musical and rhetorical offensives spearheaded by Fela—for instance, his charged *yabis* against the Olusegun Obasanjo regime in January 1977, his declaration of intention to contest the 1979 presidential elections, and the release of albums like *Alagbon Close* (1974), *Zombie* (1976), and *Upside Down* (1976). These activist interventions occurred in response to volatility caused by coups d'état in and around Nigeria and under the specter of the Cold War, which was in full swing across Africa in the 1970s. The notoriety of Fela, his organization, and the women surrounding and upholding the work reached a climax during FESTAC 77, the Obasanjo administration's landmark cultural project.

The band's musical success fueled Fela's popularity, equally spotlighting the women around him as subjects of political interest. Fela's girls had metamorphosed by 1977 into full-fledged embodiments of Afrobeat's antiestablishment politics, an evolution attributable to Kalakutans' activities and embodied art forms at a politically volatile moment and in a space pregnant with everyday violence. The women mobilized their bodies and voices through yabis, makeup, dancing, and singing to confront state agents and elite culture whenever possible; that these confrontations occurred in close physical proximity, literally, between the subculture's residence and a military barracks shaped interactions between both entities in potent and predictable ways. An unlikely outcome of this proximity and the interactions it fostered was a sense of mutual enchantment between Kalakutans and specific state actors, familiarity and, in some cases, friendship that was equally attended by the specter and materiality of violence. The spatial orientation of Kalakuta Republic in relation to other mediating entities mattered. Brothels that regularly harbored sex workers surrounded Abalti and the Afrobeat commune. In Lido Hotel, a brothel on this strip located next to the Shrine, women performers did striptease for paying clientele. The erotic nature of the women's dancing at the Shrine was inevitably read in tandem with the brothels in the surrounding area as sure evidence of prostitution in Africa 70. Linking sex work to Kalakuta women coded women in Africa 70 as deserving of harm, in much the same way that actual sex workers find themselves exposed to targeted forms of bodily and emotional harm. This chapter analyzes how sexual violence transformed Afrobeat women from salient cultural and political agents into victims, a transformation that entailed a shift from immersive creativity and ebullience into a tiring and elusive pursuit of justice and restitution from a state bent on covering its tracks. To make this claim, I recount the invasion, the intersection of macropolitical events, the everyday interactions that coalesced around those events, and some of the deeply personal aftershocks of the invasion.

Kalakuta Republic was located a mere three hundred yards from Abalti Barracks (a military base) and only thirteen kilometers from Dodan Barracks, the seat of the federal government at the time. Beginning with this proximity is crucial for refocusing mid-1970s Afrobeat performances on their literal closeness to political authorities, sanctioning the reading of the physical space of performance as simultaneously unfolding in and shaping the volatility of a military-civilian contact zone. The variety of women's erotic performances as sex workers or music performers coded this space as a zone of sexual contact between state and citizen. Modern African states are entities produced by violent imposition and endowed with powers to exercise violence, meaning that the Kalakuta-Abalti zone was coded by violent forms of sexual contact, such as sexual assault and rape. This medley of entertainment, transgression, and the ever-present threat of violence unfolded spatially to define the lived, embodied experience of Afrobeat music for the women artists who lived, played, and worked there. Ethnomusicologist Michael Veal has noted how Fela "controlled the area and right down the street you've got his enemies . . . the army."[1] This closeness posed risks to residents of the commune; it also produced a paradox. While Fela strongly criticized the government and the military in his song lyrics, the Shrine was amenable to catering to the military: it offered affordable entertainment to soldiers who lived and worked in the nearby barracks. The Shrine conveniently served soldiers. This proximity, by the same token, exposed the military to Fela's rhetorical claims to sovereignty separate from the state, claims that left Kalakutans eventually exposed to the state's brutal retaliations. The paradox produced by the physical and psychic proximity between the Shrine, Kalakuta Republic, and the military establishment—as well as how quickly this familiarity soured in moments of national ferment—is what one might call the geopolitics of intimacy. Intimacy, in this sense, underlines how the women's physical proximity to this military installation facilitated their exposure to transactional, even consenting, sexual encounters with soldiers and, conversely, to sexual violence involving state agents when the tides turned. Intimacy names a dialectic of play, pleasure and violation, given flesh by women's aesthetic and everyday performances in a specific spatial and historical context. This fraught intimacy helps us understand the unlikeliness of redress when soldier-inflicted sexual violence occurred. Invading soldiers claimed to have met the Kalakuta women already naked,[2] a claim easily refuted by the women. Singer Alake Adedipe recalled how the soldiers stripped Kalakuta women naked and casually assaulted them.[3] Soldiers lied about nudity and, in a warped logic, used it to justify the violence against the women. Top military officials peddled similar falsehoods about what really happened in Kalakuta on that infamous February day. The claims nonetheless underscored the powerful fantasies soldiers harbored about Kalakuta women and their bodies as well as the voyeuristic pleasure derived by these state agents from the soldiers' unclothing of the women, who had politicized their bodies in potent, activist ways. The Kalakuta invasion underlines how the state encounters working class, and predominantly migrant women and their bodies as sexually excessive, a crucial precursor to sexual abuse. The Kalakuta encounter illustrates how this monstrous intimacy elaborated itself in the state's assertion of sovereignty in flesh through forcible insertions, seeking to viscerally impress its power into the bodies and psyches of women-citizens. In this way, rape becomes a violent process of subject making, a method by which the state attempts to exhaust the will of certain citizens beating them into submission through terror, shame, and trauma.[4] Mbembe has described the postcolonial African state's "systematic application of pain" on its citizens, a reading that, while useful, requires a critical gender lens to understand the logics, ramifications, and aftershocks of state-sanctioned violence against Kalakuta women.[5] Rape is one method in a toolkit of statecraft by which the state makes a subject of incalcitrant women, incorporating them into the rawness of its power. Still, Amina Mama reminds us that "African women have not been passive recipients of abuse, as some authorities would have us believe. . . . they have found numerous ways of resisting the humiliations meted out to them."[6] Rooted in the colonial deployment of rape as a tool in military conquest,[7] quotidian forms of state-sanctioned sexual violence continue to define encounters between African women and the state, spurning creative modes of solidarity and resistance.

I conclude this chapter with Fela's limited appreciation for the gendered dynamics of the invasion and the differentiated nature of the women's experience of the event. By taking up the space, dominating the narratives, and assuming the face of victimhood after the invasion, Fela committed the first of three gestures of negation against the women whose experience of the event were different from his.[8] The women addressed in this chapter are neither abstract nor distant. Many are still alive and healing and reckoning with the past in different ways. I narrate my encounters with Kevwe to recast the invasion in the present tense; how she remembers the past. The life she led renders the aftershocks of this history and its silences with remarkable clarity.

Enchanting Kevwe: August 2014
It is at the museum's penthouse that I meet John (a pseudonym), a diminutive guy who speaks less than he acts and who appears to be constantly on the move. After a brief interaction, he becomes my de facto research assistant. In businesslike fashion, he lists a few Afrobeat women I might like to meet: Omowumi, who sells drinks close to Femi Kuti's New Afrika Shrine but about whom I have heard little, and Kevwe Anikulapo-Kuti, who currently works as a cleaner in the VIP toilet there. Kevwe would be easier, he reassures me, because her schedule is predictable.

She has no housing, so she resides there, her modest possessions crammed into a few bags. John asks me to return two days later, during Femi's open rehearsal. We might also meet Omowumi. My encounter with John was unplanned, but it holds utmost promise. As we part ways, I replay the comment in my head about Kevwe. The way people talk about Kevwe's situation strikes me as unsympathetic. Anxiety overcomes me as we, John and I, approach the Shrine on the appointed day. The unsettling feeling contrasts with burning anticipation. Nearly everyone we meet greets John with varying degrees of familiarity and reverence. This is an impressive aspect of how he navigates the space. He hardly spends more than a few minutes in one spot or with any one person before someone else beckons. He instructs me to follow him closely as he promptly negotiates our passage through logistic hurdles, from entry into the Shrine to proximity to the stage. He leads with such authority that I ask, "Who you be for here? / Who are you around here?" He used to work in a technical capacity with one of the bands and appears to have managed his relationships well. It is with similar efficacy that John brokers my meeting with Kevwe.

Meeting Kevwe stands as my most striking experience in searching for the Queens. It is the only moment of the day when time appears to slow down. John asks me to wait at the foot of the stairs that lead to the VIP area. After what feels like an eternity, he reemerges and instructs me to ascend the stairs. Kevwe is waiting for me, he announces with a sense of accomplishment. As I proceed to take a first step, a woman appears at the top of the stairs. It is Kevwe. She is the Kevwe I have studied carefully in photographs and concert videos. She stands with her feet planted apart, as if to allow her body take up the room it needs. Her eyes fixate on me, assessing me in a way that now feels familiar. This moment reminds me of the two other Queens I have met. They have all mastered the art of quiet and quick profiling, of sniffing out outsiders, especially journalists. The feeling of being examined for trustworthiness returns in a rush. Kevwe's examination lasts about ten seconds, although it feels like ten minutes. John is beside me, perplexed because my stillness makes little sense to him. He later informs me that I need to act faster. I know better than to heed this advice. Kevwe is reading the scene, perhaps judging the nature of my relationship to John. She breaks the silence with a simple gesture with her full right hand, "Come." I scramble up the stairs, managing not to trip. John disappears into the crowd.

I scan the VIP area. It's modest but for the privileged view it offers of the stage. In it are about twelve plastic tables, each with about four chairs. The bar holds Guinness, Gulder, Heineken, and the Ghanaian Alomo Bitters. There are no customers today, so Kevwe asks that we take one of the tables. She has on a tiny silver crown and purple necklace that show signs of wear. She also has a lilac purse that, slung around her neck, sits at the waist. But she still possesses the smile I associate with her from archival materials. John warned me about Kevwe at our first meeting. Gliding his hand along the hairs of my left wrist, alluding to romantic interest, he warned that Kevwe could do same. She could be nice, but she has "skoin-skoin," implying she is unwell. She might ask me for a lot of money or show me "craze." None of this was heartwarming information as I prepared for the meeting. John's warning was not the first I received about Kevwe. Two others earlier suggested that I avoid her altogether because her memory could not be relied on for serious research. "Fela was a sweet man!": these are her first words. It is an agreeable start to our conversation but not the one I desire. "It is just the people around him," she adds. She neither continues nor revises this statement. I introduce my research about the Queens and their contribution to Afrobeat. She shows little interest, neither nodding nor yielding any clues to reassure that my pitch is convincing. She simply listens. As we continue our conversation, the sound check begins. It is Thursday, Femi Kuti's rehearsal day. Femi has come onto the stage with his band, Positive Force. He is rehearsing a new tune. Many fans gather at the foot of the stage, some visibly high on something. The instruments are so loud that they appear to split right through the haze of lingering marijuana smoke created by the fans' collective efforts. Femi's saxophone drowns our desire to speak, to commune across age, generation, gendered experience, social class. We sit only a meter apart and can barely hear one another. We exchange several "say that again" and "ehn" and "I did not hear you."

As we strain to hold this conversation, Kevwe reaches for the lilac purse slung around her neck. She pulls out a fiercely folded paper, held together by a pen's clip. She hands it to me as if it contains the answers to all the questions I am yet to ask. I wonder what it might be as I unfold it. In it, I discover a single-page description of a dream she had. The questions pour into my head in a rush. Did she know I was coming? That anyone was coming who might consider this dream worthwhile? How long has she kept it folded in her purple pouch? Is it a personal manifesto, a poem, a diary entry ripped from its bounded form, or simply the written record of a dream, the space where she makes sense of things, where she gives form to a past that she knows intimately? I do not know what to make of it still, so I offer it here to you, reader, with Kevwe's permission. You'll notice it has its own title: "Tunlese" (fig. 4.1). Translation: Repair the home. Barely three sentences into reading, I begin to sob. She smiles, handing me a napkin from the plastic table where we sit. "Why are you crying?" she inquires. Does she know I am dealing with guilt, shame, pity, anger, all at once? Guilt and shame that I might have internalized what others have led me to believe about her? That she might pose a threat? What does her state of mind, the madness attributed to her, say about Afrobeat itself? I leave disheartened that she works in the toilet behind us, in an empire she helped build. She asks me to keep the note and the pen. I am terrified by the responsibility. How to handle this note and

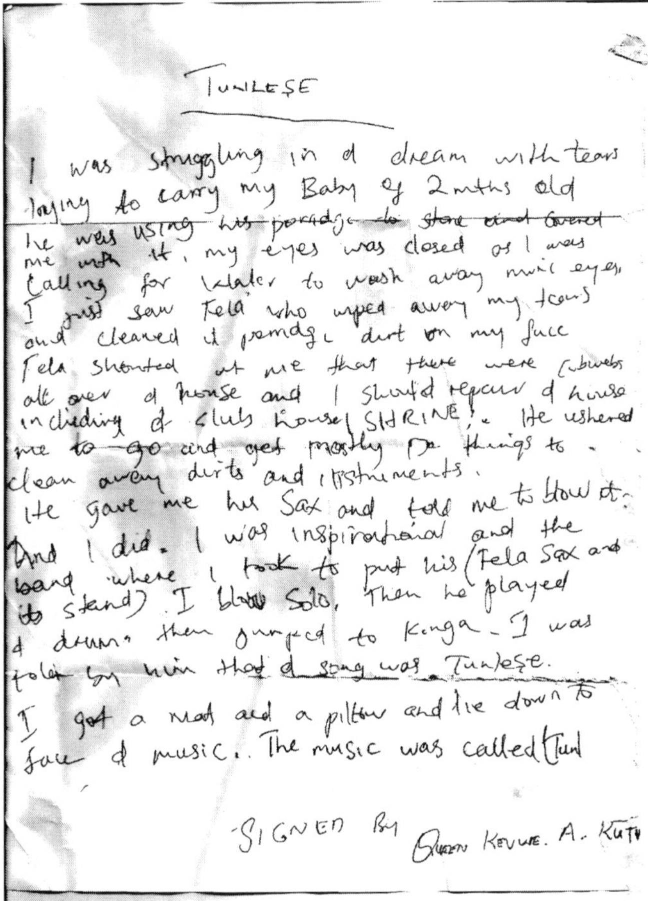

Figure 4.1. "Tunlese," Kevwe's dream written in her hand. Credit and permission: Kevwe Anikulapo-Kuti.

not enact further harm? What is the nature of my responsibility if she does not recall giving me the note but still permits me to publish it?

As we overlook the stage, time slips between the here-and-now and the there-and-then. The frames blur as the image comes into view of Kevwe onstage, flanked by four other women, singing, straining to hit notes that few Afrobeat women can. I slip into February 1977, which it seems everyone forgets by compulsive retelling. I see her here, wondering about the stories that fill this distance between her and the Afrobeat stage. We say our goodbyes and promise to meet in two days. She strikes me as kind, and perhaps to be kind is to have survived. I descend the stairs and reunite with John, whose first question to me is "How did it go?"

The Area Named Area

When Fela relocated his band to Mushin-Idi Oro in 1971, the move spurred the industry of hustlers and late-night entrepreneurs to cater to the Shrine's audience. Makeshift food stalls and bars blossomed alongside shops constructed with planks and aluminum sheets, structures that housed tailors, electricians, beauticians, and a host of other traders who serviced Kalakuta Republic and the Shrine. Marijuana sellers, as mobile as their merchandise, needed no shops. They hawked their wares in and around the area. Kalakutans patronized these businesses or floated their own to supplement their modest earnings as performers. The informal businesses that flourished in the area in turn enriched the experience for Fela's audience at hours when regular businesses had closed. An economic ecosystem flourished around the combined creative work of nightclub and commune. Fela's music attracted students and workers with disposable income, and the influx of young people to Kalakuta added dynamism to the neighborhood. The entrepreneurs benefited from the vitality Fela's work brought to the neighborhood, but they also helped his Africa 70 run more efficiently, as it could access their services without travel or strain on its resources. Spurred by the combined reputations of Fela and his people, Kalakuta and its surroundings—as a blended physical, economic, and cultural environment—became known, quite humbly, as "area."

The industry of *area* served more than civilians; part of its clientele were soldiers stationed at Abalti Barracks. Because it was so close to Abalti, area became a virtual extension of the barrack's mammy market, composed of small-scale businesses with a remarkable history found within or around Nigerian military camps.[9] Mallam Abdul Okwechime recalled that Abalti soldiers were generally "good neighbors" because at the Shrine, they paid to watch performances alongside civilians. Their reliance on the services of the Shrine and area entrepreneurs provided an incentive to not replicate the harassment prevalent in soldier-civilian relations in 1970s Lagos.[10] Crucially, too, the fact that daily cycles of work and leisure unfolded in the context of such proximity meant that everyday Kalakutans' interactions with the military were mundane. As a result, Kalakutans had a view of barracks culture at a mundane level unavailable to most Nigerians. This familiarity played no mean role in demystifying the military establishment for them. It likely also obscured for Kalakutans the lethal instruments at the state's disposal and its readiness to deploy those instruments against them. Even though it was in the soldiers' best interest to behave appropriately, they were still prone to lapses in behavior. Since soldier-civilian relationships in militarized spaces have historically been both volatile and sensitive to political shifts on the national level, soldiers were good neighbors only to the extent that political circumstances dictated so. The mid-1970s proved to be a combustible moment. A succession of coups and the atmosphere of suspicion and fear they generated shaped everyday dynamics in the Kalakuta-Abalti area. Otherwise mundane interactions devolved into publicized standoffs, contributing to the conclusion of a special commission that "Fela's house and nightclub were so close to the Abalti Army Barracks that conflict could not be avoided."[11] When the soldiers invaded Kalakuta, they also sacked area, evicting its estimated two thousand inhabitants.[12] By closing the Shrine, the soldiers effectively cut off the oxygen to surrounding businesses. Ironically, by decimating Kalakuta and area, Abalti soldiers destroyed an important outlet for their own emotional and psychological release. The soldiers, acting on orders from above, effectively shrank their options for recreation, leisure, and entertainment.

The symbolism of area was not lost on the state. That the creative activity of Afrobeat artists created area made the Fela-led commune a potentially more dangerous political organism because by spurring a previously nonexistent economy, albeit on a modest scale, it advanced implicit claims to self-sufficiency as a republic within a republic. But this was not Kalakuta's only act of territorial aggression. When Fela crossed the road for his performances at the Shrine, personal guards stopped traffic on either side of Agege Motor Road, sometimes for up to fifteen minutes, to clear the way for Fela's infamous road crossing on a donkey or on foot. Flanked by Kalakuta bodyguards and the women, who were usually heading to perform, Fela emerged from Kalakuta to chants of "Black President" and "Baba 70" from the people of area. His music was, after all, key to their livelihoods. This crossing was amusing and irksome in equal measure. Notably, the traffic buildup it caused likely impacted soldiers alongside civilian road users. These audacious acts rendered Kalakuta not simply an artist commune in a sole-standing duplex but rather a combination of neighborhood nuisance and political aggressor.

Fela's song "Zombie," released in 1976 (fig. 4.2), was a scathing satire of barracks culture and soldierly duty that exacerbated tensions between commune and state. Fela describes soldiers as unthinking and incapable of initiative or self-reflection; they blindly execute the command of higher-ups whatever the harm to themselves and others. If you tell the zombie to kill, steal, or die, it obeys without a second thought.

Fela: Go and kill
Response: *Joro jara joro*

Figure 4.2. Album cover art for *Zombie* (1976). Photo credit and permission: Lemi Ghariokwu.

Fela:	Go and die
Response:	*Joro jara joro*
Fela:	Go and quench
Response:	*Joro jara joro*
Fela:	Put am for reverse
Response:	*Joro jara joro*
Fela:	Go and quench
Response:	*Joro jara joro*
Fela:	Go and kill
Response:	*Joro jara joro*
Fela:	Go and die
Response:	*Joro jara joro*

Fela:	Put am for reverse
Response:	*Joro jara joro*
Fela:	Go and die
Response:	*Joro jara joro*
Fela:	Go and quench
Response:	*Joro jara joro*
Fela:	Go and kill
Response:	*Joro jara joro*
Fela:	Put am for reverse
Response:	*Joro jara joro*

"Zombie" is by one account "the most stinging indictment of military rule ever committed to vinyl."[13] In 1978, Fela cited *Zombie* as his most commercially successful album,[14] a potent illustration of its impact and broad reception among Nigerians and Africans living under military rule and of popular music's power to anchor lived reality for an oppressed majority. Forcing an association of the military with unthinking zombies materialized the popular desire for imageries and discourses that eluded the logic of authoritarianism or, at least, that dragged it from a totalizing sign of power to a punchline on the streets. The song "Zombie" revealed the pressure points of military life, helping Nigerians draw vivid lines around the quotidian oppressions that characterized life in a military regime. "Zombie" was Fela's and Africa 70's contribution to the desire for usable caricatures of military power, creating one of the quickest ways to provoke soldiers in real-world scenarios.

A simple but effective collage, the album art designed by Lemi Ghariokwu is equally potent. Ghariokwu juxtaposes a photograph Fela mid-speech holding a microphone with a scaled-up photograph of soldiers, one of whom appears deep in thought, his hand covering his face. Visually, Fela is rendered smaller in scale to the soldiers, and his pink, long-sleeved shirt contrasts their dusty combat gear. But the musician's stance could not be more forceful. Fela correctly predicted that the cover art would put him and the Afrobeat community in trouble.[15] (The song "Zombie" and its corresponding art likely played a decisive role in the November 1977 radio ban on Fela's songs by the Obasanjo regime.[16]) Early in 1977, the relationship between the Afrobeat community and the military spiraled. The government instituted a controversial traffic-clearing program for FESTAC 77. Police were handed horsewhips to flog Lagosians who violated traffic rules, adding to the abuse of poorer citizens. The police were also allowed to arrest traffic violators without officially pressing charges. The go-ahead to whip violators put the state in fraught contact with its citizens.

On February 12, 1977, Abalti soldiers got into a fistfight with young men in area, one whom was a member in Fela's band. The men beat up the soldiers, who retreated to Abalti but vowed to return. For context, the unthinkable notion of civilians beating a soldier has endured in the Nigerian popular imaginary as the equivalent of civilian suicide. It was no coincidence that the brawl happened on the same day as FESTAC's closing ceremony. Incensed soldiers returned to Kalakuta six days after the incendiary fistfight—but for a different reason. On February 18, a young man accidentally knocked down a motorcycle belonging to a lance corporal. To avoid arrest, the offender, who turned out to be an Africa 70 driver, took refuge in nearby Kalakuta.

Again, the contacts and conflicts between "Fela's people," as they were often called, and the military were volatile and made inevitable in some sense by state policy as much as proximity given the diametrically opposed impulses—namely, freedom and regimen—that governed them. When three soldiers asked for the driver's release, Fela and some women in Kalakuta mocked them with songs. And of all possible choices, they mocked them with "Zombie." Najite Mukoro and two other women acted as Fela's spur-of-the-moment backup singers in the balcony concert. The women sang as Fela played the saxophone. What started as an arrest backed by the authority of the state ended up being the precise opposite: a ridicule of state power. The three enraged soldiers found themselves co-opted into a concert that turned them into spectators and performers. In the "concert," they were direct addressees and ostensibly willing participants, zombies-in-action, to be viewed for pleasure. If the zombie in the song is a synecdoche for military hierarchy and not a specific soldier, these three became the actuation of zombiehood. They entered a frame that cast them as actual zombies, uniformed in flesh and blood. It was a frame they could neither easily retreat from nor eagerly inhabit. These everyday frames of performance are just as crucial to understanding the arenas of Afrobeat's subversive power as Fela's musical output or his stage acts. The presence and improvised performances of the women surrounding Fela were central to the meanings accumulated by this "concert" that likely did not exceed five minutes. The account of Faisal Helwani, Fela's longtime Lebanese Ghanaian friend, offers a more vivid rendition of the role and signification of women in the scene.

> Some soldiers then came to the Kalakuta to see Fela to ask him to let them
> have the driver so he could be charged with careless driving. Fela refused.
> A little later some officers came to make the same request. Fela in pants
> standing above them on the balcony of Kalakuta and surrounded by a group
> of scantily dressed women holding umbrella above him abused them by

playing "Zombie" on his saxophone. The officers left in a furious mood after questioning Fela's right to call his house a republic and surround it with an electric fence. They said that as far as they were concerned there was only one republic, and that was the Nigerian one.[17]

Invoking zombies as a metaphor for soldiers' blind sense of duty to totalitarian regimes might have riled up the military ranks, but singing "Zombie" live and in a semipublic space to humiliate *actual* soldiers in Kalakuta pushed Kalakutans from a "safe zone" of artistic expression to a zone of aggression. The state's next line of action suggested that a key part of its thinking was that public ridicule of soldiers by Kalakutans could be reasonably interpreted as aggression. Although soldiers might have dismissed the women's dancing at the Shrine as performance—an aesthetic event unfolding in a circumscribed space—the women's performance of "Zombie" from the Kalakuta balcony had a different and more direct tone. The scantily dressed, singing-dancing women who held an umbrella over Fela revealed themselves to be crucial agents in the political weight of the balcony concert, which must be viewed in tandem with the years of public artistic work and everyday encounters, outside of Fela, that put them in the view of the state. If they had been important agents for the subculture through individual and collective creative acts, the balcony concert became a punctum in how they deployed their bodies and voices to heighten the contact between commune and state. In their report to superiors, the soldiers quite likely mentioned the part that Afrobeat women played in the encounter. It is revealing that, in the heat of the humiliation, the uniformed men made the seemingly unrelated point to the performers on the balcony that there was "only one republic."[18] The soldiers received the improvised performance—with its gendered and sexual undertones—as an act of both emasculation and territorial aggression. For them, mocking men in uniform became another instance of Kalakuta's refusal to heed so-called constituted authority.

Little in print reveals the mindset of Obasanjo as a military leader besides his biography *My Command*, which offers a chilling justification for retaliatory violence using the apparatus of the state: "The Nigerian political tensions, conflicts and confrontations, like other human interactions, had never conformed with the law of physics that action and reaction are equal and opposite. Reaction had always been more intense and graver than action, real or imagined. Those who are the sowers of wind are usually also the reapers of whirlwind."[19] It took only a few hours after the balcony concert for the Obasanjo regime to respond in full force. Major Daudu, Abalti camp commandant, and Lieutenant Colonel Adedayo, garrison commander of the barracks (both of whose first names I could not locate), dispatched to Kalakuta "a sufficient number of soldiers with strict warning not to fire."[20] "Sufficient" implied hundreds of armed soldiers, and the instruction "not to fire" was coded to authorize the raw viciousness with which the invading soldiers enacted other forms of violence. Shooting, as it were, is not the worst conceivable form of violence that the state might inflict on citizens. The coded instruction also appeared to suggest that Kalakuta Republic had committed such an infraction that shooting them was a plausible but unwarranted consequence; framing the order in terms of shooting allowed the state to construe itself as a reasoning, even just, entity. The opposite could not have been truer. Soldiers were permitted by the exact order of "restraint" to enact violation through other means, especially in ways that yield no body count. Arson, rape, brutality, and theft were the direct outcomes of this instruction. One encounters in the 1977 invasion a vulgar display of power and the, conversely, power of playfulness to bring to the surface the hidden transcripts of Nigerian citizenship. FESTAC 77 factored meaningfully into the escalating friction between state and commune.

FESTAC 77: A National Embarrassment

For twenty-nine days, from January 15 to February 12, 1977, FESTAC brought to Lagos over fifteen thousand artists, scholars, and cultural workers from about fifty-seven nations. The festival is estimated to have attracted five hundred thousand spectators, including heads of state, diplomats, Nigerians and Africans, and cultural enthusiasts from around the world. A crowd of one hundred thousand locals cheered for the visitors at the opening ceremony at the National Stadium. Pan-African festivals on this scale were a key site of Cold War scheming, so the United States sponsored five hundred delegates, the largest contingent by any nation, a choice that might be read as part of a larger effort at eclipsing Soviet influence in West Africa.[21] State-controlled art councils sent representatives to showcase Nigeria's rich and diverse heritage in dance, theater, and music. About four thousand dancers representing Nigeria's numerous riverine communities took part in colorful regattas along the Lagos Lagoon. At least twelve thousand vehicles conveyed visitors to and from the newly constructed FESTAC Village. FESTAC's lineup of artists was impressive. The lineup included Miriam Makeba and Hugh Masekela, two of South Africa's leading musicians; Gilberto Gil from Brazil; Stevie Wonder from the United States; Bembeya Jazz National and Les Ballets Africains from Guinea; and Mighty Sparrow and Franco Luambo from Congo. The $40 million National Theatre, constructed in time for the festival, hosted art exhibitions, symposia, live-music performances, plays, and film showings. Here, Black intellectuals debated African civilization with the same verve as the future of Black solidarity and survival. It is hardly a stretch to suggest, as one commentator did, that Lagos became the mecca for Black artists from every conceivable corner of the earth.[22] "It was the largest group of African American artists ever to return to Africa as a single group," another commentator estimated.[23] FESTAC's schedule of events was as eclectic as the cast of characters it welcomed. The festival's scale and budget left no doubts in anyone's mind: it was the defining project of the Obasanjo regime. Obasanjo himself described the festival as an attempt to "recapture the origins and authenticity of the African heritage."[24] But FESTAC was more than a cultural project. It was an exercise of Nigeria's stature as a geopolitical force in the Black world, an exercise intimately linked with its oil wealth.

Full-scale cultural projects tend to accentuate the contradictions and social fault lines they work so hard to conceal. FESTAC elicited a polarized assessment from Nigerians and observers alike. Dilapidated public infrastructure, urban poverty, and traffic-congested roads were hard to hide behind the illusions of state grandeur staged by the regime.[25] One dissenting cleric comically explained that FESTAC compromised Nigeria's spiritual integrity because Obasanjo "invited people to bring their *idols* from different parts of the world" (my emphasis) to Nigeria.[26] No criticism of the festival struck the regime's nerve as much as that of Fela and his people: Fela recused himself after serving briefly on the festival planning committee on grounds of corruption and authoritarian tendencies within the committee.[27] Fela continued to voice criticism by commenting on the government's launch of Operation Ease the Traffic, the controversial initiative aimed at managing traffic congestion during the festival by handing our whips to traffic wardens. Fela was a vocal critic of the ill-conceived operation, describing it as an act of self-sabotage for a government trying to court Blacks from around the world. "What would black American visitors think of seeing these whippings, it would be like scenes from South Africa, but this time blacks whipping blacks. It would freak the Americans out."[28] Fela was responding to the contradiction of using whips to discipline Nigerian citizens to welcome descendants of the formerly enslaved, visitors whose ancestors had endured whipping as a technique of racial control. The irony was only amplified by the placement of the National Theatre, a major festival destination, about sixty kilometers from Badagry, a former major slave port. Fela and the YAP spearheaded a campaign against the ill-fated traffic program. Fela sponsored *YAP News*, an independent publication that designed and released half a million leaflets denouncing the policy. With the help of Kalakutans and

YAP members, these leaflets quickly circulated around Lagos. *YAP News* later extended its activities to the publication of antigovernment propaganda, continuing its critique of a regime whose grasp on power was tentative. "FESTAC was just one big hustle," Fela concluded, "so a whole lot of little military men and useless politicians could fill their pockets."[29]

Fela deployed more than rhetoric and publications to amplify the failures and gross contradictions of FESTAC. Over the course of the festival's four weeks, Fela hosted a run of concerts at the Shrine that he dubbed "Counter-FESTAC." The Africa 70 band performed every night for one month. "Shrine was packed with Blacks from all over the world," Fela mused, tickled by the ease with which he could steal the government's thunder.[30] As early as the second day of FESTAC, Osibisa, a Ghanaian Afropop band, and the Ivorian singer François Lougah made appearances at Kalakuta and the Shrine.[31] Many other FESTAC visitors arrived at the Shrine to pay tribute to Fela and behold the legendary dancers. Kalakuta women were thrilled to welcome these icons to the Shrine and to play the role of host. During yabis sessions in front of FESTAC guests, Fela criticized the Obasanjo administration, which had spent a fortune on creating just the right impression. Fela used these performances to lambaste Colonel Paul Tarfa, the officer in charge of the traffic program. The insults traveled quickly to the regime via a combination of newspaper reports, soldiers, and spies in the audience. The Shrine was ground zero for Nigeria's national embarrassment.

Afrobeat women singers continued to feature as vocal backup on politically charged albums such as *Confusion* (1974), *Expensive Shit* (1975), and *No Buredi* (1976), all of which testified to a festering anomie. But their collective voice independent of Fela came into occasional focus. For instance, in the song "Upside Down" (1976), a listener encounters the only published instance in Fela's musical career of a woman, Sandra Izsadore, assuming vocal lead. "Upside Down" features an all-women vocal, bringing into view Afrobeat women as a parallel and complementary political force. Soulful and clear, Sandra's floating voice delivers a scathing assessment of urban life in Nigeria while criticizing Nigerians' colonial mentality. After listing the state of public infrastructure in industrialized nations, Sandra delivers the song's venom by means of vivid contrast.

Sandra:	Communication disorganize
Chorus:	*Pata pata*
Sandra:	Education disorganize
Chorus:	Pata pata
Sandra:	Electric disorganize

Chorus:	Pata pata
Sandra:	Everything is upside down
Chorus:	Pata pata
Sandra:	Everything is upside down
Chorus:	Pata pata

With "Upside Down," Fela did something to which he was averse: he performed a song live at the Shrine after its recording and release.[32] To rehearse and record the song, Fela invited Sandra, a Black US citizen, a not-Nigerian, to take stock of the sordid state of Nigeria's infrastructure, adding insult to injury. *Upside Down* was still making its rounds in the public ear when FESTAC guests arrived. The series of pointed musical critiques, FESTAC embarrassment, and the balcony concert amplified women's profiles as key coconspirators in Afrobeat's cultural purchase. Barely a year into his term as military head of state, Obasanjo's regime sought to silence Fela and the community. It employed brute force that was decidedly gendered.

The Invasion: February 18, 1977

At about 2:00 p.m., an estimated one thousand soldiers surrounded Kalakuta Republic completely. The soldiers, who formed a perimeter around Kalakuta and its neighboring blocks, comprised officers from Abalti Barracks and the Brigade of Guards. FAK, Fela's mother, saw the number of soldiers and their cordoning formation as a bad omen. Her fears were not baseless. Dancer Omolara Shosanya claimed to have had a premonition exactly four days prior in which soldiers surrounded Kalakuta. What materialized, however, proved far worse than any dream could have revealed. Tension built with each passing minute. Some uniformed men secured the area, while others stopped traffic on Western Avenue and Murtala Muhammed, the two major roads perpendicular to Agege Motor Road, where Kalakuta Republic stood. Hundreds of pedestrians gathered to witness what would be the final moments of Kalakuta as it existed. They received instructions either to keep walking or to stand at a safe distance. Students returning from school witnessed the scene of impending violence. Some endured floggings when they brandished the double-fist Black Power salute in solidarity.[33] When the soldiers received orders to invade, they were shocked by commune's electrically fortified fence, deepening their irritation. And when the authorities subsequently shut off electricity to the area, Fela used a generator to repower the fence. It was Kalakuta's last line of defense—but the soldiers launched a counterstrike. With a single bullet, the sixty-five-kilowatt generator exploded, giving the soldiers access to the commune. The military operation, now known as the Kalakuta War or Kalakuta Invasion, lasted roughly two hours.

Some of the soldiers came to the mission intoxicated, likely to suppress any sense of restraint or compunction. Kalakuta women were the first victims of the hell the soldiers unleashed. The level of brutality implied that the soldiers felt a sense of accomplishment only from the actual rupture of skin and bones, dislodging bodily tissues from their organic attachments. The invaders sought to break the performing body, quite literally. If the body was the instrument of women's art and activism in Afrobeat, it became also the primary target of the state's revenge. Funmilayo Onilere, a dancer, had her head smashed and arm broken. She joined the first group of women to be taken to Abalti Barracks.[34] The jovial Ihase Obotu bled for days after a soldier smashed her stomach with a stone.[35] Najite, the Fire Dancer, was in a cast for weeks to support her broken neck.[36] The soldiers stripped her of clothing, marching her through the streets in broad daylight. It was on seeing the soldiers' handling of Najite that Fela assessed his own fate: "The way they beat her, today they will *kill* me." When they descended on him, he heard his bones break under the weight of their blows.[37] The semantics of the initial breach is critical: the women were the first victims and the most accurate metric of the terror well before it unfolded in full. They were the target of the operation as much as anyone else. An ambulance carted seriously injured women to a hospital while soldiers detained others in Abalti, where they awaited trial. The women did not take the invasion passively. The otherwise peaceful Fehintola put up a ferocious fight. Surprised by her guts and strength, the invading soldiers stabbed her with a broken bottle and a bayonet. After they had her wounds sewn, the soldiers transferred her to Kiri-Kiri Maximum Security Prison. When she returned to the hospital a week later, doctors discovered a splinter of bayonet still lodged in her festering sore. The soldiers did not spare Fela's seventy-seven-year-old mother, FAK. Dragging her by the hair, they shoved her through a top-floor window. When she died a year later from her wounds, even Kalakutans were shocked. A chicken never dies from a leg injury, Olaide reminisced with a Yoruba proverb, but Mama died from a broken leg.[38] The invasion might have stung a little less had it been merely about physical brutality.[39] The attack took an even darker tenor when four soldiers forced three women into an adjoining room and either raped them or attempted to. They broke a bottle on Adeola's head when she resisted.[40] Kevwe Oghomienor's experience left a deep scar: "They took me . . . two soldiers, with heavy sticks . . . took me to room . . . put stick . . . that's when I started shouting, 'Mama! Mama!' Then I fainted. They kept me between them. . . . My nose was bleeding.

I fainted then I couldn't remember anything."[41] The mark left by this encounter was indelible.[42] Kevwe chose to spend most of her time in isolation from the rest of the commune. Seeking solace, she returned to the commune a year after reuniting with her family.[43] The Afrobeat community was ill equipped to deal with the pain and devastation visited on the women. When the soldiers raped and assaulted Kalakuta women, the abuse was gender-specific, punishment for their active part in speaking up against a dysfunctional state.

The legal maneuvers that trailed the invasion furthered the violence. The state-run *Daily Times* laid the groundwork for a grand cover-up by publishing that the fifty young women arrested "were given blankets to cover up at a military camp where they were first taken to."[44] Bending to public pressure, however, the Lagos state government set up a two-person commission of inquiry led by Justice Kalu Anya to investigate the event. The commission admitted testimonies from journalists, passersby, fire brigade officers (who were prevented from putting out the fire set to the commune), eyewitnesses, and members of Africa 70. The highly publicized inquiry proved to be little more than a circus. Even when eyewitness accounts and copious evidence pointed to the state as primarily responsible for the needless violence of the day, the panel nonetheless took the government's side. It conceded that the burning of Kalakuta was not accidental but concluded that an "unknown soldier" had been partly responsible. According to the panel, this unknown individual had set a heap of rubbish ablaze, the flames of which had engulfed eight vehicles, the building, and other valuable assets. This conclusion effectively reduced a coordinated military offensive to the excesses of an unknown and unknowable agent of the state. Fela's hit album *Unknown Soldier*, released two years later, addressed the flagrant injustice of the investigation; the title evolved into a popular idiom for a litany of state cover-ups of civil violations. In a remarkable act of bravery, the women offered to show their bodily injuries as part of their testimonies. They refused to allow rape and physical assault to become a trope of state violence, insisting on testifying to the subjective experience of pain by using their scars and making rape irreducible to metaphor or abstraction.[45] Although the women were ultimately permitted to testify, the panel declined their offer to introduce visceral evidence and, following this, rejected the women's claims that they had been raped or sexually assaulted. It concluded instead that the injuries were either accidental or, revealingly, due to their resistance to lawful arrest. The commission's selective admission of the women as crucial witnesses (and of their bodies as repositories of trauma) was followed by recommendations aimed at denying the abuse that had occurred in daylight and with literally thousands of eyewitnesses. These were the panel's conclusions instead: (a) the police should have been more proactive in preventing juveniles from "falling prey to unscrupulous persons . . . engaged in certain trades"; (b) no one should be allowed to describe their residence as a republic within the Federal Republic of Nigeria; (c) the activities of the YAP must be monitored and investigated; and (d) the government should take over Kalakuta Republic and its environs, shut down the Afrika Shrine, and withdraw the Empire Hotel's liquor license.[46] Not only did the panel fail to acknowledge harm done, it also seized the opportunity of the investigation to double down on the state's position that Kalakutans were the aggressors who needed to be surveilled and punished for past and potential future infractions. The state's offensive relied first on a refusal to acknowledge harm, an acknowledgment crucial to the possibility of restitution and healing. Acknowledgment is complicated and performative, Catherine Cole argues, because without it there can be no apology and "without apology, there can be no redress. Without any of the above, what can a piece of theatre, performance, or art actually *do*?"[47] Theater became a trope as the public grappled with the moral and political fallout of the panel's report, the document's power to silence a just accounting of the invasion while repeating the violence of the state. The panel was a spectacle of a morbid kind, namely performative truth seeking, built on another morbid spectacle—the invasion—each and together greasing the machinery of absolutism. One frustrated reporter described the recommendations as "a theatrical mockery, staged at the National Theatre."[48] The shambolic investigation and its announcement sparked widespread criticism from artists and activists, many of whose careers had been shaped by protest and who recognized the panel's gesture as familiar and shocking. Wole Soyinka described official accounts of the event as "cynical." Members of Kalakuta's YAP, including Duro Ikujenyo, Mabinuori Kayode Idowu, and artist Lemi Ghariokwu, who barely escaped the attack, added their voices to the widespread disapproval of a "most inhuman act."[49] Tai Solarin, the public complaints commissioner for three southwestern states, called the administration's action "too extreme, barbaric, and brutal." The commission demonstrated the state's power to punish dissent spectacularly and relatively unscathed. These criticisms notwithstanding, two bulldozers returned to Kalakuta to demolish what the flames had not claimed. What remained of the once-vibrant commune were charred bricks, rubble, and trauma.[50] The refusal to acknowledge harm, let alone harm specific to Kalakuta women, set the tone for how the invasion entered and transformed in the public's consciousness.

Obasanjo's regime had a bloodthirst for quashing progressive forces. Protesting students at the University of Lagos, situated less than four kilometers from Kalakuta, felt the weight of a regime with a razor-thin tolerance for dissidence. In 1978, the National Union of Nigerian Students (NUNS), led by its president, Segun Okeowo, protested the dismal funding of public education, a hike in tuition and fees, and a growing military presence on Nigerian campuses. Between January and April 1978, student representatives and government officials held a series of negotiations around these concerns. Negotiations broke down, leading to nationwide campus protests. What followed is now remembered as the Ali Must Go protests, one key demand of which was the sacking of Colonel Ahmadu Ali, the minister of education. Instead of returning to the negotiation table or yielding to any of the students' legitimate concerns, the regime arrested student union leaders, shut down campuses, and stationed soldiers on campuses to control student activity. In the ensuing confrontations, soldiers shot and killed several students, including Akintunde Ojo, a student at the University of Lagos.[51] State suppression of student activism was not uncommon—in fact, Ali Must Go was the second major student political action of the 1970s. What often goes unspoken about the violent response to student protests is how soldiers' tactics were deeply gendered, reserving a different kind of punishment for the female students on campus. Soldiers raped and sexually assaulted female students during campus riots, and with no legal consequence.[52] Law enforcement and soldiers often seized moments of political ferment in an opportunistic fashion to act on sexual fantasies largely circumscribed by the stability of everyday relations. Rape became an instrument for exercising state power and fulfilling demonic fantasies of dominating civilian life. Kalakuta women were sustained targets of many soldiers' fantasies in the same way they were seen as proxies of Fela's antiestablishment politics. The dialectic of desire and retribution plays out in the practice and history of sex work around military barracks. For this reason, the area within a few hundred meters radius of Kalakuta became a contact zone, spaces of special intensification of the dialectic of desire and violation, between performers as citizens and the state.

Containing Lust

Like mines and urban centers, military bases were profitable for sex work.[53] This fact was entrenched over the arc of the two world wars, when the British colonial government established military bases that increasingly attracted sex workers from the Nigerian hinterlands, intensifying debates about empire, disease, and the sexual behavior of soldiers.[54] Migrating women who sold sex became such a staple around military establishments in Nigeria's major cities—Lagos, Kaduna, and Enugu—that they became fondly known as "ammunition wives."[55] Tolerating controlled brothels and soldiers' sexual excesses became part of the larger colonial project in Nigeria, but this tolerance contravened the narratives of colonialism as a *civilizing* project aimed at curtailing *native* excess.[56] By relocating his club to within a few hundred yards of Abalti Barracks—one of seven barracks established in Lagos under colonial rule—Fela entered a space with a fraught legacy of sex and empire in which women's bodies were fungible and understood as available for appropriation in service of the state. The afterlives of colonial policing of sex and sex work in service of the military contribute to our understanding of the 1977 Kalakuta destruction. They reframe erotic dancing as unfolding in a space historically colored by an interplay of sex, violence, and disease, a space in which contact between state and citizens, empire and colony, soldiers and civilians, was as sexual as it was anything else. But Afrobeat women used their bodies in a way that recoded the historical script of the space. Because their sexuality as well as the subversive meanings to which they attached their bodies did not operate in service of the state, their bodies were implicitly imagined as traitorous and capable of infiltrating the state through the titillation of soldiers, invading the state at its most vulnerable and most volatile: through sex. Afrobeat women boldly performed in an area where soldiers had to negotiate sexual contact with civilians. The history of sex work around Abalti Barracks recasts Fela's work beyond political ideology and locates it within the realm of the banal. The Abalti-Kalakuta area was a special zone of staged heterosexual contact between male soldiers and female civilians, as well as between artists and the state, a zone in which power elaborated itself in shifting, everyday dynamics among residents. This multilayered contact zone was not disconnected from civilians' ostensible weaponization of desire.

Afrobeat women were regularly labeled as prostitutes, but their romantic choices were more nuanced than this characterization implies. Kalakuta's sexual libertarianism meant that neither fidelity nor rigid ideological convictions governed romantic choices and sexual behavior. During live performances at the Shrine, dancers benefited from intervals between solo routines to freely interact with audience members. Interactions included sharing a drink or a joint at the latter's expense or hanging out with girlfriends who may or may not be part of Africa 70. The nature and nuance of women's interaction with other women who attended the Shrine is a little-known and exciting area of future exploration. But it is clear that the business model of the Shrine and its dramaturgical practices were designed to encourage and entrench heterosexual interaction. The Shrine was a space for women to meet and interact with club

patrons, usually men; these interactions are said to have culminated in occasional offstage romances. In this way, Afrobeat women found a close literary
parallel with the women in Tropicana, a fictional 1960s Lagos nightclub in
Cyprian Ekwensi's novel *Jagua Nana*.[57] Fela's Shrine, as Ekwensi's Tropicana,
profited from the women's presence and sexuality within and beyond the establishment. The women in both Fela's Shrine and Ekwensi's Tropicana dated
customers recreationally—but the differences between the two are also striking. Ekwensi's fictional Tropicana hosted women whose primary act was transactional romance, quite unlike the Afrobeat women whose primary role in the
Shrine was artistic work. The dance floor in the fictional club was a more prominent part of the club's architecture than the space at the Shrine, which clearly
demarcated audience from performers. Tropicana encouraged dancing; the
Shrine encouraged seeing and critical listening before dancing. Tropicana used
dance as a precoital ritual (the men *must* "crowd the floor" to meet the women
of their choosing). Barring these differences, the real and fictional nightclubs
were similar in how they set the stage for heterosexual romance as prefiguring
the gendered extraction of capital from the Lagos nightlife economy. Afrobeat
women performers, like the women in Tropicana, were not passive interlocutors in these nightclub spaces. They fashioned strategies for asserting their
individuality within these spatial confines. In the dancing cages, the dancers (and likely singers too) could target specific people in the audience and
speak to them with their bodies, inverting the gaze toward the audience and
activating a fluid register of affect. They altered neither the Shrine's architecture nor the ways it structured the live event, but they could and did disturb
how power was transacted in the club during performances. Trysts linked to
nightclub encounters remained the more sensational aspect of the women's
sexual adventures. In practice, Afrobeat women are likely to have mirrored the
sexual behaviors of their peers in larger Nigerian society; in they appear to have
involved themselves with men and stayed sexually conservative despite their
notoriety. Afrobeat women generally limited their romantic partners to within
and around Kalakuta Republic and tended to interact sexually with partners
who either shared their ideological convictions (such as students) or were
familiar with their pre-Kalakuta life social circles. A few women maintained
long-term romantic relationships within the commune with partners who were
not Fela. In fact, at least two couples married and resided within the commune,
and some women kept short-term sexual partnerships that came with material
benefits like cash and gifts. The characterization of Kalakuta as an orgy playground implies a fantasy of unrestrained, including same-sex, relationships

within the commune. Kalakuta was ripe as an incubator of same-sex desire, but actual homosexual relations, if they happened, would have been the exception; they would also have been hush-hush affairs given Fela's documented homophobia.[58] Not that homophobia precludes queerness in the commune, but the hostility likely discouraged public displays of same-sex attraction.

While Afrobeat women might have preferred to interact with students, workers, and civilians with similar ideological predispositions, consensual encounters with soldiers also occurred. Soldiers visited the Shrine in civilian clothing because doing otherwise would constitute an act of aggression, rendering an individual an obvious target of Fela's yabis.[59] A soldier who patronized the Shrine for relaxation automatically consented to civilian rules of engagement. There was the expectation that soldiers would adhere to unspoken codes of performance—maintaining silence during Fela's opening act and mid-performance rituals, grooving or singing along to familiar songs, and, on a basic level, occupying the audience section of the auditorium. Importantly, they were expected to adhere to the rituals of romance, which came with the possibility of rejection. In other words, the Shrine momentarily set the terms for social behavior for soldiers, often at odds with the regimen and hierarchies that characterized barracks culture. Of all the civilian codes they were forced to accept, soldiers struggled with only latently expressing their desire for Afrobeat women. While soldiers might have found the women desirable, they could not negotiate sex with them the same way they did sex workers (on a purely transactional basis). Afrobeat women, adorned as they were with Queen makeup, carried themselves with a dignified bearing that stoked the soldiers' irritation, paralleling a similar undercurrent evident in Kalakuta's interactions with police officers. Tejumola Olaniyan has pointed out that "wild fantasies by the police" fueled voyeurism and uncharacteristic excitement about escorting concerned parents to rescue "girls" from Kalakuta.[60] The promise of seeing topless women—more than morality or the call of duty—fueled their enthusiasm for Kalakuta. Another writer argues more explicitly that the problem was the women's mysteriousness and their desirability yet unattainability: "the beautiful girls, so loving, yet no one can come close to [them]."[61] When stories circulated that the young women stoked the imagination of state officials, the credibility of these accounts and those that portrayed the young women as sirens was not in doubt. The very logic behind the invasion satisfied the literal and figurative cravings of officers (with various levels of authority) for the "beautiful girls." When this sexual frustration erupted, it did so violently and unexpectedly, in part in the form of the commune's spectacular destruction.

State policy put uniformed men in the position of turning to sex workers, so the Empire Hotel that housed Fela's Shrine became a brothel following the sacking of Kalakuta and area. A writer visited the hotel, observing how the sex that occurred there entangled sex workers in the daily social and sexual lives of soldiers: "Located close to the Abalti military barracks, the hotel serves as a 'watering hole' for the khaki boys. Military boys come to the joint in droves to unwind and 'mess around' with the girls. . . . Even the police on patrol drop by almost every night to get some 'cigar and beer' money."[62] Because sex workers frequently lived near military barracks, there was a common misconception that all other women living in the vicinity were also selling sex or were at least sexually available and violable. That Afrobeat women asserted sexual autonomy in this spatial context was bold and risky, as living and performing there constantly exposed them to pleasure and grave danger. This precarity corresponds to Clifford Geertz's concept of "deep play," in which the risks associated with playing far outweigh its pleasure.[63] Femi Kuti's dangerous play in the song "Eregele" (1998) aligns with deep play as a form of playing in which agony attends enjoyment.

> Na play you play, you break your neck
> Play, you enter grave
> Na play you play, you break your leg
> Play, you enter grave
>
> *You were only playing, but you broke your neck*
> *Playing, but you ended in a grave*
> *You were only playing, but you broke your leg*
> *Playing, but you ended in a grave*

As illuminating as these notions of precarious play are for understanding the women's exposure to violence, they have the potential to frame the women as aggressors instead of legitimate victims of state-sponsored sexual violence and elaborate cover-ups that often followed. Instead, their play in those spaces powerfully uncovers the nature of power, the unwritten constitution of the social contract in a neocolonial context in which women's resistive acts and performances, whether in direct or oblique address to the state, puts them at grave risk that often takes a sexually violent turn. Erotic autonomy in the staged and social performances of Afrobeat women must be considered in tandem with how the colonial/military state mobilize and weaponize desire, especially in spatial contexts in which intimacy and violation run in parallel and interweaving lines.

Making Silence

Once in '53
three times in '66
Nigerians shoot civilians
through the ears
rehearsing all known tortures
murdering all males
and raping old women
forcing teenage girls in leper clinics
Hundreds butchered like goats of Ramadan.

—Onwuchekwa Jemie, *Biafra*

Routinely mistaken as a deviation from the norm, military rape illustrates a common exercise of gendered domination. Even though the invasion was not a large-scale conflict, it had the trappings of wartime violence. Soldiers raping Afrobeat women during the invasion paralleled violence during the still-fresh Biafran War, which had ended only seven years prior. The invasion operated in the same economy of freedom that came into play when soldiers invaded "enemy" territory outside the bounds of the nation-state. Unlike with the Biafra War, however, Kalakuta agitation existed more in the symbolic realm of difference; the supposed enemies of the state were artists, singers, dancers, and makeup artists hustling to make a living through art and exercising what they considered legitimate critiques within the bounds of the contract of citizenship. Still, the military hoped (as it did with Biafra) to invoke the language of war to justify extreme acts of aggression against defenseless artists.

Despite the gendered outlook of the invasion, the terms of victimhood somehow revolved around Fela. In the aftermath of the event, the public expressed sympathy for Fela and the loss of his livelihood. Fela had lost prized assets to arson and theft. His greatest material loss was the original recording of *The Black President*, an autobiographical film in whose production he had invested a fortune. The narratives that emerged among the public, however, cast a narrow loop around the circumstances of the invasion, including how Fela's subversive behavior and art might have unsettled state actors like Obasanjo. Public concern extended to how the invasion threatened civil liberties writ large. Whether critical or sympathetic, public discourse seldom took Afrobeat women into serious account or conceived of them as victims, even when their experience became public knowledge. Women's suffering was treated as collateral damage, caught in the high-profile cross fire between Fela and Obasanjo (the women themselves victims of secondary consequence). Whatever suffering the women around Fela endured, it was always framed in terms of the musician's actions or image.

Reeling from trauma himself, Fela made choices that had the effect of distorting the women's experiences in the public view. He showed little interest or appreciation for the prominence of rape in the soldiers' targeting of Afrobeat women. "Sorrow, Tears, and Blood" (1977) was his immediate response to the invasion. In the song, Fela makes no mention of the women's encounters with the soldiers. Citing "sorrow, tears, and blood" as the trademark of citizens' encounters with the police and army, he paints violence in broad strokes and ultimately casts the song as an invitation to Nigerians to resist state brutality. Perhaps the event was still too fresh for him to pursue a nuanced account that humanized the women; regardless of his reason for obscuring the gendered violence, Fela's generalization and failure to make a song showing any appreciation for the experience of the women who worked with him, particularly considering the state's elaborate cover-up, implicated him in the silencing of their stories. Fela did little to repair this omission when he addressed the subject two years later in the album *Unknown Soldier*. The eponymous song names the physical and sexual violence suffered by Kalakuta women for the first time: "Yes, dem dey fuck some of the women by force." However, musically, the reference to sexual violence is given the same weight as "Yes, dem dey burn" (Yes, they set ablaze). This is not the only issue with Fela's testimony of sexual violence in the song. The confession that rape occurred ("Yes, dem fuck some of the women by force") enacts abstractions of the encounter. Rape is made symbolically present but materially absent, evacuating at a dire moment the personhood of the women who suffered this unique form of gendered violence. The women's experience perhaps required a different musical form, vocality in a different register of horror capacious enough to contain the unspeakable and unnarratable. In a sense, the women's experience exceeded the form of Afrobeat music itself.

Fela's passing reference to sexual violence starkly contrasts with the repetitive, haunting rendition of the lines "Dem kill my mama" (They killed my mother). Overcome with emotion, Fela stumbles through the song's final call— "Dem turn green into blue" (They turned green into blue), referencing the dubious "magical" outcome of the Anya committee's findings about an "unknown soldier" burning the commune. Fela's voice creaks as words transform into a hum pregnant with mourning and loss. This minute-long rendition remains the most poignant sonic episode in the song and, arguably, in the Afrobeat oeuvre.

The women's purposefully strong singing offers a sharp vocal counterpoint to Fela's wavering lead vocals. "Unknown Soldier" was an unmistakable tribute to Fela's late mother but not to Afrobeat's lesser-known women, who, though alive, were struggling beneath the weight of trauma.

Fela only sang the women into the Kalakuta encounter two years after, couched in his mourning for his mother, FAK. Why did it take so long to acknowledge the gendered dimensions of the Kalakuta attack? One perspective is that his two-year silence was a strategic deflection, as bringing forward the narrative of the women may have fueled the perception of him as complicit in their suffering. Dancer Omolara Shosanya argued that Fela's long silence was likely due to the shock and physical brutality he suffered at the invasion, which offered little room for clarity. Yet she also implied in her explanation that the silence might have had something to do with Fela's awareness of public scrutiny about his responsibility for the women he housed and worked with: *"Ẹ mọ pé ọrùn Fela l'a wà. Nǹkan ò gbọdọ ṣe wá. Wọn mọ pé a wà nílé Fela"* / You know we were Fela's responsibility. Nothing must happen to us. Everyone knew that we lived at Fela's place.[64] Had Fela called attention to the sexual violence sooner, he would likely have elicited widespread rebuke for his culpability in leading the women in his band to harm. It bears recalling that he was serially sued for holding young women against their will in Kalakuta Republic. While he survived those legal challenges, the moral questions that underpinned them were open ended and largely unanswered. Public rebuke for his role in the women's suffering would likely have come from his own defenders, potentially deflecting public support from his pursuit of reparations, including a futile ₦25 million lawsuit he brought against the federal government.[65] These silences were complicated by two phenomena related to sexual violence involving state actors. First, of all forms of soldier-on-civilian violence, sexual violence remains the most likely to be silenced among soldiers and their civilian victims because of the burden of shame and stigma placed on victims. Second, sexual violence against women provides powerful but fleeting moral leverage in the context of conflict. Political agitators have historically seized on the sexual abuse of women within their communities to galvanize sympathy and moral support for their cause as well as to strengthen resolve against the enemy. But attention to women's suffering often vanishes "when the propaganda value of their suffering diminishes," limiting the chances of sustained redress.[66] The intermixing of solder-civilian silence and the fleeting propaganda value of sexual violence explain the passing if explicit reference made to sexual violence in "Unknown Soldier," hardly sustained in Afrobeat music in the years that followed. The tragedy of February 1977 was a punctum in a long colonial history of weaponizing sex; the nexus between the sexual violence of the invasion and coloniality could not have been clearer.

Fela's decade-long critique of the political economy of class inequality and violence was characterized by his consistent failure to account seriously for gendered violence in the colonial matrix. Sanya Osha puts it pointedly when he argues that rape operates on one register as a metaphor for violent penetration of land and territory, a trope and technique of Africa's colonization: "The colonizing gesture was a powerful maneuver of powerful phallic drives, a violent act of copulation that is often difficult to disguise."[67] In *Conflict Bodies*, one of the most exhaustive feminists treatments of the topic, Regine Michelle Jean-Charles reads rape as a colonial inheritance that women experience in both peacetime and war, an experience that lodges deep in the psychic, physical, and psychological registers of the body.[68] There has been growing recognition of the systematic use of sexual violence to deprive women of their productive and reproductive capacities. By raping Afrobeat women, Nigerian soldiers sought not only to terrorize other women in the Afrobeat ranks but also to diminish their collective capacity to produce antigovernment music and conduct the day-to-day work of sustaining the commune and its affiliated band. Choosing not to articulate a gendered perspective of the invasion aided in hiding the women's experience from the discourse of accountability. Scholarly takes on the album *Unknown Soldier* and the event it documents usually fail, by no ill intent, to account for Kalakuta women's particular exposure to state violence. Silence in Afrobeat music has yielded silence in the scholarly literature on the ramifications of the event. The absence of a rigorous class critique has produced a skewed view of how gender computed in the invasion. This misreading is pronounced by the memorialization of FAK as the invasion's quintessential woman victim.[69] FAK was indeed the only fatality directly linked to the soldiers' actions in Kalakuta, but her elite status positioned her as deserving of attention and empathy. The gendered dimension of the military incursion could simultaneously mourn the tragic end to FAK's storied life *and* account for the targeted violation of the working-class women of the commune, whose or death count for little in the public eye. Such narratives should be capacious enough to understand the social death suffered by Afrobeat's women who do not neatly meet the classed threshold for empathy. Scholarly accounts need to be intersectional and attentive to cultivating empathy through generative and class-attentive reconstructions of key events in Afrobeat.

In contrast to these mischaracterizations, the women have been forthright about how the violence of 1977 was explicitly gendered and implicitly classed. Shortly after the event, some testified, with different degrees of detail, to

Carlos Moore about the state's violation of their bodies and psyches.[70] The embodied experiences of daily trauma survival and deeply etched aftermaths permeate a story Kevwe shared of entering Abalti Barracks (recounted at the end of the chapter). The traces also endure in Omolara's recounting. She balled her right hand into a fist, as if to hold an invisible knife, before simulating how a soldier stabbed her "privates." Stories of the encounter, accounts elided in Fela's postinvasion songs and scholarship, unfurl from the women's gestures and memories. The women constructed unspoken versions of the attack, their bodies acting as vessel and witness. They shared these memories even if imageries of death trailed them, as in Omolara's account: "That day, they came to kill, that's all. They tear us, naked us. . . . I was sick because gbogbo ara mi èjè, níbi tí wón ti chook mi [my entire body was left bloody from where they stabbed me]. . . . That day, they came to wound us, and kill us, and steal. That day, mi ò mọ pé mo lè wà láyé o [I did not know that I would still be alive]."[71] The layered scars endure. Singer Alake Adedipe spoke bitterly about the traumatic event and the details she remembered. "They knocked my eye out!! I saw the man who did it. And anywhere I meet the man, I'll recognize this man," she said.[72] It was brutal to conclude, as Olaide Babayale and Omolara Shosanya did, that "you cannot fight government and win."[73] Four decades later, Olaide still has nightmares about the encounter. Kevwe's recollection of the postinvasion legal intrigue bears witness to the women's spirit as they dealt with their own traumas even as it suggests the pressure to defend Fela's legal interest: "I stood. I fought like a lion. I stood by Fela through everything. I even went to court to make witness for him . . . because they wanted to send him to fifty years in jail. That time his best friend, Kanmisola Osobu, his lawyer was begging me to become a witness. . . . He would have been in jail. . . . I was very beautiful . . . like a mirror."[74] Kevwe's vulnerability is underscored by Fela's lawyer compelling her to support him in his legal challenge even as she was nursing her own wounds. But herein lives the women's will to stage a unified front against a state bent on annihilation. If previous encounters with law enforcement had revealed anything about Afrobeat, it was that Kalakutans did not simply share Fela's deficient vision of liberation; they were also willing to defend it. What remains unclear is the extent to which women like Olaide and Omolara understood the grave risks of being an artist in Africa 70. It would be legitimate to argue that Fela's actions and ambitions led the women around him into harm's way. Following this thought, this chapter might have made a case for the women's naivete or their lack of awareness about the real dangers to which they were exposed. This is partly true, and yet to leave it there elides how the women appropriated Afrobeat music and everyday performance to insist that the state encountered them as citizens. Any conclusion that depicts the women solely as victims of Fela's whims preemptively circumscribes the feelings of accomplishment that the women felt from critiquing the state from a distance close enough to sense its unease, such as during the balcony concert. The women were a potent part of Afrobeat's challenge to the military, a fact Fela seldom acknowledged publicly. Fela drew courage from his closest allies, including women he worked with, but publicly celebrated masculine heroism. In "Fear Not for Man" (1977), citing Kwame Nkrumah's famous quote "The secret of life is to have no fear," Fela sings "Na goat dey run, na man dey stand" (It is a goat that runs, it is a man who stands his ground), lyrics that distort the truth of political courage in Afrobeat. In a genre intimately linked with misogyny, "man" echoes a celebration of male courage more than it acts as the signifier of universal humanism still in common use at the time. The public, for its part, went with Fela's heroic account of the event. It was in no position to offer any meaningful critique of the women's victimhood or of the narratives Fela attached to it in his music. The social and cultural context in which rape is made legible through representation, through rhetorical signs, themes, and narratives, is what Regine Michelle Jean-Charles calls the "paratext" of rape.[75] A central part of the paratext of rape in Afrobeat was Fela's music and the ancillary platforms over which he held sway. Distortion in Afrobeat music yielded distortion in the narratives that proceeded from it. The military culture of rape and the failure to render rape legible in the collective imaginary extended to the media establishment, which had trafficked in tantalizing images of Afrobeat women's bodies for years but went mute after those women were victimized by soldiers. Media disinterest gave implicit support to the idea that the women deserved the violence enacted against them—or, as is true in contexts where rape is excused, that they had asked to be raped by dressing *too* indecently and dancing *too* provocatively. They had, in short, seduced the soldiers. An even more insidious reading of this disinterest pertains to that idea that absolving the state of responsibility ensured that nonmilitary men could count on similar tacit consent for their own horrific acts against vulnerable women. The Nigerian public failed to comprehend that true liberation from a long century of colonialism rested on the notion that no African is free "until women's bodies are not forced to endure intimate violence, whether by partners, family members, soldiers, or actors of the state."[76]

The commune had never suffered violence on such a scale, but it remained at crosshairs with the Obasanjo regime until literally the regime's last hours in power. The regime could have relented after the destruction of Kalakuta. It did not. The force visited on the commune was trailed by continued violence at the hands of soldiers. When all else failed in Kalakutans' pursuit of redress, Fela made a desperate move to embarrass the regime on September 30, 1979, a day before Nigeria's independence celebration and transition to democracy after over a decade of military autocracy. The plan ended with another episode of brutality. Fela and a few Kalakuta women escorted an empty coffin to Dodan Barracks, the seat of the government. The coffin symbolized FAK's murder by the regime. Having caught wind of the plan, soldiers installed checkpoints on every road leading to Lagos Island, where Dodan Barracks was located. When the soldiers detected Kalakutans approaching a checkpoint at high speed, they opened fire on the vehicle, but no one was hurt. Fela recounted, "I told my boys to stay back. Only me and my wives were to carry [the] coffin up to the gate," adding that "those women are courageous-o."[77] Kalakutans ran out of luck after delivering their *parcel*. They submitted the coffin and made to escape just as word of their presence spread. Outnumbered and out-armed, Kalakutans received severe beatings and were detained. The album *Coffin for Head of State* (1981) memorializes this encounter. And in usual fashion, the narrative of the coffin episode in the album mentions nothing of the women's beating by Nigerian soldiers. These distortions in the narrative have led to a skewed view of their role in sustaining Afrobeat's agitation against authoritarianism. Explaining the women's exposure to danger as passive followership of Fela again provides too simplistic a reading. The women's serial and collective encounters with the state illustrate the risks they took in confronting injustice against themselves and, by extension, against the body politic. Even though Fela subsumed their gendered experiences narrowly under his, and while he was unjust in aspects of his band leadership, the women nonetheless considered the state to be the greater and more unjust oppressor. Kalakutans might have chosen to express their grudge with the state differently than through Fela's coffin spectacle, but they committed themselves to challenging soldiers and high-ranking military officials whenever they were required to assume a collective posture of confrontation. When the women joined the symbolic coffin to Dodan Barracks, they did so from the point of view of their grievance against the state and its acts of cruelty against them.

The Kalakuta invasion and the specific deployment of sexual violence must be understood as an exercise of state power in the historical context of military culture's structuring effects on everyday life and women's exposure to sexual violence in militarized zones. The life stories of Afrobeat women call for reattuning to the costs of male heroism embodied by Fela as well as the gendered silences woven into Afrobeat music in the invasion's aftermath. In this sense, we might understand the appeal for women's submission expressed in "Lady"

(1972) as a reinforcement of patriarchy precisely because the song, not unlike the soldiers' sense of entitlement, sees women as (sexual) property to be taken at the will of men, especially in moments of chaos and disruptions to the everyday. When we account for Fela's role in constructing the women's public personas in the years prior to the invasion, his preferred narration of the event in postinvasion songs illustrates the women being twice silenced—by state *and* by Fela. Scholars who write about women in Afrobeat should pay critical attention to the gendered face and aftershocks of the invasion, the intersecting acts of subjection it perpetuated, and the suffocation of avenues of expression and redress that followed for the women. These were some of the ruptures, fissures, and tensions that the mass wedding, a ritual of symbolic unification, sought to absorb, placate, and paper over.

Abalti Barracks in Kevwe's Recollection: Sunday, August 2014
I meet John at Kalakuta Museum, our departure point. From Allen bus stop, we board a Keke NAPEP, a yellow commercial tricycle. Kevwe is the first person we see as we disembark at the New Afrika Shrine. She is walking away from the gate. Although she seems to be in no hurry, she does not notice us behind her. John calls her, "Kevwe! Kevwe!" She does not break her stride. My first thought is that perhaps her ears are plugged with earphones. She turns only when John taps her upper arm. Her ears are not plugged. And perhaps she did hear our call. "Na now you just dey come! The whole of yesterday and day before yesterday I dey free / You are just returning? I was free throughout yesterday and the day before." The day's event is about to kick off, and she needs to supervise the VIP toilet. She cannot do an interview today, she informs us. John appeals to her to concede to a quick interview before she formally resumes her shift. She thinks quickly and asks me to wait; she'll need to catch dinner up the street. We'll be waiting at the Shrine's entrance, John informs her.

He points to a gentleman across the Shrine and whispers, "That man sef dey close to Fela. E fit tell you something / That man was also close to Fela. He could tell you something useful." He is referring to a gentleman in his seventies: Old Soldier, which I conclude is more an honorary title than a description of his past life. John introduces me as Seun Kuti's friend before disappearing. Old Soldier begins our impromptu meeting by sharing that he was friends with Seun's late mother, Queen Fehintola. He asks what state I hail from. My response, "Ondo State," leads us, too quickly it seems, to discovering our shared love for Orlando Owoh's music. We are singing our favorite Orlando songs within minutes of meeting. We cheer and slap palms like old friends, each completing lyrics initiated by the other. He mentions that Orlando occasionally performed at the Shrine, one of few Nigerian musicians to whom Fela granted the honor. Old Soldiers speaks fondly about Fehintola: she was kind and handled a lot of Fela's finances. It's the first time I learn this fact. With his permission, I turn on my voice recorder. Barely five minutes into the recording, Kevwe sprints past us. Uttering no word, she glares at me and gestures that I follow her without breaking her stride. I thank Old Soldier for his time, pay for the drinks, and chase after Kevwe, who makes a sudden left turn at the end of the street, leaving me wondering where we are headed. She leads me to a quiet compound nearby, offering me a bench behind the security post and taking the other. "I do not want all those people to be interfering in the interview," she explains. Her effort at securing a relatively quiet place is a gesture I deeply appreciate. It reinforces that she considers the interview worthwhile. She forgives too easily, Kevwe muses as we sit down. The people she's seen me with are enough reason to not speak to me. John, she reveals, was one of the "boys" the Kutis employed to evict her from Kalakuta after Fela died. My singing partner, Old Soldier, for his part, had harassed her for a relationship in the past. I was oblivious about these relationships and the tensions that have attended them, so I express my apologies for not being more alert to some of her cues. We proceed into the interview, from which the following story about Abalti Barracks (lightly edited) is excerpted:

> *Fela was looking at his wristwatch. It was already past 2 p.m., when his meeting begins. I did not leave the car. He beat me. I told him, "You will kill me." When he saw my determination, he exited the car and walked away. . . . So, I was in the car alone. One hour passed. Something told me, "Drive this car." . . . That was how I started the engine [imitates sound of running engine]. It was a Volvo. Grrrrrrrrrrh! When I turned, the car just stopped in front of Abalti Barracks. Then the soldiers said, "Ah, beautiful girl, you must be the daughter of one of these important men here." . . . Before I knew, they ushered me to where Obasanjo, Babangida, all of them, sat. O girl, see girls! Girls do not dress around here compared to these women. Prostitutes . . . beautiful girls that are also not prostitutes, girls that are undergraduates. O boy, see breasts [we both burst into laughter]. Then they asked me to take a seat. . . . Thank God Fela had just bought me a few [clothes]. I ran to the car to change. One of them asked me to sit on his lap. I sat cautiously. They said, "We have meeting. . . . when we finish, I am going to enjoy my own in a big palace, Eko le Meridien." One said, "I am going to another country." This one said, "I am going to America. I will enjoy my life." They talked about transferring money to America, London, Netherlands, Russia. O boy! Before I knew, they manhandled Fela. He [Fela] asked, likely in jest, how they could be embezzling funds without a percentage accruing to him. They replied Fela was an olófofó [a gossip or a megaphone, someone not to be trusted with confidential information]. Olófofó: that was my first encounter with that word. That was the meeting Fela

was going to attend. O boy, this story I am telling you; I could swear on the Bible. [Question: "So you sat on Obasanjo's lap?"] Yes I did, on top of his leg. What could Fela say, when they asked him to be locked in the back? When they wanted to kill him? I was telling him not to attend that meeting. True, they locked him up in the back. They then asked me to join the girls. I had to walk through the back to join the girls. . . . I told them that I needed to use the restroom. They showed me the way. The girls were saying, "O boy, we will make a lot of money today . . ." I tiptoed. O boy, about six soldiers with huge guns stood guard at the room where they locked Fela. So I put on my shoes, revealed my legs. My lipstick was glossy. I proceeded, tiptoeing but unafraid. When I approached the soldiers, they primed themselves, "Hey! Madam! Hey!" They had their guns ready. [Softens tone] I responded, "Please, I am Obasanjo's daughter. I just came from America. This is my boyfriend you held here. My father is just jealous. . . . Don't mind him." [Switches to soldiers' voice] "Really, is it true?" I responded, "Yes, I am his daughter." . . . They then said, "O boy, she is really his daughter o. Where is that mad man? Go and bring the mad man for her!" That was how they released Fela. . . . I saved Fela's life that day. Since then, Fela took me to Kalakuta and announced to everybody that I was to enjoy immunity in the commune.

What I find immediately striking are the two roughly incongruous events: the transition between Fela's joking with the soldiers and their locking him up; and the subplot associated with her claims about being Obasanjo's daughter. These two scenarios defy narrative logic and historicity, her telling "moving through a prism of possibilities, where the telling itself supersedes the veracity of the tale."[78] In contemplating the veracity of Kevwe's accounts, I could easily miss the significance the telling holds for her. Hers is a multilayered rearranging of time (and reencounter with place) that, quite like Jennifer Wenzel's thinking on the unrealized visions of anticolonial movements, scaffolds the form of its telling with past hopes and failures for use in the present.[79] It is precisely this fluidity, expressed as an incompatible and even unlikely sequence of events, that allows Kevwe to recast the past in self-affirming ways, in ways that uphold an empowering experience of self and subjectivity. If the past cannot be undone, narratives of it can at least be disordered. She approaches a site of trauma for many Afrobeat women artists and domesticates it in service of redeeming the self for an unfolding future. While Abalti figures as a space of regimen and ribaldry where women's expression of sexuality unfolds in the shadows of violence, Kevwe is able to claim rhetorical agency over these circumstances without sacrificing the erotic imaginary. It is precisely in this space colored by violence, desire, corruption, and sex that she casts her relationship to the past. Lasting seven minutes, this story of Kevwe's going to Abalti is her longest and, despite its looseness, the most coherent throughout our interview. It has a clear arc that begins and ends with her as the protagonist. She casts herself as a messiah in two instances: first, as the one who endures Fela, whom she resolves to protect; second, as the person who put her body in harm's way to retrieve him from a potentially life-threatening situation.

Trauma yields a particular relationship to time that might be disordered and recursive.[80] Kevwe's orientation toward historical time is salient. Kevwe and Fela's fight takes place close to Abalti, a first hint that the story is set before the invasion. Also, Fela's eagerness to attend the meeting implies that it may have happened during the Murtala Muhammed regime, a momentary period of truce in the ideological tussle between commune and state. In the handwritten note and in her narrative, Kevwe orients herself mostly toward the early to mid-1970s. Her choice around temporality is consequential, not because she had rosy experiences during these years—she speaks about the "war" of jealousy she had with other women in the 1970s. Rather, her orientation to that time speaks to a continued process of reconstituting the self. Her narratives gesture to a time that preceded the violent disruption of her and other women's life course. This reading of time is rehearsed in the other Queens' recurrent return to the invasion, its freshness, the clarity of the details they remember, as though it happened yesterday and not decades ago. As Kevwe rethinks and rewrites the past in the quest for healing, she relates to time and the future as ripe with promise. It is a future in which she can "blow solo" in Fela's band or earn multiple academic degrees.[81] Kevwe paints broad strokes of events or renders them in minute detail. For instance, she describes the color and texture of a doctor's medical gear and her first thoughts after regaining consciousness after the attack. "When I woke up in Abalti Barracks there was cotton wool in my ear, nose, mouth. . . . When I opened my eyes, I saw people from outer space not knowing they were Nigerians." Comfort comes when she recognizes Iyabode, another woman from Kalakuta. Throwing her hands up in mock delight, Kevwe enacts Iyabode's reaction at seeing her alive: "Ehen, I told you she would wake up. Thank God o!" Iyabode places her head on Kevwe's lap, crying. Iyabode is light in a long, airless tunnel. Rather than giving a specific historic time, she speaks flexibly of a stretched, circular, condensed time that reorganizes her complex life story. Kevwe makes time,[82] her association with "craziness" reminiscent of the popular representation of women artists as "witches" or "mad," patriarchy constructing the woman "as other in order to retain male privilege and hegemony."[83]

In scenarios of unaddressed trauma, self-narration suspends historicity. What Kevwe says and how she says it, what she remembers or chooses to forget—how these postures enter stories or fail to cohere to the story form—add to why many people recommended that I avoid her. But their warnings were anchored in no past Afrobeat event. It is as though Kevwe's life forces an uneasy reckoning. By denying Kevwe's "incoherence" a historical basis, as the outcome of a specific traumatic episode and *a practice of healing, individuals who reap the dividends of the Afrobeat women's labor and suffering rid themselves of guilt or responsibility for their current predicaments. The consistent denial and delegitimization of Kevwe's experience render her not only mentally "unwell" but also unfit to benefit from her and other women's work. The Yoruba say that the crazy person is usually best equipped to say the unsayable. Perhaps Kevwe is a custodian of cheerless stories with the potential to upset powerful Afrobeat actors. Maybe this is what she means when she says, "People might even tell you 'Don't mind her, she is a mad person.' I know everything o." After our interview, she asks me to offer the security guard a tip for allowing us to use his space. I do so; we part ways but stay in touch.*

When we reconnect again in the summer of 2022, I present her with printed copies of my recollection of our earliest meetings. By now, Kevwe has relocated from the Shrine, rented herself an apartment in Akute, where she also runs a modest business selling everyday food items. This time, we meet in a busy restaurant in Ikeja, and I fear that the noise might be distracting; I also am worried that she might find the academic parts of my writing alienating. Kevwe collects the printed stories from me, places it on the table in front of her, and begins to read. She becomes utterly quiet as her eyes travel over the words. She lets out an occasional chuckle here and there. She reads every word and lifts her gaze once to challenge me on two details: Who is John? And the references to madness. The former is a pseudonym, which she said she figured; the latter was rhetorical as she expressed full awareness of the misconceptions people hold of her. I ask if there's anything she wants me to change before publication. "You've written the truth," she responds dryly, "and I have nothing to lose." We chat over a meal, exchange gifts, and part ways.

5

"Spirit Catch Am"

Possessions, Paranoia, and the Tumultuous Egypt 80

The destruction of Kalakuta and wreckage of body and mind appeared to recede as the band regained its footing, rehearsing and performing new songs. The heavily mediatized mass wedding of February 1978 put the commune and band back in the public eye. The facade of recovery took the form of uneventful days marked by a postinvasion stasis. But daily encounters, like the following reflection on what should have been routine intimacy between Fela and dancer Adejonwo Oguntiro, punctuated the fragility of the community's recovery. Fela reflected on the encounter in his bedroom.

> I was in my bed in my room with Adejonwo, one of my queens. Then something started happening. . . . Suddenly, she said she won't have nothing to do with me.
> "Hey, Fela," she said. "Mama is here. Look! Mama! Fela, see Mama!"
> I began wondering, "Where is she? Show me. Show me."
> "There!"[1]

This encounter happened on June 10, 1981. How and why did the space of routine sexual interaction escalate into a spiritual episode, one occasioned by the possession of Adejonwo Oguntiro, a seven-year resident and dancer, by the spirit of Fela's late mother, FAK? The scene resonates in part because it departs from dominant characterizations of sex in the commune, presenting a postinvasion snapshot of the convergence of trauma, pleasure, and mourning as well as the role of ritual and surrogation in stimulating the shifting grounds of gendered power in Afrobeat in the early 1980s. In the scene, the late FAK makes a ghostly appearance in the commune, but Fela can neither hear nor see her. Adejonwo, who can, delivers FAK's message to her grieving son: the organization's travel schedule for the following day *must* be altered. Fela recalled becoming like a child before Adejonwo, who, having assumed maternal stature, delivered FAK's message and appeared endowed with physical strength. Under the weight of FAK's spirit, Adejonwo grew too strong to be physically restrained by Fela.[2] That the scene was premeditated is a distinct possibility, but the impact of Adejonwo's heightened state on Fela was total. "It was the voice of my mother," the musician declared. Scenarios such as this were not isolated, nor was Adejonwo a sole actor in Kalakuta's emerging theater of spirits. Possessions of this kind emerged as familiar, if histrionic, manifestations of African-centered spirituality in Kalakuta but were also a site of contestation among Kalakuta women as they negotiated power at a volatile time in the commune. So common were possessions of this kind that Kalakutans dubbed the four-year interval between September 1980 and September 1984 the "spirit years" and possessions as "spirit catch am" (being caught by a spirit). The spirit years were a peculiar high point in the Queens' power in Afrobeat but have remained an underappreciated episode.

Kalakuta possessions, suspended states of the faculties occasioned by catching a spirit or being caught by one, were a contested affair precisely because they were thoroughly entangled with social relations and assumed meaning in the context of the material conditions of communal life. Therefore, possessions such as Adejonwo's cannot be meaningfully interpreted outside the specific questions of who was possessed and by whom or what. The when, where, and why of the possession events further their speculative nature. To pose these questions of a spiritual event, as many Kalakutans did, is to highlight its slippery edges, moving it into the domain of play. In *Yoruba Ritual: Performers, Play, Agency*, Margaret Thompson Drewal offers a way out of the ostensibly opposed phenomenon of play and ritual. Drewal argues that, perceived through the lens of improvisation, ritual and play are not mutually exclusive categories of social action: "Whenever improvisation is a performative strategy in ritual, it places ritual squarely within the domain of play." The embodied, in-the-moment acts of revision that produce and rejuvenate ritual practice are also acts of play. The possessions witnessed in Kalakuta offer an opportunity to expand Drewal's generative read of the nexus of play and ritual because Kalakuta play reached beyond the constitution of the ritual event; Kalakuta possessions danced around the boundaries of realness and fakery, lending ritual a contested and no less generative heuristic. Possessions, or the feigning thereof, invest the performer not only with agency and symbolic importance in the moment but also with deniability and a capacity to intervene in their subjective experience of the world. Possessions are capable of altering social relations between possessed performer and witnesses. Thus, the performative power of ritual incorporated the indeterminacy of play and truth in Kalakuta possessions to produce reality, particularly when these possessions transpired over extended periods. The slippages produced opened for Afrobeat women unprecedented opportunities to invert Kalakuta's power dynamic. These slippages, the ways that the possessions bordered around notions of surrender, control, oblivion, and metacognition, rendered possession a site of possibility for refashioning relationships to Fela and to Afrobeat's gender dynamics.[3] Within these frames, the Queens imbued Afrobeat with a cultural logic in which womanhood became a subject of wonder and awe. In a stunning reversal, Fela's tendency to trivialize and satirize women's sexuality in Africa 70 songs like "Na Poi" and "Mattress" gave way to a momentary appreciation of womanhood at the dawn of the 1980s. When Adejonwo declared, "Mama is here," she conjured a slippage into an alternative domain of truth in which the very notion of reality and, by implication, of power became open, contested, and contestable. In this chapter, I demonstrate how possessions allowed specific Queens, notably Adejonwo Oguntiro and Serwaa Akosua, to garner influence and alter Kalakuta's political landscape in the early 1980s, dovetailing with continued national dystopia shaped by political coups and a society floundering under the weight of neoliberal economics.

Former Kalakutans remain divided over the genuineness of these possessions, but skeptics outnumber defenders. The general tenor of their recollection is that the possessions, as affecting as they were, were premeditated and ingenuine. One Kalakutan, Mabinuori Kayode, dismissed them as a warped game that, at its height, punished questioning bystanders; members of the commune felt forced to participate or risked being evicted.[4] The terms of participation were fraught because Fela was taken by the commune's spiritual turn and frowned on skeptics. Because possessions totally immersed daily life in the commune, distance—let alone outright criticism—implied skepticism and, to Fela's eye, betrayal of his political project. Dede Mabiakwu, a protégé of Fela, attested to the potency of these possessions. When asked about them, Olaide simply poked her nose in a gesture that summarized her utter lack of belief in the spiritual episode that gripped Kalakuta. The question of authenticity yields a limited view of the conditions that precipitated the spiritual turn as well as the material effects they produced. Spiritualism allowed some women to squeeze political power from an otherwise disempowering set of circumstances. Through possessions, some succeeded in unlocking for themselves a time-delineated, parallel reality in which patriarchy did not hold total sway, a reality over which Fela exercised little control. This chapter therefore poses a different set of questions of the spirit years, questions that reach beyond authenticity: What political opportunities did possessions present the Queens with? How does our appreciation of the locus of gendered power shift if we view possessions through the registers of ritual/play? What is gained or lost in upholding a singular truth about Kalakuta possessions? What insights do play and premeditation yield in our sensing of the women's active participation in possessions? I argue, following the posture of the women I interviewed, that the possessions were akin to what performance studies scholar Richard Schechner describes as "dark play," a mode of interactive play in which one party is in the dark, unaware they are being played with. Recalibrating the interpretive lens from authenticity to play foregrounds the paradox in which African women are symbolically upheld and revered as mothers and spiritual agents but curtailed from exercising power in key positions in many other aspects of society. In Afrobeat, they were heralded as spiritual vessels but not as intellectuals, bandleaders, or as instrumentalists. Play reveals one of the strategies by which the working-class women in Kalakuta negotiated this constraining dynamic, flexing the space of spiritualism to intervene in the material circumstances of their lives in the commune. Adejonwo's and Serwaa's immersion in possessive states—and the ventriloquism, mimicry, contortion, and bodily recalibration that proceed from these semiconscious states—illustrates the generativity of playing, the ways that dissimulation fundamentally reshaped Kalakuta's power dynamics and retuned Afrobeat music in the early 1980s. In what follows, I examine the contested politics of Kalakuta possessions and their generative role in facilitating revisions to subcultural life in the wake of the invasion alongside their double-edged capacity to elicit strong emotional responses. As generative as possessions were, they also incubated suspicion, betrayal, bitterness, and regret. The spiritual turn exposed fault lines in the commune's social fabric, occasioning the biggest wave of departures. The spirit years reached a toxic climax in 1984 with Fela's imprisonment, segueing to a hazy divorce on grounds of infidelity after his release in 1986. I begin with the spiritual turn to chart this chain of events that, one could argue, both symptomized and hastened the commune's decline throughout the decade. The ensuing narrative sustains this turn of events with the generative changes—sonic, organizational, and ideological—attributable to the women's role in the spiritual turn, actions that likely inspired Fela's humorous conclusion: "I'm surrounded by witches."[5]

Disordering the Early 1980s

In September 1980, Fela dreamed of his mother, FAK, enjoining him to "never give up the struggle"; she reassured him of her support and, critically, of her continued presence "by other means." Torrential rains, Fela came to believe, were one of FAK's manifestations, rains of the kind that fell in Abeokuta on the day of her burial.[6] Possessions were another strategy of FAK's posthumous intervention in Fela's struggle. This vivid dream and the promise of extraterrestrial powers to accompany it required more earthly agents. If FAK's appearance in Fela's dreams laid the groundwork for Kalakuta's spiritual turn, it was a Ghanaian magician, Kwaku Addai, better known as Professor Hindu, who acted as the fulcrum and public face of Afrobeat spiritualism. Often dressed in knickers or trousers and a T-shirt, Professor Hindu might have appeared to lack the pageantry of his magician peers. His most well-known Nigerian counterpart, Professor Peller, often sported a bowler hat and overcoat with matching gloves and a walking stick. If anything about Professor Hindu's self-presentation proclaimed "magician," it was his sideburns: thin at his ears, they amassed into prominent triangles that caressed the corners of his lips. Professor Hindu's bland self-presentation contrasted starkly with his magic tricks and reputation in Nigeria. And some of his most publicized acts occurred at Fela's Shrine or at concerts. At one show, Hindu conjured gold and silver wristwatches from thin air. As the audience looked on, he transformed shreds of cloth into one fully sewn piece, which, an eyewitness wrote, he gifted to a dazed woman in the crowd. The high point of Hindu's spectacle, the act that won Fela's loyalty, was his "killing" and reviving his stage assistant. Four hefty men restrained his assistant while Hindu made quick slashes across the man's throat with a saber knife. The audience gasped as blood gushed from the assistant's neck. In full view of the audience, the oft-repeated narrative goes, Hindu buried his assistant in a freshly dug grave. Hindu asked the audience to reassemble three days later, at which time he revived the once-dead, mud-caked assistant. He repeated this spectacle as part of a fundraiser event at a North London country club in 1984. This time, the burial lasted forty-eight hours. And when concerns were raised about his potential arrest in Europe if he failed to revive his assistant, he retorted, "Brother Fela wanted my capacity through the One-ness to surprise the European."[7] In an audacious expansion of his portfolio to healer, Hindu, riding on Fela's popularity and total belief, boasted to his London audience about his ability to solve any problem—from barrenness to struggling businesses. This healing came at the bargain price of purchasing a magic ring for five pounds.[8] Professor Hindu is the second Ghanaian documented to have performed magic tricks at the Shrine. His predecessor was Sir Afro-Fifi, an agile and multitalented performer who danced, did acrobatics, and performed magic tricks at the Shrine for about two years in the mid-1970s.[9] A key distinction to be drawn between Afro-Fifi and Hindu is that the former presented magics tricks in a

Figure 5.1. Fela poses with Professor Hindu onstage at the Brixton Academy, London, on November 13, 1983. Photo credit and permission: Ian Dickson via Getty Images.

repertoire of entertaining acts, all of which marked his performances unambiguously as staged. Afro-Fifi made no claims to his craft as authentic African spirituality. By contrast, Hindu did; Fela, in a moment of vulnerability, bought what Hindu sold. The domain of Kalakuta's everyday space, the real world, was Hindu's playground. Hindu became a pioneer in blurring the edges between premeditated performance and purely spiritual experience.

Hindu's magic acts onstage might have impressed Kalakutans, but they widely questioned the veracity of the dead assistant spectacle.[10] But attempts to question Hindu's growing influence came with the risk of Fela's rebuke, if not ostracism from the commune. The consolidation of Hindu's grip on Fela was enabled by the magician's keen sense for opportunity as well as by other specific events. A case in point was the false accusation of armed robbery levied against Fela in December 1981. Although lacking any merit, the accusation was enough to bring police to Kalakuta in what became yet another brutal episode. During the raid, a group of policemen repeatedly struck Fela's head with gun butts until he lost consciousness. Fela's survival, as he saw it, was nothing short of a miracle. Sensing an opportunity, Professor Hindu took full credit, claiming to have been "spiritually present when the attack occurred" and offering Fela remote spiritual covering.[11] The men grew closer afterward, so close that Fela noted, "We call ourselves brothers."[12] The magician subsequently accompanied Fela on international tours, sometimes appearing onstage before and after concerts in a vague spiritual role (see fig. 5.1). This arrangement predictably irked concert organizers, who saw Hindu as a nuisance rather than a valuable member of the Egypt 80 entourage.[13] Beyond the obvious scheming that irritated many Afrobeat collaborators, the magician's supposed powers played an important ideological role in Fela's evolving self-concept after the invasion. Hindu vindicated Fela's Afrocentric convictions about the science of African spirituality. To be sure, Hindu was not Fela's only dabbling in so-called African science via spirituality. Fela once courted a Yoruba medicine man who had the professed ability to create spiritually insulated bulletproof jackets. Initial tests at the man's shrine in Ajilete appeared to confirm the claims. Only with the timely intervention of Fela's brother Beko did the musician consent to a second round of tests on two goats. The poor goats perished instantly, leaving Fela speechless and tearful at the realization that the first round of bullets had been blanks.[14] Fela desperately sought spiritual protection at all costs, which underscored his—and Kalakutans'—posttraumatic state. As transparent as the man's claims to spiritual agency appeared to those around Fela, few appreciated the musician's traumatic state in the wake of the invasion as well as the fragility of social relationships within the resettling commune. These vulnerable states facilitated Hindu's quick and systematic power grab. During the invasion, Fela had come face to face with vulnerability and his inability to protect himself against the state, let alone protect Kalakutans, who began questioning the premise of radical social change through music and of Fela's ability to champion said change. Magic and spiritualism were reactionary tools for reckoning with the aftershocks of state violence, for smoothening out the rough edges of a harsh reality.

Hindu's ascendance conformed to Fela's long-held belief in male hegemony. But if a man triggered the spiritual turn, it was Kalakuta women who ultimately defined its outlook and trajectory. "Shortly after Hindu [returned to his base in Ghana]," Mabinuori Kayode Idowu recalled, "'spirit' men and women started to spring up within the organization, most of them claimed to have been possessed by Hindu's 'spirit' or that of Fela's late mother."[15] Adejonwo was the primary conduit for FAK's spirit. But Hindu's "spirit" found a fertile host in Serwaa Akosua. Through newfound spiritual power, the Queens influenced Fela and the organization in ways practically impossible under Africa 70. The spiritual turn was not altogether healthy for the fragile commune, as witch hunting and accusations of disloyalty flourished; alliances were brokered and broken on the whims of the spirits. No one was safe under the spirit regime. Disagreements previously resolved through *yabis* quickly degenerated into bitter retribution, including baseless accusations about plotting to murder Fela. The Ifa priest who presided over the 1978 mass wedding had warned that "for [no] reason whatsoever" should the brides share their dreams with one another.[16] The pronouncement seems to have been designed to shield Fela (and his patriarchal enterprise) from connivance, but in the context of the early 1980s, the weaponization of dreams, visions, and spirits bore out the fragile alliances that bound Kalakuta together as well as the toxic power of fantastic claims to unverifiable truth. Sightings and dreams devastated relationships in the commune.

Potent external pressures are believed to have fueled the toxicity. Fela was scheduled to perform in Milan and Naples on the invitation of *l'Unità*, the Italian Communist Party (PCI) newspaper associated with famed Marxist thinker Antonio Gramsci. The tour introduced Fela's music and ideas to the International Communist Workers. Some Kalakutans were convinced that local and international forces, particularly the Central Intelligence Agency (CIA), had attempted to thwart the tour.[17] They believed that the US agency had not only orchestrated a covert plan to sabotage their Italian tour but also planted an agent, an African American woman named Susan Findlay, in the commune. Findlay is reported to have visited Kalakuta through her connection to a Jamaican journalist based in Lagos. She quickly made the acquaintance of Kalakuta women, growing so close that she occasionally left her young daughter in their care for extended periods. It was not uncommon for nonperformers and non-Kalakutans to accompany Fela on tours, but these people tended to maintain close ties with Kalakutans. The flexibility of the band's travel roster appears to be the basis on which Findlay convinced Fela to allow her travel with the band to Milan. One week before the *Unita* tour, Findlay allegedly made a brief trip to the United States, to leave her daughter in her mother's care. She returned to Kalakuta a day before the trip bearing seven suitcases as gifts to the Queens. Those suitcases were lined with 44.5 kilograms of marijuana. When questioned, she confessed to having planted the marijuana but denied any ties to the CIA. The marijuana nonetheless caused the band problems with Italian police and immigration, generating negative publicity that led the Italian Communist Party to distance itself from Fela.[18] It was during his five-day imprisonment on this trip, in September 1980, that Fela encountered his deceased mother in a dream.[19] Whether Findlay had actual ties with the CIA is less relevant than the fear of CIA infiltration that lingered long after Findlay's departure, even coloring knowledge of past events. During this period,

Fela reflected on the 1977 Kalakuta invasion as being "a CIA plot."[20] The CIA became a spectral presence in the commune, as visitors and long-standing Kalakutans alike accused or found themselves accused of being CIA agents or police spies. Accusations of this kind offered another way to settle scores. Morale dipped as loyal collaborators, women and men alike, found themselves victimized by other people's visions, accusations over which they had little to no control.

The cracks that shaped the intimate lives of Kalakutans at the turn of the decade symptomized broader structural changes in Nigerian society. The paranoia that percolated through communal life might have been symptomatic of posttraumatic stress, but it also reflected a broader dystopia in Nigeria. In December 1983, Muhammadu Buhari led a coup that ousted the civilian regime of Shehu Shagari, whose rise to power through the 1979 elections had been greeted with optimism about Nigerian democracy. Shagari became president at a time when oil prices were again on the rise; thirteen years of military rule were followed by a welcome reorganization of the federal structure.[21] Soon enough, however, nepotism, high-level corruption, and mismanagement sank hopes for a healthy polity. Under Shehu Shagari, the National Youth Service Corps, Federal Mortgage Bank, Central Bank of Nigeria, and Federal Housing Scheme were embroiled in serious corruption scandals, all of which contributed, between 1979 and 1983, to a capital flight estimated at $14 billion.[22] Public perception saw corruption in the Shagari-led Second Republic as dwarfing the scandalous federal contracts awarded during the civil war and under cultural initiatives like FESTAC 77.[23] The colossal failures of the Shagari administration, or Second Republic, provoked not only widespread dismay but also an extensive intellectual dissection. Led by Buhari and Babatunde Idiagbon (his second-in-command), the military charged itself with "correcting" civilian excesses. "The planless, downright incompetence, and irresponsibility that characterized the current government continued," Buhari announced in his takeover speech, "the Nigerian Armed Forces could not stand idly by while this country was drifting towards a dangerous state of political and economic collapse through the continued ineptitude and insensitiveness" of a civilian leadership unwilling to change.[24] While the Buhari-Idiagbon regime was itself short-lived—lasting seventeen months, from December 1983 to August 1985— it nonetheless left a mark; Buhari notably championed the highly unpopular War Against Indiscipline (WAI) program, which focused on restoring public order and changing what Buhari called the Nigerian vices of indiscipline, tardiness, and laziness. WAI permitted soldiers to punish acts of indiscipline, from lateness to work to littering in public spaces. Disorderly queuing at banks or bus stops was punishable by fines or flogging. The imprisonment of prominent activists became a hallmark of Buhari's reign. It is no surprise that the regime's high handedness laid the groundwork for yet another coup, in 1985, by Ibrahim Badamosi Babangida (IBB). Buhari's ousting was greeted with public relief. But after the excitement of the coup subsided, IBB revealed himself to be yet another viciously crafty autocrat, a trickster contorting to the pressures of international finance institutions amid popular resistance to neoliberal transformations. The kind of trickery by which IBB became known was a social performance in which the state sought to secure political legitimacy while curtailing the terrain of cultural and artistic expression available to performers. But as David Donkor writes of this terrain of trickster performance in neoliberal Ghana, performers demonstrate exceptional skill by drawing on those same constrained repertoires to "creatively negotiate and subvert these limitations."[25] The failures of the Second Republic and the two coups that succeeded it played no small role in Nigeria's economic stagnation. Also at play was the global recession triggered by the 1979 Iran-Iraq War, which diminished demand for African exports. Trade in the value of oil dropped from $38 a barrel in 1980 to $15.10 in 1986. As the economy felt the burden of high interest rates, declining demand, and huge debt burdens, other commodities dipped in value as well. In 1982, Africa's debt service (the total cost of repaying the principal and interest on loans) rose to $8 billion, a 400 percent increase from 1975; it became $12 billion in 1983.[26] Low levels of national production and massive debt translated into high unemployment and an increased number of Africans living in absolute poverty. The global recession reverberated throughout Nigerian society. Between 1978 and 1983, Nigeria's foreign debt steadily rose from ₦3.3 billion to ₦14.7 billion, with little to no public services to show for the escalating debt. By 1983, Nigeria's nineteen state governments had a combined debt of ₦13.3 billion. The neoliberal policies of Bretton Woods institutions shaped the climate of economic precarity.[27] These institutions found a willing agent in IBB, who implemented sweeping reforms under the Structural Adjustment Program (SAP). The price was steep. Nigerians saw massive cuts to public spending, the removal of subsidies, and the termination of public programs. A market-oriented ideology supplanted pro-poor policies of the prior two decades, such as free or affordable tuition, agricultural subsidies, and free medical care. The privatization of public goods, a signature mechanism of neoliberal economics, produced a new class of uber wealthy individuals with ties to military elites, deepening the inequity while weakening public institutions tasked with welfare of the majority. The public protests that occurred against these austerity measures were met by violent suppression by the IBB regime, including across Nigerian campuses. The ramifications of the neoliberal turn were extensive, dovetailing with the rise of spiritualism in Kalakuta Republic.

From Africa 70 to Egypt 80: A Momentous Shift

In 1980, Fela renamed his band Egypt 80, marking another shift in the ideas underpinning his convictions.[28] For Fela and for Afrocentric scholars such as Cheikh Anta Diop, ancient Egypt was a site for African redemption. As early as 1978, Fela delivered a lecture at the University of Ife (now Obafemi Awolowo University) in which he lamented the corrosive effects of Christianity and Islam on Africans consciousness alongside the plunder of African wealth by neocolonial economies of extraction. But his disavowal of foreign religions was sometimes incoherent; he embraced Timbuktu, medieval city of Islamic learning in Mali, along with arguments about the African origin of humanity and the Moorish presence in Spain, not leaving out ancient Egypt's influence on Greek philosophy. These convictions were fueled in part by his studying of classic texts in the Afrocentric tradition.[29] Lectures offered Fela a public platform for sharing his critical, if evolving, views of African history, identity, and futures. His explicit goal was to challenge Eurocentric modes of knowledge production that undercut the essential project of collective healing from long histories of exploitation.[30] Fela took his emerging discoveries to campuses to make a case about the complicity of educational institutions in suppressing Afrocentric knowledge. If the demand for Fela's appearances is anything to go by, one might say he partly succeeded in his mission. Between 1980 and 1981 alone, he took part in more than sixty symposia and conferences at Nigerian institutions of higher education. Fela once declared, "I have a PhD in common sense."[31]

Few of Fela's emerging beliefs took hold in the daily rhythms of communal life in Kalakuta. But one strand of ancient Egyptian philosophy did: that of bodily transcendence, the possibility of the soul being liberated from the living body.[32] This belief found a strong equivalence in Yoruba ideas of reincarnation and ancestral worship. (Adejonwo's possession by FAK provides an illustration of this Egypto-Yoruba spiritualism, as does Fela's dedication of an altar in the Shrine to his mother and other heroes of Pan-Africanism.) By the late 1970s, Fela found an ideological home in Afrocentrism, which focused on raising consciousness around the histories of "great African empires and kingdoms, the many slave revolts, pan-Africanism, Negritude,"[33] as well as in African resistance to colonial rule and the Black Power movement in the United States. Fela ultimately distilled these ideological threads into his own formulation of Africanism.[34] While persuasive as a counterdiscourse to Eurocentrism, Fela's Africanism was less alert to its own internal structures of inequity, notably to the patriarchal basis of much of his thinking and the unresolved question of liberation for women. Tejumola Olaniyan has offered that despite his affinity with the urban underclass, Fela was selectively blind to gender.[35] But pinning this ideological shortcoming on crass masculinity and sexism fails to appreciate the full scale of Fela's gender blindness at the turn of the decade. The musician was unable to articulate an idea of African liberation that simultaneously accounted for gender *and* class. Two points suffice on this topic. First, he failed to comprehend how ideological gymnastics themselves reflected class and gender privilege and widened the inequities already embodied by these social locations. In Kalakuta, men were more likely than women to read books and engage openly in intellectual debates. Fela, who personified Kalakuta masculinity, sometimes weaponized ideology to gender segregate within Kalakuta; he did not outright dissuade women from pursuing ideological training under the umbrella of YAP, but he actively resisted the proposition on at least one occasion.[36] Fela resisted women's intellectual pursuits through YAP, concerned that exposing the women to too much critical thinking might undermine his authority and, in time, the Afrobeat enterprise.

Second, not all Queens interpreted their affinity with Afrobeat as purely political resistance. For many, Afrobeat meant upward mobility or a reliable means of artistic livelihood. Fela's search for authentic African spirituality blinded him to the fact that many of the Queens did not share the luxury of class blindness. The working-class women who performed with him likely faced material concerns such as daily survival on the wages of a performer, income insecurity considering the state's interest in thwarting their work, and economic stability. Ancient Egypt was little more than an abstraction. The women were assailed by practical questions of survival for which ideologies yielded no tenable answers. Some of the women, having grown into discerning adults, found themselves asking new questions about their relationship to Fela's work altogether. Fela expected that his working-class allies would arrive to his beliefs at his pace and with his conviction. This was *the* blindness. He learned belatedly that the women's priorities and ambitions were, quite like his own beliefs, evolving. The Queens who rode with the spiritual wave and those who felt victimized by it manifested a similar sentiment—namely, a desire for security and stability after years of giving.

A Different Chorus of Women

In a scathing review of a 1983 concert, a British writer lamented what he interpreted as Fela's self-serving style. Myriad issues piqued said writer about Egypt 80's outing, including the forty-second-long blaring of horns that announced

Fela's entrance, uninspiring saxophone solos by band members, and Fela's lack-luster go at electric piano. Songs lacked a sense of motion, he complained, "no feeling of actually going anywhere except up its own reclining read-end."[37] The writer wondered how the band could have lost its luster in the span of two years after the 1981 UK release of *Black President* and *Original Sufferhead*, both "proud members of the action faction." In the albums, the author observed, "Kuti [kept] the call-and-response interplay between his voice, horn section and female chorus moving along a cracking pace. Solos were kept brief."[38] As hard as it might be to dismiss the writer's complaint about Fela's pageantry, this was the kind of review to which Fela paid no mind because it had the ring of an entitled audience member ill equipped to appreciate the dynamism of Afrobeat music. The writer, in his detailed takedown of the show, missed one of the most critical transformations unfolding before his eyes: the emergence of a dynamic chorus of women.[39] In Africa 70 songs, the women's vocal contributions were often single words or simple phrases delivered with little melodic variation. Horns would dialogue with the chorus "in a series of tight, punchy call-and-response structures" that became increasingly interwoven as they guided the listener to the song's climax.[40] In the thirty-minute-long recording of "Zombie," for instance, the women's chorus alternates between three basic vocal responses: "Zombie," "Joro Jara Joro," and "Yes sir." In "No Agreement" (1976), the responses are "No agreement today, no agreement tomorrow" and "La la la la la." The shift by the mid-1980s could not be more striking. By the 1980s, vocal responses were not only longer but also markedly more nuanced. The women's voices unfolded in lengthier phrases and lusher imageries that conveyed the core sentiment of each song. In "Teacher Don't Teach Me Nonsense," composed in 1984 and released in 1986, the vocal responses are both long and varied, sonic dialogues between voice and instrument that convey complete thoughts.

> Teacher, Teacher o no be na lecturer be your name
> Teacher, Teacher o no be lecturer be the same
> Make you no teach me I dey know
> Person you teach finish yesterday don die today o
> Person you teach finish yesterday don die today o
> Person you teach finish yesterday don die today o
> Me and you no dey for the same category
> Me and you no dey for the same category
> Me and you no dey for the same category
> Me and you no dey for the same category
> Not the same category

That the chorus in Egypt 80 songs contains and conveys narratives has gone unmarked. In "Overtake Don Overtake Overtake (ODOO)," (1990) the chorus continues the practice and sheds new light on the women who comprised it.

> I get my money
> Plan my plan finish
> Start to go go for market
> Start to go go for shopping
> Before I reach market nko o?
> Government show don enter
> My plan don spoil o
> Government show don enter
> My plan don spoil o

The renewed spiritual power wielded by Afrobeat women coincided with and likely contributed to other notable changes, such as the introduction of a second bass and Fela's embrace of Afrocentric makeup in live performance.[41] But the musical structure itself offers a vivid illustration of the women's growing impact. The foregoing chorus in "Overtake" represents one strand in a variety of vocal responses. Drawing on now-popular motifs from earlier Africa 70 songs, Fela intersperses throughout "Overtake" vocal responses such as "Na from back," "Yeye rolling, Zombie o, Zombie yeye rolling," and "Soldier go, soldier come, soldier come, soldier go." Each of these responses accompanies distinct musical segments within the song. The Egypt 80 chorus of women has a voice all its own, and this voice is not simply a counterpoint to or placeholder for Fela's more important critique. The women's chorus, like the collective lives of the individuals comprising it, nestles powerfully into the arrangement of Afrobeat music, placing pressure on the marginal spaces allotted to women in earlier songs. If repetition in Africa 70 was a forward-moving impulse, pushing each song to its climax or ushering Fela's next polemical verse, it now served a different purpose. The Egypt 80 chorus has richness and depth. It twists, stretches, lingers with intention around musical notes that convey emotion. This chorus appears to call attention to its own narrative voice. Here, the women's voices trouble the simplicity and linearity that defined vocal responses in Africa 70. In the early 1980s, Fela's songs were more contemplative and scathing, launching pointed attacks on individuals, corporations, and specific state actors. But these songs also contained a shifting gender terrain rooted in Kalakuta's everyday life as much as in the penetrating impact of the invasion on Kalakutans' psychic lives.

Fela's tendency to dominate singing in Africa 70 diminished with time. It is quite possible that the women singers negotiated an expanded role in Fela's music in the 1980s. The backup singers once challenged Fela about their marginal presence. Kevwe recalled, for example, "I told Fela 'We singers are always at your back. You will sing, and we follow. It is as if we don't have any glory, any star. Let us singers give you one song.'" Fela is said to have obliged the singers' request to compose the chorus for "Everything Scatter" (1975), a song based mostly on the experience of "Fela's people" with police harassment. Considering this precedent, the singers might have found incentive in advocating for more vocal representation in the spirit years, as this period marked a moment of unprecedented influence by women in band activities. And yet, this kind of negotiation is insufficient to account for the seismic shift in the sonic landscape of the women's vocal roles. A more likely explanation can be found in the commune's disorienting encounter with state power in the form of serial raids on the commune. The impact of these assaults was more than symbolic. Kalakuta's destruction and FAK's death forced a reckoning with Fela's incapacity to wrestle the state. Additionally, the patent miscarriage of justice that followed the invasion called into question Fela's utopian belief in music's ability to propel systematic social change. Fela confessed years later that he contemplated suicide for the first and only time in his life shortly after the invasion, particularly after the failure to register his political party in 1979.[42] When the state struck, it aimed to seize literal and symbolic instruments of music—literally by attempting to break Fela's fingers and destroy actual musical assets and symbolically in the bodily violence enacted against Kalakutans. In "Unknown Soldier," the most comprehensive account of the invasion, Fela's voice falters with palpable emotion, a punctum in the state's penetration of the crevices of a body politic. Prior to the invasion, Fela would have considered public displays of emotion, let alone sobbing, to be a show of weakness, a retreat into the feminine. Therefore, his sharing vocal space with the Queens in the post-1977 years offers precious insight into Fela's state of mind. Other subtle and missable sonic shifts bear out this point. Early 1980s songs like "Army Arrangement" and "Coffin for Head of State" continue the practice of simple choral responses, but contained within themselves a new vocal routine, namely the blending of Fela's and the Queens' voices. A gendered separation of voices that characterized the 1970s Afrobeat music aesthetic. This separation embodied Fela's belief in the material exercise of power and social roles through gender differentiation. Early Afrobeat music, with its gendered discrimination of voices, evolved—rather undramatically—into a fluid and "ungendered" call-and-response form in the 1980s, at the precise time when the Queens were garnering influence through spirit possession, a state that implies assuming the voice of another. As the decade progressed, simple responses for women's vocals and gendered vocal segregation became increasingly obsolete aspects of Afrobeat music so that by the end of the decade, complex and blended choral responses defined the genre. "Just Like That" (1990), arguably one of Egypt 80's most sophisticated instrumentations, embodies a thoroughly deconstructed and ungendered notion of call-and-response. The song's interplay between voices and instruments become so intricate that it disorients any attempt to decipher which voice belongs to whom, let along assign them stable genders. If anything, this deconstruction of voice in early 1980s Afrobeat indexes an everyday reality in which the Queens' power waxed and Fela's waned. It is beyond coincidence that the cheeky glorification of misogyny in some of Fela's 1970s classics gave way to a more tempered treatment of the women's vocal presence in 1980s compositions.

The Queens' amplified vocal power had little to no connection to the women's liberation calls that had gripped Nigerian political life since the late 1970s.[43] As IBB sought to negotiate the economic fallout of his neoliberal policies, his regime found unlikely help in his charismatic wife, First Lady Maryam Babangida. Among several initiatives targeting women, Maryam inaugurated the Better Life Programme for Rural Women. Although Maryam Babangida was a widely influential figure in Nigerian public life, her Rural Life signature program became viewed as opportunistic, an initiative that rode the international wave of women's movements more than a true commitment to the cause of Nigerian women. The panache that Maryam brought to the office of first lady— her visibility, confidence, and elegance—arguably achieved more for women's rights than her program. The Rural Life program became a prototype for what scholars like Amina Mama have described as femocracy, an "anti-democratic female power structure which claims to exist for the advancement of ordinary women but is unable to do so because it is dominated by a small clique of women whose authority derive from being married to powerful men."[44] The dividends of such governmental and institutional initiatives are always slow to come for most working-class women, if ever they do.

"Serwaa Was Powerful"

Serwaa Akosua had distinct physical features and a warm personality. When she smiled, her shiny-white teeth contrasted with her glossy dark skin. She had large, glassy eyes and spoke quickly when nervous because she was self-conscious of her grammar. Serwaa had a fuller figure than most of her peers, uncharacteristic for an Afrobeat dancer. But when she moved to Afrobeat music, her agility combined with her well-rounded frame to produce a magnetic expression of sensuality and stamina.[45] Serwaa's dancing established her as a force among the Queens within a short period. She was eighteen when, in March 1978, she traveled from Accra to Lagos. She had contemplated moving to Lagos much earlier at Fela's suggestion that they elope, but fear of her mother's wrath had caused her to delay. When news of the mass wedding filtered to her, she decided to attend partly out of disbelief; then, she became a bride.

Solo dance routines might convey the artistic personas of the individual dancer, but the routines rarely revealed important information about the Queens' status in the Kalakuta hierarchy. Egypt 80's appearance at the 1984 Glastonbury Festival marked a striking exception. In well-circulated archival footage of the concert, Serwaa is situated in the line formation in front of Fela, who observes the women's choreography as he plays the electric keyboard. Serwaa's full body gives her a focal advantage, but she simply gyrates at the center of the group during their freestyle routines. Serwaa gracefully sways her hips to the swinging groove of "Teacher Don't Teach Me Nonsense" (1986) as her fellow dancers take turns performing solo dances to Fela's keyboard solo. Compared to the other dancers in the ensemble, Serwaa exerts herself noticeably less and yet manages to express refinement, her every move a measure of energy and grace. As the concert progresses, Serwaa becomes the only woman standing as others kneel, a position of prominence from which she skips through the pockets of space around the women, initiating what culminates in another synchronized movement of the ensemble's six dancers, including her close friend Omolara Shosanya. This performance, read in its context, offers a glimpse into Serwaa's life beyond the stage. In this instance, choreography does not simply mirror Serwaa's influence—it consolidates it. Simply put, "Serwaa was powerful!"[46] But talent was not the only factor in Serwaa's power. Keeping sight of the relationship between playing onstage and off it, we see multiple negotiations unfolding. If it can be said that a Queen dominated Afrobeat in any era, it was Serwaa in the early 1980s. Fela's daughter, Yeni Kuti, conceded that Serwaa wielded tremendous influence at this time.

Serwaa benefited from and contributed to Professor Hindu's influence. By Omolara's account, Serwaa was instrumental in Hindu's integration into Kalakuta Republic.[47] This role likely explains Serwaa's becoming Hindu's proxy when the magician needed a Kalakuta representative due to his frequent commutes between Lagos and Accra and his ultimate relocation to Ghana. The arrangement saw the magician convey spiritual messages to Fela through Serwaa, who lived in the commune. When Hindu was in Accra, Serwaa occasionally became possessed by his spirit, mediating communication between the two men as the basis of her growing influence. If Serwaa's possessions were bogus, as many Kalakutans suspected, then they offer yet another clear look into misogyny in Afrobeat. That her power derived from ventriloquizing and impersonating Hindu implies that Fela respected Serwaa only because she was possessed by the voice and vision of Hindu, an increasingly absent man. By the same token, Adejonwo garnered respect by being possessed by FAK's spirit; although a woman, FAK was an elite woman with considerate power over Fela. Like her peers, Serwaa used her newfound powers on everything from delivering visions to influencing band administration to settling scores and identifying "enemies" living in the commune. However, the timing of Serwaa's making Nigerian enemies, in early the 1980s, was less than ideal.

Ghana featured prominently in one of the volatile topics of the day: immigration. In 1983, President Shehu Shagari cited economic distress and political unrest in neighboring West African nations like Chad, Niger, Benin, and Ghana to deport 2.5 million undocumented immigrants, the largest deportation exercise Nigeria had seen.[48] The rhetoric used to justify the deportations was a familiar one. According to Shagari, illegal immigrants were not only stealing low-skill jobs from Nigerians but also threatening the nation with "criminal" activities and so-called antisocial behavior. In Shagari's eyes, immigrants had stolen factory and teaching jobs from Nigerians and, within a short span of time, had established themselves in the informal sector to become "roadside mechanics, tailors and domestics servants."[49] Shagari's anti-immigrant rhetoric and policies would disproportionately impact Ghanaians because Ghana was Nigeria's largest anglophone neighbor. Ghanaians made up a significant part of Nigeria's immigrant population, a function of similar colonial histories and attendant legacies in language, education, and legal systems. The vibrant cultural exchange made Nigeria a livable destination for Ghanaians and, when the tides changed, vice versa. Shagari's scapegoating of immigrants was a cop-out for a patently corrupt government confronted with a global recession and lacking intelligent solutions to the struggling economy.[50] Deporting immigrants proved easier than tackling a global recession or systemic rot in public service. (Wanton corruption of Shagari's government was the justification for the Buhari-Idiagbon coup.)

The immigration posture of the Shagari administration impacted the lives of West Africans who had established lives in Nigeria and called Lagos home. Random raids conducted by immigration and law enforcement officers heightened anxiety among West African immigrant communities. These anxieties echoed in intimate relationships in Kalakuta Republic, ripping at the social fabric of a commune already compromised by otherworldly sightings. A xenophobic political atmosphere, combined with Serwaa's power in the band and in commune life, stoked anti-Ghanaian sentiments among Kalakutans. During an impromptu police raid on Kalakuta, for instance, Serwaa accused a YAP member of colluding with the police to deport Ghanaians in the commune.[51] Whether real or invented, such accusations of xenophobia were taken seriously because they fueled division in an already fraught moment. Fela expressed a general sense of responsibility for Afrobeat's West African contingent and protected Ghanaians because he saw them as important allies. According to Lamiley Lamptey, he often treated Ghanaians with greater sensitivity than he did Nigerians.[52] When Fela was arrested in 1984, Kalakutans reportedly evicted Serwaa and ran Professor Hindu out of town, clearing out the commune's two most powerful Ghanaians. The eviction was less a function of their national status than of their role in Fela's imprisonment. The evictions nonetheless blurred the lines between a Kalakuta-specific grievance and the anti-Ghanaian sentiment in the air. The eviction might not have been Serwaa's last rodeo with Kalakuta. Pulchérie Ibilola Hoga recalled living with Serwaa in the years after Fela's release from prison. Not only had Serwaa returned, but she did so more with more power as she claimed the room, Hoga recounted, directly above Fela, an arrangement symbolic of the influence she wielded long after his imprisonment.[53]

Motherhood, Fatigue, and Desertion

In Lola Shoneyin's novel *The Secret Lives of Baba Segi's Wives*, chaos ensues as polygamist Baba Segi weds his fourth wife, a young, college-educated woman named Bolanle, whose profile promptly puts her at crosshairs with the three senior wives of the Alao family. The relationship between the women takes a turn for the worse when Bolanle fails to conceive, a development that reveals her education to be less salient a problem for the Alao women than it initially appeared. Concerned about his inability to father a child with his new wife, Baba Segi seeks medical help, an intervention that reveals him clinically unable to bear children. The discovery calls into question the paternity of his seven children, revealing that the wives' discomfort with Bolanle's arrival pertained to the threat she embodied to the fragile code of silence upheld by the three of them. It becomes clear that none of their children are biologically Baba Segi's, a crisis for a man who has tied his masculine self-concept to his supposed sexual prowess and fertility. Iya Tope recounts to the reader, with devilish delight, her secret path to motherhood: "For three years, that was how I lived: three days of pummeling from Baba Segi and a day of healing from the meat seller."[54] Shoneyin's novel captures with humor, clarity, and suspense each wife's clandestine stories of sex, pleasure, and pregnancy and the delicate compromises brokered between the women, each a custodian of the others' secrets. Shoneyin's work lays bare the pressure imposed on women in polygamies to bear children and hustle for favorable outcomes within the constraints of patriarchy. In Yoruba culture, a premium is placed on motherhood, so pregnancy and maternity assume more than symbolic importance. This point is made clear in one of the wives' reflections: "Iya Femi, the new wife, soon gave birth to a son and there was much celebration. The new mother clapped her knees together when she sat and strutted about like her womb was a goldmine."[55]

These scenes from *The Secret Lives* offer an entry into the value that motherhood carried for Afrobeat women in the spirit years. A mix of postinvasion trauma and a growing sense of uncertainty left many Queens searching for steady ground. The desire to become mothers increasingly factored in their growing disillusionment with the structural premise of their entanglement to Fela. Asked in 1981 if she was happy, Aduni chuckled before forming a reply: "Yes. But I want baby. Baby is number one."[56] Raised in polygamous homes and a culture that placed a premium on motherhood, the Queens were socialized into seeing motherhood as a valuable status to attain. This posture was further intensified by the Yoruba practice in which younger siblings and children, not mothers (or wives), inherit a man's wealth in the event of his demise.[57] Fela's rhetoric intensified what might have been a latent desire for some. Asked about plans for children right after the wedding, he responded with a generic interpretation of so-called African culture: "Sterility is not part of African culture. Any marriage that is not blessed with children has not received the benediction of the gods."[58] And yet with each passing month following the wedding, Kalakuta saw anything but babies. The absence of children in the first three years laid bare the Queens' precarious affinity with the Kuti family. It equally exposed the gravity of the union they had casually brokered at the mass wedding. The women's reproductive lives, which should have been personal, promptly became the subject of media speculation. Journalists began questioning the noted absence of children since the mass wedding. It took three years for "the gods" to respond. By late 1980, only Funmilayo Onilere, a dancer with a "proud, unapproachable bearing," was pregnant.[59] Funmilayo had her son in August 1981 and named him Olikoye, a choice that, as suggested in chapter 2, was intimately linked with her impersonation strategy of FAK (Olikoye was the name of Fela's elder brother). Funmilayo was devastated when, at eight months old, Olikoye died suddenly in April 1982. Motherhood was a distant possibility for most women, many of whom took flight from Kalakuta picking up the pieces of a life that began out of teenage defiance and adventure.[60] Motherhood might not have been the sole consideration in a woman's decision to separate from or remain with Fela and his work, but it appeared to be a factor. In 1983, Seun and Motun were born two weeks apart; their mothers were Fehintola and Najite, who were among the roughly five Queens still affiliated with the band well into the 1990s. In other words, no known Queen who had children with Fela made a total separation from his work. The presence of babies recalibrated the relationship between the two mothers, who grew closer as they took care of one another's children. It also offered nonmothers an opportunity for bonding as they participated in collective childcare duties.

There was a nagging perception that Fela, not unlike Baba Segi, was unable to bear children. This was a sticking point because, unlike the fictional patriarch, Fela's incapacity was self-induced, as some women were convinced that the musician used traditional herbs to manipulate his fertility. Even more sensitive was the fact that some women had abortions when they got pregnant (by Fela or perhaps other lovers). As girls and young women ostracized by family and society, the Queens had limited resources to make informed decisions about their sexual and reproductive health. They might also have been targets of sexual exploitation by medical personnel. What damage ensued from these abortions is incalculable. In a masterstroke of contradiction, the musician declared in a 1984 interview, "A woman's duties in life is to have babies and organize the home."[61] While it remains unclear whether the women felt coerced to have abortions, the question is a murky and dark aspect of their entanglement with the Afrobeat project.

A core feature of communes lies in their fragility and "the relative absence of structural underpinnings to sustain them, when, and *if*, they become problematic."[62] The 1977 attack on the Kalakuta commune rocked belief in the viability of the commune and the fragile relationships that held it together, amplifying anxieties about another impending invasion. By sabotaging the band's ability to produce and perform after the destruction, the state sought to cripple the structural foundations on which communal life rested. The spiral into rogue spiritualism had a destabilizing effect on weakened communal ties, as did the state's unrelenting assaults on the women's bodies and psyches. During the December 1981 raid of the commune on fabricated charges of armed robbery against Fela, the women found themselves on the receiving end of state violence yet again. The police arrived unannounced in five trucks, surrounded the house, and teargassed Kalakutans out of hiding.[63] They clubbed residents, whipped the women with chains, and mishandled the babies. A teary-eyed Alake stood in the wreckage left by the state invaders to share an impassioned account of events: "We do not even know what happened. We don't know what

Figure 5.2. Fehintola straps a baby to her back, likely her son, Seun, as she gazes past the camera. Photograph taken in Paris, circa 1985. Photo credit and permission: Bernard Matussière.

offense Fela has made yet now [*sic*] because they just came, beating everybody up; because this is what they've been doing. . . . They do worse things for us here in Africa, and nothing we could do about it. . . . And they know Fela it is only Fela that is preaching about all the injustice they've been doing. That is why they always bounce [*sic*] on Fela. They're always after Fela and they don't have anything to hold on him. Fela is an innocent man."[64] Visibly agitated, Lamiley Lamptey addressed the mistreatment of the women and babies. The policemen were "throwing [pregnant women] from their trucks, down and up. Five months old child for that matter; throwing him up and down." Kevwe also suffered at the hands of the police, this time in her seventh month of pregnancy. Clutching her protruding stomach from a *buba* top, she protested: "What have I done? And I am pregnant! What have I done to these people? [A] seven-month-old pregnancy! I have not done anything wrong."[65] Grappling with the gravity of the women's words requires examining the long trajectory of physical and emotional battery they endured. Kevwe's use of the personal "I" against the collective "we" as well as her repeated questioning illustrates how some women experienced state violence as simultaneously personal and collective experiences. While less spectacular than the earlier destruction of the commune, the 1981 invasion illustrates the Queens' continued persecution, endurance, and survival of relentless state-sponsored violence. This snapshot from Flori and Tchalgadjieff's documentary *Fela Kuti: Music Is the Weapon* offers one of few surviving audiovisual documents of the Queens' real-time articulation of their victimization by law enforcement. It was Alake who gave voice to this aspect of the Afrobeat experience that often goes unremarked. Unacknowledged suffering paints a grim portrait of the Queens' situation within intersecting patriarchies, illustrated on the one hand by state violence and on the other by Fela's monopoly of the postinvasion narrative, a critical outlet of emotional release and argument for victimhood, personhood and humanity. One must empathize with the Queens who, suffering violence fatigue, saw the latest attack as an opportunity to cut their losses and negotiate a difficult reunion with their families, who they had left for years. The new mothers might have seen an incentive to endure the onslaught. Others did not. They left.

The protracted improvised living arrangements after the 1977 raid likely made the decision to leave less tricky than it might have been. The architecture of the new Kalakuta Republic supplied the privacy the women needed to decide on their futures. Fela scrambled to find housing for the commune after the burning of Kalakuta Republic. After a failed attempt at resettling in Ghana, Fela and the crew returned to Lagos. Unable to afford hotels for a contingent of at least forty people, they squeezed into an apartment rented by J. K. Braimah.

(Braimah, who had been "father" of the brides at the mass wedding, continued to support Fela during these tough times, sometimes at a huge personal expense.) Existing tenants evacuated on the arrival of Kalakutans, some forfeiting what remained of their already paid rents. Tenants with children vacated especially quickly.[66] Kalakutans took over the evacuated apartments as the former occupants "voluntarily" made space.[67] It was an incursion into a relatively serene residential area in Ikeja. The new Kalakuta offered a spatial configuration ill suited to collective living. Dispersed across eight apartments, the communal arrangement was fragmented, decentralizing power. Relationships, like the apartments themselves, were amenable to compartmentalization.[68] Mothers shared an apartment as well as childcare resources. Women without babies banded together, crossing over to one another's apartment to chitchat, socialize, or exchange notes about ongoing events—not least about whatever shenanigans were unfolding in the compartmentalized commune. They interacted with Fela during rehearsals, live performance, for leisure, or by choice. The apartments made possible the choice to opt out of shared spaces; this made privacy a luxury the women could afford. Living in separate but linked apartments clarified shared interests more than it stoked opportunities for conflict that came from constantly sharing space and competing for limited resources with others. The new architecture and the social interactions said architecture allowed contributed to why Kalakuta spiritualism cut so deeply into the fault lines of communal life that emerged more clearly after the invasion. In these separate apartments, sore relationships festered. Old rivalries, already tested by spiritualism, grew more fragile. The architecture did not simply separate a group that had once thrived on close communion; the rooms became quiet connivers in stoking a sense of individualism and isolation. Kalakutans began separating themselves from Fela, his ideas, and his work, and there was no shortage of reasons to make the sometimes-difficult decision to leave: fatigue and trauma from state brutality, uncertainty about the future, the desire to become a mother (for some women), the mistrust and retribution caused by spirit possessions. The feelings produced by these undesirable turns in the Afrobeat story are captured in a pithy response by an unnamed dancer. She encapsulated the women's morale in the early 1980s when asked about half-heartedness in her dance routines: "Shortly before parting ways with Fela I remember making a criticism of one of his female dancers that she was no longer the fiery dancer she used to be and in response [sic], she asked me if I would encourage my daughter to take up a dancing career with Fela's organization as it was."[69] The exchange took place right before the asker, Mabinuori Kayode Idowu, a male YAP member, parted ways with Egypt 80. By 1981, fifteen of the twenty-seven

brides remained. This number had thinned even further by 1986, when Kalakuta housed only six Queens alongside new women performers, whose arrival
boosted the overall number of women noticeably in the early 1990s. By 1993,
Kalakuta housed an estimated seventy women, a figure resembling the commune's population, if not its spirit, from the mid-1970s.[70] Yet the most decisive
movements were those of the original Queens who separated from Afrobeat in
the early 1980s. For his part, Fela developed a renewed appreciation for the men
in his family as Queens and male comrades, like Idowu and Ghariokwu, separated from his organization. His younger brother, Beko, and his first son, Femi,
respectively had acted as Egypt 80 manager and bandleader during a period of
imprisonment; they became his most reliable allies. But Femi quickly asserted
his desire for artistic autonomy when he launched his own band, Positive Force.
Fela, who had been grooming Femi to take over Egypt 80, was unhappy with
the separation, though he later accepted his son's move toward independence.
Femi adapted his father's model by recruiting his sisters, Yeni and Sola, as his
first dancers. The women in Femi's band were not known by the now-fraught
label of "Queens"; they were "Positive Angels." Their artistic roles mirrored
those of the Queens.

As the years wore on, Fela grew understandably more cynical about music's
ability to incite revolutionary change. A close friend recalled how Fela was suddenly "found sleeping or playing sax at home with women around him or performing at the Africa Shrine . . . rarely gave press conferences or press releases
like he used to do."[71] Fela, who had once made vibrant public appearances at
campuses and symposia, voraciously consumed news, and expressed his views
in instrumental solos, became reclusive—in the words of his daughter, "a her-
mit."[72] His battle weariness shines through in "Look and Laugh" (1986), a song
in which Fela reflects on his silence on political events.

> Many of you go dey wonder why, your man never sing new song
> Many of you go dey wonder why, your man never write new tune
> My brother no be so, tabi, no be say I wan keep quiet
> My brother no be say I no wan write new song for you to make you think
> and happy
> Wetin I dey do be say
> Wetin I dey do be say
> I say wetin I dey do seh?
> I dey look and laffu

Fela and the chorus exchange a sardonic laugh—"hu hu hu hu / ha ha ha ha"—
that has a haunting quality. This laugh evolves into long, complex, ruminative

instrumental renditions in later works like "Confusion Break Bone" (1990) and "Just Like That" (1990).

Waiting: Winnie and the Queens

The peculiar combination of gendered state repression and public moral scrutiny of the private lives of activist women enables a comparative reading of the Afrobeat Queens and South African antiapartheid activist Winnie Mandela. Heroic accounts of these women's lives as activists are usually trailed by the titillating scandal of their refusal to wait for imprisoned husbands. The impossibly lengthy imprisonment of Nelson Mandela by the apartheid government and Fela's imprisonment by the Buhari regime galvanized public interest in their release. But the delicate negotiations and personal strain of these high-profile imprisonments on the lives of the women closest to these male figures has often gone unaccounted for. The stories of Winnie Mandela and the handful of Afrobeat Queens who did not leave during the spirit years illustrate how society constructs women as moral failures for ostensibly succumbing to the flesh.

Although relatively brief, Fela's imprisonment in 1984 became his longest stint in prison and it was impactful for Afrobeat women. His imprisonment by the Buhari regime was the direct culmination of Kalakuta spiritualism, triggering yet another opportunity for the remaining Queens to evaluate their relationship to the Afrobeat project. Many pinned the imprisonment on Professor Hindu and Fela's blind belief in the magician's abilities. Egypt 80 was scheduled to perform in New York, Los Angeles, and San Francisco in what was supposed to be Fela's return to the United States after fifteen years. Nigerian customs officers detained Fela, en route to the US tour, after discovering £1,600 on him. The officers claimed that he had not properly declared the cash, constituting sufficient grounds for detention. On October 8, 1984, the state charged and found Fela guilty of currency smuggling, sentencing him to five years in prison and forfeiture of the £1,600 in addition to a ₦2,000 fine.[73] It was clear that the currency smuggling charge was bogus; the cash could have been accounted for by the size of the Egypt 80 entourage, and the officers failed to produce the currency declaration form Fela had filled. And yet Fela was aware of the risks of holding such a large amount of cash in the Murtala Muhammed Airport. This is where Professor Hindu factored in: the magician had offered his assurances that the cash would be invisible to custom officers. Both men were misguided.

When men become political prisoners, their absence conjures moral predicaments for the partners they leave outside the prison walls. Fela's eighteen-month imprisonment meant different things for the remaining wives. For some, his absence offered an opportunity to make a difficult exit. Difficult because the question of *leaving to* what was not less thorny than *staying for* what? Others held on to faith about what they hoped would be a short prison time, but days and weeks dragged into months and soon, a year. In early 1986, rumors began circulating about Fela's impending release. The few Afrobeat women who had seen what was supposed to be a quick arrest become a year-long imprisonment were reasonably skeptical. Those who kept the faith promised to, on their reunion, "eat him raw" in their excitement.[74] Fela was released in April 1986 following pressure from local and international groups. One eyewitness reported how, in the company of at least two thousand fans, the women "hugged, kissed and gaped at him in one moment of uncontrollable joy."[75] A crowd of awe-stricken fans carried the musician shoulder-high, chanting his praises. Political imprisonments are often explicit attempts at containing dissident voices whose agitation lays claim to the public good. The dynamic of selflessness marks them as deserving of all kinds of sacrifice, and who better to make this sacrifice than the partners, often women, left behind? This dynamic of political imprisonment colored judgment of the women's every action in moral terms. Kalakutans, both men and women, who had been contemplating separation from the band and commune but who separated while Fela was in prison became traitors (an accusation that had become a staple of the spirit years). Those who remained but were considered disloyal also found themselves under scrutiny. The absence of a husband who had become a political prisoner somehow authorized moral scrutiny of the women; absence in this case was grounds for surveillance, by self or society.

No sooner was Fela free than a silent war began brewing. News had filtered to Fela during his imprisonment in Maiduguri that the Queens were romantically involved with other men. Even if substantiated, salacious rumors (especially of the sexual kind) that circulate around relationships infiltrated by political imprisonment derive their substance less from fact than from relentless suspicion that more must have transpired in that pesky absence and the pleasure of publicly witnessing the intimate fallouts of political activism. "I was faithful to them," Fela vented.[76] The complaint foregrounds, in its rich irony, the impossibility of innocence for the women he left behind. If it was indeed true that the women reclaimed authorship of their sexual lives in his absence, then his complaint underscores the limits Fela imagined of women's erotic freedom: they could be free and sexually liberated only on terms he authorized. This betrayal, following Fela's logic, had little to do with betrayal of a political cause per se and everything to do with the women's claiming sexual autonomy in his absence. For a long time, they had been presented as proxies of Afrobeat and extensions of his power. Their ostensible sexual lives in his absence presented a rupture to that idea. Still, the accusation of infidelity itself reveals the expectation of unfaltering fealty from women whose husbands go absent without duration, the waiting wives who face ruthless judgment when they slip or are suspected to have.

Winnie Mandela was a high-profile waiting wife. In 1964, Nelson Mandela was sentenced to life imprisonment by South Africa's apartheid regime. His sentencing was the beginning of what would become a twenty-seven-year jail term, most of which Mandela spent on Robben Island and during which he was permitted to receive letters only once every six months. While Mandela was in jail, Winnie led an armed, grassroots resistance against the racist regime that deployed a devilish array of tactics to police and systematically constrain Black South African social life. Surveillance, the disappearance of activists, and violent suppression of popular protests were familiar pastimes of the apartheid regime. Winnie continued to champion the agenda and oversaw the activities of the African National Congress (ANC), the political party committed to enfranchisement of Black Africans and mixed-race persons and, later, to the dismantling of apartheid through a combination of guerrilla warfare and political organizing.[77] The heroic ambition of ANC's early struggle and Winnie Mandela's specific role in its potency were dogged by scandals, all of which paled in comparison to a widely reported affair with a young lawyer. When Nelson Mandela was eventually released from prison in 1990, stories of Winnie's dalliance competed with and, depending on who was doing the telling, overshadowed tales of her heroic struggle against a violently racist regime. South African examples of women waiting on absent husbands abound beyond Winnie, yet she embodies the most preposterous instance. In *The Cry of Winnie Mandela*, Njabulo Ndebele poignantly describes the ache that attends this form of lingering: "Departures! They give birth to waiting. In that indeterminate space of waiting, women live through unending spells of anxiety, loneliness, longing, wishing, desiring, hoping, doubting. . . . Waiting. Sitting at the edge of the bed after a bath in the evening. Alone in the bedroom. Waiting. Letting one's hands slide over ointment spread lovingly over the body. Tarrying over the breasts. Hugging them. Sliding down the torso, over the thighs, and down to the knees. Then cutting between the knees, up through the thighs, parting them, until they yield on their own."[78] The women husbands leave behind are held to impossible standards of patience and sexual fidelity, standards from which men are forgiven or excused. In "From Penelope to Winnie Mandela: Women Who Waited," Betine van Zyl Smit reads Ndebele's novel as a feminist intervention that, in freeing Penelope (Odysseus's mythical wife in the Greek epic) from the bondage of unconditional waiting, frees women like Winnie, confronted with similar expectations.[79] Ato Quayson intervenes in reflections of Winnie's life by arguing that the true and deep conflict she confronted was the pull between iconicity and being human. Quayson, not unlike Ndebele, embraces the flesh and its dictates: "did [Winnie] ever transcend her abject solitude and manage to reach the simple delirium of being desired whole and in her entirety, with her tired and aching body, her snappy ill temper, her arrogance and pride, and all the flaws that flesh is heir to? What stray longings must have flitted tremulously across her body and soul at such moments?"[80] The Queens might not have had Winnie's stature and certainly have not been subject to extensive scholarly ruminations about their desires in Fela's absence, but they shared the moral policing of grappling with flesh when husbands become political prisoners—let alone high-profile ones. Fela's eighteen-month prison term paled in comparison to Nelson Mandela's twenty-seven years, but the toll of his imprisonment is comparable to Mandela's precisely because of the uncertain duration of absence. The Buhari regime was under no obligation and showed little interest in seeing Fela released at the end of his prison term. It took the ousting of the Buhari regime, by IBB, for Fela to regain freedom. The element of uncertainty in the question of "how long" unites the choices confronting the women in these contexts.

This said, there is a way in which emphasizing how women did not wait elides other aspects of their lives in which they likewise refused to wait—notably, their refusal to put a hold on the task of political organizing in the absence of imprisoned partners. Winnie was responsible for keeping the resistance against white minority rule alive throughout Nelson Mandela's imprisonment. Her commitment to dismantling apartheid for democracy and Black majority rule remained. "The freedom of this country," Winnie argued, "was attained by the masses of this country.... It was attained by the children who gave their lives in [Soweto in] 1976, who faced machine guns with stones and dustbin lids. It was attained by women who were left to fend for their families. They fought the enemy! We are the ones who fought the enemy physically, who went out to face their bullets. The leaders were cushioned behind bars. They don't know. They never engaged the enemy on the battlefield."[81] Winnie's charge is reminiscent of how Kalakuta inhabitants, including women, resisted a 1974 police invasion of the commune by "hurling stone, bottles, and branches."[82] Similarly, while Fela was in prison, the women sustained the band's artistic activity at the Shrine. Vivian Goldman, who witnessed an Egypt 80 performance by Femi Kuti, noted that "Fela may have been absent, but the dancers were grinding in their usual spot."[83] Important differences exist between Winnie and the Queens, but the parallels are striking. Like Fela's informants, prison guards placed in Nelson Mandela's cell newspaper clippings containing "unflattering news" of Winnie's private life. Meanwhile, they intercepted letters between Winnie and Nelson for most of his prison term.[84] The clear strategy was to feed political prisoners, desperate to hear from loved ones, negative news about their wives' conduct. In Fela's case, his male allies, many of whom may have felt sidelined during the spirit years, delivered news with evangelical fervor. Whatever story was not delivered to him in prison was served on his release. Toward the end of Fela's prison term, there were already signs in Nigeria that the apartheid regime was losing its grip and seeking out moderate elements in the ANC with whom to negotiate South Africa's transition to democratic rule.[85] It is no coincidence that the timeline of Winnie's and the Queen's wait overlapped; Nigeria and South Africa were confronting qualitatively different and yet familiar kinds of coloniality involving the modern African state, whose tactics of domination and control produced specific gendered subjects and subjectivities. Political repression through imprisonment pierced the private lives of women in ways that make for striking parallels under said conditions.

"Go NOW, Why Wait?": A Knotty Divorce

In Kalakuta, grave issues often masked themselves as trivial. A journalist, visiting the commune, painted a scene that illustrates this point quite strikingly. On the day of the journalist's visit, Kalakuta women were reportedly sleeping on mattresses or "lazily" applying facial makeup when the journalist noticed and asked about a handwritten sign on the wall: "Go NOW, Why Wait?" It was harmless, Fela responded, "Now and again a few of my wives tell me they are 'leaving' so I decided to put it there. It's all 'yabis.' . . . The notice is 'fun really,'" he added.[86] Quotation marks around "fun really" imply the journalist's skepticism about Fela's dismissal, a skepticism they ensured to document in print. The sign sat beside decorative pieces such as a painting of Kwame Nkrumah and four posters for symposia and lectures across schools. Another sign, this one less subtle, had a similar query: "Take Your Choice:—In or Out?" This one provoked one woman enough that she took it down.[87] The initial sign might have been used in jest, but it revealed the tensions that bubbled beneath the surface in the years following the invasion and, more importantly, Fela's thinly veiled anxiety about people departing his organization. In a commune that disguised much of its internal tensions, the sign spoke volumes. The disaffection that hung in the air after the destruction of the inaugural Kalakuta festered.

The sign was an attempt to name and tame the tension, a desperate effort at resolution, a desire to quickly confront a loss that seemed at once inevitable and never arriving. The improvised sign—handwritten, easily ripped from the wall, dismissed as trivial—was both performative and consequential. Whatever it hoped to achieve, its repercussion became far reaching for the women who idled around it. The precise wording "Go NOW, Why Wait?" was what Yeni, Fela's daughter, quoted when explaining Fela's divorce of the Queens three decades later. The fragile sign and its memorable words declared, for some, the disillusion of the 1978 marriage.[88]

Even if we accept the premise that Fela divorced the Queens, it remains a peculiar end to the marriage. But the sign eludes an easy reading, especially not one of definitive divorce. It ends in a question—"Why Wait?"—when "Go NOW" (with all the capitalization implies) would have sufficed. Its open-ended question defies resolution. This ambivalence, like much of social life in Kalakuta, invites and demands multiple interpretations. Could it be read as an invitation to dialogue or as Fela's absolution of responsibility, shifting the moral burden and its attendant risks to the women with legitimate reasons to not wait? Was it a flat-out separation? After said divorce, several women not only remained in Kalakuta but also continued to perform their artistic roles with no discernible change. Even Olaide Babayale, who left Kalakuta for a job at the Ministry of Health, resisted the finality implied by divorce. "I never left Fela's side," she argued, upholding an enduring affective connection with Kalakuta and the band. That she occasionally danced for Egypt 80 after her departure supports her idea of belonging even when physically separated. Her argument underscores the fluid traffic in bodies, the constant going and coming that bookmarked Kalakutan contingency, and the flexible relationships that stitched together the lives of its constituents.

The notion that a divorce happened between Fela and the Queens remains a hotly contested aspect of Afrobeat women's history. "Fela never divorced us," Olaide swore, while Fela's son Femi declared the exact opposite at every opportunity: "He divorced all his wives including my mother."[89] Omolara, a dancer, corroborated Femi's claims, but she agreed with Olaide's view of a deep affinity that transcended any settled notion of total separation: "Before Fela died, he had divorced everyone of us. . . . I remained in his house because Fela was very nice to me and to all of us."[90] Pulchérie Ibilola Hoga was a dancer in Egypt 80 during this period of exits; she had a firsthand view of life in the commune. On the ostensible dissolution of the marriage, Hoga explained: "A lot of people left, a lot of wives too. That's why Fela said that he doesn't believe in marriage anymore." Did he divorce them? I asked pointedly, to which Hoga responded in her French-inflected English, "I don't know because you you know it's, um, an African marriage. No no divorce."[91] A full-bellied laughter followed her recollection of the episode. At the heart of these disparate readings of what transpired in those years of tension and uncertainty lie deeply consequential questions with real stakes in the present. The question of divorce scaffolds questions of propriety and legacy, questions about what forms of Afrobeat coupling deserve celebration and what forms merit punishment and erasure. These questions are linked to what exact point in the past the Queens can legitimately narrate themselves into the Afrobeat story and tie their grievances. The balance of power has since tipped in favor of the influential Ransome-Kuti family, an elite lineage that has historically embodied professional excellence, public service, and Western training and deportment, values cherished by Lagos elites and occasionally rewarded by the state. To win the debate about divorce is to dictate the parameters of ownership and belonging; divorce named who was a Kuti and who had ceased to be (if ever they were)—who could stake a claim to Afrobeat wealth and who could not.

Fela's ambiguity fed the confusion. There were practical reasons for his ambivalent posture. For one, a strong declaration of intent to separate from the Queens would have spelled professional suicide. Men were critical collaborators for Afrobeat, but the women filled a distinct niche in Fela's work. For example, when disgruntled men instrumentalists separated with the band, Fela trained new ones to replace them. Fela could also learn new instruments to fill an instrumentalist's absence or convert a YAP Boy into a rhythm pianist. He deployed all these strategies when some of his finest instrumentalists separated from Africa 70 in Berlin in 1978. Although the women were fungible in the same ways, they could not be done without altogether, nor could Fela fill in for them. If the late FAK's mentorship had convinced Fela to incorporate women more intentionally into his music and live performance in the early 1970s, he retained the women because experience had shown that they—the women, with their collective personalities, individual stories, temperaments, troubles, and talents—were *the* magic of Afrobeat. Afrobeat's explosion into a cultural, Pan-African expression of Black creativity occurred only after women gave it vocal, political, and erotic edge beginning in the late 1960s with Dele Salami and the generations of women that followed her. But it had been a decade since the women had "invaded" the African popular music scene by way of Afrobeat, and with fame and wealth in the mix, their transformative and sustaining roles in Afrobeat might have become a distant memory. Still, if Fela could have sustained his work without women collaborators, he would have. The serious accusations of infidelity levied against the women provided a convenient opportunity to act, and to do so unambiguously. Fela faltered. This inability to act decisively, I would argue, was not a choice made of kind consideration but rather an admission of his own dependence on them. The indecision contained the recognition of his work's heavy reliance on the undervalued labor, sacrifice, creativity, and resilience of the women whose combined presence endowed Afrobeat music with its edge. Men instrumentalists usually maintained a degree of professional detachment from Fela's work and proclivities. The women, on the contrary, were poised to blur the boundaries of work, leisure, activism, and romance. They were more likely than the men to take risks, or to be asked, that exceeded the job description of a working artist. They occasionally worked for free or, during hard times, for low wages in exchange for housing and feeding. This expectation was practically impossible to extend to men in the band. Therefore, the wall sign that assumed retrospective significance might be read in at least two ways. It was deliberately ambiguous because such a posture absolved Fela of any compunction toward the women with whom he continued to produce music. The question "Why Wait?" authorized his retreat from responsibility. Many of the Queens needed no rhetorical gymnastics; they made their choices known with their departure. On the other hand, the sign could be taken at face value, a window into a moment of tension in the commune, a sign meaning no more than yabis.

Beyond Betrayal: Fela and Sankara

When the commune relocated into Fela's newly completed three-story home at 5 Gbemisola Street, Ikeja, it was a shadow of its former self. Its collective spirit sagged from the weight of the spirit years, relentless state violence, uncertainty, and high turnover of talents in the commune. By 1986, notable YAP Boys and most of the Queens had left the organization. A disillusioned Fela compared the exodus of his trusted allies to the betrayal of Thomas Sankara, assassinated in 1987 in a plot hatched in part by Blaise Compaoré, his longtime compatriot and second-in-command.[92] Sankara was Burkina Faso's widely beloved head of state who had set for himself the task of breaking his landlocked country's colonial ties to France and setting it on the path of self-sufficiency. The comparison that Fela made of himself to Sankara was uncannily spot-on in some ways and totally misinformed in others. The comparison was accurate because the men shared a comparable vision of African liberation that resonated widely among the oppressed class. Both men also saw in African elites the same image that Frantz Fanon did, viewing them as cowardly, intellectually lazy, and spiritually bankrupt prime agents in the tragic mishaps of African nations.[93] Sankara and Fela were mutual admirers of one another's contribution to a new order, and in spite of the progressive aspects of their political visions they also shared an unlikely impatience for dissidence within their ranks. Sankara once neutralized the efforts of teachers to unionize, responding to their demands by laying off thirteen hundred striking teachers. He instituted a grassroots justice system that became a platform for witch hunts. These blips in his stellar resume of public service notwithstanding, Sankara has remained a beacon for progressive leadership in Africa. His murder was widely attributed to Blaise Compaoré and the powerful system of patronage put in place by French neo-colonial interests.[94]

Where Compaoré betrayed Sankara, Fela felt betrayed by the young collabo-rators who deserted his work. However, the nature of betrayal was not Fela's sole reason for drawing a comparison between himself and Sankara; he viewed Sankara as a charismatic peer in the political struggle for African liberation. But the differences between them were as striking as the similarities. The two figures conceived of women's liberation in radically different ways. The Burki-nabe leader pursued a rigorous campaign for gender equality in both public and domestic life. Sankara aggressively sought out qualified women for high-rank-ing public positions, recruited them as military personnel, encouraged men to actively participate in the daily running of their homes, and undermined indigenous practices and institutions that perpetuated sexism, especially with respect to access to arable land.[95] These are arguably the most radical gender reforms pursued by any African head of state to date. Fela publicly opposed all these ideals. The political revolutions imagined by Fela and Sankara might have been derailed by their reluctance to concede to the agitations of their constitu-ents. But Fela had a legendary capacity for nihilism—a capacity summarized in his stubborn belief in a revolution that second-guessed women's liberation. This nihilism put the Afrobeat musician in a different class than Sankara.

"Before Things Were Going to Fall Apart": Arrival and Departure for Mary Umude

Serial departures exposed Afrobeat's need for amateur and low-cost perform-ers. Risk-taking young women who were likely to be sexually expressive were prime workers for Fela's brand of music. But supply of this kind of gendered labor grew less steady as the years wore on. Now mature women, Queens who had not parted ways with the commune were subdued by motherhood, fatigue, or dreams of an alternative to subcultural living. Attracting fresh female talent presented challenges, and Fela's fading charisma did not help the recruitment drive. Fela had lost luster to age, suffered fatigue and disillusion from the repeated assaults, and was simply not the musician he had once been. Clearly, physique and charm were not the only obstacles to recruiting new women. The brutality endured by the Queens had become public knowledge, as had stories of Fela's material and legal losses from the invasion. The era of starstruck young women fleeing the comfort of middle-class homes for a life of rebellion seemed over. Fela hatched a plan. "There weren't enough girls [so] Fela had to give money to his boys to recruit girls." Majemite Jaboro, who helped in Fela's postimprisonment recruitment drive, recalled that some of the new girls were likely former sex workers "who lived in local brothels."[96] Kevwe, Najite, and Fehintola, women whose journeys to Afrobeat had been characterized by rebellion, soon shared the stage with a wave of new arrivals, women mostly in their early twenties. These new arrivals infused new energy into a struggling band. Like before, few migrated from out of state.

Mary Umude (fig. 5.3), a young woman from Delta state, was among this new cohort of performers. Mary Umude arrived at Kalakuta shortly after Fela's prison release in April 1986. She traveled from Delta on the advice of her elder brother. He had written a letter to her suggesting she relocate to Lagos. The sparse letter contained an address: 7 Gbemisola Street, Ikeja. Mary boarded a bus to Lagos, discovering on arrival that the address was the third and final iteration of Kalakuta Republic. Mary's brother, whom she later advised to separate from the commune on the grounds of his misbehavior, earned a living running errands for Queen Najite (who was now known as Mama Motun, Motuns' mom). Fela welcomed Mary to Kalakuta and to Lagos. But it was "big sister" Kevwe's promise to take care of her that really counted. Sleeping arrangements in Kalakuta entailed five or six women in a room, and Mary shared a room with Kevwe, Lamiley Lamptey, Adejonwo Oguntiro, and a woman she simply remembers as Adesuwa. Kevwe eased Mary's transition into communal life, showing her around Lagos and teaching her the ropes in Egypt 80. When the question arose about becoming an Egypt 80 performer, Mary considered the choice an easy one. She convinced herself that her slender frame put her at a distinct disadvantage to the dancers with curvaceous bodies (a notable shift from Africa 70, whose women, per Fela's preference, tended to be slender). Mary became a singer, enjoying the mentorship of experienced and nurturing women performers. Her foray into backup singing began well but was not without growing pains. She struggled with sustaining Afrobeat's high-pitched melodies with precision. The task of learning the songs hardly improved over time. Mary reflected that beyond hitting the right notes in the recording stu-

Figure 5.3. Mary Umude-Haverkamp (bottom right,
in a white shirt) poses with a group of young women
alongside Fela, with an out-of-focus portrait of Thomas Sankara featured in the background. Photo credit
and permission: Femi Bankole Osunla. Permissions:
Estate of Femi Bankole Osunla.

dio, she was dealing with a mental battle that likely befell many women as they
grew more perceptive with age. Seeing through the slim veneer of freedom that
Afrobeat promised, many women questioned the reason for their continued
presence in Fela's home and work. The facade of freedom came off for Mary
after two years in Kalakuta, but she continued nonetheless in the absence of
viable alternatives. As the years wore on, working for Fela felt more exploitative
than liberating. Like many of her peers, she was barely scraping by; sometimes
they had to beg Fela for pocket money for a meal or to purchase personal effects
they could not afford on their wages as performers. Mary struggled to keep pace
with the daily rhythms of her work as a singer. These pressures exerted themselves on her artistry even as she continued to harbor fears that she might be
perceived as possessing neither the body nor the voice for Afrobeat. Fehintola
(now known as Mama Seun, Seun's mom) was by now a veteran singer and
vocal trainer herself. Fehintola helped in the ways she could, patiently teaching Mary the relevant choruses and techniques for hitting the right notes. The

fundamental question of reclaiming agency over her life lingered nonetheless. Mary now recalls her early struggle and triumph with Afrobeat singing with sardonic amusement.[97]

Younger women like Mary saw the Queens as warriors. For them, the women's stories of pain, resilience, and creativity, stories that had traveled across Nigeria and might have lured a few of them to Kalakuta, were near mythical. Averaging thirty years in age, the Queens carried themselves in a measured manner, a demeanor that came from the weight of life experience. To the new women, the Queens were also survivors. They had lived through battles that the younger women had not fought nor had any desire to fight. When asked if the new women bore the title "Queens," Mary responded pointedly, "The name was too big for us," underscoring the weight that the new arrivals accorded the older women.

Mary had a short stint with Afrobeat. In 1991, she parted ways with Egypt 80 in Thüringen, a state three hundred kilometers southwest of Berlin, during her third international tour. Her short musical career with Egypt 80 began with the album *Beasts of No Nation* (1986) and ended after *Confusion Break Bone* (1990). Her separation and emigration conformed to a larger pattern of Nigerian emigration in the late 1980s. The early to mid-1980s saw 2 to 2.5 million foreign nationals living in Nigeria (roughly 2.5 percent of the total population). Between 1987 and 1989, in a reversal of the trend from earlier in the decade, over 110,000 Nigerians sought jobs abroad.[98] Nigeria became a major exporter of highly skilled labor.[99] The numerous political and economic uncertainties that assailed Nigeria, especially the neoliberal ravages of IBB's Structural Adjustment Program, fueled these migrations. Whether taken in the context of the larger socioeconomic reality of the 1980s or the specific migratory behavior of Fela's band members, Mary's separation abroad reflected a common practice. Although separations were often unplanned, international tours offered performers a chance to chart a new course for themselves. Fela's authoritarian tendencies, normalized in everyday communal life, came into sharper focus during tours, which ironically demonstrated the limits of his authority on some level. For some, international tours offered a ticket to a new life in Europe and North America. By departing during international tours, they skipped the otherwise difficult process of obtaining visas and flight costs. Kevwe, for instance, shared a story of staying behind in the United Kingdom after a 1987 concert. While there, she relied on extreme survival tactics in the face of exploitation and racism. Kevwe tried to use aliases to secure a job and get a foothold in the economy but was ultimately apprehended by the police and deported to Nigeria in 1988.[100] Well documented are instances of absconding or separating, often impromptu, from the band in the United States and Europe as early as 1969. Fela's ambition for international fame was therefore complicated, quite legitimately, by restive laborers in his band who harbored other ambitions amid poor wages or who saw their conditions in a different, more critical light outside Nigeria. It is also true that international tours were Afrobeat's most well-paid gigs. Performers were most likely to be paid handsomely in foreign currencies when they returned to Nigeria, a further incentive for them to toe the line. Forfeiting this hard-earned pay made leaving the band rather tricky. So when Fela seized Mary's wages for the Germany tour after a disagreement, he effectively removed a key incentive for her, and other performers, to return to Nigeria. Mary weighed her options and made the decision to forge a new life in Germany.

Departures, particularly impromptu ones like Mary's, often came at a serious personal cost. Not only did performers have to abandon all their belongings, the precious little they brought on the tour, to avoid drawing attention, but they also had to confront a world with which they were totally unfamiliar and for which they were poorly equipped. Language and cultural barriers posed immediate difficulties. Timing, too, was of the essence. When they left could prove defining in the experience of the separating band members. Mary, for example, made her move in the middle of winter, knowing no one in Germany. "I had a horrible time in Germany when I left the band. . . . I remember the day I left the hotel, I left my bags, my very important photographs, and documents about myself. I left everything behind." In her early twenties, Mary contended with the ever-present risks of deportation, predation, and starvation. If deported from Germany, she would be met with ridicule or, worse, ostracism on return to Nigeria—especially if that return was to Kalakuta.

Mary recalled somberly, however, that her departure was a life-saving decision, one that she made right before "things were going to fall apart." Mary's Afrobeat journey, of an individual woman coming to Kalakuta of her volition, was becoming the exception. Sex workers were increasingly recruited as performers because work in Egypt 80 had a low bar for entry and promised a safer, more dignified alternative. This group of women brought to Afrobeat a familiar but distinct energy. Unlike the Queens, they imposed on communal life their desire for sexual and physical mobility. The third and last Kalakuta sat only a few hundred meters from Allen Avenue, an area in Ikeja whose rapid development was attributed to the inflow of drug money. By the late 1980s, Fela's entourage was increasingly associated with drug addiction, a microcosm of Nigeria's fraught global image under the leadership of General Sani Abacha (who succeeded IBB) as a hotbed of the global drug trade. Although Fela primarily encouraged the consumption of marijuana, he also began consuming what he dubbed "Felagoro," a potent mix of THC (tetrahydrocannabinol) extract and ogogoro (locally made gin). Band members consumed heroin and crack, access to which was facilitated by the commune's physical proximity to Allen Avenue, a flashpoint of crime, sex work, and drug use, reinforced Afrobeat's association with addiction and immorality and offered an excuse for renewed government interest in the 1990s.[101] Stories circulated of ex-Queens resorting to sex work to rebuild their post-Afrobeat lives.[102] A woman spoke with me on the topic on the condition of anonymity; she made a nuanced connection between sex work and poor wages. Because Fela paid low wages, some women were compelled to keep multiple male partners or, in some instances, to become (or remain) part-time sex workers to augment their work as performers. Subsidizing Fela's art with sexual labor by keeping boyfriends was not an entirely new practice. An Afrobeat woman spoke in 1977 under the pseudonym Stella about the dismal wages that Fela paid performers and how that compelled women to solicit boyfriends to buffer the shortfall: "[Fela] did not want to see any of us having whitemen [sic] friend or a boyfriend who is very rich; he will say that they will give us too much money and we would leave him. So, if he does not want us to have boyfriends, and he does not feed us, what does he expect us to do?"[103] Perhaps economic precarity in Egypt 80 inspired the women's turn, or return, to risky sexual behavior. The risks were heightened by the rising presence of HIV/AIDS in Nigerian public discourse. When HIV/AIDS made an appearance in the commune, it did so largely undetected.

The Kalakuta Republic of the late 1980s and early 1990s would have been unrecognizable to the bohemian generation of the 1970s, whose notoriety was anchored in intellectualism, discipline, and creative self-expression. Mary considered her Egypt 80 departure well timed. Her father visited her in the commune to meet Fela and urge her to hasten her departure. She recalled a heated argument between Fela and her distressed father, who had traveled from Delta to Lagos to extract his daughter from Kalakuta. The two men got into an argument when Fela declared to Mary's father, "I am not going to die." The conversation that built up to this moment is, in retrospect, dwarfed by what the statement portended. Mary begged her father to relent, reiterating her choice to remain in Kalakuta. She later reneged, renting an apartment and enrolling as an apprentice hairdresser. The transition to "normal" craft was bumpy. The demands of prolonged subservience in a formal apprenticeship bumped against the Kalakuta culture of subversion, the permissiveness that reigned supreme in the commune, and the modest prestige of being a well-traveled "Fela singer." She returned to Kalakuta but not for long. When Mary faced the threat of losing wages during the tour to Germany, she was reminded once again of the uneven and unjust labor relations that structured the making of Afrobeat music. She cut her losses and made a definitive separation from the band and from Nigeria during what became Fela's last major international tour. In the years that followed, the musician's health progressively declined amid regular raids on the commune by police and the Nigerian Drug Law Enforcement Agency (NDLEA). The heated argument between Fela and her dad, Mary recalled, foreshadowed the end. Rumors were swirling that Fela was living with HIV/AIDS. That was before things fell apart.

Queens like Najite, Fehintola, and Kevwe remained with Fela. But even for them, his ambiguous declaration of divorce and the creeping association of Afrobeat with HIV/AIDS proved devastating. The Kuti family would hold on to the divorce as a pseudo-legal basis for denying them fair treatment. A trickier terrain to navigate was the disease and the social and emotional ramifications of being publicly associated with it.

6

Facing the Music

AIDS and Alienation after Fela

When news broke in late July 1997 that Fela had fallen sick, the stories had a dark ring. The musician had fashioned a near-mythical persona that had out-lasted several death rumors. False alarms that Fela had died started in the late 1980s and continued, sporadically, for roughly one decade. But as early as 1992, Fela began canceling shows due to illness, the specific nature of which, and his specific location when his condition worsened, became the subject of feverish interest.[1] The rumors in 1997 felt different from those in the past. Days passed, and none of Fela's usual rebuttals—his flash of the double-fist Black Power sa-lute while grinning at fans—seemed forthcoming. That Fela lived in the public eye amplified the anxieties that flourished in his absence. Fear and concern gripped the Afrobeat community when credible accounts followed that the dis-sident musician was being treated at a hospital, an institution he had denounced as Western. If the rumor was true, receiving treatment at a hospital would only confirm that either Fela had either lost agency over the circumstances of his health or he was in desperate condition, as many feared. The discretion with which the Kuti family conducted affairs stoked speculation that, in turn, worked journalists into a frenzy. The speculations were powerful enough to inspire fans to camp around Kalakuta Republic, the third and final iteration of the commune. The sheer number of visitors spurred economic activity in the area. Ice cream, fast food, and newspaper vendors profited from the black mar-ket of rumor and suspicion. Commercial motorcycle (Okada) drivers claimed their fair share of the market, hiking transport fares to the area.[2] Journalists stood vigil around the commune, hounding the Kutis, the family who would define Afrobeat's story in the ensuing weeks, with questions. The media buzz lasted about ten days leading up to August 2, 1997, when the news arrived: Fela had died on a Saturday evening, at about 5:30 p.m., at an undisclosed Victoria Island hospital. The news was greeted with disbelief and grief.

Some Afrobeat women claimed to have foreseen this end. Omolara Shosanya had a premonition a decade earlier. Walking into Fela's bedroom, she found him on his side; in what seemed like a mirage, a skeleton took the place of his healthy-looking frame. Omolara interpreted the vision as a hint that darkness of sorts laid on the horizon. Her premonition metaphorized what many Kalakutans saw as early as 1980: a commune in free fall after serial assaults by the state and in the throes of rogue spiritualism. If Omolara had an epiphany, Olaide Babayale witnessed its equivalent in the flesh when she paid a courtesy visit to Kalakuta after several years working in public service. Olaide recalled meeting Fela in a subdued state. He lay weakly on his side, she narrated, more absent than half asleep in his room. He lifted his head and slowly focused on who had stepped into his bedroom. Recognition yielded a weak smile. Olaide beheld a man once full of vitality, at whose invitation she had led life at the edge. In this moment, Fela cut the opposite figure. Olaide could not stay for long, in part because the sight troubled her but also because she had work to do at the Ministry of Health. The testimonies of Olaide and Omolara offer a vivid look into the ravages of illness on communal spirit, a slump personified by Fela. And yet only a handful of women saw the tragic culmination of Fela's life with the clarity and conviction of Fehintola, one of about four wives who lived in Kalakuta until the end. There was a joke for every Kalakuta tragedy. Fela once told Fehintola, as a joke, that the day he willingly checked himself into a hospital, it was unlikely he would make a comeback. Worry overcame her when Fela personally sent for a physician. Fehintola wailed inconsolably for days, up until the minute an ambulance pulled into Kalakuta to take the musician away. It was her last time seeing him alive. Where Fehintola saw doom, others clung desperately to hope. Adejonwo Oguntiro confessed right before Fela's death: "Look at me, I cannot marry anyone else again. . . . Fela can't die."[3] Adejonwo's worry wove together the fears of many, a concern not about marriage per se but, more expansively, about what their highly public association with Fela meant for their relationship with the world without him—the source of their sustenance and the person on whom they had hedged their biggest life bets. In this sense, one must empathize with women like Adejonwo who, after twenty-four years in Afrobeat, thought life impossible without Fela. Still, fighting was precisely what would be demanded. Even the most prescient women could not have anticipated the full ramifications of the musician's melodramatic end.

The whirlwind that unfolded swept up the defenseless. The handful of Queens and army of young women who worked in Egypt 80 and resided in Kalakuta Republic were peculiarly exposed. The day after Fela's death, Olikoye Ransome-Kuti, Fela's elder brother and acclaimed former minister of health, issued a statement that sent shock waves across Nigeria: Fela had died from AIDS-related complications.[4] The public nature of the announcement was uncharacteristic considering attitudes toward HIV/AIDS, a disease that profoundly structured the sociosexual landscape of the 1990s and the global pop scene.[5] Speculation had initially surfaced in 1987 that Fela might have contracted HIV/AIDS, but his younger brother, Beko Ransome-Kuti, also a renowned medical doctor and activist, had denied the claims as "baseless."[6] For his part, Fela took delight in challenging emergent scientific knowledge on HIV/AIDS, remaining defiant even as he showed AIDS symptoms such as lesions and severe weight loss. Fela asserted that the lesions were a sign of youth.[7] There is a way to read this resistance alongside alternative "interpretations of the body" that resist the disciplinary muscle of science around HIV/AIDS.[8] Fela's denial of the HIV/AIDS epidemic dramatized tensions between researchers who cloaked racism in scientific language and African constituents who attributed local epidemics to colonialism and modernization, and witnessed how these overlapped in the scientific and global management of HIV/AIDS. A scientific and political gap developed between the two sides, revealing a lack of careful analysis of the AIDS epidemic on either sides of the debate.[9] Fela belonged to the group of Africans for whom the disease was intelligible only within uneven global relations, not as an epidemiologic fact that needed to be grappled with on its own terms. For Fela, resistance to Western discourses entailed denial of sickness and refusal to understand the social ramifications of the disease for himself and others around him. Not only did Fela continue to practice unprotected sex, but he also glamorized it in his music and rhetoric. In "Condom, Scallywag, and Scatter," one of Fela's last unrecorded songs, he mocked condoms as Western inventions designed to diminish the natural pleasures of sex—this at a time when rumors and popular misconceptions about condoms compromised public awareness about HIV/AIDS.[10] Fela's musings on gender and sexuality, Michael Veal argues, might have been considered lighthearted social observations, but they effectively laid the foundations for a hugely "problematic enactment of these positions at the end of his career."[11] The explicit repercussions of these positions for the women who surrounded him have often gone unremarked. Kalakuta Republic housed tens of young women, non-Queens, many of whom had joined Fela's band in the mid to late 1980s. Add to these numbers the girlfriends with whom Fela had affairs outside the commune—they all bore the brunt. Women in this category remained active but unaccounted for witnesses to the brutal HIV/AIDS period. Their experience of Fela's death overlapped with and diverged in important ways from that of the Queens, who bore a unique burden of Fela's decades-long foray into sexual showmanship, reactionary spiritualism, and macho populism.

The "widows of Afrobeat" endured a series of blows tied to the handling of Fela's death and the discourses that proceeded from it. Not only were the women, Queens and non-Queens alike, excluded from formal occasions for public mourning, but they also became ostracized through the cleanup that ensued. The process of isolating Fela from the women with whom he had been publicly intimate was hardly seamless. Even though the public's general posture toward the women was apathetic, the obvious could not be ignored. In a particularly revealing post-Fela era exchange, one journalist pointedly posed the question to Olikoye at the press conference where the cause of Fela's death was announced: "What are the chances that any of his wives may have contracted AIDS?" The professor's reply was snappish: "I cannot tell you. What they should however do is to go for voluntary test." His response elicited laughter![12] The exchange confirmed the struggle ahead for the women. The subtext of the professor's performance of indifference was that the women had lured Fela to his bitter fate and thus deserved little pity—this despite Fela's public sex life and flashy rhetoric about *fucking* a lot. This sinister line of thought implied that these women were directly responsible for the beloved musician's AIDS-related death, leaving them solely responsible for whatever misfortune befell them. Tying the women to Fela's fate became important because doing so made them representative of literal and metaphorical contagion, viruses corrupting family, body, and society. Fela was known to perform mock sex onstage with women dancers, in what at some point became weekly spectacles at the Shrine that supported the emerging framing of the women as contaminants. In the same way the family needed to establish morbid intimacy between the women and Fela, it required a social distance between the women and his body of work as questions of ownership, rights, and inheritance inevitably surfaced. To achieve this distance, the Kutis reiterated Fela's inchoate declaration of divorce to argue that while the women had a deep and undeniable relationship with Afrobeat, their relationship was neither legitimate nor binding in any consideration of financial and moral debt. This union might be understood as anything but marriage. A two-step dance ensued: one that portrayed the Queens as diseased bodies by virtue of social and sexual intimacy with Fela, tying them to his AIDS-related death, while distancing the women from the fruits of their collective labor in Afrobeat. They were excluded from consideration about their future and from public events, finding themselves exposed to stigma and rebuke.[13] Only few scholars like Michael Veal have expressed confusion at the women's mistreatment. His musings offer a poignant starting point for unpacking the systematic excommunication of Afrobeat women: "What is most striking about all of the discussion surrounding the circumstances of Fela's death is the absence of a sense of sympathy for [the] women's position. Ever since the 1978 communal wedding, Fela's wives had been viewed as a compromise to his own elite prestige, rather than as unequal partners with a man who—despite being persecuted—continued to benefit in many ways from his privileged origins and star status."[14] Following Veal's cue, this chapter returns to the scene of Fela's spectacular funeral to underscore how this "absence of a sense of sympathy" served a convergence of interests for the fabled Kuti family and for a public in shock at the loss of a folk hero. What Veal reads as a lack of sympathy for the Queens I read instead as a series of disciplinary actions facilitated by the intersecting mechanisms of class and gender inequity. The exact goal of the Kuti family's choices might be difficult to ascertain, but considering the intensely public press coverage around Fela's death and the highly publicized family intrigue that resulted, a central concern seems to have revolved around managing Fela's fraught public image and his association with a stigmatizing disease. A series of cultural mechanisms, activated by a momentous death, came to threaten little more than wretchedness for the women in Fela's wake. Conventional accounts of Fela's final days tend to speak of his AIDS-related death and then, with magical reflex, pick up the story with his posthumous resurgence in the critically acclaimed Broadway musical based on his fabled life. A more complicated picture emerges of family intrigue, betrayal, regret, material and social death, and survival if we turn attention away from these momentous events and to everyday exercises of gendered power—if we listen more closely and differently to the women who found themselves in the fight of their lives. When I began research for this chapter, I was interested simply in what happened to the women after Fela died and what the circumstances of his death meant for them. This was the basic question I begin with. As I studied newspaper coverage around Fela's death, I was surprised by how easily the women were being constructed as villains while Fela consolidated his posthumous status as an icon. I propose that it was not necessarily indifference toward the Queens that had the most drastic effect on their experiences after Fela's death. Instead, an accumulation of effects, decisions, and discourses combined to induce gendered misery. Resistance to these intersecting mechanisms of social dispossession became yet another terrain of struggle for the women. I argue that these outcomes unfolded through a series of mourning rituals, a host of cultural norms performed and enacted in

the wake of Fela's momentous life. As the story of Fehintola suggests, resilience
and the desire to outlive the HIV/AIDS saga provided many women with the
impetus to wade through a most trying Afrobeat episode. The staging of Fela's
funeral became a precursor to contests around family and belonging.

Spectacle and Spectators at the Funeral

Death sets in motion a plethora of cultural performances. Occasions for mourning not only produce culturally specific behaviors but also stage sometimes
fierce claims over the dead. Mourning is therefore a social act in which cultural
collectives establish new relationships with the dead. Funerals, as formal and
public stagings of the mourning act, crystallize sometimes hidden networks of
social relations between the dead and the bereaved. Not all funerals are equal.
Momentous deaths heighten both the aesthetic textures of mourning as well
as the stakes around loss and an attendant impulse toward regeneration. Fela's
funeral, like the life he led, was poised for drama. It delivered in spectacular
fashion.

When Fela died, Yeni Kuti was overcome with fear that her father had
left behind a questionable legacy.[15] But these anxieties were promptly overwhelmed by the tributes that poured in from near and far. A *New York Times*
article published two days after Fela's death hailed him as a "showy, insolent,
marijuana-smoking icon."[16] Senior officials from the American, German, and
Chinese embassies visited the Shrine to pay their respects. Afrobeat fans in
Paris, New York, and South Africa scrambled to secure copies of Fela albums.[17]
"I will go to Sam Goody first thing on Monday to pick as many Fela's CDs [*sic*]
(compact discs) as possible," one New York fan promised.[18] In Lagos, a set of
fifteen tapes including most of Fela's releases normally sold for about ₦16,000;
they started going for ₦24,000. At a whopping ten naira per wrap, marijuana
was the most lucrative merchandise of all.[19] Student leaders refused to be left
out. The University of Ibadan chapter of the National Association of Nigerian Students (NANS) declared a lecture-free day in honor of the fallen star.[20]
The Association of Catholic Media Practitioners in Lagos called for Fela's im-
mortalization as other religious entities conjured various outlandish claims.[21]
To cite one notable case, Albert Iyeke, the archbishop of the Sabbath Church
of Nigeria, chastised the Nigerian press for not publishing the prophecies of
priests, claiming that the "good Lord" had revealed Fela's death to him; the
musician might have survived had the press conveyed the prophecy quickly
enough.[22] The Alake (king) of Abeokuta granted Fela a posthumous award in
music alongside other Abeokuta indigenes like Nobel laureate Wole Soyinka

and, without any sense of irony, General Olusegun Obasanjo, the architect of Fela's greatest misfortunes.[23] A condolence register at the Shrine was filled with signatures from A-list musicians like Sir Shina Peters, Christy Essien Igbokwe, Wasiu Ayinde Marshall, and Charly Boy.[24] A Yoruba proverb captures the climate of public mourning: ọjọ́ ikú erin, ọ̀bẹ orísirísi là ń rí / *The day an elephant dies, one sees an assortment of knives.*

But the most stirring tribute did not come from the stellar lineup of dignitaries. It came instead from the throng of poor, working-class Lagosians who swarmed the streets, insisting on a people's burial for Fela. An estimated one million Lagosians gathered to pay final respects during the lying in state at Tafawa Balewa Square. At this same square, eighteen years earlier, Fela had staged a concert to declare his presidential aspirations in the 1979 elections. Now, Fela lay still, clad in a floral, long-sleeved shirt and tight orange pants in a glass casket. He is staged to clutch a jumbo-sized joint in what read as a final posture of defiance. The casket had to be snuck away after three hours, an unrelenting queue of fans still waiting to pay respects. Undaunted, the crowd escorted the hearse on its thirteen-mile journey from Lagos Island to Kalakuta Republic in Ikeja. The procession expanded, stretched, and contracted, but it never thinned out. Lemi Ghariokwu, visual artist and Fela's longtime collaborator, struggled to hold back tears as the procession passed by his office at Palmgrove bus stop.[25]

At about 11:15 a.m., the glass casket bearing Fela's remains sat on the second-floor balcony of 7 Gbemisola Street, the final Kalakuta. A banner draped over the balcony railing read "The Positive Force Mourns The Abami Eda. Fela Anikulapo-Kuti: Sun Re O," a tribute from Femi's Positive Force band. Two trumpeters exchanged somber, jazzy notes in a haunting homage. Soon after, loudspeakers blared the scathing "Unknown Soldier," musically recalling the state brutality that, visited on Fela and the Queens, marked the public's memory of a long history of neocolonial dystopia. When a group of policemen showed up, wrestling their way through the crowd and into the compound of Kalakuta Republic, the crowd began to chant "Zombie! Zombie!"—a choral arsenal gesturing to the era when state actors obsessed over inflicting naked violence on Kalakutans. The raucous call-and-response that ensued between the crowd, loudspeakers, and police rekindled public memory of state-citizen conflicts in a charged fashion. A police helicopter hovered for a few minutes before disappearing into the Lagos skies, underscoring that the policemen had come only to pay their tributes to a star they had helped to fell. Music gave way to speeches, which lent gravitas to the atmosphere of celebration, protest, and mourning. Neighbors gathered in balconies and on rooftops to catch a privileged glimpse of the proceedings, enjoying perhaps the only benefit to sharing a neighborhood with Fela and his unruly entourage. Defying protocol, the crowd pushed and pried at Kalakuta's gates. A total of fifteen people, according to an eyewitness, fainted in the frenzy.[26] Yeni opened the speeches with heartfelt remarks about her father's many struggles. Two of Fela's sons—Femi and Seun—also excited the crowd with impassioned speeches. Lagosians who could not brave the throngs, including my teenage self, sat glued to their television sets. Television channels dedicated hours and hours to live coverage. Radio stations, previously hesitant about playing Fela's songs for their length and explicit content, hosted exclusive Fela programs, some of which ran for weeks. The scene was pregnant with grief, praise, admiration, and disbelief in equal measure. The histrionic funeral cemented Fela's legacy as a folk hero.

Funerals are anything but vacant sites of collective mourning. They are social dramas where old tensions find tentative resolution or renewed intensity, where totally novel conflicts germinate over the specter of loss and longing. They curate usable narratives about the dead while fielding surrogates for the dead.[27] The literal staging of funerals—who performs what, who stands where, who says what, how, why, and who sees what—infuses this ritual of public mourning with dramatic tension. If little has been said about the women in Fela's life, it is precisely because of their actual involvement in the proceedings. Stuart Hall's reading of cultural transformation in the popular domain is instructive in understanding the dynamics at play at the funeral. Hall describes cultural change as a euphemism for the active marginalization of a particular way of life, how particular practices and ways of life are driven from the center of popular life in favor of others.[28] While Hall is interested in broader trends in popular culture, his reading clarifies the unfolding shift within Afrobeat and the underpinning class interests governing said shift. The army of working-class women who helped weave together the legend of Fela Kuti were literally sidelined at the funeral, a critical precursor to their displacement from the field of view. The intensity, glamor, and outpouring of raw emotion at the event might have offered some of the women their first real glimpse into the monumental life they had collectively fashioned in Kalakuta. But at the funeral the Queens were made to spectate. They peered from balconies and windows, watching the public's adoration of a man they had known intimately. A newspaper reporter best captured the dynamics of their location at the funeral: "Some of the women in Fela's life were seen in the compound and not at the graveside. They were not even listed by the master of ceremony among those to pay the last respects. Names that were announced and seen at the graveside include

Prof. and Mrs. [Olikoye] Ransome-Kuti, Chief and Mrs. Rasheed Gbadamosi, Mr. Femi Falana, Miss Dolupo Ransome-Kuti, Mrs. Yemisi Soyemi and Fela's seven children—Yeni, Femi, Kunle, Sola, Motunrayo, Salewa and Seun."[29] In a powerful statement that the Kutis had no interest in giving the Queens a platform to be viewed as widowed, only Fela's children were given a platform at the burial. The women belonged in the background, not unlike the roles they had played onstage, beyond the spotlight—except that now, even their voices were unheard. They became objects of journalistic gaze, a footnote in a sea of stories about a historic event. At once spectators and spectacle, the Queens and Kalakuta women watched the proceedings while being watched by perceptive journalists. A different eyewitness described how the women "stretched out their necks," monitoring "minute to minute events leading to the final burial."[30] The closest they came to Fela's remains was peering from whatever space they could fit into. The distance put between the women and the graveside cast them as spectators, indistinguishable from neighbors perched on balconies and behind windows. Ironically, those who had had the most profound effect on Fela's art, music, and lifestyle found no place at his burial. Denying the women an opportunity to pay Fela their last respects amounted to disenfranchised grief: when a relationship or the impact of a death goes unacknowledged.[31] Their exclusion from the proceedings demonstrated the belief among Fela's family that he had divorced the Queens over a decade prior. One Queen gave voice to this idea right after the burial, even if she confessed to an abiding friendship with Fela that had felt more special than the marriage itself.[32] The "divorce" constituted a basis for denying the women any social position on which to anchor their grief.[33] Divorce, as such, served more than a rhetorical function. If marriage conferred the status of widowhood at the instantiation of a death, divorce evacuated entirely the possibility of claiming the status of widowhood. Remi Taylor, Fela's legal married wife, excused herself from public proceedings, but the decision to visit the graveside was hers to make. As divorced wives, the Queens were denied marriage and widowhood and with both, a social location from which to publicly mourn Fela. They might have belonged in the compound but certainly not at the graveside, a classed space of differentiation reserved for family and venerated friends. This definition of family excluded the Queens and other "fringe elements" in the Afrobeat project. Quiet mourning was their only option. For all the pageantry that attended the funeral of Fela, Kevwe remembered it as a "dark day," one that swung between the grief of loss and the sting of disregard.[34] Fela's death accommodated legitimate expressions of public grief but was at the same time a structuring event, choreographed to publicly begin recalibrating family and worth.

"Double Wahala for Dead-i Body": Postmortem Complications

Fela paid a huge price with his life, but as Tejumola Olaniyan poignantly argues, death hardly disables the "dominant-subordinate poles in a structured inequity; death only evacuates either pole for other sets of occupants."[35] At least two crucial meetings—one right before Fela's death, one immediately after—established the parameters for Afrobeat's future, determining which social actors would assume leading roles in the unfolding drama.

The first meeting took place among the Kuti family. When Fela's illness reached an ominous point, his family, presided over by elder brother Olikoye, convened a three-hour-long meeting. The primary agenda was the "reorganization" of Fela's house, including figuring out what to do with Fela's "many wives, miscreants, and sundry dependents."[36] Beko was absent from this crucial family meeting because the Sani Abacha–led military regime had jailed him for treason and denied his formal appeal to pay Fela his last respects.[37] Intense deliberation ended in polarized positions. Fela's only sister, Dolu, and his older children voted for a radical cleanup of Kalakuta Republic. Professor Olikoye, on the other hand, favored an even-handed approach, perhaps a not-too-drastic solution allowing Kalakutans transition into more stable lives outside of Afrobeat. The question inevitably arose about who would take leadership of the commune. Femi volunteered himself since "he knows the place well."[38] This was partly true: Femi and his two sisters had frequented the commune as children and lived there for an extended period in the early 1980s. He had formally joined Fela's band in a recruitment drive for new instrumentalists following an exodus of talent. Femi had also played a leading role in managing the band during Fela's imprisonment in the mid-1980s. These experiences qualified him for the task of taking charge of Kalakuta. So did cultural patrimony, the sometimes-unearned privilege granted to first sons, and the element of force that might attend taking over the commune. The details of this first family meeting are sketchy. But the agenda of a second meeting, this one involving all Kalakutans, clarified the winning arguments from the earlier deliberation.

A second meeting took place roughly twenty-four hours after Fela died. This time, it was a meeting between Femi and the Kalakutans. Femi called an early morning meeting of all Kalakutans where he read out what amounted to a riot act: "troublemakers" risked eviction, as did women who continued the old habits that had ostensibly earned Fela a bad name. Behaviors such as noise making and hosting "delicate" visitors (likely meaning lovers) to Kalakuta would be punished.[39] Wanting to convey a decisive break from Fela's loose-handed style, Femi announced a ban on marijuana use in and around Kalakuta;

women who violated this ban could also be evicted.[40] Fela's "boys," Kalakuta's fungible law enforcement officers, were poised to execute any eviction order put forward by the Kutis. (Kevwe pointed out to me that my impromptu field research assistant, John, had helped usher her out of Kalakuta. Her confession contextualized her impatience when she found me in the company of John.) While Femi acted as the public face of the post-Fela realignment of power, he never acted without the buy-in of Fela's siblings or, crucially, of his elder sister, Yeni, who did not often address the public but wielded tremendous power as the first child. Femi gave voice to key decisions, but behind the scenes, Yeni was highly influential in every significant decision. The newspaper report of the second meeting painted the Kalakuta women with a broad brush. The report, for instance, showcased a somber-looking Fehintola but made no mention of whether she belonged to the category of "troublemaker," leaving the public to fill in the gap with negative stereotypes. Femi's riot act leveraged the momentum of the funeral in hopes of consolidating a new regime.

As would soon become clear, evicting women who had invested three decades of their productive years into Afrobeat would not be easy; the women did not accept this change without a fight. The Yoruba proverb is instructive here: ojú bọ̀rọ̀ ọ̀ ṣé gb'ọmọ l'ọmọ l'ọ́wọ́ ekùrọ́ / *A soft face does not extract the seed of a kernel*. An unnamed woman, likely a Queen, minced no words when speaking to a journalist. Riled by what was essentially a notice of eviction, she said, "I joined Fela as a student in 1974, I risked everything because of Fela. I couldn't finish schooling. But here I am today being ejected by a boy who was sucking breast when I was sleeping with his father. They have barely finished burying Fela and he (Femi) has started feeling like a king already. We are going to pull down [Kalakuta] together. All I know is that I suffered with Fela. We made his money together. We cannot be thrown away like that."[41] Tough talk was a vital arsenal in the women's moral claims to Afrobeat. And those who could threw their weight behind direct confrontation with the Kutis. It was, however, a losing battle by many indications. Although important and indispensable, the women's work with Fela had been fluid, improvisatory, and noncontractual. Fela paid daily or weekly wages in cash, leaving virtually no paper trail. What the women earned from their artistic work (and the housing that came with the nature of their work with Fela) was often framed as evidence of Fela's philanthropy instead of as wages for legitimate artistic work shaped by the particularities of talent management in Afrobeat. The long-standing practice of enlisting contingent labor transacted on fluid terms implied that the women had no formal relationships with Afrobeat music, nor did their decades-long collaboration with Fela possess legal or customary standing. This fact swayed the posthumous deliberations in the Kutis' favor, as did a narrow interpretation of Yoruba inheritance practices in which neither wives nor husbands inherit from one another; inheritances go to children and siblings. This interpretation conveniently ignored the inheritance practice that "when a man dies his property is distributed among his wives and their children; when a woman dies her property is distributed only to her children. It cannot go to the husband or his family."[42] It was clear that the Kutis were interested in the aspect of Yoruba culture that put distance between their family and the women, because as wives or widows, the women were right to assume that they could continue living in the home they shared with their late husband.[43] Public pressure might have urged the Kutis into more humane considerations, but the Kutis overwhelmingly shaped public discourse. The reporting, such as Femi's insinuation that the women gave Fela a bad name, effectively neutralized public sympathy. As was true during Fela's life, the women's continued residence in Kalakuta Republic rested on their willingness to acquiesce to a new regime and on the Kutis' kindness—but the withholding of kindness cannot be legislated in courts.

Fela's death left most of his beneficiaries frantic about their fates. The most pressing needs were acquiring food and staying housed. The women, one reporter wrote, showed "telltale signs of starvation."[44] Some organized and sought government help in a desperate move to secure financial support for themselves and some male band members, who also understood their grim fates. Speaking on behalf of all Fela's employees, Douglas Bassey, possibly an instrumentalist, pleaded with the Nigerian government to forgive their past deeds and employ them.[45] One Queen, an unnamed dancer, clearly understood that her prospects were limited. In words that fall somewhere between mourning and hopelessness, she contemplated an alternative career in catering, a vision thwarted by her lack of economic capital. In an interview with journalists, she tempered her anger with an appeal to the Kutis and their humanity. Her response is worth a lengthy quote.

> I almost collapsed when they said he's dead. Now that he is dead, that means I have to start my life all over again. The most painful thing is that I have nothing except my training as a dancer and a caterer. I will like to start life as a caterer but there is no money. And I have nowhere to go. And now they are threatening to eject us from Kalakuta. Is that the next thing they should do to us after all the years with Fela? After all we did for Fela and what Fela did to us? If the dead could truly see and know what happens on earth, I'm sure Fela won't be happy about the plan to drive us from Kalakuta. Where do they want us to go? I'm confused. . . . Leaving Kalakuta Republic? Well, I want to continue living there until they [the Kuti family] ask us to leave.

The speaker had left the Afrobeat community in 1986 but returned four years later because, she reasoned, Fela was a good husband who "gave us all the freedom on earth." She also appeared to recall, in real time, her extensive and underpaid work in Afrobeat. This realization marked a dramatic shift in her tone from conciliation to defiance: "But really why should they send us out? All these small boys and girls? I knew them when they were young at the time we were living in Moshalashi [the first Kalakuta]. I will be shocked if they drove us out. It will be the most wicked thing to do."[46] Members of the Kuti family were single-minded in their goals. They committed themselves to the task of repairing what they feared could be further dents to the Kuti name. In the days before the historic burial, they remained uncertain about what Fela's association with HIV/AIDS would mean for his legacy and for themselves. The decisions they made in those days reflect this pain and anxiety. The decisions they made after the heat of loss reflect a more strategic consolidation of power. To be sure, managing the aftershocks of Fela's public life and his unresolved private affairs were gargantuan tasks, and cleaning up after Fela would test the patience of saints. One might thus empathize with the Kutis on these grounds: there was no painless way, if even possible, to refashion the commune into a reflection of *decent* society. Because the takeover was swift, the Kutis' every move sent shockwaves of panic and suspicion across the commune, feelings that were not totally unfounded. Band members and other dependents were gripped by a heightened sense of anxiety about the future, a state that rendered dialogue difficult between them and the Kuti family. Ajimele Isesele, who played maracas and conga in Egypt 80, noted: "I was just roaming the streets of Lagos when [Fela] saw me and picked me up and gave me a new life. . . . Me now, I no get anywhere, where I dey go."[47] This tone of despair and resignation was consistent throughout Kalakuta, among the instrumentalists and the women.

Rather than seeing the Kutis as acting callously for the sheer pleasure of callousness, it might be helpful to understand them as members of an elite class protecting their interests over the dividends of labor, a tension that Fela's music powerfully obscured. Their state of mourning offered a backdrop against which to mobilize powerful cultural scripts to consolidate their grip over the spoils of Afrobeat. Behind the veil of mourning was an active recalibration of the center of Afrobeat power from Kalakuta Republic to the Kuti family, from a collective to the nuclear family form. The relationship between the Kutis and Kalakuta women had always been colored by accommodation and hostility. While the Kutis understood the women as key agents in Fela's music, the maneuvering and power play that characterized life in Kalakuta often turned personal, intensifying friction between Fela's children and the Kalakuta women over the years.

Because many Queens were roughly age-mates with Fela's children, friendships flourished between them—as did contempt. Yeni, for instance, confessed to not enjoying Fela's style of fatherhood. Femi expressed unease at the people around Fela who drained the love and attention he felt were due to the Kuti children: "He had all these people around him, two hundred people, two hundred and fifty people around him. He never wanted to show that he favored his family over anybody. So, he would give everybody something and we would have to wait, and we got the love last."[48] Years of forced accommodation between Fela's children and his "girls" blossomed into crisis. These personal dimensions should not obscure the class character of the tensions that coalesced around the early post-Fela moment.

The riot act meeting portended more trouble. Yet another complication revealed itself: Fela had died intestate. Fela's failure to leave a will that might have offered the women some legal protection—or his choice not to—deepened the trail of losses in the days following his death. The absence of a will might seem unthinkable considering that Fela kept legal counsel on his payroll for most of the 1970s (and likely throughout his adult life). It also seems curious given the scale of creative work that the women had participated in producing—more than fifty albums. Yet despite this seeming inconceivability, the absence of a will was consistent with the commune's tendency to glamorize informality in matters unrelated to the marketing of Fela's music, which was usually handled by outside entities like record labels with clearly delineated roles and expectations. While membership to a subculture might help articulate a different and distinctive cultural response to the pressures and problems of dominant society, belonging to a subculture does not protect an individual from the matrix of experiences and conditions that shape the life of the social class to which they belong.[49] Kalakutans generally behaved as though mainstream Nigerian society would ultimately evolve to mirror the subculture's expectations. The Kutis' retreat into hegemonic assumptions of kinship and family—and in the context of death, inheritance—acts as a reminder of the fragility and material limits of subcultural belonging, its weakness in subverting a rigid class hierarchy. Afrobeat women, like working-class women, were entrenched working-class subjects whose sense of ownership and belonging in Afrobeat did not change their relationship to the apparatuses of production. In fact, subcultural living might have obscured the tenacity of those hierarchies and the real fight required to successfully subvert them. Whether one interprets the absence of a will as Fela's neglect or as callousness, its gendered upshots were devastating. Most Afrobeat women did not have welcoming families to which to return. This was especially true for women who had joined as teenagers, stayed the longest, and traveled from out of Lagos, navigating city life and adulthood by trial and error and from the relative stability of communal life. After Fela's death, these women had little to show for decades of work. It became clear that they had spent much of their lives leading up to that moment building an artistic empire to which they could lay little to no claim. With no contracts in place, claims over the prolific musical output of Africa 70 and Egypt 80 were futile. Economic precarity, starvation, and the threat of homelessness were complicated by the stigma of having lived close to and loved someone confirmed to have died of AIDS-related complications.

Empathy rooted in the women's public suffering and sacrifice became the capital at their avail. The only true arsenal at their disposal were the optics and ethics of being ejected with little to nothing after all that working and living with and close to Fela had entailed. The Kutis understood the underlying moral questions posed by the few women who gave voice to their anxieties. Indeed, the question of what Afrobeat music and Fela owed to its women was present in the mind of Femi, the Kutis' spokesman, when he implied that those who felt Fela owed them should settle the score with him in the grave. For good measure, he added that the women "became his friends by association. There is really nothing at stake now that the man who brought them is dead."[50] The years of physical brutality and assault that the Queens, among many other women, had endured were ultimately rewarded by new forms of social violence.

The Kutis' behavior showed a readiness to deploy ideological and cultural arsenals and, if needed, physical force in the unfolding battle over ownership and belonging. An inflexible idea of family, marriage, and what constituted compensable labor became their preferred weapons. Despite the grave shortcomings of Fela's model, he had long publicly disavowed the idea of nuclear family in favor of an expansive notion of community forged not on blood but on shared humanity. He lived by this principle at least in how he organized communal life. The sense of giving the self to the other, of encountering one's humanity in sacrifice to the other, was, on one level, what the Nigerian masses reciprocated at the historic funeral. Yet armed with claims of divorce, Fela's immediate family came to dictate terms of exclusion based on a narrow interpretation of family. The nuclear family wielded the finality of divorce to justify alienating the women closest to Fela's work.

The public fact of the Queens' artistic labor was met by the Kutis' exculpatory response: Fela had paid the women weekly salaries and so owed them nothing in death. The women had no share in the royalties of Afrobeat music nor in Fela's estate. The argument appears reasonable at first glance, but it obscures a more complicated history of Afrobeat labor relations. There are at least two reasons why the argument is misleading. First, because the women inhabited a multiplicity of subject positions as fans, protégés, lovers, wives, coartists, and coactivists, their involvement with Fela had already been characterized by multiple and interanimating affective entanglements with the production architecture of Afrobeat music. Their artistic and political labors were always entangled with and constituted by grave personal sacrifice and trauma. The women labored under conditions that exceeded what might be reasonably argued, as the Kutis did, as strictly salaried work. The affective conditions that undergirded women's work in Afrobeat simply evolved when their subject positions changed over time, for instance when some became mothers or the transition from fan to worker. Layered entwining of labor and personal suffering complicates any simplistic reading of labor and moral debt in Afrobeat. Second, salaries became infrequent during dry spells or when Fela pursued expensive and ambitious political projects, such as running for president (a cause of friction with some male band members). Fela's personal ambitions sometimes demanded collective sacrifice in the form of unpaid wages. There were dry spells in income after the major raid of 1977; the fallout of the government crackdown was democratically shared in the form of sporadic wages. The argument that the women were paid in a traditional sense is a misleading one. Indeed, at stake was not simply a truer accounting of Afrobeat labor relations but also the amplification of a version of the past that served the Kutis in resolving many ideological contradictions that dogged Fela. Yeni might have been playing mischief when she suggested that Fela died poor, having squandered his life earnings on philanthropy. This was yet another powerful script that portrayed Fela as an unsuspecting victim and the people around him as leeches who sucked much and gave little. Fela might indeed have died penniless, but only if we limit our understanding of wealth to the piles of money he stashed in his bedroom. It would be disingenuous to suggest that Fela died in penury. True wealth in Afrobeat was obtained in creative output and intellectual property rights. By the end of his life, Fela was arguably West Africa's most prolific musician, leaving behind, by one estimate, over eighty albums featuring about 150 songs, plus a trove of unrecorded and unreleased songs.[51] International interest in Fela's music soared in the early 1980s. Bob Marley's international success demonstrated the viability of African and Caribbean music in Western markets, and Marley's death left a vacuum that Fela was well-positioned to fill.[52] One tangible outcome of interest in Fela's music was a million-dollar deal with Sony Music, which Fela turned down because of overcommercialization and the desire to control his sound. Fela's popularity might have dipped in the early 1990s, but his death revitalized local and international attention to his life and works. Evidently, whoever succeeded in staking sufficient claims over Fela would be inheriting a gold mine. Economic calculations stoked the intrigue: the Kutis had all to gain from monopolizing the spoils. They were also in the fight of their lives.

The absence of a will hung over the conflict. Practical challenges would have attended the project of delineating each woman's compensation in a will. What if Fela had desired legal protection for the women but been daunted by the complexity of pulling it off? How, for instance, could he measure each woman's contribution to Afrobeat onstage and off? How might he have located long-separated women who had played crucial roles in Afrobeat but whose whereabouts were unknown? How about bequeathing wealth to the handful of Queens who had remained until the end but not to those who had left years earlier? Should separation from Afrobeat constitute fair grounds for disqualifying women from inheritance? How about the younger women, the non-Queens? By what formula should they compute their shorter stint and relatively more peaceful years of Afrobeat work? Should they even be in the conversation, given that they, save for the sexual entanglements, came marginally closer to a conventional idea of workers than the Queens? All these questions came with complications. It might be reassuring to think that these questions at least crossed Fela's mind as his health deteriorated. But the reality remains that, if the question of protection crossed Fela's mind at all in his dying moments, he failed to act. For women whose economic survival hinged almost solely on Afrobeat, Fela's indecision, inaction, refusal, or failure was decidedly stark. And this fact should give pause. Even the women in the commune conceded that the Queens, women who had the deepest and most intimate relationship with Afrobeat music, were in a different class from the rest of them. Dismissing women's and gender issues was a recurrent theme throughout Fela's life, save for a brief period in the early 1980s. It might be in Fela's death, therefore, that we encounter the clearest act of sexism, an abdication of moral responsibility, a lack of self-awareness of gender oppression as it concerned the women in general and those who gave so much to his work specifically. It is in these structurally significant choices, not in lyrics or public spectacles, that Afrobeat's most significant gender projects are laid bare.

Fela's death signaled a denouement of sorts. For the many working-class women of Afrobeat, it heralded a new chapter of struggle. This struggle was no longer against long-standing adversaries—the state and its actors—but against fast-coalescing class interests expressed in the model of the nuclear family. The women's new, no less formidable opposition was the Kutis and elites against whose mores they had rallied for years. There was no greater embodiment of elite disdain for Afrobeat women than the Kutis themselves. Fela's death signaled a truce between state and nonstate elites, a truce that was as classed as it was anything else. The Queens struggled for recognition and meaning on this shifting ground.

Defying Social Death

Fela may have been Africa's most prominent megastar associated with the HIV/AIDS virus, but he was not the only one. The early 1990s witnessed high-profile AIDS cases that rocked the global art and pop culture world.[53] Basketball athlete Magic Johnson and Freddie Mercury, the lead vocalist of British rock band Queen, were notable examples that circulated in Nigerian public discourse. Others hit closer to home, such as Philly Bongoley Lutaaya, Ugandan musician and crooner of "Born in Africa." Through songs like "Alone and Frightened," Lutaaya dedicated his final years to promoting awareness about HIV/AIDS. "Alone" makes an impassioned plea for compassion for individuals living with the disease:

> Take my hand now
> I'm tired and lonely
> Give me love
> Give me hope
> Don't desert me
> Don't reject me
> All I need is love and understanding.

By enjoining his listeners to "stand together and fight AIDS," Lutaaya gave a face to the disease in Uganda and across Africa. Perhaps the first African to publicize his status, the musician became one of the continent's earliest AIDS activists. He died in December 1989, laboring amid cynicism and mockery for this cause.[54] The Ugandan singer embraced the reality of the disease and invested time and creativity into demystifying and destigmatizing it.

By consistently denying his sickness, Fela not only accelerated his own demise and potentially infected others in the process but also gave wind to the sails of AIDS denialism. His relationship with the disease took a dramatic turn because his death became decisive in AIDS activism in Nigeria. Doctors seized on the opportunity to educate the public about HIV/AIDS. "You don't have to live like Fela to have AIDS. . . . AIDS is just around the corner; he who has ears let him hear," one doctor warned.[55] A certain Anthonia Onyenwenyi, who convened the Society of Women and AIDS in Africa (Nigeria) Youth

Project, felt that the tireless AIDS campaigns had been vindicated by Fela's death. Nonexperts saw the need to warn about sex workers, a group whose precarious work left them susceptible to and capable of spreading the disease.[56] Increasingly, the medical community praised Fela's family for its forthrightness in publicizing the cause of his death. The Kuti family had given momentum to an important campaign, an intervention that factored in Femi Kuti's appointment as Goodwill Ambassador to the United Nations International Children's Emergency Fund (UNICEF) in 2002 in an effort to reach youth. "Kuti has been a vocal advocate of HIV/AIDS prevention since 1997, when his father, Fela Anikulapo-Kuti, founder of Afro-beat music, died of the disease," UNICEF testified. Femi affirmed this focus when asked about plans for his ambassadorship: "One of the most important actions for people in influential positions is to raise the alarm around AIDS loudly and clearly."[57] This public-facing advocacy, though important, stood at odds with the private handling of the disease in the very community over which Femi wielded power. Fela's death, quite ironically, produced a watershed moment in HIV/AIDS advocacy in Nigeria, if not Africa. In calling attention to AIDS as a factor in Fela's death, the Kuti family risked social stigma. Although the public awareness that Fela's death generated about a dreaded and still-mysterious disease failed to extend to sympathy for the women who had shared intimate moments with the late Afrobeat musician, the cause-of-death disclosure nonetheless became a critical public health intervention. It had the side effect of redeeming Fela's and the family's image, threatened by the late musician's excesses. Efforts at recalibrating the signification of disease and excess unfolded parallel to total silence about the science of contagion, the social aspect of the disease that would have inevitably centered the women closest to Fela. In death, Fela attained martyrdom as an *individual* whose death, the transparency of it, breathed life into others. The discursive framing of the death in martyred terms was an exercise in separation, isolating Fela from a network of people under his direct influence. The women he left behind became the collateral damage of this new public awakening.

The press conference at which a reporter asked Professor Olikoye about the potential exposure of Fela's surviving wives contributed to portraying them as outlaws in other critical ways. When Olikoye invited Kalakutans to the Shrine, they had no prior knowledge of the meeting's agenda or attendees. Many Kalakutans were shocked to learn only on arriving that they had been summoned to an international press conference. Local and foreign media, from the British Broadcasting Corporation (BBC) to the Nigerian Television Authority (NTA) to local newspaper outlets, had representatives at the Shrine. Olikoye's statement at the conference provided the first certified report on the late musician's demise; it was also the first time Kalakutans learned that HIV/AIDS had factored in Fela's death. Up until this moment, the disease had been quietly ransacking the commune. The Kalakutans banded together, listening to the details akin to a death sentence, at the same time as the rest of the world and in front of cameras. Wearing the hat of a medical professional, Olikoye seized the opportunity to speak on a variety of AIDS-related topics, from the dangers of having unprotected sex to everyone's vulnerability to the disease.[58] When the issue of voluntary testing arose, Olikoye gestured in the direction of the back of the hall, where the women stood. In equal parts advice and chastisement, he declared, "Nobody can force you to go for the test. . . . So it is up [to] wives and people in that category. It is up to them to decide what they will like to do regarding AIDS testing."[59] It was a moment of devastation. Dede Mabiakwu, a prominent protégé of Fela's, stood at the back of the hall. He was one of the "people in that category" who needed to get tested, according to Olikoye. Dede recalled with raw emotion in his voice how the cameras swung around, zooming in on their faces in sync with Olikoye's pronouncement, "condemned" in that moment as HIV/AIDS carriers by virtue of association with Fela.[60] Dede's accounts are replete with personal horror stories about dealing with stigma despite not having contracted the disease: "Because of the stigma that AIDS had at that time, you were like a symbol of black death. And these were women who really wouldn't know what step to take or where to go or how to make their next move. And then you just condemned them in entirety. And after that nobody gave a care about anything about these people. No psychological assistance, no medical assistance, no financial assistance of any sort whatsoever. How degenerate can one else feel?"[61] A culture of denial and secrecy surrounding HIV/AIDS in the 1990s complicated the prospects of survival after Fela's death. And dealing with the stigma required a sense of belonging and empathy. Neither the Queens nor the younger Kalakuta women could bank on emotional support—not from their families, the Kutis, or society. Dede remained one of few voices within the community advocating for the women. Professor Olikoye boasted a stellar reputation in public service, and his handling of the situation might have been intended as a broad, urgent public health intervention. It simultaneously isolated Fela from "wives and people in that category," an operation in class redemption. Dede's recollection of the press conference offers a crucial counterpoint to what might have been a well-intentioned but insensitive handling of Fela's diagnosis. Dede underscored the tangible and gendered trauma associated with the elevation of Fela at the expense of his close friends, partners, and associates who had neither family nor star status to support them in their struggle.

Orchestration: Thursday, August 2014
It's a new day of listening to Afrobeat music through headphones in a danfo bus. What gets me on this occasion is Fela's ushering in of the second bassline in "Overtake Don Overtake Overtake (ODOO)." I mouth the instruments and strum an air guitar when Fela calls "second bass jare," the cue for an orchestra of low-sounding instruments to rumble into an already complex arrangement. The groove washes delightfully over my body as I try to not draw attention to my ecstasy of mute enjoyment. The rumbling tenor of "ODOO" eases into the cheeky, airy beat of "Zombie," the former bleeding seamlessly into the latter. I am forced to snap out of my headphone-induced trance state. An actual soldier is sitting next to the danfo driver in the front seat. In Lagos, soldiers and police officers hitch free rides on commercial buses simply by donning their uniforms. The ostensible payoff is that by lifting a soldier or police officer, a danfo driver can refuse bribes to other officers he encounters on his route. Danfo drivers can refuse to pay bribes simply on the weight of carrying another officer who, riding free of charge, indicates an already paid if utterly illegal tax. It is hardly a fair trade, as declining to carry an officer is not really an option. Refusal can cost anything from being beating to being delayed from conducting business, an unbearable price for drivers who must make as many runs as possible to turn a profit on buses they rent by the hour. Cutting their losses, drivers succumb to lifting even belligerent officers. The sight of the soldier in front of me is so familiar, a commonsense transaction for public transit drivers across Lagos. But this transaction rests on the threat of violation, on the capacity of one to forcibly extract value from the other using unspoken scenarios of quotidian state violence scripted into daily commute for millions across Lagos. It's been true for decades (borne out in "Uniform Chance" in MOP 1 [Movement of the People No. 1]). I quietly listen to "Zombie," neglecting to find out whether it is still a potent observation of Nigerian life decades after its original composition. There will be no air guitars to "Zombie." I nod away the rest of the song, reflecting on scenarios and a troubling climax that does not quite happen. One must pause and consider how deeply woven quotidian violence (and the specter of violation) by soldiers and other state actors is into everyday life. The moment testifies equally to the efficacy of Afrobeat in defamiliarizing an oppressive order between state and citizens. These thoughts float around as I arrive at the Kalakuta Museum, hoping to meet John at the penthouse as planned. He is running late, so I instead chat with the young man who cleans the museum. He's rather quiet, but he occasionally makes good small talk. We've only had fleeting conversations over the past few days. He enjoys working here, he shares. There are just a few drawbacks to working at the museum. One is the Afrobeat songs that play around the clock. They might excite guests who spend a couple of hours here and leave, but they tire him. Another challenge is the smoke from the igbó; it affects his breathing. I empathize

and wonder about the solution to the two things at the Kalakuta Museum that trouble him. His last day on the job is two days away, after which he will sit for a college admission exam at the University of Ibadan.

John saunters into the penthouse. He wraps himself a joint and puffs away. He's not predisposed to joking, so it sticks when he tells me that he needs the joint for the task we have before us, namely getting Kevwe to talk to me on the second meeting. As we make our way downstairs, I ask John about how rooms were shared before the commune became a tourist destination. I want to know, for example, who lived in what room, on what floor, and in what proximity to whom. Such information could reveal something crucial about how gendered power was expressed spatially and architecturally in Kalakuta's final iteration. John obliges, attaching each room to some of its former inhabitants. He shares that a major renovation changed the dimension and number of rooms, something I did not know. Unsurprisingly, the handful of Queens in the commune shared the second floor with Fela alongside other long-standing Egypt 80 members. In the living room on the second floor, Fela welcomed friends, visitors, and the press. The configuration of the ground floor was more fluid, John explains; it contained a living area that doubled as a sleeping area as well as rooms for newbies and younger members of the commune. The penthouse had been under construction for years before Fela died, so it served—and still occasionally does—as an open-air rehearsal space for Egypt 80. I learn from John that Fehintola's room was closest to Fela's. Two other Shrine-bound gentlemen join John and I as we make our way from the museum. It's been about two hours, and I am eager to get to the Shrine to meet Kevwe. I sense another delay is underway when a sizable SUV crawls to a stop in front of us and John and the men shuffle in anticipation. Someone mutters "Dede," for Dede Mabiakwu. I keep my composure as he steps out of the vehicle with an air of royalty. The men in my company scramble to help Dede with his notepad, iPad, and cellphone. What unfortunate timing, I mumble to myself as the men escort Dede back into the compound. Dede makes a stop at Fela's tomb to pour libation and say quiet prayers. It's a brief but poignant moment. And yet I feel mildly irritated at the sudden pivot in plans; we should be on our way to the Shrine by now. John follows Dede, signaling with his head that I should come along. I'm pleased to see Dede in person but frustrated and eager to return to the urgent business of conducting an interview at the Shrine. John turns around and, without breaking stride as we ascend the stairs, whispers, "You fit use style enter am. E fit get something to tell you / You should stylishly engage Dede. He might have something useful to share." It reassures me that he's not totally abandoned the task at hand. Dede knows a lot, he adds, perhaps sensing my doubt. It is difficult to tell if John means it or is trying to compensate for the change in plans. I harbor no doubt that Dede knows about Fela and Kalakuta, but I wonder how useful he might be for my research on the Queens. It feels like turning in circles when we return to the penthouse.

Dede has an air to him: he exudes celebrity (having been a judge on the TV franchise Nigerian Idol*), blending elegance with unmistakable street smarts. He's dressed casually on this occasion, in a simple white T-shirt and slippers, and glibly codeswitches between flowery English and Warri-inflected Pidgin. Dede sometimes speaks like he has a camera trailed on him; other times, he proceeds without pageantry. I learn quickly that he speaks frankly. I pick a table a distance away as the men escort him to sit. Dede and I end up sharing a table; serendipitously, Dede needs to charge his phone, and my table is closest to the socket.*

The first few minutes of our fortuitous encounter are awkward. I am unsure of how to strike up a conversation and do not want to appear unfriendly. I am helped by one of the men in our company, who informs Dede that I am a student "wey dey do research on Fela women." Dede smiles mockingly and names me "Ashewo" (Prostitute). He asks why of every possible Afrobeat subject I would choose to study the women. He then asks what school I attend. "The University of Texas at Austin," I reply. "Really? My niece attends your school," he replies. It is a moment of connection, eased more by Dede's warmth, humor, and good fortune than by my being a savvy ethnographer. As often happens, Dede shares fond memories of Fela—"The Master," as he calls the late musician. Then he changes the subject abruptly to the Queens. "They are the engines of Afrobeat," he says, using a metaphor that implies his earlier ashewo joke concealed deeper thoughts about the women. Dede picks his words with intention, sometimes stressing syllables as much for show as to convey seriousness. "Those women hold the history of this place, men," inflecting the final exclamation. He pauses his reflection when the waiter comes around to take orders. We speak about Fela and Kalakuta spiritualism, two fond topics for Dede, I learn.

"I will paint you a picture. A vivid picture." A faint streak of seriousness flashes across his face as he speaks. But there is also a randomness with which the picture enters the discussion, as if it has only just occurred to him. He wants me to remember, to remind him about this picture; it becomes the most important aspect to our meeting. It's also his way of letting me know there's more. "Remind me when we next speak." He shares his cellphone number and address, inviting me to visit his place at eleven the next morning. Dede leaves the penthouse with the same shuffle that announced his arrival. We meet up the following day. I arrive in the middle of a studio rehearsal for an upcoming performance in honor of Nigerian reggae singer Oritz Wiliki, whom I also meet at Dede's. It is early afternoon; two hours after my arrival, we are alone in Dede's apartment. He permits me to take notes and record our conversation. We speak about international politics, Ebola, Afrobeat, and Kalakuta spiritualism. We are forty-five minutes in when he wonders why I have not brought up the picture he

talked about. It's the reason he invited me to his place. I apologize and clarify that I was hoping it would come up organically during the conversation. He pauses for a long time. When Dede finally speaks, his voice shakes with emotion. It's a stark contrast from Dede at the penthouse or Dede in the studio. He tells me a story. In the story, he recalls standing at the back of the auditorium beside some Kalakuta women. Professor Olikoye in front of the auditorium, revealing things they'd never heard before. Dede asks me to imagine the feeling of standing there as the professor delivered news of Fela's death, of the nature of his death. Dede's apartment shudders with life when he speaks, and it succumbs to deafening quiet when he doesn't. The emotions of this moment are palpable. The apartment's quiet completes Dede's picture.

—⁓—

Sociologist Orlando Patterson has famously offered the concept of "social death" to describe how chattel slavery denied the enslaved every conceivable form of social belonging. They were given no recognizable social existence outside domination and were alienated from all rights.[62] Others have conceived of social death differently, as a series of significant losses rather than a single albeit monumental event—social disconnection, loss of social identity, and the disintegration of the body.[63] These approaches to social death are instructive in understanding the mistreatment of Afrobeat women in the aftermath of the HIV/AIDS saga. Kalakuta in the 1970s hosted women from a mix of middle-class and working-class homes, giving the commune a sense of socioeconomic diversity. This class dynamics by the late 1980s was markedly different, featuring women from overwhelmingly poor and working-class backgrounds. They had weaker ties to family in Lagos or had been rejected by family. The combination of weak protective social ties and the possibility of having contracted what was widely perceived as a fatal disease condemned Afrobeat women to a state of being presumed nonexistent or already dead.[64] Olikoye's tone and orientation at the press conference took on heightened significance considering this state of vulnerability. The confluence of disease and social death was hardly a theoretical proposition. In 1997, the treatment for HIV/AIDS by one estimate cost a staggering ₦660,000 per year; for the poor, contracting the virus was a death sentence.[65] Afrobeat women found themselves incrementally stripped of a sense of belonging to Afrobeat—by family, society, and by the community itself. In addition to being denied a platform for public mourning, they were denied the right to privacy. They were discursively framed as bodies to be marked and surveilled. Dede described the feeling as having a target on your back. One prominent example of emergent discursive framing correlating to social death will suffice. The 2003 New York exhibition *Black President: The Art and Legacy of Fela Anikulapo-Kuti* became one of the biggest art events in honor of Fela's memory outside of Nigeria. Visual artist Sokari Douglas Camp contributed a piece titled *Open and Close* to the exhibition. A highlight of Camp's work was a life-sized Queen figure bearing the word "AIDS" across her forehead (fig. 6.1). Mechanized hips propelled the figure's bottom half to flap the legs in and out, conjuring Fela's dance song by the same title ("Open and Close" [1971]) and the notion of sexual abstinence—the closing of open thighs—that dominated AIDS discourse in the 1990s and early 2000s.[66] If the figure's body is the repository of a density of colonial and neocolonial imaginings around female sexual excess, the figure of the dancing Queen becomes a concrete signifier of the threat such excess poses and, once assigned a body, of the potential to behold, contain, and discipline *it*. The intention behind the work, Camp claims, was to channel Fela's spirit through the women. But the visual, mechanical, and discursive space inhabited by the figure of the Queen and the Afrobeat female body does not fully corroborate such reading.[67] Camp's expressed intention is overwhelmed by the figuration of the Queen as an embodiment of contagion, an idea circulating since Fela died. The final sentence in the description of Camp's piece conveys no sense of ambiguity about the thrust of the piece: "Fela was a symbol of West African style he had so much power [*sic*], but all of his strength could not save him from AIDS."[68] A more sensitive handling of the women's experience would demonstrate the need for the interpretation of performance related to HIV/AIDS to include its reverberations in a broader cultural context under specific historical circumstances. *Open and Close* illustrates how easily Afrobeat women, personified by the figure of the Queen, became viewed as bodies of disease, bodies so potent that Fela succumbed to their contagion. Simultaneously caricature and synecdoche, the dancing figure in Camp's work reminds us, as does David Román in *Acts of Intervention*, of the need to read AIDS performances beyond the event and for their broader effects "on the actual participants—performers and spectators."[69] One problematic outcome of AIDS representation in Afrobeat, embodied by *Open and Close*, is how the disease was attached squarely to the bodies of women in a stigmatizing fashion. This stigma hastened the women's symbolic and material excision from the Afrobeat family while fomenting a sense of disbelonging. Camp's work might be read against the public discourse that attributes blame and responsibility to women, offers few positive images of women's bodies, or considers them "too infectious" to be considered "aesthetic material for the public's imagination."[70]

Figure 6.1. Sokari Douglas Camp's kinetic sculpture *Open and Close*, exhibited at *Black President: The Art and Legacy of Fela Anikulapo-Kuti* (2003). Credit: ©2022 Artists Rights Society (ARS), New York / DACS, London.

If the handful of Queens struggled for empathy and recognition, then what fate awaited the litany of younger women who joined Afrobeat from the late 1980s onward, women who lacked even the modest social recognition some Queens managed to attain? Although this newer group was denied whatever modicum of dignity the public might have reluctantly ascribed to, for instance, Queens who were mothers, it nonetheless inherited all the disdain society reserved for Afrobeat women in general. These women also had to wrestle with AIDS-induced social anxiety and avoidance eliciting from many of them defiant resilience. So goes the story of Olanrewaju Oyeyemi, a twenty-five-year-old (at the time of Fela's death) dancer who joined Egypt 80 in 1991. After an initial visit to the Shrine, Oyeyemi was so enthralled by Fela's saxophone solos that she relocated to Kalakuta the same week. "I can't say whether I was his lover or not, but he was not my husband. I didn't have any child for him. I have my own boyfriend."[71] Oyeyemi might have been uncertain about her future, but she was certain about one thing: "I will dance until I die," whether Egypt 80 is "still alive" or "dies." Oyeyemi imagined a future with children and a family of her own. She spoke of hope—not hope in the sense of resigned optimism, but defiant hope that fearlessly embraced mortality. When asked about AIDS, she offered a piercing response: "Even if I have AIDS I don't bloody care. And I can never go for AIDS test. Over my dead body. Even if I agree to go for test, the doctor will also like to do his own. . . . Once he sees my nakedness, he would want to do."[72] Oyeyemi littered images of death through her interview, perhaps foreshadowing what was to come. She died roughly a week later, in the days between the interview and its publication. It is striking how Oyeyemi pointed to gendered abuse as a primary factor in her choice not to get tested for AIDS, underscoring the suspicion with which women who understood themselves as belonging to the underclass viewed the medical industry, even if the consequences could be fatal. A deep-seated disdain for mainstream society and its values continued to drive women like Oyeyemi to Afrobeat. It is a stinging indictment of Nigerian society that some wagered their bets on refusing to participate no matter the personal cost. Disdain for and disillusionment with Nigerian political elites and an unequal order drove young women to Afrobeat in the early 1970s. Oyeyemi implied the same to be true in the early 1990s. It is easy to characterize these women as leeches whose only salvation was Afrobeat. What often goes unsaid is how their desire for flourishing lives may have been cut short by their association with Afrobeat. Casting them as problems prevents a genuine reckoning with the full scope of their vulnerability and legitimate desire for a dignified life in the arts.

The fallout of the post-Fela saga was varied and complex. Mary Umude-Haverkamp, a former Egypt 80 singer, painted a different post-Afrobeat portrait of vulnerability and mourning. Unlike Oyeyemi, Mary parted ways with Afrobeat in 1991, six years before Fela's death. Mary recalled experiencing a deep sense of loss when news of Fela's death reached her in Germany three months after the fact: "I was shocked. I remember, I brought out one of his albums that night. I lit a candle. I just cried all night; listened to his music; got myself drunk and went to bed."[73] Mourning transformed into apprehension when she learned the cause of death. Departing the Afrobeat scene long before Fela's death did not immunize Mary from crippling anxiety, her situation made more complex by living in Germany as an undocumented immigrant. Chief among her concerns was the fear of being deported if diagnosed with HIV/ AIDS. She confided in her then boyfriend (now husband), recommending that he get tested for the disease. After two long weeks, his results arrived: negative. "I was very happy, but I was not one hundred percent sure, because I wanted to do my own test." Mary gave birth to two healthy daughters and was certain that the hospital must have done blood tests, including an HIV/AIDS test, as part of the birthing process. Yet the realization failed to offer closure about her status. Mary finally got herself tested in 2013, after becoming a citizen of Germany. She could finally breathe a sigh of relief when the results returned. The many years Mary spent waiting for a clean bill of health were nothing short of agonizing. While grateful for her sound health, Mary had new and lingering questions. "If Fela had AIDS, I would surely have it," she wondered aloud before proceeding to offer three possible explanations.[74] One, Fela contracted the disease after her departure. Two, her immune system had protected her from the disease (if indeed Fela had contracted AIDS before she left). Three, Fela did not die of AIDS, a line of reasoning that has traction in certain quarters of the Afrobeat community and certain academic circles.[75] Kevwe offered similar interrogations about her own clean bill of health: "If he died of AIDS, how come it did not affect me?"[76] A noted Afrobeat scholar claimed at a Fela symposium at the University of Lagos that the press had mischaracterized Olikoye's report of Fela's cause of death. The scholar went on to claim, quoting Olikoye, that Fela died "likely due to" complications from AIDS.[77] The transcript of Olikoye's press conference conveys no such ambiguity. The controversy around the *exact* cause of Fela's death is important, but not to a degree that eclipses stocktaking of the full implications of what AIDS meant those closest to Fela, especially for the women. For Mary Umude-Haverkamp, who lived for years engulfed by fear, it is all still a mystery. Her memories of Fela and of Kalakuta are fond but coexist with a disquieting sense of irresolution.

Oppressing Widows

This has been a story of patriarchy and its degradation of women's dignity. The story of women's post-Fela struggles resonates with a broader practice of widow oppression. Widowhood rites humiliate and disempower women. Feminist playwrights and novelists have intervened in widowhood as a site of rupture and of intense rituals that reproduce patriarchy in the instance of a death. The interventions made by these authors have rendered widowhood a well-explored subject in creative and critical sites of feminist exposition. For these authors, the death of a patriarch not only yields a feminist literary conflict but also unearths the moral bankruptcy of a society that preys on widows at their most vulnerable. The protagonists in Zulu Sofola's *Wedlock of the Gods* and Mariama Ba's *So Long a Letter* make this point. In *Wedlock of the Gods*, the experience of Ogwoma, the main character, illustrates how rituals of mourning facilitate the process of stripping widows of dignity. When her husband Adigwu dies, Ogwoma secretly reunites with her true love, Uloko. Ogwoma hated her late husband and married him only because her parents needed the money for bride price to treat her sick brother. In a single stroke, patriarchy traded her to save a brother and sold her to a man she abhorred. Ogwoma's defiant reunion with Uloko violates the customary three-month mourning period; their dalliance is further complicated by her pregnancy one month after Adigwu's death. Her romance with Uloko interrupts a tradition demanding that she marry her late husband's brother. Ogwoma rebels: "Now, you can go and tell them that their plans will fail. Tell them that I will be buried alive before I become Okezie's wife. They will see fire from me."[78] Odibei, the aggrieved mother of the late husband, manipulates Ogwoma to commit suicide through diabolical spiritual powers. Uloko follows Ogwoma's lead, taking his life in a culminating double suicide. The play's tension is forged between an individual's claim to agency and a community's determination to delegitimize that claim.

In Mariama Ba's epistolary novel *So Long a Letter*, Ramatoulaye, a Senegalese school teacher, pens a series of personal letters to her childhood friend Aisattou. The recent death of Ramatoulaye's husband, Modou Fall, spurs the letters. In them, Ramatoulaye recounts her memories, frustrations, travails, joys, pains, and especially feelings of betrayal she harbors toward her late husband. After twenty-five years of marriage and twelve children with Ramatoulaye, Modou Fall married a younger second wife. "In loving someone else," Ramatoulaye writes, "he burned his past [with me], both morally and materially. He dared to commit such an act of disavowal."[79] While living with loss and surviving gendered rituals of mourning, Ramatoulaye conveys the heaviness and irresolution she feels toward a deceased husband she resents: "Child-naming ceremonies may be missed but never a funeral. . . . Reared since childhood on their strict precepts, I expect not to fail. The walls that limit my horizon for four months and ten days do not bother me. I have enough memories in me to ruminate upon. And these are what I am afraid of, for they smack of bitterness."[80] A patriarch's death offers an occasion for mourning as much as for disciplining widows. This discipline aims to deprive mourning women of the fruits of their labor as partners while curtailing more broadly the terrain of action available to them. The custody of children and, where applicable, wealth sharing are flashpoints in the matrix of oppression.

These literary accounts foreground the space of mourning as critical to recalibrating the claim families make over a patriarch's assets. In a letter to Aisattou, Ramatoulaye reflects on in-laws who cart away "wad of notes, painstakingly topped, and leave us utterly destitute, we who will need material support."[81] The moral underbelly of gendered privation is elaborated in the event of death and mourning, the former an inescapable social fact, the latter an active process of commiseration and dispossession in which the demands to bereave under scrutiny trump the emotional well-being of the bereaved. Widow oppression binds Ramatoulaye and Ogwoma to the Queens, the closest of Afrobeat women to the category of widowhood. Each of these literary and real protagonists respond differently to their dilemma—Ramatoulaye composes letters, Ogwoma rebels and takes her life, while Najite, Kevwe, and Fehintola wrestled for recognition for their extensive labor for Afrobeat music—but a syntax of gendered control enacted at the scene of mourning connects their lives in poignant and culturally intelligible ways. HIV/AIDS emerged as a structuring force in 1990s West African public life, complicating the woes already attending the status of widowhood. And with a figure like Fela as the deceased patriarch, the stakes rose to unimaginable proportions, even as Afrobeat called into question widowhood itself. Considering these layers of social and artistic erasure, Afrobeat women questioned their very sense of the past, the vibrant and troublesome lives they had led as artists. Social death threatened to define their reality. The disease added its own complication, pressuring the women into worrying quickly about their health and, in an immediate sense, their own mortality.

In addition to bestowing a staggering body of pioneering music and a legacy of activism to Nigerians, Fela left behind a trail of vulnerable women who, having made huge compromises for the man, the music, and the subculture, found themselves clinging to life itself. Showing sympathy for or reckoning with Afrobeat women's precarious condition as possibly sick with HIV/AIDS and in need of emotional, psychological, and financial support placed a certain moral responsibility on the public as well as on Fela's immediate family. Empathy would have implied an acknowledgment of the largely working-class women of Afrobeat as crucial co-laborers in the genre's commonwealth and, by implication, as deserving of recognition (if not compensation). This form of reckoning would have demanded accounting for the possibility that Fela had had a fatal impact on the trajectories of many of the women's lives. Indeed, chances are high that Fela contracted the virus from one of the Kalakuta women. Yet little consideration was given to the idea that Fela might have played the role of vector himself, infecting many women through his sexual choices. Or, as Laura Edmondon productively frames it, to "the materialities of infection," the fact of a virus's quiet replication in human cells, which should in turn frame our read of aesthetic and social performance.[82] Rumors flourished, for instance, that an ex-Kalakuta woman had died of AIDS a few days after Fela.[83] Might Fela have been compromised by his many sexual partners while at the same time acting as an infector himself? The question is pertinent especially because economic, gender, and generational inequalities—all long-standing qualities of Fela's relationship with women—limited women's ability to self-advocate in their effort to prevent contracting HIV. Married women's "greatest risk of contracting HIV is through sexual intercourse with their husbands," and it is men who are likely to infect their wives, less the other way around.[84] Carlos Moore's speculation that "perhaps three of the women died of AIDS" hints at the social nature of transmission and the role that Fela's public posturing of masculinity may have played in the women's susceptibility to it, considering the structural inequalities that defined their relationship with him.[85] Nuance of this kind appeared incompatible with the desires and calculations at play in Fela's wake. Such discussion became particularly difficult in the narrow space between the shock of loss, asset consolidation, and the real-time martyring of Fela. Public mourning did not simply open space for grief; it inaugurated discipline and erasure. Questions of inheritance and the perception that Fela had recklessly compromised his class privilege combined with the fear of AIDS stigma to intensify the impulse to protect his legacy. This challenge required excising, in a literal and symbolic sense, the women who survived him. So when Femi retorted a few days after the burial that some of the women "brought [Fela] all the bad image and personal health problems he had,"[86] he was actively oiling the social mechanisms by which the women would be made into pariahs. Fela's death set in motion the process of reinstating him to his *proper* elite status, a move that required, above anything else, putting distance between him and the women. This narrative was repeated sixteen years after Fela's burial when Femi mused, "I couldn't understand why he married 27 wives."[87] This rhetoric implies that Afrobeat could have developed without the women's long-standing presence and participation, without their investment in episodes of the playful and the grotesque. In death, Fela reaped the benefits of maleness, stardom, and elite upbringing, even at a time of acute HIV/AIDS stigmatization. As a collective and as individuals, Afrobeat women, many disowned by kith and kin, had their activist and artistic legacy and their gendered struggles all but erased. Profound shame and regret took root in place of nostalgia. Self-censorship replaced tales of survival, gallantry, and adventure. Many distanced themselves from Afrobeat altogether, blending back into the crowd of Afrobeat fans and into mainstream society. Only a few recalled and relished the flutters of freedom that Afrobeat had offered. Rather than being part a storied account of working-class women's creative activism, the Queens became scapegoats, a spectacle of the fatal risks of nonconformity—a warning that playing might produce devastatingly gendered outcomes and that, in Nigeria, the repercussions of flirting with freedom fall unduly on women, more so if they are poor and working class. In short, yesterday's fire dancers, women who had mastered Afrobeat's pulse and groove, were asked to dance to a new and strange tune. And on this new stage, the women were tenderfeet. If for twenty years they had grown accustomed to the attention they drew to themselves as trailblazing embodiments of unfettered sensuality, as figures of idealized African beauty, now they could hardly escape the AIDS-driven surveillance and scrutiny to which they were subjected. They had spent most of their lives firing up sexual fantasies at the Shrine, but in the 1990s, they became embodiments of the dreaded aspects of sexuality. Their long-standing collaboration with Fela had been brought to an abrupt if catastrophic climax. Some succumbed, uncelebrated.

Not All Deaths Are Equal: A Requiem of Sorts

Writing about Afrobeat women takes moments of mourning. It's a requisite for the work. I begin research for this chapter with a deceptively simple question: what became of the Queens after Fela died? Stories of the lives of the women beyond 1997 and beyond Afrobeat are scant. Interviews with the Queens invariably contain moments of gratitude for being alive and references to peers who did not survive Nigeria and Afrobeat. The act of mourning that entails this work becomes even more difficult when I come across the deaths of women with whom I have cultivated a sense of familiarity. Some days of writing, I imagine daily life in Kalakuta Republic with such clarity that I visualize entire scenes. In this immersive state, I isolate specific voices from the communal banter. This of course is untrue, but it underscores a feeling of being or a desire to be there. One fallout of this immersion is that specific women coalesce in my mind from strips of stories told by many others. Like phantoms that gradually take on human dimension, these women take their form through archival photographs, concert videos, fleeting video recordings in which the camera pans away too quickly, and other women's stories about unrelated Afrobeat events. This is how some women emerge as complex persons, not just aesthetic figures. These encounters and this intimacy make learning about their deaths tough to deal with, however belatedly I come across their deaths.

I find an announcement buried in the penultimate paragraph of an untrusted online source: "Iyase [sic], Funmilayo and Fehintola, died in 2000, 2005 and 2006 respectively."[88] I should disregard the news source for reporting Fehintola as passing in 2006 instead of 2007, but I struggle to shake off how a single sentence can flatten a life, three lives. The author misspells Ihase's name in a familiar and biting disregard for who she was. This disregard, consistent with the post-Fela reporting of the Queens' misfortune, confirms, in a wicked irony, the veracity of the author's claims about their passing. The fact that they died, for the author, is less significant than weaving their obituary into the announcement that Najite had been arrested for marijuana possession by drug law enforcement. The article's title sums up the author's interest: "Fela Anikulapo-Kuti's Wife, 2 Others Arrested with Marijuana in Lagos." It is in this story that I learn of two of the three deaths. The story's intent is clearly not to mourn but to sensationalize, to extend the freak show of women's misery that Afrobeat became.

I soon learn the substance of the account is true: Najite was arrested and bailed out by the Kutis; Funmilayo died poor in Agege, a working-class Lagos neighborhood. Seun Kuti confirms the details of his mother's passing, how she mourned Fela but surely embraced life again in the years that followed. Olaide Babayale-Kuti recounted being at Fehintola's final moments at the Lagos University Teaching Hospital in 2007. A more specific account of Ihase's death comes from Kevwe. Ihase's body, Kevwe recalls with repulsion, was discovered in Ikeja. Ihase's aggrieved brother swore to avenge her death, reacting to what he felt was a targeted killing. He was called to identify his late sister's remains.[89] Her family buried her in Benin, the city wherefrom she had made an audacious sojourn to Lagos and Kalakuta in 1975.

Although we never met, I have cultivated a strange familiarity with Ihase, who walked the world with an electric personality. Onstage, Ihase's lively spirit matched her crisp voice. She was very photogenic, managing to convey joy even in the most fleeting of photographic encounters. I think of Ihase only as widely beloved, as the kind of woman to animate a room with her jovial presence. My speculations about Ihase's person are not totally unfounded. Carlos Moore, who met her in 1981, describes her in poetic language: "Ihase's strength rests in her quiet assuredness. Although youthful in appearance, she has a maturity greater than her years. Never imposing but always kind, soft-spoken and quick to smile. Oval-faced and mango-tinted brown, she spends much time on her appearance, but always in a natural unaffected manner. She is a young girl who knows what she is about, whether on stage as one of Fela's singers, or off."[90] A portrait of a beaming Ihase sits adjacent to Moore's description. Ihase has the same disposition in archival concert videos and documentaries. In a recording of the Berlin Jazz Festival, for instance, Ihase bellows the opening vocal response to "Power Show," her mouth forming an exaggerated "O" on "Show-oh." She sings as though assigned a different vocal response from her peers. In a brief snippet from the documentary Fela Kuti: Music Is the Weapon, *Ihase, conscious of the camera's focus on her, teases another woman who has failed to help braid her hair. "O ò ri pé wón ń film mi gan ńsìn-ín. Ó ò dè ̣fé ̣bá mi ṣe'run mi l'ẹ̀ẹ̀kan. Mo tún ma popular ńsìn-ín. / You see that they are now filming me well; and you did not want to help me make my hair the other time. I will now become popular."* I anticipated meeting her, wondering if she were like the other Queens I interviewed, if she were different from the image of her preserved in historical documents. My frustration mounts when, asking two other Queens about Ihase, they have little to say or simply brush the matter aside. I concede with some reluctance that there might have been tension in their relationship with her—or something else that made Ihase boringly human. Learning that she has died and the manner of her death feels like a gut punch. That an obscure, inconsequential website published news of her death and of other Afrobeat women convinces me that a meeting with Ihase will never happen. The news requires me to step away, recompose my thoughts, and quit writing for the day.

When I learn that Dodomaya has passed on, the circumstances sound eerily similar to Ihase's death. (Dodo's solo dancing is described in chap. 3.) My first, fleeting encounter with Dodo is at the wooden stall she operates opposite the New Afrika Shrine. Her face is covered in bright blue and white pastel dots, a statement to competitors along the road of her credentials. Her stock includes affordable alcohol served in shot bottles and "skoochies," a fruity alcoholic drink served with ice in a disposable plastic cup. Dodo, John assures me, invented skoochies as a potent alternative to the pricier drinks sold at the Shrine's VIP bar. Two five-ounce cups embolden the timid, John adds. I surmise that the drink is precisely what's animated the two talkative men arguing about politics at Dodo's stall. Dodo sports a bright smile when she steps aside to meet me in between fixing orders. We earn the gift of her time only after John introduces me as Seun Kuti's friend from the United States. I am impressed by the ease with which this fib rolls off John's tongue (as I have not yet met Seun). I later appreciate his will to support. Though the meeting lasts a mere four or so minutes, I am grateful for the chance to speak to Dodo amid her visibly busy schedule. We shake hands and exchange pleasantries before she refocuses on impatient customers. This meeting is the only time I set eyes on her. In 2016, Dodo's lifeless body was discovered on a street in Ikeja. After shock from the news, initial speculations were that armed robbers might have attacked Dodo on her lone commute back from the Shrine in the wee hours of the morning. Her body, claims a community of concerned Afrobeat fans on social media trying to make sense of the news, showed no signs of trauma; she seemed to have her personal belongings intact. The online community coalesces around the possibility that Dodo's asthma, a condition she lived with, might have played a role. The most probable cause goes thus: on her way from the Shrine, Dodo suffered an asthma attack and found no help.

In dying, these women, with their bodies, bear witness yet again to the banal cruelty that constitutes life in places defined by coloniality and the afterlives of *colonialism, spaces "of violence and death" that, Ato Quayson offers, are rooted in the traumas of nationhood.[91] To invoke another graphic thesis on the political economy of this state of abjection, "dumped or abandoned corpses are no exception to the rule in the postcolony."[92] Deemed unworthy of grief in life and in death,[93] the condition of Afrobeat women advances a critique of the political economy of Nigerian life: how the state and the state of things quite literally pulverizes and disposes of the vulnerable, whose bodies become metonyms of national putrescence. Dodo's is an all too familiar Nigerian story of deaths died too cheaply. I reflect on a question: what use is a revolution that cannot mourn its dead? I share a brief tribute to Dodo on social media in a post that paves the way for my meeting Mary Umude-Haverkamp, who, having known Dodo in Kalakuta, was quietly mourning the loss while recalling Dodo's uncelebrated artistic contribution to Afrobeat. Mary and I schedule a phone conversation. We devote the bulk of our initial conversation to talking about Dodomaya, and the next call, to talking about Mary.*

7

"Where We Fall Is Where We Pick Ourselves Up From"

A Legacy in Fragments

This chapter explores three discernible strands of the Queens' legacy considering the attempt to curate Fela's around their exclusion. The first strand takes on survival of the odds and the weight of sacrifice in the production of Afrobeat's male stars. This strand zooms in on the final years of singer Fehintola. Her life provides a vivid illustration of how, though estranged by the general lack of empathy for her vulnerability, she saw potential in Afrobeat's narrow definition of motherhood. Fehintola seized hold of the meager possibility afforded by the Kuti family's strategy of presenting Fela's children as proxies to suture the fractures of family that haunted Afrobeat music. The second exploration of the women's legacy revolves around the Queens' resurgence as characters of the African diaspora in Bill T. Jones's choreography of the off-Broadway production of *Fela!* When the show moved to Broadway and completed a highly successful global tour, it rekindled local and international interest in Fela's work and, collaterally, in the women who animated the music. The thrust of this strand that in spite of this interest revolving around the iconicity of the Queens, it still brought to the fore questions about their broader historical significance. The "Queens'" success on Broadway undercut concerted and previously successful attempts in Nigeria at erasing them; their labors preserved in archives in the form of concert footage and photographs mapped a template for the diasporic cast of Black women performers in the Broadway performance, who embraced the Queens as creative and political ancestors and reinterpreted the scope of the women's politics into far-flung projects. The third domain in which to read the women's legacy is in the profound if ambivalent transformation that involvement in Afrobeat came to mean for some of the original Queens themselves. All these legacies resist the ongoing erasure and distortion of their labors and the centrality of their investments in Afrobeat. To understand how these strands of legacy resist erasure, we need to consider the choreographies of memorialization that slowly took hold after Fela died and continued afterward. The chapter wraps up with provocations on Afrobeat as a haunted music genre.

Staging Family: Memorial Projects and Their Discontents

The anxieties that dogged his death and the staging of his funeral hinted at a fraught legacy. The renowned Kuti family, whose business it became to manage Afrobeat's aggrieved women artists, central constituents of the legacy, was saddled with a task that stretched beyond funeral planning. Cleaning up after Fela required curation of a kind that diminished traces of the women over time. Still reeling from two deaths—Fela's and the unexpected passing of Soladegbin (also Sola), Fela's second daughter—the grieving Kuti family planned another major public event: a memorial marking one year since Fela's death. On Friday, July 31, 1998, the late musician's children launched a three-day celebration of his storied life. As with many Kuti events, the debut memorial concert demands more than a surface look; it stands as the first public effort to reconcile some of the contradictions that dogged Fela's life. In her discussion of white grievance around the removal of confederate memorials, Juliet Hooker argues that memorials play a civic and affective function because memorialization "involves how those with political power in a given society organize public space to convey and, thus, to teach the public desired political lessons."[1] The question of what lessons the first Afrobeat memorial concert and its subsequent iterations taught might be answered by attending to efforts at casting Fela's life in messianic terms by the family that gave Afrobeat an image as close as possible to respectable society. Children served as crucial ideological agents in this project of recalibration. All of Fela's known children, except for Salewa, were the memorial concert's unlikely stars. During the finale of the three-day concert, Seun Kuti, then fifteen years old, led Egypt 80 in a performance of Afrobeat classics such as "Clear Road for Jaga Jaga (CRJJ)" and the unreleased "Government of Crooks (GOC)." Femi Kuti led the Positive Force band in a rendition of Fela's "Big Blind Country (BBC)." The bashful Kunle Kuti, who was not particularly inclined to playing music and is now the manager of the Kalakuta Museum, made an unlikely debut at the concert with the song "MASS (Movement Against Second Slavery)." Kunle's fifteen-year-old sister, Motunrayo, also battled stage fright to perform a song.[2] The three-day event represented a befitting tribute to arguably the most prolific artist in contemporary Nigerian history and signaled Afrobeat's striding into a future of which Fela's teenage and adult children would thenceforth be the champions. The concert also set the stage for "Felabration," a weeklong annual concert held at Femi Kuti's New Afrika Shrine in honor of Fela.[3] Particularly striking are the lengths to which the organizers went to showcase Fela's children, even those with minimal interest in live music performance, instead of the seasoned women artists who not only had performed with Egypt 80 but also had the deepest artistic ties to the formation of the genre itself. Given that the events of the 1998 concert ran into the wee hours of morning, it is likely that the mothers of the teenage performers escorted their children to the Shrine or observed the proceedings from the audience or backstage. They also could have excused themselves in the unlikely event that they were invited. However, the absence of Queens and other experienced women performers framed them as belonging to an era of Afrobeat from which the family sought distance. Given the tensions between the family and the women at the funeral a year earlier, ceding the spotlight to Fela's children constituted a difficult but strategic compromise at a moment of diminished reputation and weak social leverage for the women. A legible sign of this strategic compromise was Seun Kuti's highly visible participation at the memorial concert. Seun, the most musically active of the children born to the Queens, performed the unreleased "Government of Crooks" as the ultimate song for the Friday concert. He also performed what an eyewitness described as "the high point" of the Sunday concert two days later, a rousing saxophone solo that brought Fela's elder sister, Dolu, onstage. Aunt Dolu, as she is fondly called, rewarded Seun's accomplished efforts with "measured steps that elicited a deafening applause from the audience." In the ultimate gesture of appreciation of Seun's performance and his aunt's validation, the other children appeared onstage to spray the duo with "crisp naira notes," a Yoruba/Nigerian display of prestige, patronage, and validation of performance competence at social functions. Each child took turns at the end of the night singing parts of "Big Blind Country" as Femi Kuti led the instrumentation with Positive Force.[4] It was a concert by and for Fela's known children that tentatively softened the troublesome question of Afrobeat's definition of family and of Fela's legacy.

The first memorial concert and the many that followed it need to be understood as recursive attempts at giving flesh to the affective force of an abstract and nebulous concept of family in Afrobeat. This kind of commemoration demonstrates what Dwight Conquergood calls the affective power of rituals as embodied performances that transform "vague ideas, mixed feelings, and shaky commitments into dramatic clarity and alignment."[5] As contestations between nuclear and communal definitions of family sat at the heart of the post-Fela feud, the decision-making wing of the Kuti family, which gradually and reluctantly incorporated Kalakuta elements, required constant restaging for the public; public performances thenceforth inaugurated the ongoing exercise of loosening and contracting the boundaries of who was in and who was not—who was a Kuti and who was not. Public concerts were thus rituals of recursive resolution. For Afrobeat fans, nostalgia colored the live experience of the memorial concert. Egypt 80 and Positive Force indulged them in reliving Afrobeat favorites as well as songs that Fela had performed at the Shrine but not recorded. Crucially, the concert produced a transcript that was hidden in plain sight. The event signaled, quite publicly, a cautious truce between two key factions within the family: the "legal" children and the potentially restive children born to Queens, living souvenirs of how Afrobeat was joined at the hip to working-class women, and quite literally so. Children acted as proxies in mediating competing interests, their sometimes-amateur performance a portal into the uneasy compromise brokered between the Kuti family and the "excess" women. Public performances of this kind became one way for Afrobeat to paper over a fraught past and, with it, unresolved questions of debt and fairness. But fielding children as *the* performers also showcased Afrobeat as a genre that, while still in flux in Fela's wake, was certainly, to draw on Malik Gaines's reflection on amateurism, "liberated from the coercive mastery of production and style."[6] Watching amateurs onstage asked the audience to suspend their scrutiny as of both aesthetic performance, technical execution of the concert, and cultural performance, the tentative reconstitution of family. Spotlighting Queens' children publicly implied a sketchy integration of their mothers into the family, a truce of sorts. Public staging of Afrobeat memory, orchestrated by the family, imagined a future that elided Afrobeat's historical entanglement with women—specifically the Queens, many of whom had been marginalized by varying combinations of trauma, poverty, intimidation, disbelief, and death. As such, the amateur concert performance had a double temporality: it gestured to a future absence of Queens while circumscribing the scope of inquiry about the past. Implied in the Queens' and women's exclusion from post-Fela public proceedings, from the funeral to the memorial concert, was the insistence that they were marginal actors in Afrobeat's success—put differently, that public celebrations of Fela's life would have included the women had they been worthwhile agents of said past. Here, absence measured worth. But this fiction of the past and future needed to be recursively restored, constantly reenacted albeit also by beginners to take hold as cultural truth.

The impulse to consolidate a narrow version of family and worth lay behind yet another concert, this time by Fela's grandson Made Kuti, who in 2021 performed his debut album at Terra Kulture, Lagos. With COVID-19 protocols such as masking and distancing in place, Made performed songs from his debut album, revealingly dubbed *For(e)ward* (2021). The album was published collaboratively with his father, Femi Kuti. Like Made's forward-looking debut album, the joint album with Femi is titled *Legacy+*. The gesture of looking back to move forward is embodied by Made's band name, The Movement, harkening back to Fela's party, "Movement of the People." The mix of Africa 70 songs and Made's compositions at the concert cleared space to construct him in a storied genealogy of Kutis, a line of distinguished men artists—"Afrobeat royalty" or "a chip off the Kuti block," as one writer described him.[7] In *For(e)ward*'s fourth song, "Different Streets," Made makes the case patently: "I truly respect those who rise through hardship, defying all odds through hard work and good leadership. My family is one of those. That's why I know the difference between making an honest living and corrupt embezzlement." The act of clearing space for one version of Afrobeat's future is clearly an act of exclusion. Who is included in Made's glib mention of "my family"? Who does the possessive "my" not include? The concert offered some hints. Indeed, just as striking as the strategic return to the past and the rhetorical construction of family and legacy was the restaging of a version of what constitutes the Kuti family itself. Seun Kuti, no longer a teenager but now an internationally acclaimed artist in his own right, continued to embody the compromise vision of family tentatively inaugurated at the 1998 concert and performed virtually every year at Felabrations. In 2021, Seun, the virtuosic teenage son of Queen Fehintola whom Aunt Dolu had sprayed with money at the 1998 memorial concert, was beckoned as a crucial figure in the restaging of family. Seun was called to act as an ill-fitting surrogate for his mother and, by extension, for the unaccounted for women whose stories drips out of every note of Afrobeat music. It was precisely the staging of the stitching together that struck an eyewitness. Their recounting of the moment Seun joined Made onstage stands out for its uncanny resemblance to the moment Aunt Dolu had invited herself onstage twenty-three years earlier. "As the crowd giggled and gyrated to the young Kuti's electrifying performance," the eyewitness writes, "a key highlight for the night was when Made brought on his uncle, Seun Kuti, and his father, Femi Kuti, for separate duets. In fact, his father performed twice on stage with him, bringing back some of the iconic Fela Kuti tunes such as 'Trouble Sleep Yanga Go Wake Am,' 'Zombie,' among others."[8] The truce with a still-unresolved past signaled an even deeper cultural operation. Hershini Bhana Young offers an insightful analysis of beauty pageants and freak shows that is instructive here. Beauty pageants are ambivalent rituals of femininity that conflate national bodies and women's bodies in the staging of unattainable, idealized femininity. Freak shows are spectacular embodiments of the odd, the ugly, and the grotesque. Yet these performative genres, Young argues, are more intimately linked than might appear at first glance. The central point is the mutually constitutive nature of ostensibly dissimilar genres of performance, the inextricability of the bodies that enact them. Pageants "stage the unimaginable ideal against the specter of the aberrant" body, requiring repeated restaging to lend form to the ideal and vice versa.[9] Pageants derive their aesthetic and cultural essence in relation to freak shows, whose ugliness, in turn, props up and parodies beauty pageants. One performative form emerges from the shadow of the other. Young's generative discussion on their coconstitutive nature, the reliance of the one on the other for its essence, is immediately relevant to reading the modalities of post-Fela memorial and legacy performances. Repeated stagings of the ideals of respectable family that proceeded from the first-year memorial became meaningful and potent only because they existed against the backdrop of the public attachment of women's bodies to the HIV/AIDS freak show that preceded it. The Kuti-led concerts have been powerful, if also shaky, showcases of the ideal, heteronormative family against graphic imagery of the women's bodies in artworks such as Sokari Douglas Camp's kinetic sculpture (discussed in chap. 6) and against the material privation and serial deaths of the Queens with each passing year. At these concerts, Kuti men came to embody musical mastery, professionalism, discipline, and staying power (sometimes quite literally in the physical and sweaty exertions that their performances often command); offstage, the women's lives were in tatters, the very antithesis, or so it seemed, of what the Kuti men had constructed for themselves and those included in their definition of family. Restaging the grandeur of the Kuti legacy implied that the family's inability to redeem the restless, uncouth, and potentially diseased women of Afrobeat was further evidence of the moral failings of those women and not a result of their economic deprivation by a powerful class of individuals. Indeed, in constructions of Afrobeat's past, women might be valued for their capacity to birth children befitting the Kuti name. More specifically, women who produced laborers, read male, qualified for partial recognition for their decades of labor. To not be included in this criterion was to be condemned to the cadre of freaks. The most vivid realization of this thinking is found in the idea that the children receive a portion of the royalties from Fela's music; it is at their discretion whether to share their portion with their mothers.

The problem of this practice should be obvious. If Seun and other children acted as stand-ins for Afrobeat *mothers*, then who and what stood in or could stand in for the many women—the majority—who refused to or were denied having children? What or who could stand in for women who prioritized artmaking and childlessness over fecundity? Even the women who mothered children within the Afrobeat community have been remembered by this distorted lens. Tying the women's labor to fecundity in this way not only excluded most women (only a handful of Queens mothered children by Fela) but also pacified a tiny group of Queens whose children, when mature, could publicly advocate for their mothers, stretching out an issue the Kutis wanted resolved sooner. The truce was a long and bumpy road. This conscripting notion of inclusion, grafted onto a narrow conception of motherhood, became a source of angst for certain Queens, leaving them challenging their denial of recognition or a place in contemporary Afrobeat music. "Why won't *I* be recognized?" Olaide asked, her voice shaking with frustration and disappointment. "Why won't *I*, Olaide Babayale-Kuti, be recognized?" she emphasized, pointing to herself this time and staring me square in the eyes to underscore the sheer absurdity that she and many other Queens are excluded from formal reward and recognition.[10] During our first hour-long interview, Olaide called my attention at least three times to a framed photograph, one among several hanging on her sitting room wall. The photograph was of a toddler, a girl, sitting on a sofa. "That is my daughter in Fela's house," she explained each time she drew attention to the photograph, sometimes in the middle of another story or during a pause between questions. Although Olaide had a child in Kalakuta, hers was not fathered by Fela. Interspersing our interview with reminders of her daughter in Fela's house, sitting in "Fela's chair," and narratives of her everyday economic struggle illustrated Olaide's intimate knowledge of the significance ascribed to children in defining the legacy of the few Queens who had children *with Fela*. She gestured later in the interview to the furniture in her sitting room, sparse and worn, asking if it befits "Fela's wife": "Give us money. Let us live well. Let us enjoy the fruit of our labor. Many people have died, but some of them have their children living. . . . I have worked. I worked and worked and worked. . . . Look at my old car that you saw me driving in. Is that what I am supposed to be driving in? Look at my house. Fela's wife. I am only telling the truth, if not, *ìrònú á ti p'ọ́tá mi* / I might have died from misery." Olaide sought to drive home the dissonance between surging global interest in Fela's life and Afrobeat music and the material lives of the many working-class women who gave meaning to the art. Her everyday struggle indicates at once a personal and a collective reality, offering a most poignant illustration of the persistent fault lines and fallouts of Afrobeat's dominant gender ideology and thinly obscured class operations. Yet Olaide counts herself among the fortunate. She lives in a home bequeathed to her and her siblings by her late mother; she rents out other apartments in the building, generating income to augment her modest monthly pension from the Ministry of Health.

(She credits the Kutis' goodwill for the ministry job and for the modest pension it generates, which allows her scrape by.) She considers her time working as a dancer in Fela's band as the most meaningful but least materially rewarding years of her life. "How can one hand be eating, and the other is hungry?" Olaide punctuated her view of Afrobeat injustice with the expression. She continued to articulate the injustice of the Afrobeat enterprise in economic terms—the absurd reality that those who sowed the most have been the least rewarded. Olaide's critique should not be reduced to bitterness; it is a matter of correcting a wrong. She stands out in her fondness of the Kuti family, but like the other Queens, retains a scathing rebuke of their treatment of the women who worked with Fela. "I love *all* Fela's children," she recounted their names from the oldest to the youngest, "but why can't we enjoy what they are enjoying too." The juxtaposition of love and rebuke as well as her description of herself as "Fela's wife" underscore her reading of this situation as a family affair, except that her more capacious definition of family sits at odds with what the Kutis have repeatedly projected in public. She sees herself as part of the Kuti family on revised terms; she critiques them, in other words, because she loves them. These feelings, the desire for inclusion, are hardly universal among the women I interviewed. Indeed, Olaide's conciliatory tone and feelings of warmth toward the Kutis are outliers and need to be read as inclusion preceded by reparation and economic justice. Where anger and frustration punctuated the Queens' narratives, even Olaide's, I read the emotions as justifiable responses to an evident outrage. Any universal expectation of love from the aggrieved women without accountability from the Kutis would amount to deepening the wounds of injustice.

Seun Onstage and In Person: March 2012 & July 2015

Fehintola's life powerfully illustrates how Afrobeat women resisted despair. She committed herself to flourishing even when confronted with the probability of dying, even as her health showed signs of decline. This refusal of despair toward mortality mirrored Fehintola's general outlook on life when she shared these thoughts in 1982: "I want to enjoy my life, if I can before I die."[11] It was several years before there were immediate reasons to question her mortality. Fehintola lived up to this dream in some ways, seeking out new purpose when confronted with declining health. In so doing, Fehintola charted a particular legacy for herself, one vividly captured by the life and trajectory of Seun Kuti (fig. 7.1), her only son and star artist of Egypt 80.

In 2012, Seun Kuti and the Egypt 80 band perform at the annual South by Southwest (SXSW) music festival in Austin, Texas. Drenched in sweat, Seun commits himself to impassioned renditions of saxophone solos, producing a pleasing performance that leaves the audience disgruntled when the club closes at two o'clock in the morning. Seun's live performance energy is infectious, particularly in this compact club space. He leaps around the stage, contorting his body during musical hooks to construct a duplicate vision of Fela. When he turns his back to the audience, which he does often, the words tattooed to his upper back—"Fela Lives"—become visible. The words and his musculature construct a palimpsest that conjures nostalgia for Fela. This is true for me, as I never met Fela nor witnessed him perform live. Seun will have to suffice in satisfying this longing. And he, his body, fills this ineffable sense of loss. Lekan Animashaun (aka Baba Ani), Fela's long-standing manager, also performs in the band, connecting Seun in a direct line to a history of Afrobeat performance dating to Fela's 1960s Koola Lobitos band. In the intimate space of a packed Copa nightclub in downtown Austin, the Egypt 80 band delivers an electrifying performance. Photographs with Seun and his two talented women dancers reward my tenacity alongside that of friends and fans who are UT Austin students.

In summer 2015, three years after the Austin performance, I am sitting across Seun Kuti in a hotel lobby in downtown Houston. This meeting happens a day after the second time I see Seun perform live, at the Miller Outdoor Theatre. The event forms part of an intercontinental tour spanning Africa, Europe, and the United States. Seun looks a little jaded from last night's exerting performance, but he keeps spirits high as usual. He pays for lunch, marking a transition into our interview. The band is scheduled for travel to its next show in Netherlands. His tour manager peeps in every ten or so minutes, implying that the chat needs to be brief. I quickly articulate my real interest: Fehintola, not necessarily Fela. In the hour-long chat, Seun speaks about Fehintola's influence on him as an artist. I leave the chat with the strong impression that Seun's successes testify to his mother's vision and resourcefulness as much as to his own hard work and creativity.

Fehintola: A Final Act

Public concerts assumed a false and timeless sense of harmony even in their projection of an unsettled notion of family. These concerts conjured a sense of integration that obscured the struggle of the proxy accommodation of the few Queens who were mothers. Often unremarked are the personal sacrifices the Queens made to be even marginally acknowledged, sacrifices that a figure like Fehintola embraced to set a different basis for her own legacy. Based on the same notion that the women brought little value to Afrobeat was the common portrayal of them as perpetual amateurs with little to no artistic or administrative skills, let alone skills with use outside Kalakuta. This image misses the fact that some Queens had decades of experience as performers, markedly

Figure 7.1. Seun Kuti and Egypt 80 performing at Miller Outdoor Theatre, Houston, on July 1, 2015. Photo credit by author.

more than required for apprenticeships. In other professions, the women would be celebrated as masters of their craft. In Afrobeat, they are perpetually conscripted to the status of the child and the unskilled, a status attributable to a combination of Fela's consistent monopoly of Afrobeat's public platforms, the seemingly repetitive artistic roles they played over extended periods, and the tendency to traffic in aesthetically pleasing images of Afrobeat women performers in their youth despite their patent maturity. The construction of them as perpetually young, as amateurish, produced by the symbolic distance between the women as figures and as actual persons, not only is infantilizing but also distorts the material conditions in which they lived. This distortion obscures their capacity as savvy cultural managers. As with many things Afrobeat, the multifaceted picture marinates beneath the surface appearance. Fehintola spent a total of thirty-one years as an Afrobeat performer. The first two decades of her artistic life were spent working as a backup singer in the Africa 70 and Egypt 80 bands. In a little-known story, she spent the last decade of her life rebuilding the band after Fela's death. The final decade of Fehintola's life paints the portrait of a woman who evolved from her early years as a starstruck, amateur teenage singer into a bona fide professional equipped with a range of artistic and managerial skills. She committed her final years to transferring those skills to her only son, Seun.

After Fela's death, the responsibility of leading the band fell to Femi, the most accomplished Kuti at the time. But it was Seun Kuti who, amid the post-Fela family feud, ultimately inherited Egypt 80 as a teenager.[12] After Femi formed his Positive Force band, he had neither the interest nor the capacity to keep Egypt 80 alive—nor was he particularly thrilled about playing Afrobeat classics despite pressure from fans grieving Fela's death. Femi opted to play his own original songs independent of Egypt 80.[13] There was yet another compelling reason for Femi to create distance between himself and Fela's Egypt 80, a band with a public image at odds with the image Femi had developed.[14] A more conservative manager than his late father, Femi had little interest in running an overstaffed organization nor in duplicating roles already performed by Positive Force staff members. These calculations underscored the vacuum created by Egypt 80's unfolding leadership crisis. The band needed more than shows; it needed an identity, a face after Fela. Confronted with hostility and cynicism, Fehintola rose to the challenge by guiding her "underage" son, as Femi described the emerging teenage bandleader in the heat of the post-Fela feud, to leadership of Egypt 80.[15] With twenty-one years of Afrobeat experience under her belt, Fehintola had witnessed and survived her fair share of gendered struggle. She had seen organizational and ideological shifts within Afrobeat. Like many of her fellow Queens, her encounters with the state were far from abstract. Scars on her belly bore witness to the rawness of state power, the banality of its reprisals, and the potency and possible limits of subversive artmaking. The state left its mark on her skin and, as with her peers, in her psyche. As a Nigerian citizen, Fehintola understood with brutal clarity the gendered logics of neocolonial state violence, the lowest depths to which the state could descend to reassert itself, as well as the boundless possibilities of being and belonging, of social citizenship, in a subculture lodged at the margins of society. Fehintola helped Seun gain a firm grasp of the band's inner workings, the politics of show business, and the art of managing a band whose essence placed it outside the orbit of state largesse and, by extension, the direct patronage network of powerful elites. As a long-standing member of the Afrobeat subculture, Fehintola had lost friends, sisters, and comrades to the pursuit or seduction of freedom. But in 1997, as a thirty-eight-year-old mother, she identified her singular task: condense these life lessons on citizenship, discipline, entrepreneurship, and activism for fourteen-year-old Seun, who stood tentatively on the cusp of stardom. Fehintola had been three years older than Seun when she embarked on that definitive journey from Ipoti-Ekiti to Lagos in 1976 in pursuit of an earnest vision of life as a singer. That journey, like many others by pop-enchanted young women, moved the needle of Afrobeat music in ways we may never fully account.

Fehintola endured life under patriarchy, a struggle her son would likely never experience. Under Fehintola's guidance, Seun avoided potential missteps as a bandleader. A lesser-known fact is that Fehintola performed as Seun's backup singer at the outset of his career, just as she had for decades with Fela. Seun released his debut album, *Think Africa*, in 2007, the year Fehintola died. It was a cruel twist of fate: Fehintola sang in *Think Africa*, but she did not live long enough to witness its release. She had left her stamp on Afrobeat and on her son's art, setting the foundation for the many achievements he later enjoyed. The following year, the young Egypt 80 bandleader released a second album, *Many Things* (2008). At twenty-four, he debuted at Sounds of Brazil (SOBs), a live-music venue in lower Manhattan, New York. Seun has since performed at important live-music festivals across the world, leading regular tours across Europe, Africa, and the United States. In what has arguably been Seun's greatest feat, his album *Black Times* (2018) was nominated for a 2019 Grammy Award in the category of Best World Music. When Seun celebrates his successes, it is not without a nagging sense of loss about his mother's inability to bear living witness: "It took the band ten years to get our deal. It is one of the biggest sorrows and disappointments . . . that my mum did not live to see my first record. She worked so hard for me and as soon as I made it, she passed. So, I think that the interval between my dad's death and my mom's death was the making of my career. That was what she dedicated the last ten years of her life to."[16] Mary Umude-Haverkamp worked briefly as a backup singer with Fehintola in the late 1980s, and she shared Seun's sadness on this issue: "It pains me that the woman just died without even enjoying her son and her grandchild now. It is very painful. Fehintola was a good woman. She was good. She was good. Yeah!"[17] What went unspoken for so long, publicly at least, was that Seun's art is a testament to his mother's vision and quiet struggle. Perhaps driven by love as much as by mourning and rectitude, Fehintola doubled down in focusing on her only son in her final years. "You don't want to be any woman's only child," Seun quipped. A mother's undivided focus is the consequence of such misfortune.[18] He punctuates his joke with a full-bellied laugh. It is notable that in those years, Fehintola shielded Seun from witnessing the full range of her emotional struggles and feelings of betrayal after Fela's death. And she did so while dealing with grief, survival, and existential questions. "My mom must have taken [Fela's death] hard for sure. There was the usual mourning. But she never put that pressure on me because she understood that I was going through my own grief and mourning period [when Fela died]."[19] The question of mortality, which many women found themselves confronting, likely took on a different intensity in the last few years of Fehintola's life. But she shielded her grief from public view in a fashion reminiscent of Kevin Quashie's exploration of interiority and the notion of quiet. Quashie writes that quiet encompasses "the full range of one's inner life—one's desires, ambitions, hungers, vulnerabilities, fears."[20] Seun recalled how Fehintola intensified her efforts to see him secure leadership of the band in which she had invested many years of her life. Perhaps these final years were characterized by hope, dread, anxiety, love, and an uneasy sense of accomplishment. We will never fully know the scope of Fehintola's inner world during long years of vulnerability and possibility.[21] Fehintola's final years raise the specter of quiet that both mirrors and transcends the likely-viral deaths that coursed through the Afrobeat commune.[22]

Fehintola's legacy slinks through the crevice afforded only a few Afrobeat women. Motherhood frames her entry into Afrobeat history. Children like Seun have shown themselves more than capable of shaping their mothers' legacies. And yet it bears underlining the many women excluded by this parameter. Upholding motherhood as the measure of worth or personhood silences Afrobeat women more than it invites an expansive engagement with their lives. And motherhood limits the broader range of subjectivities the women inhabited as artists, social beings, and as political agents. For example, Fehintola's continued artistic and organizational work are little known compared to her having mothered Seun. To be clear, we encounter critical aspects of Fehintola's personhood, vision, and struggles in her son's success. And this is a feat in which she would likely take pride. Still, understanding the broad and complex range of identities, selves, and investments requires looking through and beyond the lens of motherhood.

Fehintola's final years call to mind another gendered dynamic in the construction of women's labor in Afrobeat. In Fehintola, Afrobeat vividly reveals itself as a genre that thrives on familial and affective ties that bind Afrobeat women in sacrificial relationships to their male kin, leaving women to bear an outsized burden in the making of men's success without sharing its rewards. To be clear, the employer-employee dynamic implied to have governed women's labor relations with Afrobeat would fail to inspire the kind of selfless, invisible labor required to produce stars in the stature of the genre's men artists, from Fela to Femi to Seun Kuti. How, for instance, might we compute the repeated exposure to state violence in weekly wages, which some in the Kuti family insisted Fela had paid? The entanglement of labor, romance, trauma, and value run deep in Afrobeat, often to the women's disadvantage. The dynamic of selfless labor and gendered dispossession encapsulates the women's story over the arc of Fela's career, but it was powerfully consolidated the 1978 mass wedding. Their collective marriage to Fela came at a time of uncertainty and dwindling fortunes for Africa 70. Becoming wives—for some, very young—bound them to a sacrificing relationship to Fela and to Afrobeat. To be clear, involvement in Fela's band at great personal expense was, for some, the only ticket to the semblance of a career in the music industry. And we might assume that some were grateful for the exposure. Yet the entanglement of filial love, romance, and business, integral to the careers of Afrobeat's male stars, should be upheld for feminist critique. Like many uncelebrated Afrobeat women, Fehintola's labor and commitment to a dignified life is worth underscoring in a genre thoroughly invested in mischaracterizing women's labor and distorting their worth. (Recall how the manager of the Kalakuta Museum commented that the women have added no value to themselves and have consequently earned their place in the margins of memory.)

Fehintola's influence transcends training her son and getting him going on a debut album. She enlisted and mentored her niece, Iyabo Adeniran, to become an Egypt 80 performer. Iyabo learned the art of the Queens' makeup under Fehintola's mentorship, ensuring continuity not only in Egypt 80 vocals but also in crucial aspects of Afrobeat's visual aesthetics. Iyabo juggled the combined roles of Egypt 80 singer, dancer, and makeup expert, a multivalent exhibition of performance competence embodied by Fehintola and successive generations of women performers. The relationship between Fehintola and her niece was composed of understated acts of solidarity, alliance, and mentorship among women who found ways to advance their interests in a male-dominated genre and at an especially fraught moment. As mother and coartist to Seun, Fehintola embodied the genre's tentative split between play and work, between professionalism and personal sacrifice, entangling labor, intimacy, and family. At the onset of Seun's now celebrated career, he was joined not only by his mother and Iyabo, his cousin, but also by his half sister Motunrayo (daughter of Queen Najite), who performed as a singer-dancer on his debut album. Women with deeply affective investments in Seun's success and in their own legacy played crucial roles in keeping Egypt 80 afloat. A similar pattern occurred when Femi Kuti broke away from Egypt 80 to found Positive Force. Femi's elder and younger sisters, Yeni and Sola, were the first backup acts in his newly formed band (fig. 7.2). Funke Kuti, who married Femi and mothered Made Kuti, completed the trio of Positive Angels. Women shepherded their male kin to artistic success as Afrobeat stars and helped to subsidize costs of fledgling bands but have not always received credit for their efforts. This is due in large part to the invisibility of their labor, the entanglement of work with filial love. The weight of sacrifice unduly borne by women in crafting iconic Afrobeat men deserves complication. The sense of stability provided by women's labor helped midwife, rather than disrupt, gendered division of labor across generations. Afrobeat scholars must keep sight of this gendered labor dynamic and its reward system even as they laud the disarming story of a mother's selfless sacrifice for her only son. Fehintola might not have survived until Seun's stardom, but she set him firmly on the path to success. Her legacy endures in Afrobeat songs: Fehintola left fragments of herself in Afrobeat music, in her son's band, and in spontaneous offstage singing unmoored from the particularities of time and place. If one leans in closely enough, one might catch a glimpse of her face in a tattoo on his torso. Seun embodies Fehintola's struggle; it is quite literally etched into his body. Her dispersed presence in Afrobeat destabilizes discourses of abjection that threatened to become her legacy after Fela's death.

Women played yet another crucial role as post-Fela Afrobeat male stars were beginning their careers. The Kuti family women became moral and ideological buffers when Fela's two sons struck out to forge their own artistic and political profiles. The women performers in Seun's Egypt 80 and Femi's Positive Force had blood ties with their bandleaders, quite unlike the Queens' relationship with Fela. So when the Kuti men appeared onstage alongside women who were sisters, cousins, or mothers, the women's presence insulated them from public scrutiny. The women inhabited familiar and respectable social roles that cast (or recast) them as Queen-surrogates, whose artistic identities did not invite titillating assumptions about their sexuality. In this subtle and revised role for women in Afrobeat, Femi and Seun fended off prying moralists to focus on building their artistic profiles. In short, the women in their families provided a curtain behind which the rising artists could create work largely unburdened by Afrobeat's sullied legacy around the ruthless conflation of art, political activism, and sex. This conflation found its most problematic expression in the ravages of HIV/AIDS within the Afrobeat community. While these men artists required the talents of women to survive, they drew on the support of women with whom they shared strong familial ties and, as such, could be assumed to have no sexual entanglements. Femi tried particularly hard to project a sanitized image of himself and to redefine Afrobeat professionalism and personal responsibility outside of his father's shadow.[23] (The "Positive" in his band name was no coincidence.) The presence of his sisters and Funke Kuti (his now ex-wife) helped to temper Afrobeat's history of moral dubiety, which derived largely from scrutiny around Fela's romantic and sexual relationships with the many young women who worked for him.

Figure 7.2. Femi Kuti's Positive Force band poses at Tivoli in Utrecht, Netherlands, on June 29, 1998. Yeni Kuti, Sade Jokotade, Femi Kuti, and Funke Kuti (married to Femi at the time). Photo credit and permission: Frans Schellekens / Redferns via Getty Images.

Queens on Broadway

In 2009, the Queens made an unlikely appearance in New York in an off-Broadway musical choreographed by Bill T. Jones and coproduced by Jay-Z, Will Smith, and Jada Pinkett Smith. Marketing for the performance insinuated Fela's macho posturing. Sahr Ngaujah, an award-winning Sierra Leonean-American actor and director, played Fela in the Chicago performance I attended. Ngaujah's animated monologues in the first act cut the familiar image of Fela as an iconoclastic activist on a mission to take down corrupt state actors. Extensive saxophone solos punctuated a visual contrast between his shirtless, muscular upper body and the heavily ornamented dancing women around him. Together, Ngaujah and the off-Broadway Queens appeared to be restaging the image of an African avenger on a lone, righteous pursuit of justice against the odds. The Queens in this telling run the risk, at least on the surface, of becoming decorative pieces in contrast to the grandiloquent and dynamic lead character, who moves between playing virtuoso saxophone solos, directly addressing the audience, and inviting them in the opening moments of the show to join the transgression at his Shrine. The character, in other words, has humor and flair, muses a lot, plays the instrument, orchestrates the movement of others, shows interiority by falling in love (with the character Sandra Izsadore), and poses philosophical questions about Nigeria's fate. Fela's robust internal life and dramatic arc might be read as eclipsing nonspeaking characters, notably the women. But there is an affective register that the women's singing and dancing bodies conjure and sustain throughout the performance, defining the character of Fela himself. This aliveness percolates through the show, complicating the familiar construction of individualism and machismo that suffuses Afrobeat's visual and discursive fields. In collaboration with Maija Garcia, a Cuban American director and choreographer, Jones reimagines the dancing Queens as diasporic Black women subjects endowed with a vitality of their own. The choreography itself contains what Nadine George-Graves describes as diasporic spidering, the active process of identity construction emerging from "many points of intersection and modes of passage" around a core, a person, or a sojourner.[24] The panoply of sonic and choreographic registers index this spidery, diasporic performance work: the music derives from 1950s and 60s highlife, jazz, calypso, Afrobeat, and Yoruba spiritual soundscapes. The movement styles range from salsa, soukous, soul, acrobatics, and partnered and solo movements, moving from regimented and fluid to esoteric and grounded. The cast itself comprised a diasporic set of Black women dancers including Nicole de Weever, a dancer and arts activist from St. Maarten, and Rujeko Dumbutshena, a Zimbabwean-born dancer, choreographer, and scholar. Other dancers, much like the original Queens, came to the show from an array of places and with a broad range of personal histories: De Veaux hails from Chattanooga, Tennessee; Koomson's parents are from Ghana, but she grew up in New England. Wodobode was born in the Central African Republic and grew up in Paris. Iris Wilson was raised in Queens; McClendon was born and raised in the Bronx.[25] In close collaboration with an ensemble of dancers, Jones and Garcia reanimated the Queens, who had been largely erased in Nigeria or narrated as afterthoughts in stories of Fela's genius and gallantry. The show's seven Queens sported brilliant makeup and took center stage in intricate solo and group choreographies that established them as aesthetic and political forces. De Weever recalled that while they might not have had speaking roles, they "embodied power and strength onstage in the way we sang and chanted those songs, with complete ownership of the text. We sang the songs and used our bodies, so we had to embody the feeling." De Weever speaks here of the affective power and potency of Black women's embodiment. The Broadway performance became a palimpsest of feminist possibilities encapsulated in de Weever's later statement that the Queens stood "almost like his soldiers in a sense, [Fela's] strength."[26] In a complicated history of women's resilience and creativity, Jones's intervention may have been imperfect considering how little was known about the Queens' lives at the time. Yet judging by the scholarship and creative output the Broadway show has since engendered, Jones's effort is welcome following a long history of gendered erasure. Francesca Royster argues that the production's complicated exploration of biography, politics, spirituality, and sexuality dovetails with Jones's exploration of these themes in earlier choreographic works.[27] Despite the overt intersections in Jones's and Fela's personal and artistic lives, Jones's handling opens space for feminist tellings of the Afrobeat story; he achieves more than simply recounting the familiar tale of Fela's activism. He gives renewed potency and attention to the subversive politics of the Queens' body movements across space, their crisp vocals, and the suggestion of women's freedom encapsulated in their fierce bodily gyrations, a signature aspect of the show's choreography. Jones sidesteps Afrobeat's fraught sexual and marriage politics by casting fewer Queens and steering the musical away from "the trap of this being a fascination with polygamous lifestyle."[28] Still, some view the women as strong and beautiful bodies wanting in depth and character.[29] On at least two fronts, such critiques have simultaneously clarified and understated the scope of Jones's intervention as well as the research resources at the team's disposal. Jones made a pioneering attempt at resuscitating the Afrobeat Queens as historical subjects. By naming the seven Broadway Queens after the original Afrobeat women, he invited the possibility for recognition, a modest but critical effort at reanimation. Each woman plays a specific character so that even ensemble movements reveal subtle aspects of the women's individuality. The production team relied on the familiar literature and archival materials that existed on the Queens at the time of the production. "All that we had to refer to was the book, um . . . ," Rujeko strains to remember. "Carlos Moore's *This Bitch of a Life*?" I interject. "Yes, yes," she confirms. So besides a 1992 recorded concert that allowed Rujeko to see Egypt 80's women perform live, Moore's book offered Rujeko her first and most meaningful engagement with Fela's work and with the Queens. Carlos Moore worked briefly as a consultant on the Broadway production. Nicole de Weever relied on Moore's work to glean important details about her character, Adeola. "She was sixteen when she met Fela, very young. She was born in 1958. I got a glimpse into her family life a little bit but also what her aspirations were. That was the conflict that I worked with, in terms of being able to have a speaking role. The Queens did not have speaking roles. All we can do is embody the knowledge that we got from who we know them to be in the book." Combining Moore's work with concert videos and documentaries allowed de Weever to excavate details about personality, relationships, and motivations that served her character development.

Broadway dancers like de Weever deepened their political voice through the experience of performing as the Afrobeat Queens. Nicole de Weever offers a poignant description of the confluence of her political transformation from playing the role of a Queen: "I walked the world differently after being in the show. It sparked the activist within me. I started my own foundation called Art Saves Lives, because I understood how important art was in changing and shifting the life of people, so it really ignited the activist in me. It shifted my lives in many ways, and, as a result, the people around me."[30] Art Saves Lives is a nonprofit that teaches critical thinking and self-awareness through visual and performing arts programming in the United States and St. Maarten. De Weever considers these artistic and programming efforts part of a larger impulse to decolonize her home country of St. Maarten, a Caribbean island still a colony of France and the Netherlands. In channeling the Queens' artistry and politics, the Broadway dancers animated a notion of diaspora that dance scholar Jasmine Johnson has argued uncovers the "contingencies and diverse cultural influences" that shaped Fela's music to begin with.[31] Johnson's reading of the diasporic contingencies undergirding Fela's work is a critical anchor for other points of convergence between the Afrobeat Queens' and Broadway performers' personal lives and their positionality as historical subjects in the circulation of symbols and historical ties that constitute and shape African diasporic subjectivity. De Weever shares a deeply affecting moment of their tour of the production that tied her to the Afrobeat story.

> The play was very heavy. We carried a coffin at the end of the show at the same time as I lost my dad, and I was dealing with my grief. So every day, I had to walk with the coffin and I was grieving. We were in London performing and opening in Washington, DC, one week after that. I could have chosen to not go back but I believed so much in the work, and that my dad would have wanted me to do what I love. I everyday carrying this coffin onstage, and it was almost like a physical manifestation of the grief that I held in my body, the pain I was carrying everyday. In some way, it helped me with my character onstage. It became a way for me to sit with my heavy feeling about what that song ["Coffin for Head of State"]
> stood for.[32]

Black grief was a dominant force driving racial politics in the US during the Obama years. Public mourning of Black death and loss manifested in the eruption of the Black Lives Matter movement, a political moment that triggered white grievance and with it, white nationalist movements in the United States.[33] Grief and grievance take root in the history of slavery, colonialism, and ongoing forms of dispossession. Black performance ruffles the sediments of these histories, often distorted in dominant discourses; muscle memory and the affective registers of embodiment dissolve rigid boundaries of time, event, and place that attends dominant framings of race. Black loss is compounding and cumulative; the grief de Weever experienced and from which she forged her character was not simply the coincidence of a death in her family and an emotionally charged moment in the performance. Neither was it simply a deep sense of empathy derived from identifying with Fela's musical narration of the loss of his mother. Rather, this grief is compounded, collective, and historical, signifying a logic of violence that, once rooted in the constitution of the colonial state in Africa, was exacerbated by neocolonial systems on the one hand and racialized violence that suffuses the afterlives of slavery on the other.[34] It is grief, as de Weever explains it, "that I held in my body, the pain I was carrying everyday." The coffin that de Weever participated in carrying in the second act of the Broadway show repeated Fela's grim protest at the killing of his mother by Nigerian soldiers. The context of de Weever's show matters in that the performance coincided with the killing of Trayvon Martin and the ensuing protests and outpouring of rage. Grief from state violence in 1970s and contemporary Nigeria simultaneously prefigure and echo the overpolicing of Black bodies in the United States. Both instances of anti-Blackness converged in a moment of clarity in October 2020 with the #EndSARS movement of Nigerian youth against police violence, a movement that ended in a brutal crackdown on protesters. Trayvon's killer and the "unknown soldier" responsible for FAK's death both rehearsed and reenacted the impunity of state-sanctioned violence against Africans and people of African descent. Rooted in personal loss, the public grief around the two deaths might be read in tandem. And in playing a Queen, de Weever's body became a site of compounded, historical loss bringing together the afterlives of slavery with the afterlives of colonialism.

When it came to Fela's shows, only a few visitors confessed that the dancing women left a more indelible impression on them than the musicians. While the women in the Fela-led bands did not stage overtly resistive acts nor explicitly challenge patriarchy in a highly public or consistent sense, their embodiment of sensuality and vigor onstage and their notoriety offstage underscored the ambivalent politics of visibility that trails women performers, admired as trendsetters and reviled as morally suspect.[35] The embodied presence of Afrobeat dancers paired with the piercing and animated vocals of backing singers, preceded by and adding to a circuit of public images in print, coded the women's bodies, voices, and presence as already political precisely because to dance publicly and sensually was to assert a presence in Nigerian society; to sing subversive songs, even misogynistic ones, was to insert a voice in a space claimed as the preserve of men; to participate in calling out the state's moral bankruptcy was to render tangible and embodied the elusive concept of citizenship. For many other women artists, this nexus of interventions coalesced in live performances, in the moment when the Afrobeat woman dancer seized control of the dancing cage or the center stage, giving bodily vibrations that unleashed lust in some and dread in others. The instant when the dancer had the entire ensemble behind her, or when, through her moves, she directed the Afrobeat ensemble, even if for a fleeting moment, felt like an exercise of power in a contemporary Nigerian society that otherwise constrained women's bodies and voice. Other women artists understood the freedom and affective power that such moments in live performance had the capacity to generate. Musician and costumer Wunmi Olaiya cites the dancing women as her creative ancestors, recalling an early memory of witnessing the dancing women perform live.

> Leaving Nigeria and going to England, I finally got to see Fela onstage at the Brixton Academy [she screams]. You've got to be there to see it. I think I spent the whole day so excited waiting for that show. I don't know how I stood that night watching it. . . . And then the dances, I love the fact that the women controlled it. They controlled it. They controlled it. You can talk about Fela all day long, but when you went to the show, you went to check the women out. So, as a female artist stepping in myself and doing what I do with music and dance it made it very easy for me because I did not have to explain myself to anybody.[36]

Olaiya offers an important rearticulation of the Queens' dancing bodies in a live performance event designed ostensibly to showcase Fela's mastery and, sometimes, his dominance over the band. Certainly, Fela intended for the women's dances to appeal to a largely male audience and to ensure continued patronage of the club. But solo dancing also occasioned surprises and spur-of-the-moment revisions that, in turn, constituted instances of inspiration for others, if not completely for the performer herself. Improvisations generated in the heat of performance had the capacity to infuse spaces saturated by misogyny with the seeds of feminist and queer encounter. Consequently, it would be reductive to limit reading the political import of the women's performances to their overt appeal to the male gaze. Rujeko Dumbutshena powerfully underscores how the Broadway dancers drew inspiration from the original Queens to unleash the power of the erotic on conservative US audiences invested in containing Blackness or in a specific mode of respectable Black performance: "We would see people in the front row of the audience, who wouldn't be in their seat when the second act came on because they couldn't take it. It was too much in their face." She found authority to embrace the sensualness of Naa Lamiley Lamptey, who she played in the Broadway performance. Rujeko's thoughts powerfully echo those of Wunmi, who witnessed the actual Queens perform live.

> I think for me, really, it is more like drawing from my own experience of women, African women, Zimbabwean women. What is our expression of sexuality? What is the sensual nature of African women? Maybe the best example was the wedding scene [in the Broadway show]. I think that my expression of sexuality, how does it differ and how was it expressed in the context of the Queens? Maybe it's less demonstrative and more subtle. Drawing from my experiences of African women was helpful in the character of [Naa Lamiley] that I built around, because there's a real dignity and a strength and resilience, and the things that I admire about African women. That's always a source of inspiration for me, in what I create about myself. My writing or my choreography is always highlighting women and their resilience, the spaces that they create, how they attain power.[37]

This too, this surging through the bodies of other young women finding their way in the world, is the legacy of the Queens. Rujeko was struck by the sense of solidarity between the original Queens, a gesture powerfully underscored by their shared embrace of subcultural living despite their diverse ethnic and socioeconomic backgrounds. "It was helpful to understand why they made the choices that they made; that it was a rebellious act. That was admirable, and that they lived in such a diverse community. That was beautiful. They seemed to coexist in a way that only African women could," Dumbutshena laughed at the joke. "I admired that it was an act of rebellion."[38] At least in the 1970s, women from privileged backgrounds shunned the comfort and luxury of well-paved futures to work as artists and live in Kalakuta Republic, Rujeko reflected, and those from more humble socioeconomic circumstances sought to escape the grips of poverty. "They therefore had like minds."[39] Dumbutshena's attention to class offers an important jumping off point for a deeper conversation about how class might have shaped the material circumstances of the Queens' lives long after their public, iconic Afrobeat lives.

An exploration of the material lives of the women is especially urgent considering the familiar construction of the Queen as a figure of African female pride and strength. Women's transformation of the sonic, performative, and political contours of Afrobeat, a decidedly political genre rooted in Pan-Africanist ethics, needs be reconciled with the material lives of the women behind the figure. Compelling as it is at first glance, the construction of the Queen as principally a Pan-African figure risks romanticizing the women's lives and struggles. Admiration and praise are the substrates of this pride-and-strength thesis. Consistent with this spirit, Iris Wilson, a dancer in Bill T. Jones's musical, poetically described the Broadway Queens as "warriors of the words." Bright, Afrocentric makeup and costumes complement the dancers' athletic and skillful reinterpretation of Afrobeat's vibrant hip-centered choreographies. The potent blend of precision, skill, and stamina executed by dancers with "Amazon-like" bodies help visualize the poise and power of Afrobeat women. For most of the show's first act, the design is colorful and invites audience participation, eliciting applause at the acrobatic execution of patently complicated moves. Jones manages to balance the Broadway aesthetic of spectacle in the first act with the grimness of the Afrobeat story in the second, where the narrative pivots to themes of trauma, violence, loss, and a different conception of endurance. In the end, however, it is the story of Fela and the women's resilience that prevails. While this celebratory aesthetic is an important counterpoint to a history of silence around the Queens, it runs the risk of failing to interrogate the Queens' lived experience, the contradictions in the story, the cracks in the narratives. When asked during an interview if they had met any of the original Queens, dancer Iris Wilson revealed that she had met Najite, whose character she played on Broadway, as well as Kevwe, who, she recalled, seemed pleased with the show and came onstage to dance at the end of the performance at the Shrine.[40] The encounter between the Broadway Queens and the original Queens illustrates that the American dancers had little chance to interact with the women whose lives they performed. This lack of interaction is no fault of the American performers, as their Lagos tour was heavily restricted for security reasons and came after the show had been fully developed, leaving few opportunities for major changes to the story or the show's structure. Nonetheless, there was an opportunity to reconcile the idealized image of the figure of the Queen with the reality of the lives many Afrobeat women led in the wake of Fela. "I would have preferred to meet her in person, rather than read from a book. It would have been a better, more authentic, storytelling," says de Weever, explaining the challenges of developing her character from a slim body of research resources. De Weever's ruminations imply that upholding the Queens as figures of beauty and strength might be productively juxtaposed against or complicated by a full accounting of the nuances of their lives as an ongoing process. Imagining the

Queens only as liberated agents in a figurative sense perpetuates a misleading sense of harmony while circumscribing a rich rendering of how Afrobeat
music weaves together the grotesque and the beautiful—how, in the women's
memories, ambivalence underwrites indescribable pain and transcendent enjoyment as cohabiting realities. New chronicles of the Queens' stories might
celebrate beauty and resilience without pursuing parallel narratives that we, or
the women themselves, might not recognize. It is a testament nonetheless to
the power of Jones's intervention that artistic surrogates of the Queens have,
in the wake of the Broadway musical, flourished in African diaspora communities. Women of color, especially Black women, have drawn inspiration from
the Queens by seizing the opportunity of Afrobeat concerts, photoshoots, and
nightclubs to inhabit the persona of the Afrobeat Queens, forging tentative
manifestations of a Black diaspora that potently decenters Fela.[41] The Queens'
circum-Atlantic travels made a return stop in Nigeria when Bolanle Austen-
Peters, a Nigerian director and filmmaker, produced and directed *Fela and
the Kalakuta Queens*, a successful musical that traveled to London and South
Africa after a successful run in Lagos. Austen-Peters's work was inspired by
Bill T. Jones's musical; its marketing insinuated it was a Nigerian response to
Broadway, a homecoming of sorts for the Afrobeat story. Austen-Peters sought
more nuance in her telling by inviting two Queens, Olaide and Omolara, with
the blessing of Fela's estate, to serve as consultants on the project. But like
Jones's musical, Austin-Peters's script leans heavily on Carlos Moore's work,
rendering the performance more a narrative of fascination with Kalakuta life
than a complex portrait of Afrobeat history. Austen-Peters's invitation of the
Queens nonetheless played a validating role for them. It was a major Nigerian
production about their lives, and they were invited to be part of it. Despite
repeating familiar missteps in representation of the Queens, the musical has
remained the most dignifying representation of the Kalakuta women to be
produced *in* Nigeria.

Beyond the Binary: How Afrobeat Shaped the Queens' Lives

Stories are capacious enough to contain the processual, dialectical, and in-
tersubjective experience of life and gendered struggle in one of Africa's most
vibrant subcultures of the twentieth century. Stories also cut across the victim-
agent binary that has dominated narratives about the Queens' lives. As girls
and young women joining a subculture at a politically volatile moment, many
were naive about the political economy of gendered violence in Nigeria and
the profound risks to which Fela and their affiliation with him exposed them.

Many of them escaped into Afrobeat in pursuit of largely unrealized fantasies of freedom. The power asymmetry between women artists and Fela, as well as between the women and the famed Ransome-Kuti family, also paints a bleak picture of their autonomy. The lens of victimhood underscores how the life-altering decisions they made as teenagers, such as choosing subcultural living over conventional paths, defined the rest of their lives—and not always in a wholesome way. The power inequities that governed their artmaking, decision-making, and life options accumulated as gendered losses. Most still nurse psychological and physical wounds from the backlash occasioned by their participation in Fela's subversive art. Their victimization by state, society, and subculture inaugurates a lucid view of injustice and gendered injury in Afrobeat. If we view the young women as "girls," which many were at the outset of their Afrobeat careers, and understand their risky albeit audacious choices as exercises in teenage exuberance, then we might welcome the possibility of forging alternative moral discourses around the complicated legacies and trajectories of Afrobeat activism. Such an accounting might enable a clear-eyed reassessment of the value of Fela's brand of activism in the ongoing struggle for African freedom. Victimhood by itself presents too narrow a frame to appreciate the scope of gendered subjectivities inhabited by women in Afrobeat as teenagers in the 1970s; as spiritual actors in the early 1980s, a period of heightened influence for Afrobeat women; as mothers, for some; as deserters of a derailed movement and former wives; in the early 1990s, as veteran artists who commanded the respect of younger women; as widows and targets of a moral discourse of HIV/AIDS in the late 1990s; as former artists; or as sexagenarians in the 2020s. The multiple, compounding subjectivities implied by this protracted temporality become critical for reading their lives and shifting relationships with and investments in Afrobeat. Many of the women I interviewed did not simply read their circumstances in light of youth and innocence (or a lack thereof) at the time of joining the Afrobeat community but rather as a lifelong struggle for a more just Nigerian society and, specifically, for due recognition for their critical contributions to Afrobeat and African popular culture. Quite unlike the implications of the category of victimhood, the sheer brazenness and publicness of their craft marked them as creative vanguards. Their presence declared women's capacity as agents in transforming popular culture and articulating citizenship in the interstices of patriarchy. They boldly staged an idealized African womanhood, presenting themselves as figures of strength and resilience. Their public posturing—onstage, on album art, and in everyday life—unsettled the notion of the women as powerless victims. The audacity and volatility of these expressions were equally animated by, but irreducible to, their youth.

The lives of women in Afrobeat exceed loss or triumph, even though these are constitutive of their experience. The binary that undergirds loss and triumph assumes a narrative finality that fails to account for the myriad ways that social movements transform those who participate in them and find themselves persuaded by their ideas, ethos, and style.[42] The Queens were transformed by the Afrobeat experience as much as they transformed Nigerian and West African popular culture. Their stories contain a range of sentiments—from nostalgia, pride, and satisfaction to disbelief, regret, and profound hurt. When not scheduled to perform a solo or in the cages, Olaide recalled her penchant for sitting backstage and listening, weed in hand, to the band play live music. She listened deeply, in a near meditative state, not as an outsider but as a witness to ideas she knew had germinated from Kalakuta Republic, tested in everyday discourse before assuming musical form. Olaide takes pride in her role in making space for the germination of now-widely cited lyrics, ideas, metaphors, quips, scats, and hooks that Fela disseminated from the Shrine's stage. The women I interviewed express a profound sense of pride for having stood as dissenting voices at a critical moment in Nigeria's history. Although virtually none of the remaining Queens earns a livelihood in popular music or the performing arts, they continue to cite Afrobeat as a deeply transformational episode. They possess an unmistakable sense of self-assurance and political clarity, which they credit to Afrobeat. Olaide is nicknamed "Ìya Ibẹ̀" ("The Mother There" or "Mother in the Area") in her neighborhood. When asked to clarify how she got the name and what it means, she revealed that she earned it from her involvement in grassroots politics. Candidates running for local positions come to solicit her support. A few weeks before our meeting, she championed a drive to repair her street in Ogba, Lagos, an act that, she explained, earned her radio mentions (on Bond FM). Historian Meghan Healy-Clancy elaborates on the idea of public motherhood to describe how South African women activists leveraged idealized conceptions of maternity in their assumption of activist roles.[43] As Ìya Ibẹ̀, a public mother, Olaide garnered the political capital and lived experience, of having been a Queen, as the basis for her role, brokering political power long after her formal ties to Afrobeat.[44] As we negotiated the short distance between a junction and her apartment for our first interview, shop owners and neighbors saluted Olaide as Iya Ibe, as if anticipating the stories she would later tell me of her influence. Najite credits Afrobeat for her cosmopolitan outlook on life. International tours, she explained, afforded her an opportunity to forge experiences outside Nigeria and meet "important people," which she might not have been able to on her own. She "shines" whenever she visits her village from Lagos. Najite takes pride in her work as an Afrobeat dancer, relishing having had the opportunity to pursue her love for the arts while being part of an important movement. These experiences place her one peg ahead of her contemporaries in her hometown, Warri, who view her admiringly.[45] Omolara Shosanya, for her part, is ambivalent about her entanglement with Fela and Afrobeat. While she expresses fondness for Fela and hails him for being a great teacher, she repeatedly wondered how differently her life might have turned out had she been presented with the conditions to make more affirming decisions as a teenager and aspiring artist. Omolara's stories oscillate between funny, ruminative, and somber, her memories a labyrinth of questions and musings rather than answers. Omolara continues to weigh the dividends and scars left from her work as an Afrobeat dancer.[46] For these women, transforming Afrobeat music occasioned a profound transformation of their lives and sense of self.

Theirs is also a tale of sisterhood and solidarity. Olaide spoke these words to Omolara on my first meeting with them: "Ibi tí a bá ti ṣubú l'a tí ń dìde" (Where we fall is where we pick ourselves up from). Omolara expressed resistance to participating as a coconsultant with Olaide on Austen-Peters's production of *Fela and the Kalakuta Queens* despite the financial incentive. She wanted Afrobeat put firmly behind her as she continued to forge ahead with her life. It was Olaide who, having recommended and introduced Omolara to the production team, convinced her to reconsider the modest financial reward from the production as one of the dividends of their struggle with Fela. Omolara expressed gratitude for Olaide's framing, in part because it unambiguously named the fall and recognized the injury that came from their work with Fela. She was also grateful for the opportunity to participate in potentially rebuilding the Queens' public image. The friendship between Olaide and Omolara takes the form of occasional visits and sleepovers during which they catch up on old memories while making new ones. It was at Olaide's home that I met Ifeanyi Abuah (whose nickname in Kalakuta was Okokomaiko). Ifeanyi folded her legs on "Aunty Laide's" seater sofa, lit a cigarette, and reminisced about Kalakuta. She interjected her stories with headshaking to signal her disbelief at the incredible world that was communal living. Both women interjected one another's stories, filling gaps in the other's memory, refuting some accounts, or laughing at unspeakable memories that only the two of them and fellow Kalakutans knew about. Being in Kalakuta produced a bond that few would truly understand or appreciate. A shared experience of artistic transcendence, ecstasy, risk, pain, love, betrayal, abandonment, fear, and, in the end, survival has strengthened these relationships. The need for solidarity has, of necessity, stretched into their present lives. Having walked similar life paths and having *fallen* within close range of one another, these women know that getting up, however shakily, was their only choice. It is the choice they have to make each day. Marginalized people, bell hooks explains, "resist by identifying themselves as subjects, by defining their reality, shaping new identity, naming their history, telling their story."[47] The Queens have resisted erasure by telling their stories to whoever cares to listen, granting formal and informal interviews, maintaining friendships, swapping life stories, and testing one another's memories of communal and personal experiences in Kalakuta Republic. The complexity of the stories told by these women to one another is yet to be fully documented. The love and empathy they share is also an unspoken legacy of the Afrobeat movement. When Olaide celebrated her sixtieth birthday in May 2018, she reminisced about the journey that brought her there. This act of still living, of having enjoyed and survived life, constitutes her long struggle. The women will continue to rise and fight until they feel a greater sense of justice has been achieved. Their lives recall the opening verse of Maya Angelou's poem "Still I Rise": "You may write me down in history. . . . You may trod me in the very dirt / But still, like dust, I rise."[48]

On Haunting

The gap between gendered labor, sacrifice, and historical erasure troubles repressed histories of Afrobeat as well as barely concealed wrongs of the Nigerian state. The presence of the Queens, a collective force, continues to unsettle dominant narratives of gender in Afrobeat music. The women's voices linger in songs; their bodies decorate and punctuate album art, concert videos, and historical photographs. Their unapologetic presence dares efforts at silencing the uneasy reality of their irrefutable public labor and intimate sacrifice. The women's presence interrupts the conventions of academic discourse where at conferences befuddled and curious scholars pose "unacademic" questions: Where are the Queens now? Did they have children for Fela? How many? Are those women still alive? These are some of the most asked questions to have been posed of this research. The presence of silent and silenced Afrobeat women trails memorial projects such as the Kalakuta Museum and the annual Felabration, which construct quasi-official histories that locate women at the margins. Afrobeat music is a haunted genre in this sense, a musical form populated by the ghostly lives of its many women. The animated state that constitutes this kind of haunting, Avery Gordon reminds us, occurs when repressed or unresolved social violence reveals itself directly or obliquely through vivid eruption or a gentle presence that refuses to go away while also refusing to fully revealing itself. Historical erasure and the failure to redress or atone for injustice compound the trauma of events to render history unfinished. They haunt the present.[49] Catherine Cole contends in *Performance and the Afterlives of Injustice* that unresolved history, especially histories marked by profound injustice, take on afterlives that accumulate a toxic excess and impose a force field on the now, interrupting "our times in ways that we cannot always predict or control."[50] These articulations of haunting readily illuminate the affective reverberations of state-sanctioned violence and large-scale historical injustices such as genocide, wars, and slavery. The story of the Queens suggests that unresolved histories of injustice can produce the effect understood as haunting in more intimate contexts, such as in the material shocks of patriarchy in an artist commune. When these microcosmic spaces are impacted as much by state-sanctioned violence as by misogyny, they intensify and accumulate in toxicity precisely because they are crucibles for the quieter and less spectacular violence of everyday life, rendering them less amenable to redress and reckoning than haunting produced by mass atrocities. A puzzling gap exists between the women's injuries and sacrifice on the one hand and attempts after Fela's death to minimize them as problems. Yet another gap exists between the wealth of their collective creativity and their current abjection, whose most potent form is the women's daily struggle of living in near penury and homelessness. Afrobeat becomes a cultural field of untenable dissonance.

Let Us End with Another Reflection on Haunting

I finally find my break after a long struggle for a framework or cogent concept to narrate the Queens' historiographical situation in Afrobeat, something that will make sense to readers of this book. The break I have long sought comes in an unlikely form: a painting in Femi Kuti's New Afrika Shrine. It's a Thursday, and Femi Kuti is conducting his open rehearsals at the Shrine. Throughout my fieldwork, I contemplate continuities between Fela Kuti's Queens and Femi Kuti's Positive Angels, the young women who now gyrate in cages to Femi's music just as the Queens did at Fela's Shrine. The erotic quality of the choreography is blatant. Sandra Swazzi, a Positive Force dancer likely in her early thirties, moves with such intensity that the dancing cage vibrates as if it might fly off its base. Both hands suspended, Sandra vibrates her lower body with feverish precision. My de facto research assistant, John, wonders why I am not taking photographs; he assures me that it's okay. I take a few before awkwardness overcomes me. No one else appears to be taking photographs, at least not with a professional-looking camera. I wonder if the dancers really feel comfortable being photographed. Soon I decide to retire for the day. But then, on my way out of the Shrine, I encounter an artwork on a wall at the back of the auditorium (fig. 7.3). It hangs unremarkably among several other works of art, historical photographs, enlarged newspaper clippings, and witty sayings by the late Chief Priest. Most displays in Femi's Shrine gesture in some way to Afrobeat's legendary past, but they make claims on the present. The artwork decorating the club makes obvious gestures to continuity by conjuring the aesthetic of Fela's Shrine. This piece of art stops me in my tracks. It signals to the past but does so sideways. It is a portrait of Fela entitled Pouch with Seven Lives. In the piece, Fela peers into the camera in a way that conveys the officialness of a passport photograph. He looks uncharacteristically serious, his demeanor in contrast with the portrait's digitally constructed vegetal ambience; leaves and random scribbles fill the spaces on either side of his head, while an ornate pouch with heavy beads hangs around his neck. The area around his eyelids is reddish brown, outlining a circumference from his eyelashes to his cheekbone in dots of white paint. If you stand still and pay attention to a haunted place long enough, it reveals its ghosts. The ghosts in Pouch demand such stillness. Details materialize the longer I observe. The lavish beads hanging from the pouch appear needlessly heavy. They have a feminine quality but also resemble dead weight around the musician's neck, immediately invoking a presence the artist may or may not have intended.

I linger there as my heart rate picks up. The artwork has a restless quality. The face belongs to Fela, but the eyes conjure the Queens, as though the musician is wearing a mask. John wonders why I have taken interest in this work more than the numerous historic and didactic art pieces throughout the Shrine that call attention to Femi's commanding live rehearsal. He's passed by this piece perhaps hundreds of times and has likely found it no more remarkable than the other, more meaningful pieces. I might have missed it myself had I left through the opposite exit. I ask John about the artist. Does he know who created the piece? Does he know where I might locate the artist? Why did the Shrine's management include it in the collection? Because it is a striking piece? Or because, like many other works, it appears to be honorific art? It holds Fela, but it also contains other competing presences, a person or story buried just beneath the surface, deep enough to be missed but surfaced enough to be beheld. The author, I later learn, is Nigerian digital artist, photographer, and publisher Weyinmi Atigbi, who created Pouch with Seven Lives as part of a collection of four pieces for the 2011 Lagos exhibition Art of Rebellion. My hunch about Pouch's aura is vindicated by an eyewitness who, having visited the exhibition, described Fela's face in Pouch as "shrouded in shades that seem to reflect mystery and mystique." The feminine presence suggested in the piece is elaborated in the three other artworks, whose ornamentation explicitly depict Afrobeat women.[51] I had none of this context when I was stopped by the restive quality of the piece at the Shrine as a gift or an acquisition. In my mind, the Queens appeared uninvited in a place *invested in their erasure. Perhaps I am reading too much into an innocuous artistic rendering of Fela. But I cannot shake the feeling, so I take several photographs as I stand before the piece, adjusting my camera settings so that the flash does not bounce off the surface. Satisfied, I take what I think is the best shot in the poor lighting. I return to the photograph every now and again. I see a woman, or women, peering mischievously through Fela's eyes, looking back at the space they built. They show up here, not through the women dancing in cages but as ghosts, specters of Afrobeat's checkered past. Stillness. Stillness is what this art demands. And the women seep through the canvas, despite the loudness, and from the walls. Peering, they quietly propose another look at Afrobeat's awkward silencing of its others.*

The title remixes Fela's adopted name: Fela "Anikulapo" (one who has death in a pouch), invoking his professed invincibility, becomes Fela who bears a "pouch with seven lives." Like the photograph, the title oozes with meaning. The pouch, not Fela, contains or is endowed with seven lives. But whose lives? What other lives, in other words, weigh down on the pouch? Unlike the enlarged photograph of the Queens on the Kalakuta Museum's wall, this piece embraces irresolution. It raises the possibility of contesting familiar narratives. The artwork becomes a palimpsest in which lies a history that demands a continued revision of the past. It haunts. It also asks the single most repeated question that audiences have posed to me at academic conferences: Where are the Queens now? In this digital reimagination, the Queens are entangled in a dialectical situation, seeing through Fela's gaze but constantly resisting erasure by it. For the past four decades, the women have continued to struggle against the erasure that defines much of how the history of Afrobeat is told.

The Queens exist in an animated condition in which unresolved social violence presses on the present, "when the people who are meant to be invisible show up without any sign of leaving."[52] *They are suspended between iconicity and absence, a state that transforms them into figures of beauty and resilience, of idealized African womanhood, but fundamentally occludes any material engagement with their lived experiences in and since Afrobeat. The trope of iconicity that has continued to punctuate the Queens' presence flattens a complicated and unresolved history and the subjectivities of its various actors into sometimes meaningless marsh. While these tropes of memory present the Queens (through vibrant photographs, art installations, or computer-generated Queen faces), their ultimate effect is one that distorts the Queens beyond recognition and circumscribes an understanding of Afrobeat in rigorously historical terms. These invocations rarely name the women, let alone provide a modest biography that grants them personhood. However, historical silencing is hardly surgical; ghosts seep through the ruptures of vexed stories that insist on retelling a single hegemonic truth. Each telling of Fela's life without a full*

Figure 7.3. *Pouch with Seven Lives,* a digital portrait of Fela Kuti by Nigerian artist Watigbi (Weyinmi Atigbi), initially showcased at 2011 exhibition *Art of Rebellion* in Lagos. Photo credit and permission: Watigbi.

and conscientious accounting of the women's place in it, each instance of iconizing the Queens without the substance of their lived experience finds itself in a troubled relationship a basic question: where are the Queens now? It is a question we are bound to keep asking until we muster the courage to hear what answer the question yields, what bodies it exhumes, what ghosts it calls forth. Haunting foregrounds an understanding of the Queens as historical subjects caught in a cross fire of histories, agendas, ambitions, modernities, and, above all, patriarchies.

Almost four decades later, the mass wedding continues to dominate public memory of the Queens. The Nigerian public has constructed the women into unknowable subjects with bodies that render them simultaneously hypervisible and incapable of sentience or agency. The question "Who were those women?" encapsulates the fundamental problems around subjectivity, fungibility, and power the Queens and other Afrobeat women artists have come to embody. The women were fungible in that their bodies were substitutable, eclipsing the possibility of individuality. Fungibility, Sadiya Hartman argues, transforms a body into "an abstract vessel vulnerable to the projection of others' feelings, ideas, desires, and values. . . . [It also acts as] the surrogate for the master's body since it guarantees his disembodied universality and acts as the sign of his power and dominion."[53] To describe the Afrobeat Queens using the language of fungibility is not to imply that they share the ontological status of the enslaved, the subject of Hartman's analysis. Rather, it is to illuminate the gap between the women's subjective existence and the dominant deployment of the figure of the Queen, a figure into which others put their feelings, ideas, desires, and values. Fungibility underscores how their bodies have been mobilized not only to visually reify Fela's masculine body but also to act as artistic surrogates for Fela, a fact that complicates the possibility of conceptualizing their individuality as historical subjects. Extending Hartman's use of fungibility, I suggest that the interchangeability of Afrobeat women, and the Queens in particular, allowed for anonymous, collective action. This fungibility delayed the possibility of a rich historical rendering of their lives, but in real time it sanctioned opacity in ways that let the women project through performance their own desires and aspirations onto a dystopic political order. In this way, fungibility becomes a site of both erasure and possibility. My hope is that the reader finds this book to have achieved a little more of the latter.

Conclusion

What Afrobeat Owes Women It May Never Repay

There is no denying the Queens' critical transformation of Afrobeat music; the distinct tenor of the chorus was heard in the very first notes of "Lady"'s choral response (1972), piercing and urgent voices wafting from vinyl to transistor radios and across living rooms and music shops across Lagos to define a moment in African music history. Their agile and restive bodies at the Afrika Shrine interrupted the visual aesthetic of vinyl art covers and, more audaciously, unleashed a feverish eroticism in live performance in the Shrine's dancing cages. Whether as cultural agents or figures of moral controversy, these women artists left a permanent stamp on the sonic, visual, haptic, and affective vibrations of African popular music and the textures of popular activism in the early years of Nigerian social and cultural life in the wake of colonialism. A sustained accounting of how girls and young women made such a profound cultural and political impact—let alone of the shifting contours of their vocality, sensual embodiment, and unruly self-presentation over time—has remained largely elusive in histories and analysis of Afrobeat music. That little has been written about such a pioneering and enigmatic group of women artists derives partly from a general underappreciation of women's work as cultural producers, a silence about which much has been written and for which much more lies waiting to be excavated. But the silence pertains also to methodological and critical blind spots and to what interpretive habits have been brought to bear on their acts and contributions to culture and activism. First, the focus on stage and public-facing performances has offered insightful but inadequate analysis into the worlds Afrobeat women inhabited, slices of which unfolded onstage in full view of the audience but also bled into or circulated in the domain of other publics. From the very early moments of conceptualizing this project, I thought

I would be making an intervention that inserted the women into existing histories of the genre, an intervention in the modality of a historical corrective. While I understood that little had been written about women in Afrobeat, I understood that to fill in this gap in history would require posing a different set of questions than was being asked about Fela and Afrobeat at the time. I refined the standard opening questions for my interviews after speaking to one or two women. The questions included: "Describe when and how you joined Kalakuta Republic." "Describe what a typical day looked like when you had tours/performances." "Describe a typical day when you had no tours/performances." "What did it feel like being on stage as a dancer/singer?" "How did you interact with the audience, the band, and with Fela?" "How did you interact with other Queens?" "Were you close to any one or to group of women?" "What was your favorite song/fondest memory?" To pose and to find answers to questions such as these and to craft a narrative that did more than recount the familiar narrative of Fela's accomplishments required looking for and talking to the women instead of drawing on secondary sources or secondhand narratives from people who had worked with Fela. The task of locating them, earning their trust, and listening respectfully to their life stories, the aspects they cared to share with me, revealed not only the historical erasure I had suspected but also a staggering level of distortion in popular narratives and commonsense assumptions about their multiple and sustained entanglements with Afrobeat music. The project quickly morphed from one of filling gaps in history to one of pursuing a feminist critique of Afrobeat: its archives, its mythologies, its aesthetic products, its self-narratives, its curatorial impulse, its imagined futures. In each and all these fronts, Fela acts as a formidable center of gravity. My task became that of historian of the multitude and subaltern, forced, Sadiya Hartman offers, "to grapple with the power and authority of the archive and the limits it sets on what can be known, whose perspective matters, and who is endowed with the gravity and authority of historical actor."[1] I needed to negotiate the limits of Afrobeat's conventional archive, the familiar forms of Fela's rhetoric documented in books and other multimedia formats, biographies on his life, the curation and content of the Kalakuta Museum, and the body of songs containing Fela's contemporaneous musings on the political economy of Nigeria as a neocolonial formation. Rereading and exceeding these frames would make space for new stories about women's experiences in Afrobeat, but doing so demanded that I look for the women where they were and speak to them. My first attempt at meeting a Queen unfolded when I visited the beer joint run by Najite Mukoro, a respected Afrobeat dancer in her day; the joint was a few meters from the Kalakuta Museum, whose peace, I learned, she occasionally disrupted with one-woman protests. One gentleman explained that Najite's protests had been more frequent and intense with the creation of the museum, a process that facilitated evicting her and the commune's final residents. The two times I heard this story told at the museum, it ended with her being forcefully removed from the premises. (The eviction is ironic considering that the management converted parts of the commune into rentable hotel rooms to be charged per night.) Najite's protests, the sentiment of which came across in virtually all the interviews I conducted with the women, threw into relief the contributions-to-Afrobeat thesis, which, at its core, posits a false sense of resolution and harmony within Afrobeat and, more specifically, between Kuti family and working-class women performers who made the genre into a culture goldmine. Whatever story I had to tell needed to grapple with eviction as a material and figurative act and the outsider status the women now occupied. The story also needed to take seriously the moral and philosophical claims made by the women's rupture, at different scales, to the peace of settled narratives about Afrobeat music. In addition to Najite, I met and forged relationships with other Queens, whom I met in physical locations and at different stages in their current lives. While formal interviews averaged one to two hours per sitting, I had the benefit of interviewing some Queens (and other Afrobeat-affiliated women) multiple times and, with some, during random check-in phone calls that almost inevitably contained new stories or never-before-disclosed details. I have continued to visit them when I am in Nigeria and check in via phone; this relationship began in 2014. These meetings have occurred over a period of years. I have met some alone or, on rare but eventful occasions, in the company of another Afrobeat-affiliated woman. For our second interview, Olaide invited me to her home, where I met Ifeanyi Abuah (a younger Kalakuta regular), who was visiting at the same time. It was also at Olaide's place that I met and video interviewed Omolara, whom Olaide invited to the recording session. I reunited with Omolara two years later for a one-on-one chat at her aunt's home. My first two meetings with Kevwe occurred at and around the New Afrika Shrine; these meetings have been followed by a succession of phone chats and in-person meetings. My encounter with Najite was at a daughter's home, following our initial encounter at her shop.

A striking pattern emerged after speaking with a few Queens. They spoke at greater lengths, with less prompting and far more ease and animation, about social life in Kalakuta Republic than about their heralded work as dancers or backing vocalists. Of all they shared about their audacious journey, confrontation of the state, and critiques of society, it was what unfolded in and around Kalakuta that unleashed a glint in the eyes, raised the voice a few decibels, elicited animated slaps of the thighs, invited profanities of all sorts, and roused the deepest emotions. They relished the rule breaking; leisure; improvised living of all sorts; *yabis*; as well as dramatic retellings of invasions by police and other state agents and occasional successes registered in resisting them; self-beautification; illicit and liberating sexual adventures in and beyond the commune; pleasures of all kinds; the feeling of freedom of solo dancing; the satisfaction of relistening to one's voice woven into a chorus replaying all over the country (all over the world); being seen, recognized, and occasionally re-spected as a Queen; dealing with loss and doubt; departures and tentative re-turns; friendships forged and trust broken; acknowledgment as activists against an autocratic state; unresolved memories of the past; enduring traumas; and a sense of irresolution about the Afrobeat project. These experiences, gener-ously captured in the women's oral narratives, exceed the formal and aesthetic character of Afrobeat music even if songs contain fragments of those stories. Events of national consequence were often anchored in a personal memory, something that unfolded in their lives or in the commune that imbued the event with intimate meaning. Overlooking the quotidian, in other words, has meant losing sight of the dynamic arenas of self-making as citizens and as moral and political subjects. The everyday world of communal living nourished narratives and self-crafting strategies that endured in bodies and memories as much as—if not more than—formal, aestheticized stage performances. *Queens of Afrobeat* attempts to expand the archive of Afrobeat by enriching biographical narra-tives about the art, aesthetics, politics, and contemporary lives of women who subscribed to Afrobeat and permanently transformed it without due credit to themselves. I have sought to contribute to the growing archive of the Queens' presence and contribution to Afrobeat as well as the associated gendered strug-gles they experienced and endured as a result. When scholars look solely to Afrobeat lyrics as evidence, they come to the unsurprising conclusion that Af-robeat music is Fela's genius ruminations on the nation's perennial struggles in the shadow of empire. But the effect of privileging this form of text as primary historical evidence has been to elide women's roles in germinating Afrobeat ideas and elevating its power to persuade listeners, friends, and adversaries of the music. Also unremarked has been the women's own affective investment in the meaning and import of Afrobeat songs, how they saw their lives intimately documented in the songs, sometimes reappropriating lyrics for personal use in negotiating everyday life in, outside, and after communal living, as well as how songs rejigged their memories of challenging or succumbing to the hegemony of the state. For them, "Unknown Soldier" documents a deeply personal ex-perience of trauma, sisterhood, resistance, and survival as it narrates an event of public and national importance. The song "Everything Scatter" embodies a personal memory of state overreach at the same time as it marks preliminary troubles with law enforcement. The sources we privilege need to account for patterns of musical recycling within Afrobeat that illuminate how women practiced worldmaking in the everyday.

Following their lead, I offer narratives rooted in new readings of familiar songs and less-considered print and popular culture sources. *Queens of Afrobeat* has been informed by the women's memories of their lives, from their professional work to narratives of everyday life, their stories excavating the fluid spaces between activism and enjoyment. It has favored a processual and contingent approach that embraces shifting centers and multiple possibilities. Public and private experiences rooted in structural inequity can and do stand alongside historically contingent moments when Afrobeat women marshaled a plethora of aesthetic and social moments or cultural resources to exercise control over otherwise disempowering circumstances, including their unequal entanglements with Fela. It is precisely for this reason that there can be no singular history of Afrobeat or of Fela's life, only recursive narratives that fold one into the other, cutting through, complicating, extending, and enriching what we know about the past. There can and should be plural histories of Afrobeat, each narrative rigorously researched but alert to shifts in the scope and elasticity of its margins. Additionally, apart from two women (Najite and Kevwe) who spent over two decades working in Afrobeat, not one person I interviewed appeared to have remained with the commune or in the band from the early 1970s through the post-Fela period. Fela's older children, possible exceptions, were daily visitors to Kalakuta Republic for much of the 1970s and, as such, were largely excluded from expectations and embodied experience of work, play, and rebuke that governed everyday life. While many people related stories of the same experiences—and many stories contained the same basic elements—the perspectives and level of detail were often different, shaped heavily by the teller's positionality. Narratives were heavily inflected by gender identity, social class, relationship to the Kuti family, longevity in Afrobeat (how long they lived in Kalakuta Republic or performed in Afrobeat bands), period and timing (when they worked in Fela's band, considering the massive shifts in the commune's ideological character across decades), as well as responsibility (what roles they played in the commune and band).

The Queens have earned their rightful place in the history of Nigerian popular culture and in postindependence social movements. The women in Afrobeat bequeath to us a powerful but hauntingly imperfect rendition of freedom. By means of Afrobeat music, they cut through layers of moral, social, and aesthetic constraints to forge tiny, precarious spaces that allowed for the flourishing of complicated gendered, classed, sexual, national, and Pan-African subjectivities. The Queens recalled their Kalakuta experience as bittersweet: bitter when they reflected on their injuries from calling out social ills, their sense of being forgotten by Nigerians, and their exclusion from "the fruits of their labors," as Olaide Babayale-Kuti unambiguously framed it. Their recollections were sweet when they spoke of their abiding friendships with other women; their sense of freedom and adventure, of travel, of the funny, extraordinary Kalakuta events that did not become Afrobeat lyrics; and of Afrobeat songs that comprised their lives as teenagers and young women. Indeed, as young working-class women, gender, experience, and social class intersected to overwhelmingly define their capacity to self-advocate. These intersections also influenced how society determined their worth, including the parameters of remembering and forgetting. Their positionality has dictated the women's ability to publicly contest Afrobeat narratives or to generate and mobilize resources to lead fulfilling lives in the present.

—⁓—

There are two central domains within which to read Afrobeat's cultural incursion and its gendered implications for African feminist cultural history: as popular culture and as a subculture, both male-dominated domains that impinge on a robust accounting of the creative lives and subjectivities of women who actively shape their outlook and lend them political meaning. The sexism and misogynoir of postwar popular music have been hostile to and exploitative of meaningful participation by racialized and working-class women. Even when concessions are made, they turn out to be marginal opportunities that hardly harness the full range of women's talents. By the same token, because subcultures as distinguishable social formations are often dominated by men and media coverage leans toward areas dominated by men, documenting the creative genius, interests, and lived experiences of girls and women has fallen on the shoulders of feminist scholars.[2] The marginalization of women in subcultures and popular music culture is doubly amplified in Afrobeat because of Fela's personification of the genre alongside the misogynistic imageries and discourses that saturate Afrobeat's lyrical, visual, and discursive fields. The moral scrutiny the women confronted over the deployment of their bodies and voices in sometimes resistive and often morally ambiguous ways added to their cultural power in the same way the discomfort they elicited underscored popular music and subcultures as double-edged spaces of creative agency for women who dare to venture in as active participants. Their retreat from public view in Fela's wake, the precise moment when the most influential histories of Afrobeat were being crafted, might reinforce the misconception that they were marginal actors in Afrobeat. And yet their enduring cultural impact remains unimpeachable even when the precise language for narrating their contribution and struggles might be tentative.

Afrobeat music drew its cultural keep from its capacity to combine a Pan-African sensibility, a materialist analysis of culture and of Black nationalist discourse rooted in an urban youth culture that strategically reclaimed real and imagined African cultural aesthetics. Fela's insistence on strengthening the pillars of patriarchy as part of his cultural nationalist project led to a string of contradictions when juxtaposed against his expressed desire to deploy music to challenge oppression. The possibility that Fela exaggerated his opposition to feminism to upset Western liberal sensibilities did little to blunt the material effect of his position on the women who, having participated in upholding his views on gender, had to wrestle with it in and outside the Afrobeat community. As such, even fierce critics of Fela's gender politics often neglect the most damning aspects of Afrobeat's gender politics, namely how songs like "Lady" (1972) and "Mattress" (1975), which deride women through music and imagery, prefigured long-term misogynistic effects on the material circumstances of the women who worked in his bands. The material impact on the women's lives and life chances can be attributed in part to the unprotected labor extracted from them in service of Afrobeat music. To subordinate everyday life to Fela's music or rhetoric is to lose sight of a rich dimension of women's lives: how their identities leading to Afrobeat interloped their experience and susceptibility to dispossession within it. As such, critiques of Afrobeat misogyny would do well to ask new questions: To whom and what did Fela orient his misogyny, and when? How did age, class, nationality, and education (and the forms of social capital attached to it) shape each woman's ability to respond to or absorb the aftershocks of Fela's excesses? How did responses evolve over time and under what circumstances? These questions separate Sandra Izsadore, Remi Ransome-Kuti, and Funmilayo Ransome-Kuti (FRK) from the army of young women artists (some of them Queens) whose identities rendered them uniquely susceptible to social backlash occasioned by Fela's lackadaisical posture toward gender.

Fela's razor-sharp musical critiques on race and class as primary categories of oppression obscured gender and sex-based oppression. Consistent with nationalist thinking at the time, Fela harbored rudimentary and polemical ideas about precolonial African gender relations. One of his most glaring failings on the topic was his consistent glamorization of female subservience, an idea he mapped onto an imagined African woman little in evidence even in the commune he led, especially considering the varied challenges to his authority by the women in the band. That this fantasy of women was as much a colonial invention as it was a neocolonial male fantasy of African womanhood would be comical had it not lent itself to deleterious applications in Kalakuta's everyday contestations over value and opportunity. Fela's misconstruction of a pristine and pliable womanhood constitutes a classic example of the reactionary traditionalism that rigidifies indigenous culture either by purging it of European contact or by stereotyping it as pristine. As a part of this purgative cultural project, reactionary femininity scrupulously adheres to a cultural ideal of femininity purged of any hint of degeneracy projected onto colonized women.[3] The posture was resistive to colonialism, but the stereotype of African womanhood as subservient and nurturing was one of the tropes of this project, becoming one of several levers African men pulled in controlling women and consolidating the gains of colonial patriarchy. Paul Tiyambe Zeleza makes the point more forcefully when he writes of cultural decolonization: "Colonialism and globalization make the recuperation of precolonial African cultures, which were themselves neither static nor uniform, idealistic gestures at best. The structures, categories, discourses, and performative styles, idioms, and rituals of colonial cultures were indigenized in varied and uneven ways according to the inscriptions of class, gender, race, religion, location, and their specific intersections. It cannot be overemphasized that cultural decolonization will not be achieved through the negation of simple rhetorical or ideological pronouncements."[4] The Afrobeat community's failure to advance a radical gender politics underscores how African subcultures, even of the progressive ilk, risk reifying sediments of colonial pasts in the imaginative landscape of cultural decolonization. Subcultures that emerge on the trails of colonialism confront the dilemma of identifying and responding to its legacies without adopting its tactics and system of values.[5] Afrobeat, led by Fela, struggled on this front.

The existing frames for reading gender identity, discourse, and gendered performance in Afrobeat have proven inadequate to approaching the contours, shifts, and contradictions that define Afrobeat music. Debates over musical misogyny, for instance, obscure what is owed by Fela to a host of women, especially young, working-class women and, in the 1970s, girls. As I have suggested throughout the book, neither Fela nor his music should be taken as reliable narrators of Afrobeat's shifting gender relations or of the material stakes around upholding a rigid gender binary that benefited men.

African modernity and nationalist projects saw elites feverishly contain women's bodies through social discipline, surveillance, and legislation. The disciplining of women on the altar of morality in colonialism's wake relied as much on earlier colonial scripts on the female body, morality, and forced civilization as on the continued and intertwined operations of gender, class, and public anxiety around HIV/AIDS. Male hegemony, once institutional-

ized under colonialism, only deepened in a Nigerian society that saw a major war on the cusp of colonial rule, successive military regimes shaped by
Cold War politics and neocolonial calculations, and a general exacerbation
of social relations resulting in a fizzling of the social contract between state
and citizens. The colonial script that rendered African bodies bizarre—and
a correction of this script in its wake—produced the same reactionary effect
of policing women's sexuality and the terms on which their bodies entered
public spaces.[6] If Nigeria's conservative elites concerned themselves with the
morality of the Queens' provocative embodiment of freedom, the frenetic
military establishment located its unease in their participation in a dissident
music subculture that targeted the state and its bumbling elite for ridicule.
Connected to this insult was the notion that young women had been not
simply complicit but central to the notoriety and formulation of Afrobeat's
trenchant critique of the state (of affairs), a particularly potent locus of patriarchy in the wake of colonialism. This form of gendered defiance was met with
sometimes spectacular disciplining that relied on a combination of moral and
autocratic methods by society and state. Implicit consent from disapproving
elites authorized the state's infliction of lasting injuries on the women, their
host, and their Kalakuta peers. Some women in Afrobeat became high-profile
scapegoats, held up as embodying the cruel fate that awaited defiant women.
The ostensible ruination of their lives before and after Fela's wake, the reasoning appeared to be, would deter girls from contemplating similar paths
of social deviance. This rebuke supported the unspoken notion that society
benefits when women adhere to hegemonic notions of conduct and decency
and that deviating from this script could prove damning. The framing of the
women as diseased bodies in what was perhaps the most elaborate attempt
at disciplining them from within the commune, following Fela's dramatic
death from AIDS-related complications. When AIDS tore through Kalakuta
Republic in the mid-1990s, it did more than ravage bodies. AIDS became a
cultural and moral force, as much as an epidemiological reality, that deepened
existing inequities in Afrobeat and in broader Nigerian society. The stigma
and threat of social death of AIDS allowed the Queens and many other Afrobeat women artists little room for privacy or public support. Thus, the disease
dealt a huge blow on the legacy of women in Afrobeat music. That Fela's life
culminated in public spectacle around AIDS came to shape the women's view
of their own relationship to Afrobeat. In response to AIDS' impact on the arts,
David Ansen writes, "It is about . . . artists who would never get the chance to
grow, music silenced."[7] AIDS silenced the women in a few ways, not least of
which through sickness itself. The social and moral effects of the disease and
its gendered dimension led many women to seek distance from the genre. In

the Queens, Nigeria sought to silence one of the most forceful eruptions of female creativity and expressivity in modern history. While Fela's unrelenting assault on dominant social codes made him an icon, Afrobeat women's parallel gendered defiance earned them derision and erasure. Michael Veal concludes, in perhaps the clearest reading of the aftershocks of Fela's reckless life on the women around him, that "women of the Lagos underclass likely shared the ultimate price for his ideological linkage of hypersexualism, populism, and cultural revitalization."[8] The women have led lives that project a lifelong defiance of these coordinated assaults on their voices, bodies, memories, and self-expression. They have shown themselves to be social visionaries who, enduring the psychic scars of HIV/AIDS, penury, social isolation, judgment, and classification as "promiscuous, reckless, wild, and wayward," have reclaimed Afrobeat music as painful and "beautiful experiments," to quote Hartman once again, of resisting and surviving patriarchy, surveillance, and coloniality in its psychic, bodily, and intimate effects.[9]

The inculcation of binary thinking about gender has witnessed historically situated and seemingly perpetual attempts at subordinating women through a variety of machinations. Popular culture has emerged as a powerful space for the inscription of these hegemonic ideas but also as the vanguard, the cultural laboratory, of subverting those cultural machinations.[10] Africa 70 and Egypt 80 women exceeded the conventional understanding of "working artists." Their creative labor as dancers, singers, and Afrobeat makeup connoisseurs enabled them to break new ground in the music industry, paving the way for other women artists—including of a different generation—to express themselves in artistic and sensual ways that many perceived as subtly defiant. While the dancers' bodies staged a visual metacommentary on Afrobeat politics, Afrobeat's background singers came to embody the dialogic discourse of call-and-response central to the Afrobeat style. Controversy and sensationalism set them apart from peers in other bands, as did unique experiments with live performance that ruffled the tedium of early 1970s popular culture. The women's creativity animated Afrobeat music and culture for decades, even as they endured bodily and emotional trauma from law enforcement and the armed forces. Despite being exposed to violence, they continued to explore artistic and activist passions that gave Afrobeat music and activism oomph. This investment in Afrobeat might have amounted to giving themselves up for a false promise. But most of them considered it a meaningful contribution at mobilizing art in service of an alternative if unfulfilled order.

It would be cynical to conclude that Afrobeat's failing of women posits the fundamental incompatibility of popular culture and inclusive radical politics. To my mind, its failure and Fela's unique role in it illustrate what happens when radicalism anchors itself squarely on the flamboyance and ever-shifting grounds of the popular, in the tendency for spectacle and controversy over vigilance, stillness, and the slow work of undoing toxic traditions, habits, beliefs, whether of indigenous or colonial extraction. The popular and radical are not fundamentally incompatible; indeed, if Afrobeat music reveals anything important, it is precisely the persuasive power of the former in conveying the ethos of the latter, which might be indigestible via other means. Instead, it is living in the public eye and weaving mythologies around a man that yields little more than a self-defeating posture. Not only do myths lend themselves to hegemonic co-optation, but they also distort the exigencies of imagining a more just society. The women's struggles in the post-Fela intrigue provide vivid illustrations of the tragic fallout of a partial revolution, one that, even by playful inversion, considered and deemed certain forms of gendered oppression permissible and natural. Popular or otherwise, revolutions (loosely defined) promise a reordering of the structural premise of society. They aspire to dismantle all oppression while asserting the unimpeachable dignity of life.

So what does the moral and ideological misfiring of Afrobeat—as a musical genre, a subculture, a band, an aspiring movement (at least in the late 1970s), or a combination of these configurations—lend itself to? What possibility is there in Afrobeat's failures, derived from a potent mix of Fela's ideological inconsistencies and active gender management as well as from the repressive overtures of the Nigerian military establishment? And what futures might emerge from these failures? Following the question posed by Jennifer Wenzel about the flourishing of resistive political imagination, we might ponder: How do anticolonial visions survive defeat "to become repositories of aspirations for later movements"? How might such movements and fractured histories of resistance accumulate afterlives with political meaning that reanimate them as potent repositories for contemporary struggles?[11] What energized feminist politics might emerge from the spectacular failure of true and broad liberation in the Afrobeat project, a failure lucidly captured by the memories, narratives, and present debilitating circumstances of the women who sacrificed the most for the actuation of a skewed political vision anchored as much in political critique and communal and collaborative worldmaking as on blasé showmanship, self-indulgence, and an embrace of charismatic patriarchy? What flavor of feminist imaginings and visions of egalitarian futures might rise from the ashes of Afrobeat's gender politics (or lack thereof)? The Queens are lodestars in the space of galvanizing possibility in the throes of erasure and ostensible defeat.

Figure Concl.1. Olaide Babayale-Kuti poses for a photograph with author in front of her home in Ogba, Lagos. Photo credit by author.

Figure Concl.2. Najite Anikulapo-Kuti sits down for a photograph at her daughter's home. Photo credit by author.

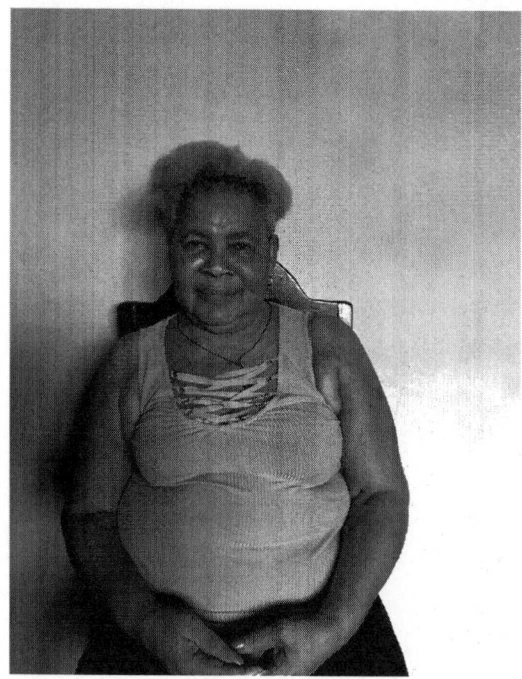

Figure Concl.3. Dele Salami, Fela's first dancer, sits for a photograph at her home in Ajegunle, Lagos. Photo credit by author.

Figure Concl.4. Omolara Shosanya (at Olaide Babayale-Kuti's home) responds to questions about her Afrobeat experience. Photo credit by author.

Figure Concl.5. Kevwe Anikulapo-Kuti poses for a photograph with Dotun Ayobade opposite the Shrine, Ikeja. Photo credit by author.

NOTES

Preface

1. Moore, *Fela*, 10.

2. Carlos Moore clarifies that he did not write these biographical descriptions himself. Shawna Moore and Nayede Thompson jointly wrote them. Moore, *Fela*.

3. LaRay Denzer's essay "Fela, Women, Wives" profiles the women adjudged to have had an impact on Fela's life and career. Denzer contextualizes within a sociocultural frame the Queens' artistic and domestic work, the controversies they inspired, and their contributions (111–34). Vivien Goldman's "Thinking Africa: Afrobeat Aesthetic and the Dancing Queens" intervenes in a comparable fashion, pointing out the political undertones of the women's erotic dances. Goldman understands the Queens' dancing and makeup as carrying aesthetic and ideological significance in Afrobeat music and politics. For her, the sensuality of the women's bodies constituted key apparatuses in crafting Fela's public persona and activist work (105). Important interventions have also been made by scholars such as Michael Veal, Tejumola Olaniyan, and Sola Olorunyomi, all of whom have tackled the thorny question of gender in Afrobeat music alongside an accounting of the women behind the sound.

Introduction

1. Akindele, "Fela Weds," 1.

2. Neither Lemi Ghariokwu nor the Queens I interviewed were in possession of a copy of this marriage certificate. When asked if they still owned a copy, their reaction hovered between laughter and disbelief. They found it ridiculous that I expected them to still have the document after several decades. Their response further underscored how the wedding lived between spectacle and caricature

even for those who partook in it—an event whose paraphernalia was unworthy of keep in the same way as, say, a birth certificate and yet that nonetheless impacted the young women's sense of self in profound ways. For a snapshot of Lemi's role in extending the aural to the visual in Afrobeat, see Olorunyomi, "Lemi Ghariokwu on the Afrobeat Tradition," 80–83.

3. Akindele, "Fela Weds," 11.

4. See Coly, "Un/Clothing African Womanhood."

5. Mann, "Dangers of Dependence," 41–43.

6. Following Catherine Cole's invitation in *Performance and the Afterlives of Injustice*, I use afterlives as an analytic frame for exploring social and political life in the wake of colonialism. While generative, "postcolonial" posits a time *after* colonialism even when its structural underpinnings remain largely intact. Where appropriate, I use "the neocolony" and "the afterlives of colonialism" to denote the postindependence period. See Cole, 22–25.

7. Gaunt, *Games Black Girls Play*, 1.

8. McFadden, "Becoming Postcolonial," 4.

9. McRobbie and Garber, "Girls and Subcultures," 211–12.

10. McRobbie and Garber, "Girls and Subcultures," 216–20.

11. See Drewal, "The State of Research on Performance in Africa," 2, for a discussion of the temporality of performance and attention to processual and temporal dimensions. Also relevant here is Nigerian/Yoruba feminist thinking about the contextual nature of gender performance. Oyèrónkẹ́ Oyěwùmí argues in *Gender Epistemologies in Africa*, for instance, that "if structures of gender emerge out of particular histories and social contexts, we must pay attention to the continuous ways in which gender is made and remade in everyday interactions and by institutions" (2). Lorelle Semley's study of motherhood and gender relations among to the Yoruba lends credence to this position. She states that "the dominant position of husbands and fathers was not absolute; neither were all mothers and wives disempowered." See Semley, *Mother Is Gold*, 6. Margaret Thompson Drewal challenges the notion that power resides permanently on the male axis in Yoruba ritual performance. She argues that an asymmetrical model of power rooted in a Western binary understanding of gender yields biased results and "creates the impression that women universally are in a rather hopeless position of eternal subordination" (Drewal, *Yoruba Ritual*, 174). Attending to process dissolves the victim/agent binary and refocuses attention on the sustained making and unmaking of gender and gendered subjectivities in Afrobeat.

12. Olaniyan, *Arrest the Music!*, 175.

13. See Gaunt, *Games Black Girls Play*, 1. For a more extensive treatment of the links between Black urban cultures, commercial hip-hop music, and constructions of Blackness in the United States, see Rose, *Hip-Hop Wars*.

14. "What Kind of Man," 64.

15. Moore, *Fela*, 162.

16. Nwankwo, "So Fela Ran Away?," 34.

17. Solarin, "Open Letter to Fela Anikulapo-Kuti."

18. Fela's confession that a band member, Steve Udah, had hatched the original idea for the wedding gave rise to this position. Udah thought that such an occasion would generate public excitement to match Kalakuta's notoriety. And he was right. Moore, *Fela*, 156–57.

19. Shosanya, interview.

20. Clark, *Hubert Ogunde*.

21. "The 12 Wives of Chief Ogunde."

22. Babayale-Kuti, interview.

23. Ezenekwe, "Hell That Was."

24. Shosanya, interview.

25. For Achille Mbembe's description of play, see Mbembe, *On the Postcolony*; "Provisional Notes on the Postcolony," 3–37. To play in the postcolony is to not to decolonize, as scholars like Ngũgĩ wa Thiong'o have famously argued. Ngũgĩ wa Thiong'o is the most prominent African thinker on decoloniality. In *Decolonising the Mind: The Politics of Language in African Literature*, he cites culture as a site of imperialist domination and indigenous language as a tool for anti-imperialist resistance. However, Ngũgĩ, like Mbembe, fails to account for differential access to the resources of cultural resistance. My use of play considers this unequal access as well as the pitfalls of fetishizing resistance because the oppressed can become oppressors themselves under different circumstances. Also, this focus on decoloniality as the object of resistance elides how resistance struggles can easily become masculinized, producing casualties of women, the uneducated, and the poor.

26. Mbembe, *On the Postcolony*, 108. Other scholars have explored how the figure of the trickster in popular theatre authorized and facilitated this kind of shapeshifting by perceptive actors. See, for example, Donkor, *Spiders of the Market*; Shipley, *Trickster Theatre*.

27. Diouf, "Engaging Postcolonial Cultures," 6.

28. Mbembe, *On the Postcolony*, 102–41.

29. Cox, *Shapeshifters*, 5.

30. Moore, *Fela*, 156.

31. When I posed the question pointedly at Najite about her age when she moved into Kalakuta, fifteen, she offered an equally pointed response underscoring the cultural practices the women mobilized from their and other Nigerian cultures to justify their involvement with Fela: "No, fifteen years dey young? For village dem dey marry fourteen, thirteen, fifteen. If na the Hausas, as dem born you, na im dem dey marry you." Indeed, Fela was aware of these cultural practices and drew on them to justify his undue sexual and romantic entanglement

with teenagers even though he also preached the principles of equity and fairness; this was precisely the core of his brand. His choice to weaponize the former is what is in question.

32. Turner, "Brain, Body and Culture," 31.

33. Clarke et al., "Subcultures, Cultures and Class," 13.

34. In *Tactical Performance*, Bogad describes protesters as "tactical players" who scavenge, repurpose, and sabotage the words and symbols of the powerful in pursuit of activist goals. A key difference between Bogad's thinking about serious play and mine lies in Bogad's emphasis on "tactics" as the cornerstone of social movements. While the Queens deployed tactics, they did not always do so with activist ends in mind nor necessarily for public witnessing. On this front, some scholars might be reluctant to read as political the women's use of facial makeup to activate certain registers of beauty. I argue instead that the Queens' mundane, "apolitical" acts remained fundamental to the character and formation of Afrobeat activism. The continued process of experimentation, reflection, copying, and repetition consolidated the makeup style as a cornerstone piece of Afrobeat aesthetics, a bodily practice that has inspired other Black women toward their own enactments of racialized self-fashioning across the African diaspora. For how Black women embody the Queen makeup, see Ayobade, "Queens in Flight." The makeup, now a globally recognized aspect of Afrobeat music, emerged out of the women's everyday improvisations. Their everyday practices of play as resistance are consistent with scholarly takes on everyday life as the stage upon which artists and oppressed groups rehearse and elaborate resistance.

35. Statler et al., "Serious Play," 237. See also Backett, "Getting Serious about Play."

36. Statler et al., "Serious Play," 238–39.

37. Allen and Veal, *Tony Allen*. Lemi Ghariokwu repeated the war zone metaphor during my interview with him.

38. For an extensive discussion of Fela's musical style and politics, see Grass, "Fela Anikulapo-Kuti." See also chapters 4 and 5 in Veal's *Fela* as well as the introduction and chapter 4 in Olaniyan, *Arrest the Music!*

39. Marre, *Konkombe*.

40. Segun Bucknor, Afropop bandleader of Revolution, described Fela's house as the "first genuine commune he knows in Nigeria," where the inhabitants lived by the philosophy of "all for each and each for all." See "Counter Culture."

41. Fairfax, *Fela, the Afrobeat King*, 260.

42. One such ritual is captured in the documentary *Fela Kuti: Music Is the Weapon* by Jean-Jacques Flori and Stéphane Tchalgadjieff.

43. Women attended for free during ladies' night on Tuesdays. Fela delivered lecture-style speeches on current affairs on Fridays, known as Yabis Night. The comprehensive show on Saturday was a full-band concert and variety night. It

featured a host of acts, from magicians and contortionists to upcoming musicians. Comprehensive shows, unlike other nights, saw Africa 70 performers bedecked in uniformed costumes. The Shrine played host on Sunday afternoons to Sunday Jump, a show targeted at younger audiences who could not attend mid-week late-night shows because of school. Mondays and Thursdays were reserved for rest and rehearsals. Only government raids, tours, and infirmity disrupted this schedule.

44. "Counter Culture."

45. Goldman, "Thinking Africa," 105.

46. Goldman, "Thinking Africa," 108–109.

47. Haastrup, "Teenage Girl Caused Kalakuta 'War,'" 15.

48. Haastrup, "Teenage Girl Caused Kalakuta 'War,'" 15.

49. No minimum legal age for marriage and sexual consent existed under statutory or customary law in 1978. Only in 2003 did Nigeria adopt the United Nations Convention on the Rights of the Child. What would become the Child's Rights Act passed into law after ten years of "heated debates by parliamentarians" who contested its national application to different cultural and religious groups. The act defines a child as a person below the age of eighteen and, among other provisions, prohibits "the betrothal and marriage of children." Passing the law at the national level did not automatically translate into adoption by state legislatures. As such, there is variation in the adoption of the act between regions and ethnic groups across Nigeria, particularly with respect to the age of marriage and consent. Certain groups continue to uphold customary law, which is more permissive about these limits. Instead of age, adherents of customary law take the period "after puberty" as indicative of a child's preparedness for marriage. In customary marriage, however, parental consent is of critical importance, and its absence can delegitimize and nullify a marriage. By the same token, parental consent can legitimize child marriage, even under the most problematic of circumstances (such as marriage for economic reasons). Fela claimed that the mass wedding was conducted according to customary law and asserted his right to marry on this basis. This was a disingenuous position. Customary law may be fluid about the question of marriage age, but it remains largely inflexible about the centrality of parental/familial consent. Fela not only failed to secure parental consent, but he also understood that consent could not be easily obtained for three key reasons. First, some of the brides might have been deemed too young, a fact that some critics raised in questions of his moral standing. (For moral arguments against the wedding, see Solarin, "Open Letter," and Nwankwo, "So Fela Ran.") Second, asking for the consent of about thirty families would present a logistical and cultural nightmare. Third, Fela's general conduct was at odds with that of a respectable groom, setting aside the fact that he was still legally married to his first wife. The perceived flexibility of customary law offered Fela a weak cop-out from these

complicated requirements. Specific Nigerian states have leveraged the Child's Right Act to more forthrightly implement the Child's Rights Act and protect children from abuse that might arise from the gray areas between legal and customary marriage. In 2007, for instance, Lagos promulgated the act into law—not early enough to prevent the 1978 wedding. For local adoption of the Convention on the Rights of the Child, see UNICEF, "Information Sheet."

50. Ghariokwu, interview.

51. Moore, *Fela*, 187.

52. Conquergood, "Performance Studies," 146.

53. Bridge, "Gendering Music."

54. This is ethnography that goes beneath surface appearances and brings "to light underlying and obscure operations of power and control." See Madison, *Critical Ethnography* (1-11).

55. Acholonu, *Motherism*, 28.

1. Birth of a Restless Collective

1. Diouf, "Engaging Postcolonial Cultures," 5.

2. Schechner, *Performance Theory*, 11.

3. McRobbie and Garber, "Girls and Subcultures," 208–22.

4. Mudimbe, *The Invention of Africa*, 9.

5. Veal, *Fela*, 17–18.

6. Olaniyan, *Arrest the Music!*; Allen and Veal, *Tony Allen*.

7. See the Queens' interviews in Moore, *Fela*, 176–232.

8. See, for instance, Nwankwo, "So Fela Ran Away?"

9. Solarin, "Open Letter to Fela Anikulapo-Kuti."

10. Solarin, "Open Letter to Fela Anikulapo-Kuti." Critics and commentators like Solarin continued to qualify the young women as "girls" even when many were adults by legal and customary standards. Aggrieved parents sought redress through the courts, relying on claims that their daughters were innocent. Partly because of the nature of these complaints, child abduction cases accounted for a majority of the musician's myriad court appearances in the 1970s. Meanwhile, the absence of federal legislation on child marriage made indictment practically impossible. That some daughters testified before judges in Kalakuta's favor presented the most damning indictment against not only the parents but also the social status quo. Parental and feminist insistence on girlhood functioned as tacit appeals for public intervention considering the limited legal options.

11. See Abosede George's *Making Modern Girls* for an extensive discussion of the tensions between colonial and indigenous conceptions of girlhood in Lagos from the late nineteenth century to the mid-twentieth century.

12. Babayale-Kuti, interview.

13. See Murphy, "Performance of Pan-Africanism."

14. Hay, "Queens, Prostitutes and Peasants," 433.

15. See Hebdige, *Subculture*, 29.

16. For an overview of the economic impulses that, in addition to racism, governed the outlook and actions of Teddy Boys, see Clarke et al., "Subcultures," 35–37.

17. For an extensive discussion of the racist impulse behind the rise of postwar British subcultures and the Caribbean cultural responses to these collectives of white youth, see Hebdige, *Subculture*, 39.

18. Pruitt, "How the Vietnam War."

19. Pruitt, "How the Vietnam War."

20. See Peniel Joseph's essay "Dashikis and Democracy" and Martha Biondi's *The Black Revolution on Campus*.

21. Bhandhukravi, "Notting Hill Riots."

22. Bhandhukravi, "Notting Hill Riots."

23. Flori and Tchalgadjieff, *Fela Kuti*.

24. Attempts were made to avert a full-scale war—of note was Kwame Nkrumah's convening of the 1967 Aburi Accord, to which he invited Chukwuemeka Ojukwu, the leader of the Biafra movement, and members of the Supreme Military Council led by Yakubu Gowon. But the seeds of conflict had been sown decades earlier in 1914, with the forced amalgamation of the northern and southern protectorates under the British colony. The merger of disparate ethnic groups ranked colonial expediency above local interests or historical dynamics.

25. Okolie, "Margaret Ekpo."

26. Christopher Alan Waterman has argued that songs like "E Sa Ma Miliki" by Ebenezer Obey (Just Keep Rocking, 1970) reflect anxieties produced by the civil war. Such political reflection through music foreshadowed Fela's more explicit ruminations about Nigerian social life in the 1970s. For Waterman, see *Jùjú*, 121.

27. Fela quoted in Moore, *Fela*, 110.

28. Osoba, "Corruption in Nigeria," 376.

29. Cohen, "Subcultural Conflict."

30. For a discussion of the correlation between commodity prices and popular culture production, see Barber, *Generation of Plays*. For a specific exploration of how changes in crude oil price shaped popular music in Nigeria, see Waterman, *Jùjú*. Also, because of the invention of microgroove discs, Fela could experiment by the early 1970s with musical arrangements that lasted up to thirty minutes. The coincidence of technological advances in music consumption and a local landscape fueled by petrodollars served his rise to stardom.

31. In "Trading Virtue for Virtuosity," Leslie Nicole Braun presents this paradox in the value attached to women's dancing in Congolese dance music (48). The same dynamic applies to the Nigerian music scene, in which women dancers, while vital to bands' survival, attracted low wages for their craft and wielded little power in band management.

32. Wale Owoade, "Kehinde Lijadu's Death: Five Essential Songs from the Legendary Sister Duo." *Pan African Music*, November 16, 2019. https://pan-african-music.com/en/kehinde-lijadus-death-5-essential-songs-from-the-legendary-sister-duo-2/.

33. Akano, "The Scene."

34. The Sisters began their careers as session vocalists in recording studios. They released their first album, *Iya Mi Jowo*, in 1969. The duo followed this release with approximately one album every two years until the mid-1980s. See Larkin, "Lijadu Sisters."

35. Ogunyemi, "Marriage Today," 4.

36. Ogunyemi, "Marriage Today," 4.

37. Marre, *Konkombe*.

38. With so much money in government coffers, Gowon created the Udoji Commission, whose primary task was to increase salaries and benefits for upper-level civil servants. This poorly conceived policy resulted in inflation with ripple effects on the consumption of Nigerian pop music. For example, cassette players, once considered luxury items, became widely affordable, expanding the market for cheap cassettes and, with weak regulation, the illegal proliferation of vinyl-to-cassette copying. Unfortunately, artists suffered the shortfall for the boom in affordable music technology. For a discussion of the changing technologies of the 1970s and how Nigerian bands responded, see Waterman, *Jùjú*, 118.

39. Hale and Sidikou, "New Perspectives on Women's Songs."

40. Waterman, *Jùjú*, 31.

41. In the essay "African Thought Leadership," Patricia McFadden makes a similar case about the persistent neglect of women's literary contributions. In 1978, Ama Ata Aidoo famously made the case in the essay "To Be an African Woman Writer."

42. Redmond, *Anthem*, 245.

43. For a more extensive discussion of Makeba's mobile activism through music and live performance, see Shana Redmond's *Anthem* (245). The documentary *Mama Africa: Miriam Makeba* by Mika Kaurismaki presents an evocative narrative of Makeba's life and activism. Particularly striking is the film's handling of her Pan-African activism and transnational ties. For briefer introductions, see Cagnolari, "Miriam Makeba" and Sizemore-Barber, "The Voice of (Which?) Africa."

44. See the documentary *Mama Africa* for a detailed treatment of Makeba's musical career in the United States as well as her storied relationship with Kwame Touré.

45. Tejumola Olaniyan offers an astute reading of the song "Jeun Ko Ku" with attention to how its inventive instrumentation and humorous take on the culturally recognizable figure of the drunkard aided its commercial success; see Olaniyan, *Arrest the Music!*, 34–36.

46. "Counter Culture."

47. Veal, *Fela*, 17.

48. "Counter Culture," 60.

49. Dalley, "The Idea of 'Third Generation.'"

50. Nzegwu, "School Days in Lagos," 138.

51. jegede, "Dis Fela Sef!," 82–83.

52. Fairfax, *Fela, the Afrobeat King*, 324.

53. Allen and Veal, *Tony Allen*.

54. "Boy Who Plans a Jazz Revolution," 17.

55. Webster, "Communes," 127.

56. See Coly, "Un/Clothing African Womanhood."

57. Olaniyan, *Arrest the Music!*, 169.

58. Campt, *Listening to Images*, 72.

59. Campt, *Listening to Images*, 94.

60. Campt, *Listening to Images*, 94.

61. It is entirely reasonable to imagine the transaction at the site of photographic capture as having been initiated by the press's photographer, who likely requested an "action" pose. Topless photographs of "showgirls" (young women who worked as dancers in Lagos nightclubs) were common in the Nigerian press, and a few magazines are said to have lobbied Afrobeat women to pose on their "Page Three" features. Another blatant example of media voyeurism can be found in a different photograph of a young, topless Kalakuta woman in a 1976 article in a major magazine, *Spear*, that routinely carried Afrobeat stories. In this example, the photographed girl does not look at the camera. The photographer captures her with Fela's dog, Wokolo. The girl laughs at something beyond the frame of the photograph, but her bosoms are made prominent by its composition. The same story features a photograph of six young, bikini-clad Kalakuta women in a swimming pool. These photographic practices gave prominence to the nudity of girls and young women in Afrobeat, illustrating the coordinated exploitation of their bodies for sensationalism onstage and in print. Chapter 2, "From FRK to 'Lady': A Revised Genealogy of the Music's Other Women," demonstrates how the print media extended this practice to coverage of young women artists, especially dancers, in other Afropop bands. For the photograph of the young girl and Fela's dog, see *Spear Magazine*, July 1976, 7. I am more interested in the critique the photograph facilitates than in its reproduction here, which carries the risk of resensationalizing.

62. For a discussion of the gendered underpinnings of the production and circulation of newspaper writings in Africa, see Newell, "Afterword," 425–33.

63. See Clark, *Hubert Ogunde*; Barber, *Generation of Plays*; "The 12 Wives of Chief Ogunde."

64. Alcendor, "Fela."

65. Moore, *Fela*.

66. Coly, *Postcolonial Hauntologies*.

67. These accounts of Najite and Ihase come from a combination of my interviews and interview responses in Moore, *Fela*.

68. Waterman, *Jùjú*, 133–34.

69. Moore, *Fela*.

70. Moore, *Fela*, 199.

71. Moore, *Fela*, 177.

72. Yeni Anikulapo-Kuti, interview.

73. Moore, *Fela*, 178.

74. This kind of autonomy was precarious because of its reliance on Fela's financial support. Fela expected undivided loyalty from the women with whom he maintained relationships. The musician is said to have cleaned out the apartment of a girlfriend (of things he got her) when he visited unannounced and saw she was not home, reading her absence as evidence of unfaithfulness. Lamiley's education and professional exposure likely immunized her from this kind of treatment. Her hotel room came in handy as a transitory space when, following Kalakuta's destruction, Fela needed shelter for the displaced commune. Kalakutans moved into the hotel that had housed Lamiley for years.

75. Kalakuta's intellectual pull for students bound for or enrolled in university has not been fully considered in Afrobeat scholarship. Scholars have identified that this demographic constituted a key segment of Afrobeat music listeners; however, they often forget to underscore how some students eschewed formal education in favor of a Kalakuta "education." The commune was, in other words, more than an intellectual haven—crucially, it was a place of education. A few examples will suffice on this account. Under the mentorship of a babalawo, Duro Ikujenyo took to herbalism in an effort to relearn the Yoruba secrets of herbs. Lemi Ghariokwu, a self-taught artist left his training at Yaba College of Technology to become an album art designer. Ghariokwu fondly dubbed his years as a Kalakuta artist (between 1974 and 1978) as his own "tertiary education." Mabinuori Kayode Idowu's mother accused Fela of brainwashing her son, who stopped attending school. Together, these three young men formed the Young African Pioneers (YAP), the youth wing of Fela's political party, Movement of the People (MOP). Although a predisposition toward intellectualism was evident among Kalakuta women, it was largely the precinct of an elite group of its young men.

76. Kalakutan phrases such as "Johnny just come," explored in Fela's album *Johnny Just Drop*, described the susceptibility of newcomers to the sharp wits and competitive spirit of city life. A popular 1989 Nollywood film, *Lagos Na Waa*, dramatizes the experience of the new arriver. *Lagos Na Waa*'s humor exaggerates the ignorance of the traveler against the backdrop of a city notorious for impatience and antipathy.

77. For an important critique of the dominant notion of rituals as timeless actions, see Drewal, *Yoruba Ritual*.

78. Najite Anikulapo-Kuti, interview.

79. Denzer, "Fela, Women, Wives," 131. The theme of freedom also emerged consistently in the interviews I conducted with the women.

80. Bauman, *Liquid Modernity*, 17. It is important to underscore that Kalakuta lionized self-indulgence as a model for resistance; it failed, however, to take questions of gender and patriarchy seriously. This partial approach to resistance produced, among other things, feelings of freedom that culminated in disastrous outcomes. Here, it is worth underlining Audre Lorde's injunction about the master's tools and the master's house. See Lorde, "Master's Tools."

81. Kalakuta youths might have been exposed to various addictive behaviors by the community's potent concoction of music, marijuana, and mobility—or their resistance to such behaviors may have been disarmed by immersion in this space. Many women became hooked on Kalakuta and its combination of substances and freedom from responsible adult guidance, making the prospect of leaving their family more attractive and the possibility of reuniting with their estranged family much more difficult. Indeed, stories abound of women who, having said their final goodbyes to Kalakuta, reappeared only after a few weeks or months because they had been thrown out from their homes. Many women found themselves trapped in this cycle. Fela witnessed enough of this oscillation to predict a parting woman's impending return. The musician was, sadly, often proven correct. Still, the women's imperfect association with Afrobeat signified flurries of the imagination amid an intersection of gendered constraints.

82. Kelley, *Freedom Dreams*, 5.

2. From FRK to "Lady"

1. For FRK, see Johnson-Odim and Mba, *For Women and the Nation*; Byfield, "In Her Own Words"; UNESCO, *Funmilayo Ransome-Kuti*. For Sandra Izsadore, see Izsadore and Oyekunle, *Fela and Me*. Remi Ransome-Kuti joins these women alongside the Queens in the essay by Denzer, "Fela, Women, Wives." Dele Salami is virtually nonexistent in Afrobeat scholarship, save for mentions in Allen and Veal, *Tony Allen*.

2. The erasure of subaltern groups from colonial histories of popular uprisings sparked extensive debates in subaltern and postcolonial studies. For an introduction to these debates, see pioneering works such as Guha and Spivak, *Selected Subaltern Studies*. Also part of this intellectual tradition is Gayatri Spivak's germinal essay "Can the Subaltern Speak?" For the conjoining of archival authority with state power, see Derrida and Prenowitz, "Archive Fever."

3. Foucault, "Nietzsche, Genealogy, History," 76.

4. Oyěwùmí, *Gender Epistemologies in Africa*, 2.

5. Except where otherwise specified, this section on Funmilayo Ransome-Kuti derives from Johnson-Odim and Mba, *For Women and the Nation*. Chapter 1, "Historical Background," and chapter 4, "Lioness of Lisabi," are especially relevant to the discussion in this section.

6. Johnson-Odim and Mba, *For Women and the Nation*, 9–11.

7. Johnson-Odim and Mba, *For Women and the Nation*, 54–55.

8. Johnson-Odim and Mba, *For Women and the Nation*, 72.

9. Johnson-Odim and Mba, *For Women and the Nation*, 67.

10. Johnson-Odim and Mba, *For Women and the Nation*, 88.

11. Veal, *Fela*, 112.

12. Cheryl Johnson-Odim and Nina Mba note that FRK permanently abandoned Western clothing beginning in the late 1940s, wearing Yoruba dress as a mark of "class allegiance as of cultural pride and unity with the market women." See *For Women and the Nation*, 66–67. Her name change therefore needs to be read as solidarity with both her son's radical politics and with her own personal journey toward the self in community with others.

13. Babayale-Kuti, interview.

14. Babayale-Kuti, interview.

15. Yeni Anikulapo-Kuti, interview.

16. Eludoyin, interview.

17. Roach, *Cities of the Dead*, 2.

18. These descriptions of Funmilayo's life are drawn from Carlos Moore's *Fela*, 191–95.

19. Moore, *Fela*, 191–93.

20. Moore, *Fela*, 96.

21. Moore, *Fela*, 98.

22. Moore, *Fela*, 102.

23. Moore, *Fela*, 104–105.

24. Moore, *Fela*, 103.

25. Moore, *Fela*, 183.

26. Johnson-Odim and Mba, *For Women and the Nation*, 82–83.

27. Moore, *Fela*, 198.

28. In chapter 6 of *For Women and the Nation*, "'For their Freedoms': The International Sphere," Johnson-Odim and Mba detail how FAK's rising international profile and the frequent travels it entailed were attended by tensions in her domestic relationship, especially when her husband fell ill and eventually died. The authors capture FAK's later ambivalence toward the exacting demands of public activism for a woman and the personal relationships she held dear, including toward a husband who was immensely supportive of her work (125–54).

29. Mbembe, "Variations on the Beautiful."

30. Kwame Nkrumah makes a poignant distinction between moral responsibility as constituted in colonial and neocolonial relations. Nkrumah argues: "For

those who practise [neocolonialism], it means power without responsibility and for those who suffer from it, it means exploitation without redress. In the days of old-fashioned colonialism, the imperial power had at least to explain and justify at home the actions it was taking abroad. In the colony those who served the ruling imperial power could at least look to its protection against any violent move by their opponents. With neocolonialism neither is the case." See *Neo-Colonialism: The Last Stage*, xi.

31. "How I Escaped Death," 3.

32. *Newbreed*, May 1975, 28. Funmilayo Ransome-Kuti, quoted in Denzer, "Fela, Women, Wives," 118.

33. Johnson-Odim and Mba, *For Women and the Nation*, 56.

34. Johnson-Odim and Mba, *For Women and the Nation*, 51.

35. Moore, *Fela*, 41.

36. For a snapshot of Remi's life, see Denzer, "Fela, Women, Wives," 120–24; Moore, *Fela*, 169–74.

37. Moore, *Fela*, 171.

38. Moore, *Fela*, 173.

39. "Boy Who Plans a Jazz Revolution," 17.

40. Oroh, "'I'm Still Scratching the Surface,'" 20.

41. Moore, *Fela*, 169.

42. Haastrup, "Fela's Wife Okays," 24.

43. Spencer, "Fela Kuti Remembered."

44. "Birth of a New Sound," 11.

45. "Interview: Femi Anikulapo-Kuti and Jerome Sandlarz," 43.

46. See, for example, Denzer, "Fela, Women, Wives."

47. This description comes from Sandra Izsadore talking about Dele's effect on the audience. See Goldman, "Thinking Africa," 106.

48. This reading of Congolese *danseuses* and the creative and generative tension between drumming and dancing in Congolese popular music has benefited from Leslie Nicole Braun's "Trading Virtue for Virtuosity," 56.

49. Allen and Veal, *Tony Allen*, 70.

50. Hay, "Queens, Prostitutes and Peasants," 434–39.

51. Braun, "Trading Virtue for Virtuosity," 50.

52. Allen and Veal, *Tony Allen*, 70.

53. "Meet Fela's Ex-Girlfriend."

54. See Daniel Koranteng's interview in Collins, *Fela*, 43.

55. Salami, interview.

56. Salami, interview.

57. Morgan, "Is This an Invasion?"

58. Salami, interview.

59. These dancers do not appear in the list of Afrobeat dancers compiled by Michael Veal in *Fela*, 262.

60. Goldman, "Thinking Africa," 109.

61. Salami, interview.

62. Palmer, *Ginger Baker in Africa*.

63. Braun, "Trading Virtue for Virtuosity," 49.

64. *Guardian*, "Lighting Up Lagos."

65. Morgan, "Is This an Invasion?," 11.

66. See the footage of Segun Bucknor's performance in the documentary *Ginger Baker in Africa*.

67. Akano, "Gondola," 23.

68. Akano, "Ozzidi Is a Success Story."

69. "Star in Her Eyes."

70. The raunchy lyrics and imagery that supported Africa 70's notoriety indicate that Fela was in fact sitting in the company of several men musicians whose work, aided by print media, actively trafficked in the gender and sexual tropes that characterized social life in Lagos. His archrival, King Sunny Ade, whose career took off in 1963 and who had his big break in 1967, composed "Wa Woyan" (Come and Behold Breasts) to widespread appeal. The song captured a perception held by Yoruba male urbanites that rural Yoruba women were easily seduced and generally more trustworthy and less demanding than "sharp-eyed" city women (Waterman, *Jùjú*, 133–34). Male artists and a male-controlled media projected these working women artists in sexually suggestive ways that, beginning on nightclub dance floors, clearly transcended the stage.

71. In the essay "Invented Dances," I expatiate on the intimate entanglement between beat making and embodiment in the production and circulation of Nigerian popular music. For a specific refence about Fela's deployment of instrumentation to elicit dance in the early 1970s, see Ayobade, "Invented Dances," 9–11.

72. Olaniyan, *Arrest the Music!*, 170.

73. Since at least the 1920s, popular culture in West Africa had been dominated not only by men (in the changing landscape of colonialism that redefined public cultural life) but, crucially, by masculine vocals. Different variants of highlife music consolidated male hegemony in public life, whether dance band highlife, performed in elite Ghanaian nightclubs in the 1920s and 1930s, or proletarian forms such as palmwine music, highlife, and Konkomba highlife of the same period. These musical forms pervaded anglophone West Africa, reflecting and cultivating popular music as the domain of young men. In Nigeria, *jùjú* music did not simply traffic in Christian and Yoruba tropes of gender—it was also overwhelmingly produced by men who trafficked in images compatible with male hegemony. See Waterman, *Jùjú*.

74. I am indebted to Tejumola Olaniyan for pointing out in an early iteration of my analysis of the cover art of *Shakara* the striking connection between *Shakara* and Hendrix's *Electric Ladyland*.

75. Washington, *Our Mothers, Our Powers.*

76. Jackson, "Don't Teach Me Nonsense."

77. See Nzegwu, "School Days in Lagos," 141. For a discussion of the embrace of and turn away from Victorian notions of marriage (and their attendant ideas of spousal submission) among elite Lagos women, see Mann, *Marrying Well.* For a comprehensive survey of Yoruba women's history, see Denzer, "Yoruba Women."

78. Ethnomusicologist Derek Stanovsky urges scholars to heed the sometimes-racist ways in which Western media portrayed Fela in obituaries by emphasizing his polygamy and sexual eccentricities; Stanovsky also suggests that we discuss Fela's legacy without reinscribing the racist and sexist tropes that undergird invocations of him as an embodiment of Black male excess. (We could read Stanovsky's warning about excess against Francesca Royster's embrace of the term to pursue a generative reading of the Black [queer] male body alongside choreographer Bill T. Jones.) *Huffington Post* columnist Kirsten Savali cites "Lady" to make the case for critical ambivalence toward Fela's legacy. She argues that Fela's music and lifestyle influenced the proliferation of misogyny in hip-hop and rap; although the claim is not well supported by the evidence. The lesson as I read it from these divergent but important assessments of Fela's life is that a sensitive Afrocentric accounting of Fela's legacy can and should coexist with principled critique of his fraught relationship with women. See Stanovsky, "Fela and His Wives"; Savali, "Life and Legacy"; Royster, "Fela Kuti, Bill T. Jones, and the Marketing."

79. Washington, *Architects of Existence,* 224.

80. Washington, *Architects of Existence,* 227.

81. Margaret Ekpo served as a legislator in the Eastern Regional House of Assembly, becoming one of the first women elected to political office in postindependence Nigeria. Her political life began much earlier, when she took women's issues to Nnamdi Azikiwe's party, National Congress of Nigeria and the Cameroons. Ekpo's political networks were formed through allegiance to Aba market women. Her rising political profile included representing Nigeria in two constitutional conferences in 1944 and 1956; negotiations during those conferences proved crucial to Nigeria's independence struggle. Ekpo's life encouraged more women in politics. See Okolie, "Margaret Ekpo."

82. See George, "Within Salvation"; George, *Making Modern Girls.*

83. See, for example, Ochonu, "Male Anxieties, Cultural Politics"; Coly, "Un/Clothing African Womanhood."

84. Newell, "Afterword," 430–31.

85. For a sampling of such articles, see Tshwala-Amadi, "Liberation and the African Woman"; Lewis, "Is Virginity out of Fashion?"; "When a Wife Starts to Kick"; Thomas, "Devious Rules of Being a Girl." These anxieties suffused the

creative writing of male authors at the time. See Newell, "Representations of Women," 169–88.

86. Coly, "Un/Clothing African Womanhood," 12.

87. See, for example, Pierce, "Farmers and 'Prostitutes'"; Ochonu, "Male Anxieties, Cultural Politics."

88. Newspaper columnists who visited Kalakuta Republic in the 1970s often conveyed surprise at the freedom commune women appeared to enjoy. Another refrain was the sense of discipline that governed communal life, quite the antithesis to the chaos and disorder that many Nigerians imagined. For examples, see Folayan, "Fela"; Ezenekwe, "Hell That Was."

3. To Improvise a Precarious Freedom

1. Moore, *Fela*, 225.

2. Moore, *Fela*, 225

3. Ezenekwe, "Hell That Was," 22.

4. Some speculate that perhaps out of fear of the prospect of a Fela-led presidency, the Federal Electoral Commission (FEDECO) introduced requirements that disqualified the musician and several politicians. It is quite true that Fela's MOP failed to meet FEDECO's requirement of having functional offices spread across Nigeria to be registered in the election. Fela had little success in formal politics, but his ambition earned him the nickname Black President.

5. Lemi Ghariokwu learned of this high-profile meeting through a tip-off from his parents' social circle, finding out that he, as an artist and contributor to *YAP News*, had been named alongside others. Ghariokwu, interview.

6. Moore, *Fela*, 170.

7. Barber, *Generation of Plays*, 10.

8. Jones, *Theatrical Jazz*. Jones writes of *àṣẹ* as animating forces that, when placed with other properties, materialize something that did not previously exist. In collaborative performance, one individual does not have a monopoly over this creative potentiality of *àṣẹ*; rather, it is a shared, coanimated responsibility: "When the *àṣẹ* of one is depleted, others are required to replenish it" (200).

9. "What Kind of Man," 60.

10. Collins, "Fela and the Black President Film," 69.

11. Collins, "Fela and the Black President Film," 57.

12. Fairfax, *Fela, the Afrobeat King*, 370.

13. Johnson, "Black Performance Studies," 454.

14. This definition of yabis comes from Fairfax, *Fela, the Afrobeat King*, 272.

15. Olaniyan, *Arrest the Music!*, 78.

16. Fairfax, *Fela, the Afrobeat King*, 272–73.

17. Fairfax, *Fela, the Afrobeat King*, 272.

18. Adetiba, "Face-to-Face with Muyiwa Adetiba," quoted in Fairfax, *Fela, the Afrobeat King*, 370–71.

19. Yeni Kuti, interview with author.

20. Johnson, "Black Performance Studies," 454.

21. Olaniyan, *Arrest the Music!*, 213.

22. Bhabha, "Of Mimicry and Man," 126.

23. Conquergood, "Lethal Theatre: Performance, Punishment, and the Death Penalty," 343.

24. Ezenekwe, "My Experience Inside Kalakuta Republic," 33.

25. Gaunt, "YouTube Search and Twerking Videos," 1.

26. Flori and Tchalgadjieff, *Fela Kuti*.

27. Hoga, interview.

28. Yeni Kuti, interview.

29. Babayale-Kuti, interview.

30. Jones, *Theatrical Jazz*.

31. jegede, "Dis Fela Sef!," 87.

32. Mbembe, "African Modes of Self-Writing," 9.

33. Lowe, *Intimacies of Four Continents*.

34. Reflecting on the moral landscape of leadership in postcolonial Africa in a manner germane to my reading of relationality in Kalakuta Republic, Eze Chielozona argues that "the most important question or task [for the postcolonial African] is not how to liberate oneself from Western imperialism but rather how to relate to other Africans, fellow victims of oppression." Eze's charge sheds a different light on how individuals interact with one another and the commentary Kalakuta Republic made on the ethics of relations within Africa in the wake of colonialism. See Chielozona, "Decolonisation and Its Discontents," 416.

35. Simone, *City Life from Jakarta*, 60–62.

36. Ayobade, "Fela Kuti."

37. Ghariokwu, interview.

38. Veal, *Fela*, 91.

39. Mabiakwu, interview.

40. The notion that Fela committed "class suicide" as a fundamentally altruistic act, that he stood to benefit little or nothing from fraternizing with the underclass, still carries traction. In a recent Fela Studies conference at the University of Lagos, at least two speakers, one a Fela scholar, echoed this sentiment with the support of several other attendees. This scholar made the comment during the Q&A session of a panel in which Gloria Emeagwali presented a paper comparing the ideas and styles of Fela Kuti to that of Sun Ra. See Fela Studies Group, "Rethinking African History."

41. The discs were likely recycled from broken *jigida* waist beads, composed of circular plastics that some Queens incorporated into their fashion.

42. Goldman, "Thinking Africa," 108.

43. Goldman, "Thinking Africa," 108.

44. Goldman, "Thinking Africa," 108–109. Also, see Piot, *Remotely Global* for an extensive discussion of village modernity.

45. Nzewi, "How the Art Takes Shape," 81.

46. Zeleza, "Towards a Cultural Economy."

47. Apter, *Pan-African Nation*, 6.

48. Ayobade, "'We Were on Top of the World.'"

49. Caillois, "Definition of Play," 136.

50. Ayobade, "'We Were on Top of the World,'" 12.

51. Ezenekwe, "Hell That Was," 22.

52. Okome, "Nollywood, Lagos, and the Good-Time Woman," 180.

53. Moore, *Fela*, 167.

54. Tejumola Olaniyan offers an extensive discussion of the texts, authors, activists, thinkers, and events that fomented Fela's ideological evolution from the early 1970s to the early 1980s. Olaniyan has also been credited with reading Fela's artistic and political pursuits in the early 1970s as those of an "apolitical hustler." See Olaniyan, *Arrest the Music!*, 31–38, 114–18.

55. Olaniyan, *Arrest the Music!*, 114–18.

56. Olaniyan, *Arrest the Music!*, 118.

57. See, for example, Baron, *Egypt as a Woman*. See also Coly, "Un/Clothing African Womanhood."

58. Kevwe, for instance, registered her discomfort as the singers' dresses grew shorter and shorter over the years. Kevwe Anikulapo-Kuti, interview.

59. Goldman, "Thinking Africa," 108.

60. Nzegwu, "School Days in Lagos," 137.

61. "Wunmi - Thoughts on Fela."

62. Roholt, *Groove*, 2.

63. Goldman, "Thinking Africa," 105.

64. Najite Anikulapo-Kuti, interview.

65. Olorunyomi, *Afrobeat!*, 162.

66. Drewal, "The State of Research," 43.

67. Drewal, *Yoruba Ritual*, 7.

68. The Yoruba proverb "eégún ńlá ní í gbẹ́hìn ìgbàlẹ̀" (The biggest masquerade emerges last from the grove) underscores the significance of the last dancer.

69. Drewal, *Yoruba Ritual*.

70. For instance, see DeFrantz, "Black Beat Made Visible"; Drewal, *Yoruba Ritual*, 7; Villepastour, *Ancient Text Messages*.

71. Villepastour, *Ancient Text Messages*, 120.

72. Dodomaya, interview with Mallam Abdul Okwechime.

73. Najite Anikulapo-Kuti, interview.

74. Moore, *Fela*, 120.

75. Ghariokwu, interview.

76. His fellow inmates helped him replace his stool on two consecutive nights while his mother supplied vegetables to neutralize the marijuana in his system.

77. Moore, *Fela*, 140.

78. Moore, *Fela*, 223.

79. Moore, *Fela*, 223.

80. Collins, "Fela and the Black President Film," 68.

81. Moore, *Fela*.

82. Siollun, *Oil, Politics and Violence*.

83. In November 1977, for example, the Ghanaian Flying Squad Police conducted a raid on Hotel President in Accra, where Fela and his band members were guests. Seven of Fela's people, including two women, were arrested for marijuana possession in the sting operation Fela described as a "second rape" of Kalakuta Republic. Fela concluded, based on a tip-off, that Ghanaian law enforcement had coordinated efforts with the Nigerian government to prevent Fela from playing a caustic new tune, "VIP (Vagabonds in Power)," in Ghana. See Kehinde, "Fela Raided in Ghana."

84. Anikulapo-Kuti, "Manifesto of the MOP," 23.

85. Olaniyan, *Arrest the Music!*, 124–26.

86. Backett, "Getting Serious about Play," 12.

4. Unknown Soldier

1. Michael Veal in the documentary *Finding Fela*. See also Edwards, "Crossroads Republic." The author describes how "many considered 'Fela's boys' to dominate the neighborhood by fiat" (101).

2. *Daily Times*, February 21, 1977. Cited in Fairfax, *Fela, the Afrobeat King*, 311.

3. Moore, *Fela*, 200–201.

4. This nexus of forcible sex and subject-making is one in which the neocolonial state rehearses, repeats, and requires gendered, racialized domination of women; this dynamic is reminiscent of Christina Sharpe's reading of monstrous intimacies in the constitution of slavery. The monopoly of violence imbued in the constitution of neo/colonial state power was cut from the same cloth that upheld so-called property rights that authorized violence in plantation economies. For Sharpe's offering on the quotidian horror of rape in the political economy of plantations, see *Monstrous Intimacies*.

5. Mbembe, "Provisional Notes on the Postcolony," 4. For a detailed treatment of rape and its representation in post/colonial francophone Africa and the Black diaspora, see Jean-Charles, *Conflict Bodies*.

6. Mama, "Sheroes and Villains," 61.

7. Mama, "Sheroes and Villains," 51–53.

8. The three acts of negation were (1) the discursive framing of the invasion squarely around Fela's loss, (2) *divorcing* the Queens, and (3) making no legal provision for their welfare, as was discovered after his death in 1997.

9. Mammy traders sell food, drinks, and petty goods that soldiers require for day-to-day subsistence. The concept of mammy markets is thought to have begun in the late 1950s with Mammy Marian Ochefu, the wife of a noncommissioned soldier, who became famous for brewing and selling *enyi*, a nonalcoholic dairy drink. If mammy markets were a place for soldiers to hang out, refuel, and procure items for their daily needs, the emergence of Kalakuta's "area" and the Shrine nearby Abalti Barracks helped stretch out the landscape of recreation available to soldiers stationed there. For a brief history of the mammy market, see Abah, "Meet Grandma."

10. Okwechime, interview.

11. Fairfax, *Fela, the Afrobeat King*, 321.

12. This estimate comes from the lyrics of "Unknown Soldier."

13. See Graham, "Fela: The Full Works."

14. Aliu, "I Can Cope."

15. Ghariokwu, interview.

16. Teniola, "Ban on Fela's Records," 1.

17. See Collins, *Fela*, 69.

18. Collins, *Fela*, 69.

19. Obasanjo, *My Command*, 159.

20. Fairfax, *Fela, the Afrobeat King*, 314.

21. Pan-African festivals became a crucial site for the elaboration of Cold War politics as the superpowers vied for advantage among Africa's influential artists and cultural officers. See Murphy, "Performance of Pan-Africanism."

22. Monroe, "Festac 77," 34.

23. Monroe, "Festac 77," 34.

24. Monroe, "Festac 77," 35.

25. Andrew Apter argues that the festival not only laid uncritical claim to a pristine culture (which had emerged, in fact, partly under colonialism) but also obscured fundamental inequities at the heart of Nigeria at the time of the oil boom. In other words, the windfalls from oil funded a spectacular invention of culture. See Apter, *Pan-African Nation*.

26. Ekanem, "Festac 77 Responsible."

27. See Moore, *Fela*, 135–36.

28. Collins, "Fela and the Black President Film," 58.

29. See Moore, *Fela*, 131. Lieutenant Colonel Buka Suka Dimka cited similar instances of government corruption as crimes to justify his failed but fatal coup against the Murtala-Obasanjo administration.

30. Moore, *Fela*, 131.

31. Collins, "Fela and the Black President Film," 67.

32. Moore, *Fela*, 70.

33. *New Nigerian*, February 19, 1977. Cited in Fairfax, *Fela, the Afrobeat King*, 310.

34. Moore, *Fela*, 193.

35. Moore, *Fela*, 216.

36. Moore, *Fela*, 208.

37. Moore, *Fela*, 140.

38. Babayale-Kuti, interview.

39. Carlos Moore's description of the invasion in *Fela* can be found in two separate sections: 135–41 and in the Queens' narratives, 163–233. See also Collins, "Fela and the Black President Film," 69.

40. Moore, *Fela*, 209.

41. Moore, *Fela*, 187.

42. Moore, *Fela*, 187.

43. Moore, *Fela*, 187.

44. *Daily Times*, February 21, 1977, 1.

45. Regine Michelle Jean-Charles offers a potent critique of rape discourses in francophone literary and cultural representation. Jean-Charles troubles a pervasive representation that subordinates the subjective experience of the trauma of rape to tropes about rape that absent the bodies of the victimized. By testifying with their fresh injuries from physical and sexual violence, the Afrobeat women insisted on making transparent the lived experience of state-sanctioned violation. At the tribunal, some women offered their brutalized bodies as graphic evidence to convey the scale of unprovoked brutality so that that neither the state nor the public could easily reduce the physical and sexual violation to familiar tropes of rape representation. See Jean-Charles, *Conflict Bodies*, 13–14.

46. Fairfax, *Fela, the Afrobeat King*, 322.

47. Cole, *Performance and the Afterlives of Injustice*, ix.

48. This description of the Anya probe comes from an unattributed *Daily Express* newspaper article cited in Fairfax, *Fela, the Afrobeat King*, 323.

49. The most thorough narration of the Anya probe and its dubious findings can be found in Fairfax, *Fela, the Afrobeat King*, 316–43.

50. The Lagos state government claimed ownership of the land and replaced Kalakuta Republic, quite cynically, with the Ransome-Kuti Memorial Grammar School. See Debekeme, "Kalakuta Falls," 1.

51. See Akintola, "Perils of Protest," 107–108.

52. See Balsvik, "Student Protest."

53. Aderinto, "Colonialism and Prostitution," 110.

54. Since barring soldiers from having sex altogether was not an option, colonial officers sought out practicable solutions, one of which was the introduction

of "controlled brothels" where sex workers could be screened and monitored. Supporting sex work around military installations helped solve the twin problem of keeping soldiers within close perimeter of the barracks while allowing for the control of venereal disease (by tracking sex workers believed to carry infections). For an extensive treatment of the conflicting discourses attached to sex work in service of the military as well as the medicalization of soldiers' sexuality in Nigeria, see Aderinto, *When Sex Threatened the State*, 93–112.

55. Aderinto, "Colonialism and Prostitution," 110–11.

56. In *When Sex Threatened the State*, Saheed Aderinto clearly maps the conflict between soldiers' sexuality and the colonial enterprise: "While sexual recklessness and prostitution could be tolerated among the soldiers, their civilian counterparts, in the colonialists' conviction, had to be sexually disciplined in order to be modern or to maximize the gains of imperialism—civilization." The state's implicit support of soldiers' violence (including sexual assault and rape) against defenseless civilians was supported by the widespread belief that such violence was necessary for the greater good, especially since soldiers were deemed more disciplined and farther ahead on the ladder of civilization than "natives" (95).

57. This scene from *Jagua Nana* paints a vivid picture of the configuration of the dance floor as a space of fetishized cross-racial, heterosexual encounter.

> Jomo Ladi and his Leopards always played well, though rather loudly, but dance *High-life* must be loud to fire the blood. White men and black men, they all rose, and crowded the floor. The black men chose the fat women with big hips; the white men clung to the slim girls with plenty of collar bone and little or no waists. There were girls here, and women, to suit all men's tastes. Pure ebony, half-caste, Asiatic, even white. Each girl had the national characteristic that appealed to some male, and each man saw in his type of woman a quality which inspired his gallantry. So the women enticed their victims and the *Tropicana* profited.

Ekwensi's characterization of women as devious objects of male desire and conquest reflects his broader approach in the novel to city life, sex work, and the antics of an aging sex worker, the novel's eponymous protagonist. Ekwensi, *Jagua Nana*, 14.

58. Moore, *Fela*, 237.

59. Midway through one of his counter-FESTAC performances, Fela addressed the issue of 160,000 Nigerian Muslims traveling to Mecca for hajj. His argument was that religious tourism such as hajj was depleting the Nigerian economy, but the issue only arose when he spotted a man in the audience dressed in Islamic garb. Such direct addresses were not unusual, so a soldier in military

wear could easily have elicited similar rebuke. This event is documented in John Collins's essay in the *Glendora Review*, "Fela and the Black President Film," 70.

60. Olaniyan, *Arrest the Music!*, 169–70.

61. Alcendor, "Fela," 36.

62. Idam, "Sodom and Gomorrah," 2009.

63. Geertz, "Deep Play."

64. Shosanya, interview.

65. Fela and two members of his family sued the government for damages incurred during the invasion. The presiding judge at the Lagos High Court, Lateef Dosumu, dismissed the case on the grounds of Fela's lackadaisical attitude toward the courts and because Fela had not provided accurate documentation for the precise losses. Justice Dosumu thought the ₦25 million claim was inflated. This ruling stood even though Dosumu conceded that Fela and his family had sustained losses. In a rather revealing addition, Justice Dosumu argued that the constitution made no provisions for damages for the violation of a citizen's fundamental human rights. See "Fela Loses"; "Fela: No Appeal." In a separate account of the ruling, Justice Dosumu dismissed the suit on the basis that "the Federal Government was not liable for the action of its servants" and could only use its discretion in compensating parties aggrieved by state officials. See Graham, "Fela: N25m Suit." It is telling that the lawsuit filed by Fela and his family did not include the state's injury of Kalakuta women, illustrating the strategic subordination of the women's issues to Fela's.

66. United Nations, "Sexual Violence and Armed Conflict," 1.

67. See Osha, "Unravelling the Silences," 93. Mongo Beti's novel *The Rape of Cameroon* also illustrates the metaphorization of rape in African literature. For a critique of the representational limits of rape as a trope of domination, see Jean-Charles, *Conflict Bodies*, 23.

68. See Jean-Charles, *Conflict Bodies*, 10. In her reading of postapartheid performance, Catherine Cole makes an equally compelling case for understanding trauma as recursive, lodged in and entangled with the body's cells and tissues. Cole writes this of Jay Pather's *Body of Evidence*: "The wounds and scars and traumas of the past live on in the bodies of now, in today's bodies, in their flesh and bone and skin and psyches." Jean-Charles and Cole call our attention to the lingering afterlives of harm, which disrupt linear temporal frames that impose a before/after frame, privileging the passage of time since the traumatic event or, conversely, that tie healing, magically, to political transitions, as in as the *post-* in *post-*apartheid or *post-*colonial. For Cole, see *Performance and the Afterlives of Injustice*, 76–77.

69. Mojubaolu Olufunke Okome's essay "'Unknown Soldier': Women's Radicalism, Activism and State Violence in Twentieth-Century Nigeria" emblematizes this approach to class. Okome rightly points out the gradual erosion of

women's exercise of political citizenship in twentieth-century Nigeria, as well as their exposure to state violence. However, to make this case, Okome mobilizes the example of elite women with tremendous social and political capital, such as Efunsetan Aniwura, the famed Ibadan merchant, and Mrs. Ransome-Kuti. In *Insidious Treasons and Beyond: Forty Years of Alternative Theatre in Nigeria*, renowned Nigerian playwright and theater scholar Femi Osofisan laments flagrant human rights abuses of the Olusegun Obasanjo regime. The list of infractions by the regime includes "the devastation of Fela's Kalakuta Republic and the fatal wounding of his hero mother." See Osofisan, *Insidious Treasons*.

70. Moore, *Fela*, 177–205.

71. Shosanya, interview.

72. Moore, *Fela*, 200.

73. Babayale-Kuti, interview.

74. Babayale-Kuti, interview.

75. Jean-Charles, *Conflict Bodies*, 9.

76. Jean-Charles, *Conflict Bodies*, 3.

77. Moore, *Fela*, 244.

78. Jones, *Theatrical Jazz*, 39

79. Wenzel, *Bulletproof*, 5.

80. Crossley, "Narrative Psychology," 539.

81. Kevwe implied that she earned a BA in English and a diploma in computer science. She also said she had a degree from the University of Texas, a notion that she revealed to coincide with her learning that I studied in Texas.

82. See LaMarr Jurelle Bruce's *How to Go Mad without Losing Your Mind: Madness and Black Radical Creativity*, particularly chapter 7, "Songs in Madtime," for the generative illogic and temporal reordering that madness allows and embraces in Black feminist sounds.

83. Bridge, "Gendering Music."

5. "Spirit Catch Am"

1. Moore, *Fela*.

2. Moore, *Fela*, 248.

3. Feminist scholarship has explored how certain African women find space within trances and possessions to upend everyday sexism. See Cornwall, *Readings in Gender*, 10.

4. Idowu, *Fela*, 312–13.

5. Peretu, "I'm Surrounded by Witches."

6. That Funmilayo's death left a mark on Fela is not in question. He once explained: "I wanted to see her. It finally dawned on me: fuck, I will never see this woman again. She's gone, man! Gone!" See Moore, *Fela*, 246.

7. Goldman, "Resurrection Shuffle," 38.

8. Goldman, "Resurrection Shuffle," 39.

9. Collins, *Fela: Kalakuta Notes*, 16.

10. Idowu, *Fela*, 311–12.

11. Bonner, "Fela and the Secret of Eternal Youth," 47.

12. Bonner, "Fela and the Secret of Eternal Youth," 47.

13. Professor Hindu can be seen, for example, in the much-circulated video of the 1984 Glastonbury Festival in England. See Marks, *Fela Kuti Live*.

14. Idowu, *Fela*, 308–10.

15. Idowu, *Fela*, 312.

16. Akindele, "Fela Weds."

17. The ordeals and suspicions that surrounded the Italian tour are captured in Idowu, *Fela*, 251–60.

18. Idowu, *Fela*, 261.

19. Moore, *Fela*, 246.

20. Bonner, "Fela and the Secret of Eternal Youth," 46.

21. The military's creation of nineteen states was expected to counteract the centripetal regional forces that had led to the death of the First Republic in January 1966 and to the Nigerian civil war (1967–1970). See, for instance, Suberu, "Problems of Federation," 29.

22. These statistics on Nigeria's foreign debt and capital flight estimates come from Metz, "Second Republic."

23. Metz, "Second Republic."

24. Buhari, 1983 speech.

25. Donkor, *Spiders of the Market*, 2.

26. Moyo, *Dead Aid*, 18–19.

27. Fearing a global economic meltdown, the Bretton Woods institutions obligated African and Latin American nations to restructure their economies. National debts were restructured or forgiven based on radical reforms that shrank public spending mostly to the detriment of the masses. See Moyo, *Dead Aid*.

28. For Fela, the early 1970s was defining; it was a period that marked his transition from what Tejumola Olaniyan has described as "apolitical hustler" to cultural nationalist. This transition was influenced heavily by Fela's racial awakening through the Black Power movement in the United States. The political and intellectual works of Marcus Garvey, W. E. B DuBois, and Edward Blyden popularized a Pan-Africanist sentiment that advocated for institutions that would cater to the interests of Blacks globally. However, it was the writings and policies of Kwame Nkrumah that gave wind to Fela's investment in Pan-Africanism, a political philosophy steeped in belief in the shared histories of Blacks across the world as well as the need for racial unity. Nkrumah, who became Ghana's first president in 1957 and was a fierce advocate for African unity (a sentiment expressed in his establishing the Organization for African Unity), was also a

friend of the Kutis. Tejumola Olaniyan offers an extensive discussion of the texts, authors, activist, thinkers, and events that fomented Fela's ideological evolution from the early 1970s to the early 1980s. See Olaniyan, *Arrest the Music!*, 114–18.

29. For Fela's quotation, see Idowu, *Fela*, 297. Some works cited by Fela include *Civilization or Barbarism: An Authentic Anthropology* and *The African Origins of Civilization* by Cheikh Anta Diop, *The Moors of Spain* by Stanley Lane-Poole, *Black Cargoes* by Daniel Manyx, *History of Nations* by Peter Furtado, *Black Man of the Nile* by Yosef Ben-Hochannan, and *How Europe Underdeveloped Africa* by Walter Rodney.

30. Veal, *Fela*, 18.

31. A full transcript of Fela's speech at a Nigerian university can be found in Idowu, *Fela*, 275–300.

32. Idowu, *Fela*, 283.

33. Olaniyan, *Arrest the Music!*, 79.

34. Olaniyan, *Arrest the Music!*, 114–18.

35. Olaniyan, *Arrest the Music!*, 119–20.

36. Ghariokwu, interview.

37. Barber, "Live in Amsterdam," 31.

38. Barber, "Live in Amsterdam," 31.

39. This said, it is crucial to point out what the critic's analysis overlooks about the musician's approach to live performance. Live performances of Africa 70 and Egypt 80 were more loosely arranged than albums. "His European performances," Randall Grass writes, "were a presentation of those things he considered relevant—the spiritual inspiration of Professor Hindu, his own didactic preaching, and, of course, his new music." See Grass, "Fela Anikulapo-Kuti," 147. It might be productive to see the reviewer as an unwitting witness to a band in transition. The early 1980s were a moment of great logistical challenges. Fela's presidential ambitions—his diversion of resources to fund his campaign and his documented lack of sensitivity to the material needs of Africa 70 collaborators—forced away some of his most talented musicians. To replace them, Fela recruited Kalakuta boys without musical training. It was during this time that Duro Ikuje-nyo, a YAP Boy more interested in ideology than learning a musical instrument, joined the band as a rhythm pianist. The experiment, spotty at first, paid off by 1985, after the band hit its stride in songs like "Army Arrangement."

40. See Veal's description of Afrobeat's typical structure in the 1970s in *Fela*, 96–97.

41. It was at this time that Fela initiated the practice of using *efun* to paint white rings around his eyes and motifs across his face. The painted eyes, for Fela, signified extraterrestrial vision. Fela introduced into his songs the expression "Underground Spiritual Game," a phrase that signaled his embrace of the metaphysical. The phrase was often queued by a sonic shift, such as a distinct second

bass line. Afrobeat from the 1970s typically has a single bass line constituting the sonic foundation on which all other instrumental and vocal components are built. The bass line begins, cuts through, and ends each composition. With the lyrics, it provides the signature of each song. Whether a funky or a ruminative tune, the bass line dictates if and how the listener should move. The introduction of a second bass complicates this established musical tradition. Beyond lyrics and stagecraft carrying a spiritual valence, the second bass introduced a new sub-structure, a dialogue between background sounds. Beneath the lyrics and instruments, a second bass line signified a new interactive possibility. If the bass line functioned as a solid, dependable part of Afrobeat's sonic architecture, it became animated and infused with the restlessness of the artists who gave it life in the first place. The introduction of a second bass line featured among spirit-inspired aesthetic changes, but perfecting it required time and practice. Afrobeat music took on a contemplative, looping character, a style Fela refined as the decade progressed.

42. In a 1993 interview, Fela talked about contemplating taking his life: "One day I felt like committing suicide. I just dey tired. That was shortly after they did not register Movement of the People in 1979, but I come dey read for inside book say if you die you go still come back." See Onanuga et al., "Fela."

43. Fela retained an aversion for "women's lib" for most of his life, once describing it as an example of "imperialist thinking" that ran afoul of nature's course. See Bonner, "Fela and the Secret of Eternal Youth," 46.

44. Mama, "Feminism or Femocracy?," 41.

45. These descriptions of Serwaa's physical features are partly adapted from Carlos Moore's observations of Serwaa in Moore, *Fela*, 229–31. They are supplemented by my own reading of her attributes in photographs.

46. Yeni Anikulapo-Kuti, interview.

47. Shosanya, interview.

48. Russel and Teitelbaum, *International Migration and International Trade*, 20–21.

49. Shagari, *Shehu Shagari*, 330.

50. Shagari's policy notably violated a fundamental mission of the Economic Community of West African States (ECOWAS), established to facilitate movements of people, goods, and services across the boundaries of these nations. (ECOWAS hoped to temper the effects of colonial boundaries on mobility and economic activity in the subregion.) The political exigencies faced by the Shagari regime trumped regional allegiances.

51. Idowu, *Fela*, 321.

52. Moore, *Fela*, 180.

53. Hoga, interview.

54. Shoneyin, *The Secret Lives of Baba Segi's Wives*, 96.

55. Shoneyin, *The Secret Lives of Baba Segi's Wives*, 96.
56. Moore, *Fela*, 184.
57. In "The Dangers of Dependence," Kristin Mann explains this practice in some detail.

> During their lives Yoruba polygynists took care to share their time and wealth roughly equally among their wives and children, hoping to minimize conflict among them. Yoruba inheritance practices were complex and may have been changing in the late nineteenth century. It seems clear, however, that according to Yoruba custom husbands and wives did not inherit from one another, although wives had a right to remain in their deceased husbands' residences. Men's property passed to their younger siblings and children, and women's property passed to their children. All a man's children had the same rights to inherit, including illegitimate children as long as he had acknowledged his paternity (41).

58. Aliu, "I Can Cope."
59. Moore, *Fela*, 191.
60. Denzer, "Fela, Women, Wives," 128.
61. Bonner, "Fela and the Secret of Eternal Youth," 46.
62. Webster, "Communes," 129.
63. Fela was charged for armed robbery but released on bail ten days later. He subsequently composed "Authority Stealing" and "International Thief Thief (ITT)," songs critiquing hierarchies of class and nation that frame popular discourses of theft and corruption. Neither exploitation of wealth by multinational companies nor systemic corruption by highly placed Nigerian officials earns the label "theft"—this debasing qualification belongs to the petty robber.
64. Flori and Tchalgadjieff, *Fela Kuti*.
65. Flori and Tchalgadjieff, *Fela Kuti*.
66. Dodomaya, interview with Mallam Abdul Okwechime.
67. A legal battle ensued between Fela and the aggrieved landlord, who found himself caught in moral cross fire between Fela Kuti and the state. Fela argued that the government that destroyed his home lacked the moral authority to enforce his eviction from his temporary home. The gradual takeover of the entire eight apartments saw the birth of a new Kalakuta Republic.
68. The previous Kalakuta had a shared area; the new one did not, as it was eight apartments spread across two separate buildings. A key feature of the previous commune was that it allowed for a collective experience of space and time. The new Kalakuta, born out of desperate circumstances, held no such promise. The patriarch occupied a two-bedroom ground-floor apartment. J. K. Braimah took the apartment opposite Fela's. Remi, Fela's first wife, moved back to living

close to him after a protracted separation. She shared an apartment with her mother. The musician's three older children—Yeni, Femi, and Sola—also returned to living within close quarters of their father. Yeni and Sola, the daughters, claimed one apartment. Femi Kuti, Fela's son, shared an apartment with Dele Shosimi, a pianist in the organization. The Queens, YAP Boys, band boys, and other Kalakutans occupied the remaining flats. This arrangement sanctioned new relationships and consolidated old ones.

69. Idowu, *Fela*, 325.

70. Denzer, "Fela, Women, Wives," 125.

71. Idowu, *Fela*, 323.

72. Yeni Anikulapo-Kuti, interview.

73. Grass, "Fela Anikulapo-Kuti," 144–45.

74. Onyebadi, "Fela's Release," 8.

75. "Fela Released from Prison," 176.

76. Yeni Anikulapo-Kuti, interview.

77. See Britannica, "African National Congress."

78. Ndebele, *Cry of Winnie Mandela*, 7.

79. van Zyl Smit, "From Penelope to Winnie Mandela," 404.

80. Quayson, "What It Means to Be Winnie."

81. Smith, "Mandela."

82. Haastrup, "Teenage Girl Caused Kalakuta 'War,'" 15.

83. Goldman, "Thinking Africa," 104.

84. In an interview with *Frontline*, Ahmed Kathrada, a close friend of Mandela and coprisoner on Robben Island, recounted how prison guards attempted to demoralize Mandela with news of his wife: "What I remember, for instance, there was some unflattering newspaper report about Winnie. So what they did is they made a cutting, when we were not allowed newspapers, and they just put it on his desk. So they did do that from time to time." Kathrada, "Long Walk of Nelson Mandela."

85. "Anc," 8.

86. Fadugba, "Fela Flays Times," 7.

87. Fadugba, "Fela Flays Times," 7.

88. Yeni Anikulapo-Kuti, interview.

89. Ohakah, "War at the Shrine," 7.

90. Oshunkeye et al., "Fela, Sex and Showbiz," 13.

91. Hoga, interview.

92. Idowu, *Fela*.

93. Fanon, *Wretched of the Earth*, 149.

94. The institution of the People's Tribunals of the Revolution (TPR), a grassroots court system that dispensed justice sometimes indiscriminately, stoked disaffection. The TPR became a tool for witch hunting at the grassroots

level, which, combined with growing opposition, ultimately derailed the Sankara-led revolution. Growing popular dissent fueled factions within the military, leading ultimately to Sankara's assassination. For details on Sankara's assassination, see Shuffield, *Thomas Sankara*.

95. Shuffield, *Thomas Sankara*.

96. Jaboro, *Ikoyi Prison Narratives*, 71.

97. Mary laughed for something close to two minutes during our phone interview. These accounts of Mary's arrival in Kalakuta come from this interview. Umude-Haverkamp, phone interview.

98. Russel and Teitelbaum, *International Migration and International Trade*.

99. Russel, "International Migration," 301.

100. Kevwe Anikulapo-Kuti, phone interview.

101. Barrett, "Fela Kuti," 40; Veal, *Fela*, 235–36.

102. Veal, *Fela*, 206–208.

103. Ezenekwe, "Hell That Was."

6. Facing the Music

1. Veal, *Fela*.

2. "Snippet, as Fela Marches On," 17.

3. Omozokpia, "Rumours."

4. "'Fela Left It Too Late,'" 8.

5. Ansen, "David Ansen Recalls."

6. Nwosu, "Fela's Last Journey," 16.

7. Veal, *Fela*, 237–38.

8. Román, *Acts of Intervention*, xx.

9. Patton, *Globalizing AIDS*, xii–xiii.

10. Smith, "Modern Marriage," 1002.

11. Veal, *Fela*, 112.

12. "'Fela Left It Too Late.'"

13. For example, when asked how Fela managed so many wives, Femi Kuti responded in a 2013 interview: "It was very stressful for him. Do not forget that he divorced all of them. They were not faithful to him." See Atoyebi and Adeniji, "Punch Interview."

14. Veal, *Fela*, 238.

15. Gibney, *Finding Fela*.

16. Herszenhorn, "Fela, 58."

17. Semenitari, "Fela Forever!," 34.

18. Sonowo, "New York Stands Still for Fela," 2.

19. "Mementos Turn Gold."

20. Sotunde, "Musical Jam for Fela's Fans," 3.

21. Sonowo, "New York Stands Still for Fela."

22. "He Might Not Have Died," 16.

23. Arowojolu, "Alake Honors Fela," 3.

24. Arowojolu, "Alake Honors Fela," 3.

25. Ghariokwu, interview.

26. Okpara et al., "15 Fans Faint at Fela's Burial," 3.

27. Roach, *Cities of the Dead*.

28. Hall, "Notes on Deconstructing 'the Popular,'" 442–43.

29. "Wives Absent at Burial," 16.

30. Okpara et al., "15 Fans Faint at Fela's Burial," 3.

31. Williams, "Disen-Whaaaat??," 2017.

32. Oshunkeye et al., "Fela, Sex and Showbiz," 13.

33. For instance, Femi said to reporters a few days after the burial: "Fela was not married when he died. He divorced his wives including my mother, and it was popular knowledge." Also see Njoku, "'I Can't Understand Why My Father Married 27 Wives.'"

34. Ohai and Onyema, "Fela Slept."

35. Olaniyan, *Arrest the Music!*, 180.

36. Omozokpia, "Rumours."

37. Okpara, "Beko Asks to See Fela."

38. Omozokpia, "Rumours."

39. Ohakah, "War at the Shrine," 7.

40. "Fela's Burial Plans in Top Gear," 1.

41. Ohakah, "War at the Shrine," 7.

42. Drewal, *Yoruba Ritual*, 187.

43. Kristin Mann offers a useful discussion of Yoruba inheritance rights in "The Dangers of Dependence," 41.

44. "Snippet, as Fela Marches On," 17.

45. Okpara et al., "Fela's Dancers Petition Govt," 1–3.

46. Oshunkeye et al., "Fela, Sex and Showbiz," 13–15.

47. Oshunkeye et al., "Fela, Sex and Showbiz," 15.

48. Gibney, *Finding Fela*.

49. Clarke et al., "Subcultures, Cultures and Class," 15.

50. Ohakah, "War at the Shrine," 7.

51. Veal, *Fela*, 12.

52. Veal, *Fela*.

53. Ansen, "David Ansen Recalls"; Amaechi, "Celebrities on AIDS List."

54. Mugabe, "Remembering Uganda's 'AIDS Face.'"

55. Amaechi and Iheh, "Doctors React to Fela's Death," 6.

56. Babalola, "Endangered Lives of Part-Time Prostitutes," 22.

57. United Nations, "UNICEF Names."

58. Parts of this moment are captured in Gibney, *Finding Fela*.

59. "'Fela Left It Too Late,'" 8.

60. Mabiakwu, interview.

61. Mabiakwu, interview.

62. Patterson, *Slavery and Social Death*, 5–7.

63. See Králová, "What Is Social Death?," 237; and Norwood, *Maintenance of Life*.

64. Borgstrom, "Social Death," 5.

65. Ukwuoma, "Pharmacists Seek Govt Subsidy," 3.

66. The figure in Camp's work sits on a platform approximately the size of Fela's dancing cages. Her legs are bent at the knees in such a way that they look buckled beneath the weight of her fragile frame. The rest of her body lacks the artistic detail of her face, which is covered in dots of white paint and the word "AIDS." This work can be found on the artist's website: http://sokari.co.uk /project/open-and-close/.

67. Sarah Adams echoes this skepticism in a review of Camp's kinetic sculpture: "While it is likely that Sokari was concerned with the stigmatization and possibly the infection of Fela's wives through their association with their husband who died of AIDS, the piece felt misguided." See Adams, "This Is Lagos," 83.

68. See Sokari Douglas Camp's website.

69. Román, *Acts of Intervention*, xxiii–xxiv.

70. Harrington and Bellamy, *Positive/Negative*, 28.

71. Oshunkeye et al., "Fela, Sex and Showbiz," 14.

72. Oshunkeye et al., "Fela, Sex and Showbiz," 14.

73. Umude-Haverkamp, phone interview.

74. Umude-Haverkamp, phone interview.

75. See, for example, Segun Osunla's explanation in Olaniyan, *Arrest the Music!*, 202. Osunla, Fela's personal photographer from 1975 to 1997, claimed that the musician was killed by a combination of overexposure to air conditioning during one of his final arrests and the injection of a slow-killing poison.

76. Ohai and Onyema, "Fela Slept."

77. Fela Studies Group, "Rethinking African History."

78. Sofola, *Wedlock of the Gods*, 22.

79. Ba, *So Long a Letter*, 12.

80. Ba, *So Long a Letter*, 8.

81. Ba, *So Long a Letter*, 7.

82. Edmondson, "Faustin Linyekula," 406.

83. Oshunkeye et al., "Fela, Sex and Showbiz," 13.

84. Smith, "Modern Marriage," 1002. See also 997.

85. Lee, "Finding Depth in Fela's Women."

86. Ohakah, "War at the Shrine," 7.

87. Njoku, "'I Can't Understand Why My Father Married 27 Wives.'"

88. "Fela Anikulapo-Kuti's Wife, 2 Others Arrested with Marijuana in Lagos."

89. Kevwe Anikulapo-Kuti, interview.

90. Moore, *Fela*, 215.

91. Quayson, *Calibrations*, 77.

92. Adebanwi and Obadare, *Encountering the Nigerian State*, 9.

93. I am thinking here about Judith Butler's articulation of precariousness and grievability; she writes that "an ungrievable life is one that cannot be mourned because it has never lived, that is, it has never counted as a life at all." I am compelled by Butler's argument that a greater apprehension about precarious lives is gained by "asking whose lives are considered valuable, whose lives are mourned, and whose lives are considered ungrievable." It is rather befitting for this analysis that Butler cites the war on terror and the early years of the AIDS crisis in the US as monumental events that produced and laid bare the intimacies between precariousness and grievability. See Butler, "Precariousness."

7. "Where We Fall Is Where We Pick Ourselves Up From"

1. Hooker, "Black Grief / White Grievance."

2. Onwuneme, "Shrine Stirs for Fela," 24.

3. The brainchild of Yeni, Felabration now takes place simultaneously across key cities around the world. Felabration has welcomed A-list African artists, intellectuals, and activists since its inception. Some past episodes of Felabrations are archived on the website http://www.felabration.net/.

4. This scene is described in Onwuneme, "Shrine Stirs for Fela," 24.

5. Conquergood, "Lethal Theatre: Performance, Punishment, and the Death Penalty," 342–43.

6. Gaines, "Amateur."

7. See "Made Kuti Steps Outside."

8. "Made Kuti Steps Outside."

9. Young, *Illegible Will*, 123.

10. Babayale-Kuti, interview.

11. Moore, *Fela*, 224.

12. Adeniji and Uhakheme, "Life without Fela Is Challenging," 28.

13. Adeniji and Uhakheme, "Life without Fela Is Challenging," 28.

14. Olaniyan, *Arrest the Music!*, 263–71.

15. In an interview, Femi suggested that Seun's mother had to bear the responsibility of raising him: "Seun is underage. . . . He has a mother. If she does not know what is proper for her son, sorry for her. But she better know what to do for her son to become a good human in this world. If they do not allow him grow, he will just find that five years have passed, he has achieved nothing." The extensive interview can be found in Adeniji and Uhakheme, "Life without Fela Is Challenging," 28.

16. Seun Anikulapo-Kuti, interview.

17. Umude-Haverkamp, phone interview.

18. Seun Anikulapo-Kuti, interview.

19. Seun Anikulapo-Kuti, interview.

20. Quashie, *Sovereignty of Quiet*, 3.

21. Quashie, *Sovereignty of Quiet*, 8.

22. Here I find Laura Edmondson's invitation that we attune our sensibilities beyond the seductions of crisis and emergency and to consider instead "the slow seepage of damage and dispossession" (407). Attunement to the quiet frequencies of contagion and disease productively complicates the spectacular and the visible in narrating the afterlives of Fela. See Edmondson, "Faustin Linyekula."

23. Olaniyan, *Arrest the Music!*, 264.

24. George-Graves, "Diasporic Spidering," 37.

25. Lee, "Finding Depth in Fela's Women."

26. de Weever, interview.

27. Royster, "Fela Kuti," 495.

28. Lee, "Finding Depth in Fela's Women."

29. Lee, "Finding Depth in Fela's Women."

30. de Weever, interview.

31. Johnson, "Queens' Diaspora," 2.

32. de Weever, interview.

33. Hooker, "Black Grief / White Grievance."

34. See Mbembe, *On the Postcolony*, chapter 1 ("Of Commandment").

35. Braun, "Trading Virtue for Virtuosity."

36. "Wunmi—Thoughts on Fela."

37. Dumbutshena, interview.

38. Dumbutshena, interview.

39. Dumbutshena, interview.

40. earthcandyarts, "Earthcandy*Food.Fashion.Flyness."

41. See, for example, Ayobade, "Queens in Flight."

42. Reed, *Art of Protest*, xvi–xvii.

43. Healy-Clancy, "Family Politics."

44. Babayale-Kuti, interview.

45. Najite Anikulapo-Kuti, interview.

46. Shosanya, interview.

47. hooks, *Talking Back*, 43.

48. Angelou, *Complete Poetry*, 159.

49. See Gordon, *Ghostly Matters*, xvi. My reading of haunting has also benefited from Cho, *Haunting the Korean Diaspora*, 1–49.

50. Cole, *Performance and the Afterlives of Injustice*, 27–28.

51. "Art of Rebellion," Nigeria Content Online.

52. Gordon, *Ghostly Matters*, xvi.

53. Hartman, *Scenes of Subjection*, 21.

Conclusion

1. Hartman, *Wayward Lives, Beautiful Experiments*, xiii.

2. For example, see Griffin, *If You Can't Be Free*; Brooks, *Liner Notes*; the Makeba and Simone chapters in Redmond, *Anthem*; Feldstein, "Nina Simone."

3. Hogan, *Colonialism and Cultural Identity*, 21.

4. Zeleza, "Towards a Cultural Economy for African Liberation."

5. Hostert, *Passing*, 59.

6. Coly, *Postcolonial Hauntologies*.

7. Ansen, "David Ansen Recalls When AIDS Silenced the Arts."

8. Veal, *Fela*, 238.

9. Hartman, *Wayward Lives, Beautiful Experiments*, xiv–xv.

10. Barber, *Readings in African Popular Culture*.

11. Wenzel, *Bulletproof*, 2–3.

BIBLIOGRAPHY

Abah, Hope. "Meet Grandma Who Established First 'Mammy Market.'" *Daily Trust*, January 28, 2017. https://www.pressreader.com/nigeria/weekly-trust /20170128/281801398682567.

Adams, Sarah. "This Is Lagos: Yabis Night, Music and Fela." *African Arts* 37, no. 1 (Spring 2004): 83–85, 95.

Adebanwi, Wale, and Ebenezer Obadare, eds. *Encountering the Nigerian State*. New York: Palgrave Macmillan, 2010.

Adeniji, Olayiwola, and Ozolua Uhakheme. "Life without Fela Is Challenging, Says Femi." *Guardian*, August 2, 1997.

Aderinto, Saheed. "Colonialism and Prostitution in Africa." In *Encyclopedia of Prostitution and Sex Work*, edited by Melissa Ditmore, 110–12. Westport, CT: Greenwood, 2006.

———. *When Sex Threatened the State: Illicit Sexuality, Nationalism, and Politics in Colonial Nigeria, 1900–1958*. Bloomington: Indiana University Press, 2015.

Adetiba, Muyiwa. "Face-to-Face with Muyiwa Adetiba—'Why My Mother's Death Hurt Me'—Fela." *Sunday Punch*, June 25, 1978.

Aidoo, Ama Ata. "To Be an African Woman Writer: An Overview and a Detail." In *Criticism and Ideology: Second African Writers' Conference Stockholm 1986*, edited by Kirsten Holst Petersen, 155–72. Uppsala: Nordiska Afrikainstitutet, 1988.

Akano, Remi. "Gondola." *Newbreed*, January 1974.

———. "Ozzidi Is a Success Story." *Newbreed*, 1987.

———. "The Scene: Some Like It Hot." *Newbreed*, January 1974.

Akindele, Laja. "Fela Weds." *Daily Times*, February 21, 1978.

Akinnibosun, Yinusa. Interview by Dotun Ayobade. August 10, 2014. Lagos, Nigeria.

Akintola, Bukola. "The Perils of Protest: State Repression and Student Mobilization in Nigeria." In *Encountering the Nigerian State*, edited by Wale Adebanwi and Ebenezer Obadare, 99–121. New York: Palgrave Macmillan, 2010.

Alcendor, Patricia. "Fela: A Societal Phenomenon." *Happy Home*, July 1977.

Aliu, Adams. "I Can Cope with My Two Dozen Wives—Fela." *Punch*, March 4, 1978.

Allen, Tony, and Michael Veal. *Tony Allen: An Autobiography of the Master Drummer of Afrobeat*. Durham, NC: Duke University Press, 2013.

Amaechi, Iyke. "Celebrities on AIDS List." *Daily Champion*, August 4, 1997.

Amaechi, Iyke, and Uche Iheh. "Doctors React to Fela's Death." *Daily Champion*, August 5, 1997.

Amkpa, Awam. *Theatre and Postcolonial Desires*. London: Routledge, 2004.

"Anc." *Vanguard*, April 28, 1986.

Angelou, Maya. *The Complete Poetry*. New York: Random House, 2015.

Anikulapo-Kuti, Fela. "The Manifesto of the Movement of the People (MOP)." Lagos: Kalakuta Museum, 1978.

Anikulapo-Kuti, Kevwe. Interview by Dotun Ayobade. August 17, 2014. Lagos, Nigeria.

———. Phone interview by Dotun Ayobade. December 15, 2018.

Anikulapo-Kuti, Najite. Interview by Dotun Ayobade. June 15, 2017. Lagos, Nigeria.

Anikulapo-Kuti, Seun. Interview by Dotun Ayobade. July 2, 2015. Houston, TX.

Anikulapo-Kuti, Yeni. Interview by Dotun Ayobade. July 14, 2014. Lagos, Nigeria.

Ansen, David. "David Ansen Recalls When AIDS Silenced the Arts." *Newsweek*, 2012. http://www.newsweek.com/david-ansen-recalls-when-aids-silenced-arts-63481.

Apter, Andrew. *The Pan-African Nation: Oil and the Spectacle of Culture in Nigeria*. Chicago: University of Chicago Press, 2005.

Arnfred, Signe, ed. *Re-Thinking Sexualities in Africa*. Uppsala: Almqvist and Wiksell Tryckeri AB, 2004.

Arowojolu, Ayo. "Alake Honors Fela, 49 Egba Indigenes." *Daily Champion*, August 6, 1997.

"Art of Rebellion." Nigeria Content Online. Updated April 4, 2011. Accessed June 30, 2022. http://nigeriang.com/entertainment/art-of-rebellion/9013/.

Atoyebi, Olufemi, and Gbenga Adeniji. "Punch Interview: Why I Didn't Talk to Fela for Six Years—Femi Kuti." *Sahara Reporters*, March 31, 2013. http://sahara reporters.com/2013/03/31/punch-interview-why-i-didn%E2%80%99t-talk-fela -six-years-%E2%80%93-femi-kuti.

Ayobade, Dotun. "Fela Kuti: Kalakuta Was the Spirit." *Art Africa*, March 2017.

———. "Invented Dances, or, How Nigerian Musicians Sculpt the Body Politic." *Dance Research Journal* 53, no. 1 (April 2021): 5–22.

———. "Queens in Flight: Fela Kuti's Afrobeat Queens and the Performance of 'Black' Feminist Diasporas." In *Gendering Knowledge in Africa and the African Diaspora: Contesting History and Power*, edited by Toyin Falola and Haliso Yacob, 143–63. London: Routledge, 2017.

———. "'We Were on Top of the World': Fela Kuti's Queens and the Poetics of Space." *Journal of African Cultural Studies* 31, no. 1 (2017): 24–39.

Ba, Mariama. *So Long a Letter.* Johannesburg: Heinemann Educational, 1989.

Babalola, Ademola. "Endangered Lives of Part-Time Prostitutes." *Saturday Champion*, August 30, 1997.

Babayale-Kuti, Olaide. Interview by Dotun Ayobade. August 14, 2014. Lagos, Nigeria.

Backett, Paul. "Getting Serious about Play." *Design Management Institute Review* 24, no. 1 (2013): 12–19.

Balsvik, Randi Rønning. "Student Protest—University and State in Africa 1960–1995." *Forum for Development Studies* 2 (1998): 301–25.

Barber, Karin. *The Generation of Plays: Yoruba Popular Life in Theatre.* Bloomington: Indiana University Press, 2000.

———. *Readings in African Popular Culture.* Bloomington: Indiana University Press, 1997.

Barber, Lynden. "Live in Amsterdam." *Melody Maker*, March 12, 1984.

Baron, Beth. *Egypt as a Woman: Nationalism, Gender, and Politics.* Berkeley: University of California Press, 2005.

Barrett, Lindsay. "Fela Kuti: Chronicle of a Life Foretold." *Wire*, September 2011. https://www.thewire.co.uk/in-writing/essays/fela-kuti_chronicle-ofa-life -foretold.

Bauman, Zygmunt. *Liquid Modernity.* Cambridge: Polity, 2000.

Bhabha, Homi. "Of Mimicry and Man: The Ambivalence of Colonial Discourse." *October* 28 (1984): 125–33.

Bhandhukravi, Alice. "Notting Hill Riots—50 Years On." *BBC*, August 21, 2008. http://news.bbc.co.uk/2/hi/uk_news/england/london/7571879.stm.

Biondi, Martha. *The Black Revolution on Campus.* Berkeley: University of California Press, 2014.

"Birth of a New Sound." *Daily Times*, July 29, 1970.

Bogad, L. M. *Tactical Performance: The Theory and Practice of Serious Play.* Abingdon: Routledge, 2016.

Bonner, Leslie. "Fela and the Secret of Eternal Youth." *New African*, January 1984.

Borgstrom, E. "Social Death." *QJM: An International Journal of Medicine* 110, no. 1 (2017): 5–7.

"The Boy Who Plans a Jazz Revolution." *Drum*, December 1963.

Braun, Lesley Nicole. "Trading Virtue for Virtuosity: The Artistry of Kinshasa's Concert Danseuses." *African Arts* 47, no. 4 (Winter 2014): 48–57.

Bridge, S. K. "Gendering Music in Popular Culture." In *The International Encyclopedia of Gender, Media, and Communication*, edited by K. Ross, I. Bachmann, V. Cardo, S. Moorti, and M. Scarcelli, 1–10. Hoboken, NJ: John Wiley & Sons, 2020.

Britannica, The Editors of Encyclopedia. "African National Congress." In *Britannica*, edited by The Editors of Encyclopedia Britannica. Chicago: Encyclopædia Britannica, Inc., 1998. https://www.britannica.com/topic /African-National-Congress/additional-info#history.

Brooks, Daphne A. *Liner Notes for the Revolution: The Intellectual Life of Black Feminist Sound.* Cambridge, MA: Belknap Press, 2021.

Bruce, La Marr Jurelle. *How to Go Mad without Losing Your Mind: Madness and Black Radical Creativity.* Durham, NC: Duke University Press, 2021.

Butler, Judith. "Precariousness and Grievability—When Is Life Grievable?" Verso, 2015. https://www.versobooks.com/blogs/2339-judith-butler -precariousness-and-grievability-when-is-life-grievable.

Byfield, Judith. "In Her Own Words: Funmilayo-Ransome-Kuti and the Auto /Biography of an Archive." *Palimpsest: A Journal on Women, Gender and the Black International* 5, no. 2 (2016): 107–27.

Cagnolari, Vladimir. "Miriam Makeba: How 'Miss Makeba' Became 'Mama Africa.'" *Pan African Music.* https://pan-african-music.com/en/miriam -makeba-how-miss-makeba-became-mama-africa/.

Caillois, Roger. "The Definition of Play, the Classification of Games." In *The Game Design Reader: A Rules of Play Anthology*, edited by Katie Salen and Eric Zimmerman, 122–55. Cambridge, MA: MIT Press, 2006.

Camp, Sokari Douglas. *Open and Close.* Sculpture with wood, cowries, and electric steel. Exhibited at *Black President: The Art and Legacy of Fela Anikulapo-Kuti*, 2003.

Campt, Tina M. *Listening to Images.* Durham, NC: Duke University Press, 2017.

Chielozona, Eze. "Decolonisation and Its Discontents: Thoughts on the Postcolonial African Moral Self." *South African Journal of Philosophy* 34, no. 4 (2015): 408–18.

Cho, Grace. *Haunting the Korean Diaspora: Shame, Secrecy, and the Forgotten War.* Minneapolis: University of Minnesota Press, 2008.

Clark, Ebun. *Hubert Ogunde: The Making of Nigerian Theatre.* Oxford: Oxford University Press, 1980.

Clarke, John, Stuart Hall, Tony Jefferson, and Brian Roberts. "Subcultures, Cultures and Class." In *Resistance Through Rituals: Youth Subcultures in Post-War Britain*, edited by Stuart Hall and Tony Jefferson, 9–74. London: Hutchinson, 1976.

Cohen, Phil. "Subcultural Conflict and Working-Class Community." In *Culture, Media, Language: Working Papers in Cultural Studies, 1972–79*, edited by Stuart Hall, 61–69. London: Routledge, 1972.

Cole, Catherine M. *Performance and the Afterlives of Injustice: Dance and Live Art in Contemporary South Africa and Beyond*. Ann Arbor: University of Michigan Press, 2020.

Collins, John. "Fela and the Black President Film." *Glendora Review: African Quarterly on the Arts* 2, no. 2 (1997): 57–73.

———. *Fela: Kalakuta Notes*. Amsterdam: KIT, 2009.

Coly, Ayo A. *Postcolonial Hauntologies: African Women's Discourses of the Female Body*. Lincoln: University of Nebraska Press, 2019.

———. "Un/Clothing African Womanhood: Colonial Statements and Postcolonial Discourses of the African Female Body." *Journal of Contemporary African Studies* 33, no. 1 (2015): 12–26.

Conquergood, Dwight. "Lethal Theatre: Performance, Punishment, and the Death Penalty." *Theatre Journal* 54, no. 3 (2002): 339–67.

———. "Performance Studies: Interventions and Radical Research." *Drama Review* 46, no. 2 (2002): 145–56.

Cornwall, Andrea. *Readings in Gender in Africa*. Bloomington: Indiana University Press, 2005.

"The Counter Culture." *Newbreed*, December 1973, 59–64.

Cox, Aimee Meredith. *Shapeshifters: Black Girls and the Choreography of Citizenship*. Durham, NC: Duke University Press, 2015.

Crossley, Michele. "Narrative Psychology, Trauma and the Study of Self/ Identity." *Theory and Psychology* 10, no. 4 (2000): 527–46.

Dalley, Hamish. "The Idea of 'Third Generation Nigerian Literature': Conceptualizing Historical Change and Territorial Affiliation in the Contemporary Nigerian Novel." *Research in African Literatures* 44, no. 4 (2013): 15–34.

Debekeme, Zee'Tei. "Kalakuta Falls." *Punch*, October 30, 1978.

DeFrantz, Thomas F. "The Black Beat Made Visible: Hip Hop Dance and Body Power." In *Of the Presence of the Body: Essays on Dance and Performance Theory*, edited by Andre Lepecki, 64–81. Middletown, CT: Wesleyan University Press, 2004.

Denzer, LaRay. "Fela, Women, Wives." In *Fela: From West Africa to West Broadway*, edited by Trevor Schoonmaker, 111–34. New York: Palgrave Macmillan, 2003.

———. "Yoruba Women: A Historiographical Study." *International Journal of African Historical Studies* 27, no. 1 (1994): 1–39.

Derrida, Jacques, and Eric Prenowitz. "Archive Fever: A Freudian Impression." *Diacritics* 25, no. 2 (1995): 9–63.

Diouf, Mamadou. "Engaging Postcolonial Cultures: African Youth and Public Space." *African Studies Review* 46, no. 2 (2003): 1–12.

Dodomaya. *Kalakuta Chronicles.* By Mallam Abdul Okwechime. *iGroove Radio,* December 26, 2014.

Donkor, David. *Spiders of the Market: Ghanaian Trickster Performance in a Web of Neoliberalism.* Bloomington: Indiana University Press, 2016.

Drewal, Margaret Thompson. "The State of Research on Performance in Africa." *African Studies Review* 34, no. 3 (1991): 1–64.

———. *Yoruba Ritual: Performance, Play, Agency.* Bloomington: Indiana University Press, 1992.

Dumbutshena, Rujeko. Online video interview by Dotun Ayobade. June 1, 2020. Providence, RI.

earthcandyarts. "Earthcandy*Food.Fashion.Flyness. "Episode 6 (Part 1 of 2):" Felabration." February 2, 2012. YouTube video, 9:46. https://youtu.be /_XKutaVjXRE.

Edmondson, Laura. "Faustin Linyekula and the Violence of Plague." *Theatre Journal* 72, no. 4 (2020): 405–23.

Edwards, Brent Hayes. "Crossroads Republic." *Transition* 97 (2007): 94–119.

Ekanem, Etop. "Festac 77 Responsible for Nigeria's Woes—Cleric." *Vanguard,* April 2013.

Ekwensi, Cyprian. *Jagua Nana.* London: Hutchinson, 1961.

Eludoyin, Elutunde. Phone interview by Dotun Ayobade. August 8, 2014. Lagos, Nigeria.

Ezenekwe, Arthur. "The Hell That Was 'Kalakuta Republic.'" *Spear,* September 1977.

———. "My Experience Inside Kalakuta Republic." *Spear,* October 1977.

Fadugba, Nick. "Fela Flays Times: Defends His Music and Politics." *Daily Times,* September 29, 1979.

Fairfax, Frank Thurmond. *Fela, the Afrobeat King: Popular and Cultural Revitalization in West Africa.* Ann Arbor: University of Michigan, 1993.

Fanon, Frantz. *The Wretched of the Earth.* New York: Grove, 1963.

"Fela Anikulapo-Kuti's Wife, 2 Others Arrested with Marijuana in Lagos." Editorial. *SaferNigeria,* July 24, 2011. https://saferafricagroup.wordpress .com/2011/07/24/fela-anikulapo-kuti%e2%80%99s-wife-2-others-arrested -with-marijuana-in-lagos/.

"'Fela Left It Too Late'—Olikoye." *Saturday Champion,* August 9, 1997.

"Fela Loses." Editorial. *Nigerian Tribune,* February 11, 1978.

"Fela: No Appeal." Editorial. *Nigerian Tribune,* February 14, 1978.

"Fela Released from Prison." *Drama Review* 30, no. 2 (1986): 176.

"Fela's Burial Plans in Top Gear." *Daily Champion,* August 11, 1997.

Fela Studies Group. "Rethinking African History: Knowledge Production and Political Sustenance in Post-Colonial Africa." Paper presented at the Fela Kuti

International Conference on African Homelands and Social Theory, Institute of African and Diaspora Studies, University of Lagos, July 5–7, 2019.

Feldstein, Ruth. "'I Don't Trust You Anymore': Nina Simone, Culture, and Black Activism in the 1960s." *The Journal of American History* 41, no. 4 (March 2005): 1349–79.

Flori, Jean-Jacques, and Stéphane Tchalgadjieff, dir. *Fela Kuti: Music Is the Weapon*. Film. Universal Import. 2004.

Folayan, Dele. "Fela: The Woman Humanizer." *Sunday Punch*, December 1, 1974.

Foucault, Michel. "Nietzsche, Genealogy, History." In *The Foucault Reader*, edited by Paul Rabinow, 76–100. New York: Pantheon Books, 1984.

Gaines, Malik. "Amateur." In *In Terms of Performance*, edited by Shannon Jackson and Paula Marincola. The Pew Center for Arts & Heritage, Philadelphia and Arts Research Center, University of California, Berkeley. Accessed September 15, 2023. http://intermsofperformance.site/keywords/amateur /malik-gaines.

Gaunt, Kyra. *The Games Black Girls Play: Learning the Ropes from Double-Dutch to Hip-Hop*. New York: New York University Press, 2006.

———. "YouTube Search and Twerking Videos: Music, Misogynoir, and Technology as a Weapon." Academia.edu. Accessed August 31, 2023. https:// www.academia.edu/36177633/Music_Misogynoir_and_Technology_as_a _Weapon.docx.

Geertz, Clifford. "Deep Play: Notes on the Balinese Cockfight." *Daedalus* 134, no. 4 (2005): 56–86.

George, Abosede A. *Making Modern Girls: A History of Girlhood, Labor, and Social Development in Colonial Lagos*. Athens: Ohio University Press, 2014.

———. "Within Salvation: Girl Hawkers and the Colonial State in Development Era Lagos." *Journal of Social History* 44, no. 3 (2011): 837–59.

George-Graves, Nadine. "Diasporic Spidering: Constructing Contemporary Black Identities." In *Black Performance Theory*, edited by Thomas F. DeFrantz and Anita Gonzalez, 33–44. Durham, NC: Duke University Press, 2014.

Ghariokwu, Lemi. Interview by Dotun Ayobade. July 25, 2014. Lagos Nigeria.

Gibney, Alex. *Finding Fela*. Film. Kino Lorber. 2015.

Goldman, Vivian. "Resurrection Shuffle." In *Fela: From West Africa to West Broadway*, edited by Trevor Schoonmaker, 36–40. New York: Palgrave Macmillan, 2003.

———. "Thinking Africa: Afrobeat Aesthetic and the Dancing Queens." In *Fela: From West Africa to West Broadway*, edited by Trevor Schoonmaker, 103–10. New York: Palgrave Macmillan, 2003.

Gordon, Avery. *Ghostly Matters: Haunting and the Sociological Imagination*. Minneapolis: University of Minnesota Press, 2008.

Graham, Ronnie. "Fela: The Full Works." In *Fela: Kalakuta Notes*, edited by John Collins, 123–30. Amsterdam: KIT, 2009.

Graham, Roy. "Fela: N25m Suit, No Way." *Punch*, February 11, 1978.

Grass, Randall F. "Fela Anikulapo-Kuti: The Art of an Afrobeat Rebel." *Drama Review* 30, no. 1 (1986): 131–48.

Guha, Ranagit, and Gayatri Chakravorty Spivak. *Selected Subaltern Studies*. New York: Oxford University Press, 1988.

Haastrup, Kehinde. "Fela's Wife Okays Mass Wedding." *Punch*, February 14, 1978.

———. "Teenage Girl Caused Kalakuta 'War.'" *Punch*, March 13, 1975.

Hale, Thomas A., and Aissata G. Sidikou. "New Perspectives on Women's Songs and Singing in West Africa." In *Women's Songs from West Africa*, edited by Thomas A. Hale and Aissata G. Sidikou, 1–8. Bloomington: Indiana University Press, 2013.

Hall, Stuart. "Notes on Deconstructing 'the Popular.'" In *Cultural Theory and Popular Culture*, edited by John Storey, 442–53. London: Prentice Hall, 1998.

Harrington, Imani, and Chyrell D. Bellamy. *Positive/Negative: Women of Color and HIV/AIDS: A Collection of Plays*. San Francisco: Aunt Lute, 2002.

Hartman, Sadiya. *Scenes of Subjection: Terror, Slavery, and Self-Making in Nineteenth-Century America*. Oxford: Oxford University Press, 1997.

———. *Wayward Lives, Beautiful Experiments: Intimate Histories of Social Upheaval*. New York: W. W. Norton, 2019.

Hay, Margaret Jean. "Queens, Prostitutes and Peasants: Historical Perspectives on African Women, 1971–1986." *Canadian Journal of African Studies/Revue Canadienne des Études Africaines* 22, no. 3 (1988): 431–47.

Healy-Clancy, Meghan. "The Family Politics of the Federation of South African Women: A History of Public Motherhood in Women's Antiracist Activism." *Signs* 42, no. 4 (2017): 843–66.

Hebdige, Dick. *Subculture: The Meaning of Style*. London: Routledge, 1988.

"He Might Not Have Died—Priest." *Sunday Champion*, August 10, 1997.

Herszenhorn, David M. "Fela, 58, Dissident Nigerian Musician, Dies." *New York Times*, August 4, 1997. https://www.nytimes.com/1997/08/04/arts/fela-58 -dissident-nigerian-musician-dies.html.

Hoga, Pulchérie Ibilola. Interview with Dotun Ayobade. March 21, 2023. Paris, France.

Hogan, Patrick Colm. *Colonialism and Cultural Identity: Crises of Tradition in the Anglophone Literatures of India, Africa and the Caribbean*. Albany: State University of New York Press, 2000.

Hooker, Juliet. "Black Grief / White Grievance." In *Faculty for Faculty Lecture Series*, hosted by Brown University, 2019. https://www.youtube.com/watch?v =XenOhROq5Mg.

hooks, bell. *Talking Back: Thinking Feminist, Thinking Black*. Boston: South End Press, 1999.

Hostert, Anna Camaiti. *Passing: A Strategy to Dissolve Identities and Remap Differences*. Translated by Christine Marciasini. Cranbury, NJ: Rosemont, 2007.

"How I Escaped Death, by Mrs. Funmilayo Ransome-Kuti." *Sunday Punch*, December 1, 1974.

Idam, Jossy. "Sodom and Gomorrah – Where Old Prostitutes Live." *Nairaland*, May 17, 2009. https://www.nairaland.com/273361/sodom-gomorrah -where-old-prostitutes.

Idowu, Mabinuori Kayode. *Fela—Phenomenon and Legacy*. Black Art Productions, 2012.

"Interview: Femi Anikulapo-Kuti and Jerome Sandlarz, Zooz, Paris." In *Fela: From West Africa to West Broadway*, edited by Trevor Schoonmaker, 41–54. New York: Palgrave Macmillan, 2003.

Izsadore, Sandra, and Segun Oyekunle. *Fela and Me*. Ibadan: Kraft, 2019.

Jaboro, Majemite. *The Ikoyi Prison Narratives: The Spiritualism and Political Philosophy of Fela Kuti*. Self-published, lulu.com, 2017.

Jackson, Marissa A. L. "Don't Teach Me Nonsense: On Bill Cosby, Fela, and Other Wrongly Exalted Misogynists." *For Harriet*, December 10, 2014. http:// www.forharriet.com/2014/12/dont-teach-me-nonsense-on-bill-cosby.html.

Jean-Charles, Regine Michelle. *Conflict Bodies: The Politics of Rape Representation in the Francophone Imaginary*. Columbus: Ohio State University Press, 2014.

jegede, dele. "Dis Fela Sef! Fela in Lagos." In *Fela: From West Africa to West Broadway*, edited by Trevor Schoonmaker, 78–102. New York: Palgrave Macmillan, 2003.

Jemie, Onwuchekwa. *Biafra: Requiem for the Dead in War*. West Papua: Port Moresby, 1970.

Johnson, Jasmine Elizabeth. "Queens' Diaspora." *African and Black Diaspora: An International Journal* 9, no. 1 (2016): 44–56.

Johnson-Odim, Cheryl, and Nina Emma Mba. *For Women and the Nation: Funmilayo-Ransome-Kuti of Nigeria*. Urbana: University of Illinois Press, 1997.

Johnson, Patrick E. "Black Performance Studies: Genealogies, Politics, Futures." In *The Sage Handbook of Performance Studies*, edited by Soyini D. Madison and Judith A Hamera, 446–63. Thousand Oaks, CA: SAGE, 2005.

Jones, Omi Osun Joni L. *Theatrical Jazz: Performance, Àṣẹ and the Power of the Present Moment*. Columbus: Ohio University Press, 2015.

Joseph, Peniel E. "Dashikis and Democracy: Black Studies, Student Activism, and the Black Power Movement." *Journal of African American History* 88, no. 2, History of Black Student Activism (Spring 2003): 182–203.

Kathrada, Ahmed. "The Long Walk of Nelson Mandela: Interview, Ahmed Kathrada." Interview by John Carlin. *Frontline*, PBS. 2014.

Kaurismaki, Mika. *Mama Africa: Miriam Makeba.* Film. ArtMattan Films. 2019.

Kehinde, Tayo. "Fela Raided in Ghana." *Punch*, November 16, 1977.

Kelley, Robin D. G. *Freedom Dreams: The Black Radical Imagination.* Boston: Beacon Press, 2002.

Králová, Jana. "What Is Social Death?" *Contemporary Social Science* 10, no. 3 (2015): 235–48. https://doi.org/10.1080/21582041.2015.1114407.

Larkin, Colin. "Lijadu Sisters." In *Encyclopedia of Popular Music*, edited by Colin Larkin, 817. London: Oxford University Press, 2006.

Lee, R. Felicia. "Finding Depth in Fela's Women." *New York Times*, December 17, 2009. https://www.nytimes.com/2009/12/17/theater/17fela.html.

Lewis, Yomi. "Is Virginity out of Fashion?" *Happy Home*, 1977.

"Lighting Up Lagos: The Stars of 1970s Nigerian Rock Music—in Pictures." *Guardian*, June 6, 2016. https://www.theguardian.com/artanddesign/gallery /2016/jun/06/1970s-nigerian-rock-music-stars-wake-up-you#img-14.

Lorde, Audre. "The Master's Tools Will Never Dismantle the Master's House." In *Sister Outsider: Essays and Speeches*, 110–14. Berkeley, CA: Crossing Press, 2007.

———. "Uses of the Erotic as Power." In *Sister Outsider: Essays and Speeches*, 87–91. New York: Ten Speed Press, 2007.

Lowe, Lisa. *The Intimacies of Four Continents.* Durham, NC: Duke University Press, 2015.

Mabiakwu, Dede. Interview with Dotun Ayobade. August 15, 2014. Lagos, Nigeria.

"Made Kuti Steps Outside the Shrine with The Movement." *Guardian Life*, 2021. https://guardian.ng/life/music/made-kuti-steps-outside-the-shrine-with -the-movement/.

Madison, D. Soyini. Critical Ethnography: Methods, Ethics, and Performance. Second Edition. Thousand Oaks: Sage Publications, Inc, 2012.

Mama, Amina. "Feminism or Femocracy? State Feminism and Democratisation in Nigeria." *Africa Development/Afrique et Développement* 20, no. 1 (1995): 37–58.

———. "Sheroes and Villains: Conceptualizing Colonial and Contemporary Violence against Women in Africa." In *Feminist Genealogies, Colonial Legacies, Democratic Futures*, edited by M. Jacqui Alexander and Chandra Talpade Mohanty, 46–62. New York: Routledge, 2012.

Mann, Kristin. "The Dangers of Dependence: Christian Marriage among Flite Women in Lagos Colony, 1880–1915." *Journal of African History* 24, no. 1 (1983): 37–56.

———. *Marrying Well: Marriage, Status and Social Change among the Educated Elite in Colonial Lagos.* Cambridge: Cambridge University Press, 1985.

Marks, Denis, dir. *Fela Kuti Live: Fela Anikulapo-Kuti and the Egypt 80 Band.* Film. Yazoo. 2000.

Marre, Jeremy. *Konkombe: The Nigerian Pop Music Scene.* Film. Shanachie Entertainment Corp. 2000.

Mbembe, Achille. "African Modes of Self-Writing." *Identity, Culture and Politics* 2, no. 1 (2001): 1–39.

———. *On the Postcolony.* Berkeley: University of California Press, 2001.

———. "Provisional Notes on the Postcolony." *Africa: Journal of the International African Institute* 62, no. 1 (1992): 3–37.

———. "Variations on the Beautiful in the Congolese World of Sounds." *Politique Africaine* 4, no. 100 (2005): 69–91.

McFadden, Patricia. "African Thought Leadership: Writing as/for Resistance." *Africology: The Journal of Pan African Studies* 10, no. 2 (2017): i–v.

———. "Becoming Postcolonial: African Women Changing the Meaning of Citizenship." *Meridians: Feminism, Race, Transnationalism* 6, no. 1 (2005): 1–18.

McRobbie, Angela, and Jenny Garber. "Girls and Subcultures." In *Resistance Through Rituals: Youth Subcultures in Post-War Britain,* edited by Stuart Hall and Tony Jefferson, 209–22. London: Hutchinson, 1976.

"Meet Fela's Ex-Girlfriend and Afrobeat Queen, Dele Salami, Who Also Dated Ebenezer Obey." *iCampus.* Accessed May 12, 2015. http://www.icampusng .com/meet-felas-ex-girlfriend-afro-beat-queen-dele-salami-who-also-dated -ebenezer-obey/.

"Mementos Turn Gold." *Daily Champion,* August 13, 1997.

Metz, Helen Chapin. "The Second Republic, 1979–83." United States Library of Congress, 1991. http://countrystudies.us/nigeria/29.htm.

Monroe, Arthur. "Festac 77—The Second World Black and African Festival of Arts and Culture: Lagos, Nigeria." *Black Scholar* 9, no. 1 (1977): 34–37.

Moore, Carlos. *Fela: This Bitch of a Life.* London: Allison and Busby, 1982.

Morgan, Mac. "Is This an Invasion of Entertainment by Women Artistes?" *Daily Times,* May 12, 1971.

Moyo, Dambisa. *Dead Aid: Why Aid Is Not Working and How There Is a Better Way for Africa.* New York: Farrar, Strauss and Giroux, 2009.

Mudimbe, V. Y. *The Invention of Africa: Gnosis, Philosophy, and the Order of Knowledge.* Bloomington: Indiana University Press, 1988.

Mugabe, Faustin. "Remembering Uganda's 'Aids Face,' Philly Lutaaya." *Daily Monitor,* December 12, 2014. https://www.monitor.co.ug/artsculture /Reviews/Remembering-Uganda-s--Aids-face---Philly-Lutaaya/691232 -2554112-13856e5/index.html.

Murphy, David. "The Performance of Pan-Africanism: Staging the African Renaissance at the First World Festival of Negro Arts." In *The First World Festival of Negro Arts, Dakar 1966: Contexts and Legacies,* edited by David Murphy, 1–42. Liverpool: Liverpool University Press, 2016.

Ndebele, Njabulo. *The Cry of Winnie Mandela.* Oxfordshire: Ayebia Clark, 2003.

Newell, Stephanie. "Afterword." In *African Print Cultures: Newspapers and Their Publics in the Twentieth Century,* edited by Derek Peterson, Emma Hunter, and Stephanie Newell, 425–33. Ann Arbor: University of Michigan Press, 2016.

———. "Representations of Women in Popular Fiction by Nigerian Men." *Journal of African Languages and Cultures* 9, no. 2 (1996): 169–88.

Njoku, Benjamin. "I Can't Understand Why My Father Married 27 Wives— Femi Kuti." *Vanguard*, October 12, 2013.

Nkrumah, Kwame. *Neo-Colonialism: The Last Stage of Imperialism*. New York: International Publishers Co., Inc., 1966.

Norwood, Frances. *The Maintenance of Life: Preventing Social Death through Euthanasia Talk and End-of-Life Care - Lessons from the Netherlands*. Durham, NC: Carolina Academic Press, 2009.

Nwankwo, Caro. "So Fela Ran Away with 27 Girls?" *Spear*, August 1978.

Nwosu, Iheanacho. "Fela's Last Journey: Controversy, the Name Is Fela." *Sunday Champion*, August 10, 1997.

Nzegwu, Nkiru. "School Days in Lagos: Fela, 'Lady,' and Acada Girls." In *Fela from West Africa to West Broadway*, edited by Trevor Schoonmaker, 135–48. New York: Palgrave Macmillan, 2003.

Nzewi, Ugochukwu-Smooth C. "How the Art Takes Shape: Old Forms/New Idioms in Our Fashion." *Art Africa*, March 2017.

Obasanjo, Olusegun. *My Command: An Account of the Nigerian Civil War, 1967– 1970*. Nairobi: East African Educational Publishers Ltd, 1999.

Ochonu, Moses. "Male Anxieties, Cultural Politics, and Debates over Independent Womanhood among Idoma Male Migrants in Late Colonial Northern Nigeria." *Interventions* 13, no. 2 (2011): 278–98.

Ogunyemi, Gori. "Marriage Today Is Keeping a Glorified House Girl." *The Punch*, August 15 1977.

Ohai, Chux, and Ada Onyema. "Fela Slept with Me More Than His Other 27 Wives." *Modern Ghana*, October 30, 2010. https://www.modernghana.com /nollywood/9342/fela-slept-with-me-more-than-his-other-27-wives.html.

Ohakah, Chibisi. "War at the Shrine: Femi Vs. Fela's Girls." *Saturday Champion*, August 16, 1997.

Okolie, Chris. "Margaret Ekpo: The Voice of Courage." *Newbreed*, March 1974.

Okome, Mojubaolu Olufunke. "'Unknown Soldier': Women's Radicalism, Activism and State Violence in Twentieth-Century Nigeria." In *Gender and Power Relations in Nigeria*, edited by Ronke Iyabowale Ako-Nai, 239–66. Lanham, MD: Lexington Books, 2013.

Okome, Onookome. "Nollywood, Lagos, and the Good-Time Woman." *Research in African Literatures* 43, no. 4 (2012): 166–86.

Okpara, Anthony. "Beko Asks to See Fela." *Daily Champion*, August 8, 1997.

Okpara, Anthony, Emeka Uwaezeoke, Geoffrey Anyanwu, Victor Ogbonnaya, Victor Owe, and Henrietta Obozuwa. "15 Fans Faint at Fela's Burial." *Daily Champion*, August 13, 1997.

Okpara, Anthony, Emeka Uwaezeoke, Iheanacho Nwosu, and Efre Akpabio. "Fela's Dancers Petition Govt." *Sunday Champion*, August 10, 1997.

Okwechime, Mallam Abdul. Interview by Dotun Ayobade. June 13, 2017. Lagos, Nigeria.

Olaniyan, Tejumola. *Arrest the Music! Fela and His Rebel Art and Politics*. Ibadan: Bookcraft, 2009.

Olori, Toye. "Repossessing the Late Fela Kuti's Property." *Inter State Service*, January 12, 1999. http://www.ipsnews.net/1999/01/music-nigeria-repossessing -the-late-fela-kutis-property/.

Olorunyomi, Sola. *Afrobeat! Fela and the Imagined Continent*. Trenton, NJ: Africa World Press, 2002.

———. "Lemi Ghariokwu on the Afrobeat Tradition." *Glendora Review: African Quarterly on the Arts* 3, no. 3 & 4 (2001): 80–83.

Omozokpia, Chris. "Rumours." *Felaweb*, July 24, 1997. https://cvanpelt.incolor .com/Felaweb/rumours.html.

Onanuga, Bayo, Seye Kehinde, Dapo Olorunyomi, and Akin Adesokan. "Fela: A Prison Interview" *The News*, March 1993.

Onwuneme, Sony. "Shrine Stirs for Fela." *Thisday*, August 14, 1998.

Onyebadi, Uche. "Fela's Release: Victory for Conscience." *Vanguard*, April 28, 1986.

Oroh, Abdul. "'I'm Still Scratching the Surface.'" *African Guardian*, October 17, 1988.

Osha, Sanya. "Unravelling the Silences of Black Sexualities." *Agenda: Empowering Women for Gender Equity* 18, no. 62 (2004): 92–98.

Oshunkeye, Shola, Wale Sokunbi, Aliu Mohammed, Eric Osagie, Ndidi Oka-for, and Joy Onuoha. "Fela, Sex and Showbiz: Where Do We Go from Here?" *Weekend Concord*, August 16, 1997.

Osoba, Segun O. "Corruption in Nigeria: Historical Perspectives." *Review of African Political Economy* 23, no. 69 (1996): 371–86.

Osofisan, Femi. *Insidious Treasons and Beyond: Forty Years of Alternative Theatre in Nigeria*. Ibadan: Bookcraft, 2016.

Oyěwùmí, Oyèrónkẹ́. *Gender Epistemologies in Africa: Gendering Traditions, Spaces, Social Institutions, and Identities*. New York: Palgrave Macmillan, 2011.

———. *The Invention of Women: Making an African Sense of Western Gender Discourses*. Minneapolis: University of Minnesota Press, 1997.

Palmer, Tony. *Ginger Baker in Africa*. Film. Eagle Rock Entertainment. 2006.

Patterson, Orlando. *Slavery and Social Death: A Comparative Study*. Cambridge, MA: Harvard University Press, 1982.

Patton, Cindy. *Globalizing AIDS*. Minneapolis: University of Minnesota Press, 2002.

Peretu, Thomas. "I'm Surrounded by Witches—Fela." *Lagos Weekend*, September 24, 1993.

Pierce, Steven. "Farmers and 'Prostitutes': Twentieth-Century Problems of Female Inheritance in Kano Emirate, Nigeria." *Journal of African History* 44, no. 3 (2003): 463–86.

Piot, Charles. *Remotely Global: Village Modernity in West Africa*. Chicago: University of Chicago Press, 2008.

Pruitt, Sarah. "How the Vietnam War Empowered the Hippie Movement." *History*, September 14, 2018. https://www.history.com/news/vietnam-war -hippies-counter-culture.

Quashie, Kevin. *The Sovereignty of Quiet: Beyond Resistance in Black Culture*. New Brunswick, NJ: Rutgers University Press, 2012.

Quayson, Ato. *Calibrations: Reading for the Social*. Minneapolis: University of Minnesota Press, 2003.

———. *Postcolonialism: Theory, Practice or Process*. Cambridge: Polity, 2000.

———. "What It Means to Be Winnie." *Africa Is a Country*, February 15, 2014. https://africasacountry.com/2014/02/what-is-it-to-be-winnie-mandela.

Redmond, Shana L. *Anthem: Social Movements and the Sound of Solidarity in the African Diaspora*. New York: New York University Press, 2014.

Reed, T. V. *The Art of Protest: Culture and Activism from the Civil Rights Movement to the Streets of Seattle*. Minneapolis: University of Minnesota Press, 2005.

Roach, Joseph. *Cities of the Dead: Circum-Atlantic Performance*. Twenty-fifth anniversary ed. New York: Columbia University Press, 2022.

Roholt, Tiger C. *Groove: A Phenomenology of Rhythmic Nuance*. New York: Bloomsbury Academic, 2014.

Román, David. *Acts of Intervention: Performance, Gay Culture, and AIDS*. Bloomington: Indiana University Press, 1998.

Rose, Tricia. *The Hip-Hop Wars: What We Talk about When We Talk about Hip Hop—and Why It Matters*. New York: Basic Books, 2008.

Royster, Francesca T. "Fela Kuti, Bill T. Jones, and the Marketing of Black Masculine Excess on Broadway." *Biography* 34, no. 3 (2011): 492–517. https:// doi.org/10.1353/bio.2011.0049.

Russel, Sharon Stanton. "International Migration." In *Demographic Change in Sub-Saharan Africa*, edited by Karen A. Foote, Kenneth H. Hill, and Linda G. Martin, 297–349. Washington, DC: National Academy Press, 1993.

Russel, Sharon Stanton, and Michael S. Teitelbaum. *International Migration and International Trade*. Washington, DC: World Bank, 1992.

Salami, Dele. Interview by Dotun Ayobade. July 7, 2019. Lagos, Nigeria.

Savali, Kirsten West. "The Life and Legacy of Fela Kuti." HuffPost, December 14, 2011. https://www.huffingtonpost.com/kirsten-west-savali/fela-kuti-wives -aids_b_1009593.html.

Schechner, Richard. *Performance Theory*. New York: Routledge, 1988.

Semenitari, Ibim. "Fela Forever!" *Tell*, August 18, 1997.

Semley, Lorelle D. *Mother Is Gold, Father Is Glass: Gender and Colonialism in a Yoruba Town*. Bloomington: Indiana University Press, 2010.

Shagari, Shehu. *Shehu Shagari: Beckoned to Serve*. Ibadan: Heinemann Educational, 2001.

Sharpe, Christina. *Monstrous Intimacies: Making Post-Slavery Subjects*. Durham, NC: Duke University Press, 2010.

Shepard, Benjamin. *Play, Creativity, and Social Movements: If I Can't Dance, It's Not My Revolution*. New York: Routledge, 2011.

Shipley, Jesse Weaver. *Trickster Theatre: The Poetics of Freedom in Urban Africa*. Bloomington: Indiana University Press, 2015.

Shoneyin, Lola. *The Secret Lives of Baba Segi's Wives*. New York: William Morrow, 2011.

Shosanya, Omolara. Interview by Dotun Ayobade. June 19, 2018. Lagos, Nigeria.

Shuffield, Robin. *Thomas Sankara: The Upright Man*. Film. ZORN Production. 2006.

Simone, Abdoumaliq. *City Life from Jakarta to Dakar*. Global Realities, edited by Charles C. Lemert. New York: Routledge, 2010.

Siollun, Max. *Oil, Politics and Violence Nigeria's Military Coup Culture (1966–1976)*. New York: Algora, 2009.

Sizemore-Barber, April. "The Voice of (Which?) Africa: Miriam Makeba in America." *Safundi: The Journal of South African and American Studies* 13, no. July–October (2012): 251–76.

Smith, Daniel Jordan. "Modern Marriage, Men's Extramarital Sex, and Hiv Risk in Southeastern Nigeria." *American Journal of Public Health* 97, no. 6 (2007): 997–1005.

Smith, Stephen W. "Mandela: Death of a Politician." *London Review of Books*, January 2014. https://www.lrb.co.uk/the-paper/v36/n01/stephen-w.-smith /mandela-death-of-a-politician.

"Snippet, as Fela Marches On." *Saturday Champion*, August 2, 1997.

Sofola, Zulu. *Wedlock of the Gods*. Ibadan: Evans Brothers, 1972.

Solarin, Tai. "Open Letter to Fela Anikulapo-Kuti." *Nigerian Tribune*, February 17, 1978.

Sonowo, Biodun. "New York Stands Still for Fela." *Daily Champion*, August 5, 1997.

Sotunde, Iyabo. "Musical Jam for Fela's Fans at Ibadan." *Guardian*, August 13, 1997.

Spencer, Neil. "Fela Kuti Remembered: 'He Was a Tornado of a Man, but He Loved Humanity.'" *Guardian*, October 31, 2010. https://www.theguardian .com/music/2010/oct/31/fela-kuti-musical-neil-spencer.

Spivak, Gayatri Chakravorty. "Can the Subaltern Speak?" In *Marxism and the Interpretation of Culture*, edited by Cary Nelson and Lawrence Grossberg, 271–313. Urbana: University of Illinois, 1988.

Stanovsky, Derek. "Fela and His Wives: The Import of a Postcolonial Masculinity." Appalachian State University. 1998. https://legacy.chass.ncsu .edu/jouvert/v2i1/STAN.HTM.

"Star in Her Eyes." *Spear*, 1966.

Statler, Matt, Loizos Heracleous, and Claus D. Jacobs. "Serious Play as a Practice of Paradox." *Journal of Applied Behavioral Science* 47, no. 2 (2011): 236–56.

Suberu, Rotimi T. "Problems of Federation in the Second Nigerian Republic and Prospects for the Future." *Africa: Rivista trimestrale di studi e documentazione dell'Istituto italiano perl'Africa e l'Oriente* 47, no. 1 (1992): 29–56.

Sutton-Smith, Brian. "Play and Ambiguity." In *The Game Design Reader: A Rules of Play Anthology*, edited by Katie Salen Tekinbas and Eric Zimmerman, 296–313. Cambridge, MA: MIT Press, 2006.

Tamale, Sylvia, ed. *African Sexualities: A Reader.* Cape Town: Pambazuka Press, 2011.

Teniola, Eric. "Ban on Fela's Records Condemned." *Punch*, November 17, 1977.

Thiong'o, Ngugi wa. *Decolonising the Mind: The Politics of Language in African Literature.* Oxford: James Curry, 1986.

Thomas, Dupe. "The Devious Rules of Being a Girl." *Happy Home*, August 1977.

Tshwala-Amadi, Gina. "Liberation and the African Woman." *Happy Home*, August 1978.

Turner, Victor. "Brain, Body and Culture." *Performing Arts Journal* 10, no. 2 (1986): 26–34.

"The 12 Wives of Chief Ogunde." *Ebony*, October 1969.

Ukwuoma, Ben. "Pharmacists Seek Govt Subsidy for Aids Treatment." *Guardian*, August 13, 1997.

Umude-Haverkamp, Mary. Phone interview by Dotun Ayobade. January 26, 2016.

UNESCO. *Funmilayo Ransome-Kuti and the Women's Union of Abeokuta.* Paris: UNESCO, 2015.

UNICEF. "Information Sheet: The Child's Rights Act." August 2007.

United Nations. "Sexual Violence and Armed Conflict: United Nations Response." April 1998.

———. "UNICEF Names Nigerian Musician Femi Kuti as New Special Representative." *UN News*, June 12, 2002. https://news.un.org/en/story/2002/06/37412-unicef-names-nigerian-musician-femi-kuti-new-special-representative.

van Zyl Smit, Betine. "From Penelope to Winnie Mandela: Women Who Waited." *International Journal of the Classical Tradition* 15, no. 3 (September 2008): 393–406.

Veal, Michael. *Fela: The Life and Times of an African Musical Icon.* Philadelphia: Temple University Press, 2000.

Villepastour, Amanda. *Ancient Text Messages of the Yorùbá Bàtá Drum: Cracking the Code.* Franham: Ashgate, 2010.

Washington, Teresa N. *The Architects of Existence: Aje in Yoruba Cosmology, Ontology, and Orature.* Self-published, Oya's Tornado, 2014.

———. *Our Mothers, Our Powers, Our Texts: Manifestations of Aje in African Literature.* Bloomington: Indiana University Press, 2005.

Waterman, Christopher Alan. *Jùjú: A Social History and Ethnography of an African Popular Music.* Chicago: University of Chicago Press, 1990.

Webster, Colin. "Communes: A Thematic Typology." In *Resistance Through Rituals: Youth Subcultures in Post-War Britain,* edited by Stuart Hall and Tony Jefferson, 127–34. London: Hutchinson, 1976.

Wenzel, Jennifer. *Bulletproof: Afterlives of Anticolonial Prophecy in South Africa and Beyond.* Chicago: University of Chicago Press, 2009.

"What Kind of Man Is Africa Shrine Chief Priest, Fela Anikulapo-Kuti." *Newbreed,* January 1974.

"When a Wife Starts to Kick." Dear Oyin Adviser: The Intimate Problems. *Punch,* August 18, 1977.

Williams, Litsa. "Disen-Whaaaat?? Understanding Disenfranchised Grief." *What's Your Grief.* 2017. https://whatsyourgrief.com/disenfranchised-grief/.

"Wives Absent at Burial." *Guardian,* August 13, 1997.

"Wunmi - Thoughts on Fela." October 17, 2013. YouTube video, 4:16. https://youtu.be/VtyM_ovlGgY.

Young, Hershini Bhana. *Illegible Will: Coercive Spectacles of Labor in South Africa and the Diaspora.* Durham, NC: Duke University Press, 2017.

Zeleza, Paul Tiyambe. "Towards a Cultural Economy for African Liberation." In *3rd Kwame Nkrumah Pan-African Cultural & Intellectual Festival.* kwamenkrumahonline.com, 2021. https://kwamenkrumahfestival.com/session-recording/towards-a-cultural-economy-for-african-liberation/.

Compaoré Blaise, 200–201
"Condom, Scallywag, and Scatter," 210
Confusion Break Bone (1990, album), 146, 204
"Confusion Break Bone" (1990, song), 193
Conquergood, Dwight, 105, 245
consent, 4, 96, 133, 154, 161, 174, 284, 295
Cosby, Bill, 91
cosmopolitanism, 2, 44, 46, 49, 59, 93, 120, 268
Côte d'Ivoire, 146
Counter-FESTAC concerts, 146, 312n59
coups, 5, 30, 41, 97, 129, 132, 139, 170, 176–77, 185, 310n29
COVID-19 pandemic, 246–47
Cox, Aimee Meredith, 17
creative activism, 18, 33, 139, 143, 239
Criminal Investigation Department, 127
"Cross Examination" (1985), 104–5

Dakar, 38
"dancing girls" discourse, 34–35, 43
Danjuma, T.Y., 98
danseuses, 82, 303n48
dark play, 171
Daudu, Major, 143
Davis, Angela, 73
Decade of the Woman, 92
Decca Records, 44–45
decoloniality, 111, 261, 283, 293n25
deep play, 155
Delta, 202, 206
Democratic Republic of the Congo, 38, 82, 144, 297n31, 303n48
Denzer, LaRay, 59, 291n3
De Veaux, Lauren, 259
de Weever, Nicole, 26, 259–62, 265

diasporic spidering, 259
Dimka, Buka Suka, 129, 311n29
Diop, Cheikh Anta, 178
Diouf, Mamadou, 33
divorce, 171, 197–200, 207, 211, 216, 222, 310n8, 320n13, 321n33
Dodan Barracks, 132, 162
Dodomaya/Dodo/Ndudi, 123–25, 241–42
domestic violence, 16, 94
Donkor, David, 177
Dosumu, Lateef, 313n65
the dozens, 101, 103
Drewal, Margaret Thompson, 169, 292n11
DuBois, W. E. B., 119, 315n28
Dumbutshena, Rujeko, 26, 259, 263–64

Ebola, 63, 230
Economic Community of West African States (ECOWAS), 317n50
Edmondon, Laura, 237, 324n22
Egba, 67–69
Egba Native Authority, 67
Egypt, 46, 115; and Egypt 80 name, 178–79
Egypt 80, ix, 106, 191, 196, 204–6, 210, 229, 252, 285, 316n39; after Fela's death, 222, 244–46, 250–51, 253–54, 256–57, 260; dancers, 106, 123, 198, 202, 233–34; entourage, 174, 193; Femi leaving, 192, 256; at Glastonbury Festival, 184; musicians, 25, 220; name, 178–79; song choruses, 180–83
Ekpo, Margaret, 92, 305n81
Ekwensi, Cyprian, 153, 312n57
Elutunde, Eludoyin, 25, 58, 71
Emeagwali, Gloria, 307n40
EMI Records, 44

Dotun Ayobade holds a joint appointment as Assistant Professor in Performance Studies and Black Studies at Northwestern University. He studies how embodied forms of popular culture shaped the contours of community, justice, and activism in late twentieth-century West Africa.

For Indiana University Press

Tony Brewer, Artist and Book Designer
Gary Dunham, Director and Acquisitions Editor
Sophia Hebert, Assistant Acquisitions Editor
Brenna Hosman, Production Coordinator
Katie Huggins, Production Manager
Nancy Lightfoot, Project Editor and Manager
Dan Pyle, Online Publishing Manager
Pamela Rude, Senior Artist and Book Designer
Stephen Williams, Marketing, Publicity, and Rights Manager